Praise for *1941: Fighting the Shadow War,*
A Divided America in a World at War

"Engrossing . . . Wortman's brisk narrative takes us across nations and oceans with a propulsive vigor that speeds the book along like a good thriller." —*Wall Street Journal*

"Admirable work . . . superbly depicted." —*Winnipeg Free Press*

"Even readers familiar with the broad history of the era are likely to find new insights and new details of the behind-the-scenes maneuvering that preceded Pearl Harbor. An engaging and well-researched look behind the scenes of an important historic era. Highly recommended."
—*Kirkus Reviews* (starred review)

"A fascinating narrative of a domestic conflict presaging America's plunge into global war." —*Booklist* (starred review)

"Like the rumble of thunder before a storm, Marc Wortman's *1941: Fighting the Shadow War* creates a mesmerizing sense of ominous and terrifying foreboding. This is the fascinating story of the global war that most Americans know almost nothing about: the bitter and even deadly struggle pitting American against American as the United States confronted Hitler and Japan before our country's actual entrance into World War II. There were heroes and villains and, as Wortman depicts so richly up to Pearl Harbor, nobody knew who would win."
—Nathaniel Philbrick

"Marc Wortman's *1941: Fighting the Shadow War* tells the story of America's plunge into World War II in a way that is smart, suspenseful, and full of surprising historical twists. *1941* has the sweep and intimacy of an epic novel and the pace of a military thriller."
—Debby Applegate

"With the skills of a mosaicist, Marc Wortman creates a fresh portrait of the most crucial year of the war, when the United States became the 'arsenal of democracy,' when Hitler invaded the Soviet Union, and when the nation had its rendezvous with destiny at Pearl Harbor. Wortman brings into a single view both the war abroad and the 'shadow war' at home between supporters and opponents of American intervention, a battle that continued until the end of that tumultuous year."

—Susan Dunn

"The story of Mr Roosevelt's Hidden War on Nazi Germany and support of the British effort in 1940-1941 has been told before, of course, but not I think with such verve and delightful panache as in Marc Wortman's new book. Its strength lies in his blend of characters high and low, from FDR and his highest confidantes to a normal family at Pearl Harbor to the U.S. journalists in Berlin as they saw war advancing across Europe and, then, towards America itself. It's a smart book, and a great read."

—Paul Kennedy

"Narrated with panache and a fastidious eye for detail, Wortman's *1941: Fighting the Shadow War* tells how FDR ingeniously helped Churchill by any means he could without breaking the Neutrality Act. Beset by furious, powerful domestic rivalries, who had the country in their grip, they were bested only when Pearl Harbor was attacked. An on-the-edge-of-your-chair thriller."

—Geoffrey Wolff

1941

Fighting the Shadow War

Also by Marc Wortman

*The Millionaires' Unit: The Aristocratic Flyboys
Who Fought the Great War and Invented American Air Power*

The Bonfire: The Siege and Burning of Atlanta

1941

Fighting the Shadow War

A Divided America in a World at War

Marc Wortman

Grove Press
New York

Published simultaneously in Canada
Printed in the United States of America

First Grove Atlantic hardcover edition: April 2016

First Grove Atlantic paperback edition: April 2017

ISBN 978-0-8021-2667-2
eISBN 978-0-8021-9032-1

Grove Press
an imprint of Grove Atlantic
154 West 14th Street
New York, NY 10011

Distributed by Publishers Group West

groveatlantic.com

17 18 19 20   10 9 8 7 6 5 4 3 2 1

For my children, Rebecca and Charlie,
thoughtful readers

". . . public sentiment is everything. With public sentiment, nothing can fail; without it, nothing can succeed. Consequently he who molds public sentiment goes deeper than he who enacts statutes or pronounces decisions. He makes statutes and decisions possible or impossible to be executed."

—Abraham Lincoln
First Lincoln-Douglas Debate,
August 21, 1858

Contents

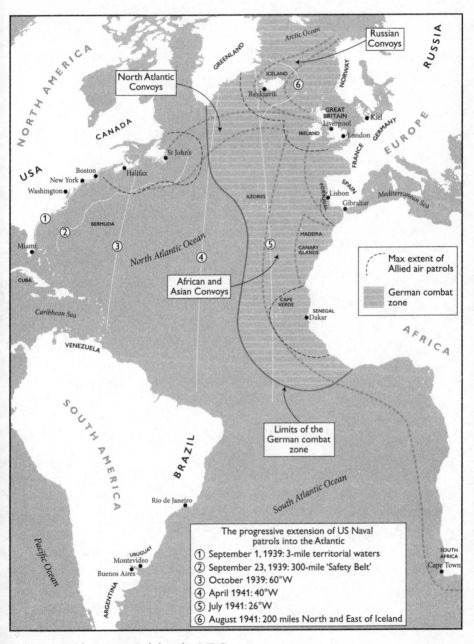

North Atlantic
Convoys

Russian
Convoys

ARCTIC OCEAN

GREENLAND

ICELAND

Reykjavik

RUSSIA

NORTH AMERICA

CANADA

GREAT
BRITAIN

Liverpool

NORWAY

Kiel

GERMANY

EUROPE

St John's

IRELAND

London

USA

Boston

New York

Halifax

FRANCE

Washington

SPAIN

Lisbon

PORTUGAL

Gibraltar

Mediterranean Sea

①

②

BERMUDA

AZORES

③

North Atlantic Ocean

④

⑤

MADEIRA

CANARY
ISLANDS

Miami

African and
Asian Convoys

Max extent of
Allied air patrols

German combat
zone

CUBA

Caribbean Sea

CAPE
VERDE

SENEGAL

Dakar

AFRICA

VENEZUELA

SOUTH AMERICA

Limits of the
German combat
zone

BRAZIL

Pacific Ocean

Rio de Janeiro

South Atlantic Ocean

URUGUAY

Montevideo

Buenos Aires

SOUTH
AFRICA

Cape Town

ARGENTINA

The progressive extension of US Naval
patrols into the Atlantic
① September 1, 1939: 3-mile territorial waters
② September 23, 1939: 300-mile 'Safety Belt'
③ October 1939: 60°W
④ April 1941: 40°W
⑤ July 1941: 26°W
⑥ August 1941: 200 miles North and East of Iceland

Map © 2016 by Martin Lubikowski, ML Design

1941

Fighting the Shadow War

Introduction
1941

On September 1, 1939, a million and a half Nazi German troops poured across the border into Poland. Two days later the United Kingdom and France declared war on Germany, and World War Two began. Two years, three months, and four days later, December 7, 1941, 353 Japanese aircraft launched from six carriers attacked Pearl Harbor. Much of the United States Navy's Pacific Fleet lay in ruins, and 2,403 Americans were killed. The following day, December 8, 1941, President Franklin Delano Roosevelt told the world that "the United States of America was suddenly and deliberately attacked by naval and air forces of the Empire of Japan." On a date which still lives in infamy, a shocked and aroused America was thrust into the Second World War.

Or so the most widely accepted and oft-told story of the start of the Second World War goes. In reality, the story of America's entry into the war was complex, contentious, and portentous, a tortuous and rocky trail too easily overlooked in the dazzling light of the four years of war that followed. Long before the attack on Pearl Harbor, the United States had been caught up in the war, fighting in the gray zone between its self-imposed neutrality as a nation officially and lawfully at peace with every nation on earth and its president's declared intention to destroy Hitler and Nazism, drive Japan's military out of China and Indochina, and liberate conquered lands from tyranny. The Axis powers of Germany, Italy, and Japan, and their collaborating leaders and nations, would not roll back quietly within their prewar borders in response to FDR's demands. Far from it.

Thus, at his behest, throughout 1941 American military leaders strategized for victory against the Axis, set up liaisons with unofficial allies in London and China, and began training American forces to fight overseas wars. The government started the process of building up its army, navy, and air forces in order to possess the firepower and heft capable of eventually winning global wars against massively mobilized, war-hardened great powers. The White House also pushed American military forces farther and farther into harm's way and held summits with the leadership of unofficially allied nations, including Prime Minister Winston Churchill of Britain and Soviet leader Joseph Stalin. The country declared war after bombs dropped on Pearl Harbor, but well before then U.S. military personnel had come under fire, and had shot back. Americans had died in combat. America had been at war in all but name.

That story has not been told. Not in this way. That's because Americans before Pearl Harbor refused to see themselves at war. In his famous and widely read February 17, 1941, *Life* magazine essay, "The American Century," the powerful and influential Time, Inc., founder and publisher Henry R. Luce declared, "We are in the war. The irony is that Hitler knows it—and most Americans don't." Luce tried to pull the wool off his nation's eyes. "We are not in a war to defend American territory," he was brazen enough to admit. Even the term "defense," he said, was "full of deceit and self-deceit." Hitler understood this; so did Japan's Imperial Council. Most of Luce's countrymen did not.

While the United States became, through FDR's astute leadership and at times constitutionally questionable maneuvers, "the Arsenal of Democracy" and its military engaged in undeclared combat, the large majority of Americans wavered over supporting, or refused to support, anything that ran the risk of full-scale war. Most had yet to choose sides—even as FDR sought to persuade the country that its fate depended on turning back Hitler and Japan. Most Americans hated Hitler, and most sympathized with the people of Europe and China who were crushed under his and Japan's boots, but poll after poll made plain that they hated foreign wars even more. Most Americans hoped the Allies would win, but many more were unwilling to offer more than hope: They would not let the U.S. military do any of the fighting to ensure victory.

Americans fought among themselves at home, instead, caught up in an increasingly bitter war of words. The passionate isolationists had plenty of support in Congress, which passed legislation expressly forbidding direct trade with belligerent nations and, even while creating the first-ever peacetime draft army, prohibited conscripts from fighting overseas. To deal with trade, military, and geographical restrictions, FDR learned to interpret the Constitution and read a map in ways no president ever had before him. And through speeches, fireside talks, and press conferences, he pursued what he called "longtime education" to awaken his nation to the possibility of war and all that might entail. At the same time, he recognized the political realities of a balky Congress and a resistant citizenry, and refused, he said, to bind his nation to "anything which would require a definite response or action on the part of anybody."

This repeated contradiction between foreign affairs goals and national means, a desire to see democracy and freedom triumph and an unwillingness to enter the world war, drove Americans to fight among themselves. Often secretly, the contesting forces overseas promoted their sides in the proxy fight for the hearts and minds of Americans still safe in their homes. These disputes were carried over the airwaves and in the press and were taken up at the ballot box, in the streets and arenas, and sometimes through violence—a shadow war of its own. On December 7, 1941, the Greatest Generation would finally step from the shadows into the explosive glow of real war, but before going to war, this was the Most Conflicted Generation, led by a president who was willing to do anything short of firing the first, decisive shot that would lead the United States into war.

This book tells the story of how America went to war while still caught up in its own bitter fight over its role in World War Two before

Pearl Harbor. This shadow war darkened the American scene. Journalists who had witnessed the war firsthand, such as CBS radio correspondent William Shirer and fascist proponent Philip Johnson (the latter much better known for his architectural work) and political and government leaders (most famously the transatlantic aviator Charles Lindbergh and the president's alter ego and personal envoy to Winston Churchill and Joseph Stalin, Harry Hopkins) came back from Europe to tell contradictory stories about the war and express opposing visions of the world's future. Unsure which way to turn, a divided America stumbled, argued, and fought, while searching for its place in a world at war.

War on a scale never before seen finally came to America in 1941. To understand this turning point in human history, we must step back to the first days of the war, riding along with the mighty German army on its dash into Poland in September 1939.

1

Foreign Correspondents

Poland, 1939

The motorcade of trucks and cars roared and jolted over the ripped-up, unpaved road that cut like a jagged blade through the Polish Corridor. Even in bright daylight, the pall of war cast its gloom over the men knocking about inside the vehicles as they dodged the tread cuts and bomb craters in their path. Since leaving Berlin with its payload of foreign correspondents before dawn, the German Propaganda Ministry caravan had motored fitfully northeast toward the Baltic seacoast and the remains of the war. The blinking men looked out impassively at the seemingly endless, moving green column of *Wehrmacht* troops and grim-faced Polish refugees who choked the road. The soldiers were jubilant. It was September 18, 1939, less than three weeks since Germany's invasion of Poland and Great Britain and France's declaration of war against the Third Reich. Thousands of German troops were heading *home*. Many rode atop "tanks, tanks, tanks," a soldier in those lines chanted, proudly hailing "the row of tanks [with] no end," now grinding along beneath a locomotive cloud of exhaust, on the drive *out* of Poland.

As the press corps drove along the road to Danzig (today's Gdańsk), the vehicles bucked and then stopped and then, gears grinding, lurched ahead again like fish running upstream. The reporters covered their faces and coughed against the swirling black exhaust, powdery dust, acrid smoke from smoldering bombed-out towns, and the urge to puke.

One of the reporters recorded later how they held their noses against "the sickening sweet smell of dead horses and the sweeter smell of dead men," the remains of a suicidal Polish cavalry charge against the German panzers strewn in the forest and fields along the road.

Paired together by the German Propaganda Ministry, two Americans among the foreign correspondents shared much in common as they looked out on the war zone four thousand miles from home. They were about the same age and shared similar American beginnings, and each had spent most of his adult life in Europe. They loved its life and culture, especially Germany's; and both men had won fame by reporting on what they saw in Europe for Americans back home.

The slightly older of the two could easily have been taken for a middle-American banker or a college professor rather than a dashing, hard-bitten foreign correspondent, an image already firmly etched into the American consciousness. He was phlegmatic, tall, balding, and prematurely gray, round-faced and comfortably paunchy. Beneath his dark, carefully trimmed brush mustache, his small mouth clinched continuously on a pipe. A ski accident had blinded him in one eye, leaving the pupil a bit off kilter. He appeared to take in everything behind his round, thick spectacles as though through a gun sight. He spoke plainly and dressed conservatively in a pinstripe Savile Row three-piece suit and tie beneath a rumpled gabardine trench coat. His style was to have little style at all.

His companion in the press pool was all style. He looked straight out of central casting—slicked-back, dark hair with streaks of gray, clear hazel eyes, and angular cheekbones descending to a deeply cleft chin. A costly custom-made camera dangled from carefully selected bespoke fashion over a lithe frame. He bore a passing resemblance to his near contemporary, the English Shakespearean actor Laurence Olivier, and the register of his emotions covered almost as much range. His good looks and personal taste seemed as carefully and artfully tended as the words in his articles. However, he was anything but scripted. He talked on and on, nervously exhilarated at the prospect of seeing the world war up close.

The other reporter, much the stonier of the two, felt only cynicism about what lay ahead. He was repulsed at the prospect of reporting on a war that he knew had barely begun.

But each man had his job to do.

The day before, the Red Army had swept into eastern Poland, joining the Germans in filleting the former Polish nation, to be gobbled up like a pig's haunch between them. The world watched as Europe, almost exactly twenty-five years after its first unimaginably cataclysmic war, leaped vertiginously into the bottomless chasm of a second great war. Being among the very first journalists to witness the start of the Second World War marked a momentous climax for the two men. The reporting trip to the front culminated parallel personal and professional journeys they had traveled for the better part of the past decade.

Not only were the two men nearing the end of a long day's drive and a winding road through life, they had also started out from similar places in the industrial Midwest. The somewhat older of the two reporters was now thirty-six. Born in Chicago, he moved as a boy to Cedar Rapids, Iowa, where the simplicity of family life amid the endless surrounding acres of cornfields had left its mark on him. Three years younger, the other American correspondent grew up in a mansion overlooking Cleveland and at a private boarding school in the East. Both could point to fathers who had been successful city attorneys. Each held college degrees, still relatively unusual at the time. Like so many educated and restless young Americans of the 1920s, they were drawn like iron filings to the magnet of postwar Europe's sophistication and its overthrow of tradition and reinvention of life and art.

Both loved the cosmopolitan, smart, highbrow, cynical, and uninhibited erotic life they made in Paris, Berlin, Rome, Vienna, and other capitals of Europe. Each quickly felt as at home there as in the United States. Voracious learners, they could read and speak several languages—and shared a particular fondness for German language, culture, and life.

Both started out with artistic and literary ambitions, but then turned, in different forms, to journalism, passionate and committed to scouting out and being on hand for the latest turn of events. They were in love with the new. As a result they had managed to witness some of the Continent's most momentous occasions over the past decade while cultivating ties among the famous men and women who shaped those events.

Each reporter in his way had traded on his love for Europe and his deep and intimate acquaintance with leading Europeans to win fame back in the United States. The two men shared a loose professional association, too, through the power of radio networks to reach inside American homes. The older reporter's reedy, uninflected voice had grown familiar to millions of Americans through his frequent radio broadcasts on European tensions. The younger man had won renown, too, originally as a tastemaker in the world of the arts, bringing back news from Europe about the new and austere modernist aesthetic that had conquered contemporary design and architecture. He traveled to Poland as a freelancer for a national weekly magazine that served as the print voice for one of America's most influential radio personalities.

That night, along the fast-eroding edge of the Baltic coast battlefields, their Nazi minders insisted that they share a room in the sumptuous beachfront Kasino Hotel in the Danzig Bay resort town of Zoppot (Sopot). It was a return there for the two men: Both had anticipated the war and, in August, had separately visited, driving through the Polish Corridor just days before the German invasion. Their return to the Hanseatic League port towns and cities, with their famous medieval Gothic guild houses lining cobbled streets as in some fairy tale made real, would serve as their personal farewell to an ancient and tottering Europe going up in flames.

And that brought them here together this day.

Any similarities between the two men ended with that. They took an almost immediate, poisonous dislike to each other.

*   *   *

Even the day before the war started, neither man could believe that Hitler would actually invade, until World War Two began at four forty on the morning of September 1, 1939. That was when twenty-nine *Luftwaffe* Ju 87 Stuka dive bombers came screaming from the sky over Wieluń, a small city of no conceivable military or industrial value near the German border. More aerial strikes followed, and when the first German troops streamed into Wieluń that afternoon, they found three quarters of the town leveled and twelve hundred people dead in their beds. The world war began with a terror bombing, fulfilling the special instructions Hitler gave to his generals before sending nearly a million and a half men, twenty-four hundred tanks, and twenty-five hundred aircraft into battle against a smaller, partially mobilized, and relatively poorly equipped Polish army. "Go, kill without mercy," the German chancellor purportedly declared. "Only in such a way will we win the living space that we need." He reminded any who might pause at such orders, "Who remembers the annihilation of the Armenians?" A war for territory marked the start of an unremitting campaign of racial destruction.

Within just days of the opening attacks, German panzers thundered through open country toward Warsaw. Poland, though, was not merely knifed; it was ripped in two. Under terms of the mutual nonaggression pact reached a week before the German invasion by Soviet foreign minister Vyacheslav Molotov and his Nazi counterpart, Joachim von Ribbentrop, the Red Army invaded. The day before the two correspondents entered Poland for the last time, Russia announced it would annex the eastern half of its territory.

The front lines advanced so fast that the foreign correspondents could not catch up with them that day. That was no surprise for the older of the two men, Berlin-based CBS radio's chief continental correspondent, William Lawrence Shirer. Shirer had sardonically noted the night before that he was "off to the 'front' . . . if we can find one."

Shirer's reedy introduction—"Hello, America. This is Berlin."—at the start of his weekly segment on CBS World News Roundup, and of late his frequent breaking-news reports on the rising tensions and outbreak of the war reached tens of millions of Americans. That was a great leap for a man who had worked his way to Paris pitching hay on a cattle boat a decade earlier. He landed a job in the *Chicago Tribune* Paris bureau and covered major events, including Charles Lindbergh and the *Spirit of St. Louis*'s arrival at Le Bourget Airport at the end of his epochal transatlantic solo flight, royal coronations, Olympic games, and other sporting events. In 1932, Shirer became chief of the *Tribune*'s Central European bureau in Vienna. He married an Austrian woman. In 1934, CBS's European chief, Edward R. Murrow, hired him to report for his radio network from the volcanic continent's molten-hot center, Berlin.

Once there, Shirer made it his business to get to know this fast-rising strongman who had just become chancellor and then almost immediately, as head of state, consolidated all power in his own hands.

On September 5, 1934, not two weeks after Shirer's arrival in Berlin, he watched the National Socialist leader in action for the first time. He went to the annual weeklong *Parteitage*, the Nazi Party rally, in Nuremberg. The week proved to be a "sort of baptism in Nazi Germany," he wrote in a diary he secretly kept. At the outset, he was inadvertently swept into "a mob of ten thousand hysterics" gathered outside Hitler's hotel. When Hitler stepped onto the hotel balcony, Shirer watched as "they went mad . . . their faces transformed into something positively inhuman." He was baffled, seeing nothing in this small and haggard man prone to nervous tics worthy of such adoration and outright hysteria. However, before the week's end, he better understood Hitler's genius at orchestrating a theater of mass frenzy and blind loyalty.

The rally at Nuremberg was, he noted later, "like a scene in a Wagner opera. . . ." The grand spectacle reached its crescendo on the Zeppelin Field, the immense parade grounds where a quarter-million people gathered to show their undying support for their Führer. Brilliant as a speaker and at bolstering unity among his people, Hitler cast what Shirer called his "spell" on the thousands gathered before him.

"Man's—or at least the German's—critical faculty is swept away. . . ," he recorded, "and every lie pronounced is accepted as high truth itself." At the end of the week in Nuremberg, Shirer and other reporters met with the German chancellor. Shirer recorded that Hitler explained that the party-rally format was part of a deliberate, highly rehearsed "technique" employed to orchestrate the annual renewal of his followers' emotional support. By the end, Hitler explained, they would go "back to their towns and villages [to] preach the new gospel with new fanaticism."

He did not think much of Hitler, but after that week he understood far better the wellsprings of his power. He later wrote, "One had to remember though—and I sometimes forgot—that Adolf Hitler was a consummate actor." After what he'd seen, the young reporter feared "that European civilization . . . might not survive Hitler's dictatorship."

As Shirer continued to report from Germany, restrictions grew more severe and violent, and he was obliged to accept the German Propaganda Ministry's strict oversight and censorship of his radio broadcasts. They controlled the feeds and could cut him off at any time. His broadcast scripts were read by three censors and two German-Americans listened in as he read them out for transmission. To describe what he was witnessing to Americans who might not believe the truth even if he could tell them, he said later, he "used every ruse of voice and double meaning to dodge the Nazi censorship." American listeners often heard him say, "The German people are reading today in their papers," which were well known to be tightly controlled by the government, conveying in his deadpan manner that he could only tell half-truths about life under Hitler. Even on his rare trips back to the U.S., despite his wishes to speak out, he could not report more, if he was to get permission from Berlin to return to his job.

In a veiled attempt to convey to his American listeners the dangers he foresaw, he also translated from Hitler's own harangues about the need to suppress Jews, Slavs, and other so-called inferior peoples and their nations. He described the military buildup and the huge war industry Germany possessed. He shared Hitler's intention to overturn the Great War's Versailles peace limitations placed on Germany. Many people at home discounted what he reported, either in sympathy to the Nazis or out of lack of concern about those they oppressed or any potential threat they represented to American interests and security. "This is a truth obvious to all of us here," he noted privately, "but when we . . . report it we [are] accused of making [anti-]Nazi propaganda."

The censorship steadily tightened, to the point that microphones were covered to prevent the sounds of British bombing raids and return antiaircraft fire from reaching American audiences' ears. Frustrated by his inability to report fully and truthfully, Shirer jotted down his daily impressions of life in Nazi Germany. After his early-morning broadcasts for the evening news at home, he'd stumble through Berlin's blacked-out streets to his room at the Adlon Hotel, neighboring the Brandenburg Gate, the Reichstag, and other government buildings. Here he'd scrawl out a diary on small sheets of paper. After making each day's entry, he carefully tucked those pages within stacks of other papers, magazines, and books piled high on his desk. He knew the maids and porters worked for the Gestapo and sifted through his belongings while he was out. If the Gestapo found his diary, filled as it was with the daily truth censored from his radio broadcasts, he'd be tossed out of the country or put in a Gestapo prison, or worse. However, he found that the spies "didn't have the patience to dig through my stuff." Day by day, his secret diary grew.

Every few weeks he gathered up its loose pages and passed them to a friendly diplomatic courier who smuggled them to Washington, D.C.—though even in later years he never revealed just who carried or sent out the diary. Among those who may have helped him for a period were the former American ambassador William Dodd and his pretty and vivacious daughter, Martha, who thought of Shirer and his Viennese wife, Tess, as "my closest and dearest friends" during her final year and a half living at the embassy in Berlin. Thanks to some unnamed conspirator, hundreds of smuggled pages reporting about life in Germany under

Hitler's murderous totalitarian rule awaited Shirer's eventual return to Washington, D.C.

One day he expected to return home for good. Once there, no longer forced to submit to German censorship, he could tell his countrymen the truth. That truth was indeed frightening. He was certain that war with the Third Reich was coming for America. "The clash," he secretly recorded, was ". . . as inevitable as that of two planets hurtling inexorably through the heavens towards each other." He needed to warn his countrymen. America remained caught up in a political struggle at home over its role in the European war, the menace Hitler posed for Americans thousands of miles overseas, and whether fascism might ever prove a true danger to the nation. Shirer thought the United States should mobilize for war. Now. The dangers of waiting were all too obvious to him.

Just how obvious became clear during an encounter with a haughty, high-ranking German military official. When Shirer asked him about Hitler's ultimate intentions toward the U.S., he coyly asked Shirer back: Would not "'a master at timing . . . choose the moment for war with America—a moment which he thinks will give him the advantage?'" War, Shirer feared, "may come sooner than almost all Americans at home imagine."

He feared war for personal reasons, too, particularly with his wife and young daughter still living in Berlin. If war came before they got out, they would likely be interned. He knew what that might mean.

The press contingent racing after the German army in Poland reached the final Baltic battleground. From the German command post on a Gydnia hilltop, Shirer surveyed the front along a ridge two miles distant—"where the killing was going on," he told American listeners in a broadcast a few days later. He had refused the offer of a German helmet, he wrote down in secret, finding it "repellent" and "symbolic of brute German force." The battle was too far off to spot individual fighters, but he

Shirer broadcasting to America for CBS Radio from Berlin. The metal canister contains his gas mask.

could see the Polish positions and that the Germans surrounded them on three sides and cut off escape with their artillery fire on the fourth. The din of battle, the shocking detonations of the big German shells, the flash-bang of artillery and rattling of machine-gun fire, echoed and reechoed through the city. With "nothing but machine guns, rifles, and two anti-aircraft pieces which they were trying desperately to use as artillery," the Poles slowly fell back into buildings where other fighters had taken up positions. German infantry moved toward them behind advancing tanks. Overhead a seaplane spotted for the *Schleswig-Holstein* as the battleship, anchored off Danzig ten miles to the rear of Shirer's viewing post, lobbed huge, sibilant shells overhead that burst against the Polish positions. Flames shot up from the roof of a building that burned down upon the defenders within. Polish troops kept hidden,

Shirer covering the election of a new Pope from St. Peter's Square, Rome, in 1939.

not daring to expose themselves to the Stukas bombing and strafing their lines. The screaming airplanes dove within 150 feet of the ground and soared away unmolested. It was, said Shirer, "as if they'd been target practicing."

He could not help feeling awed seeing the Nazi military in action. Sea, air, and land arms "all seemed to work as a precise machine," he said. The officers in the observation post "remind[ed] me of coaches of a championship football team who sit on the sidelines and confidently watch the machine they've created perform as they knew all the time it would." That night, he saw the Polish Corridor's last fifteen thousand Polish fighters surrender.

Normally happiest and most at ease in the company of his many friends among the press corps, Shirer instead felt uneasy on this trip. It was not only the day's events that disturbed him. He was worried about his assigned traveling companion in the press pool.

The German Propaganda Ministry forced him to share a room with Philip Cortelyou Johnson. Despite the two men's similar age and American pasts, shared love for Europe, and the overseas camaraderie war reporters might normally enjoy, "None of us can stand the fellow," Shirer noted at the end of the day, in one of his rare diary entries critical of a fellow reporter. He wanted only to slip away from Johnson. The reporters in the pool felt more than an intense dislike for the talkative and frenetic Johnson, already among the most prominent evangelizers for modernism in architecture, though not yet among the most famous architects in the world. They had reason to fear this flighty, off-putting American who seemed uncomfortably close to their German Propaganda Ministry minders.

2

A New World

For Philip Johnson, following the German army as it wiped out the last resisters in Poland seemed like he was living within a dream. As with Shirer, witnessing Poland's death throes climaxed Johnson's life's journey. He, too, had watched Hitler clasp the German people's heart to his own and the Third Reich rise as a relentlessly aggressive military power. In fact, he had come to report on the German scene and first encountered the Führer's spellbinding rhetorical brilliance even before Hitler became the country's leader. His reactions were as different from Shirer's as night from day: Shirer's nightmare scene was fantasy come true for Johnson.

Articulate and passionate about anything modern, new, artful, and monumental, Johnson was stunningly brilliant, socially incandescent, and passionately opinionated on all matters of taste. He had a coruscating, irresistibly arrogant wit, and relished table talk and wicked gossip about art and ideas and the people who made them. Margaret Scolari Barr, the wife of the influential art historian Alfred Barr, Johnson's mentor and founding director of the Museum of Modern Art in New York City, recalled him in the period as "handsome, always cheerful, pulsating with new ideas and hopes. He was wildly impatient, could not sit down. . . . His way of speaking, of thinking—that quickness and vibration" brought him many friends, wide attention and early success. Whatever faults he may have had, penny-pinching wasn't one of them. While still in college at Harvard, his prominent Cleveland lawyer father gave him a large cache of Alcoa company stock shares that would skyrocket in value. He never worried as he spent freely on the luxuries he loved, like European fashion and American Packards and Cadillacs, and supported numerous less-well-off friends.

That fortune endowed Johnson with endless opportunity and the ability to make and entrance friends not only with his charm and intellectual gifts, but with his material ones, too. He knew everyone in the art world who mattered and made a home among Manhattan's artistically minded high-society crowd. At most gatherings, that scene centered on him.

Enamored of Europe as the result of boyhood summers spent there with his mother, Johnson returned often to the Continent's great cities and monuments to deepen his college education in ancient Greek culture and European philosophy. Along with rich artistic and intellectual exposure, those trips gave him his first chance to explore his sexual longing for men. The smartest of the smart set, Johnson never lacked for offers to attend society's finest salons or to share his bed with lovers.

Consumed by the idea then foreign to most Americans that architecture and design were fine arts in their own right, he used his own money to establish the new Museum of Modern Art's Department of Architecture, making it the first major American museum to exhibit contemporary architecture and design. At age twenty-six, he collaborated in curating MoMA's landmark 1932 show "The International Style: Architecture Since 1922." The groundbreaking exhibition introduced Americans to masters of modern European architectural style, such as Walter Gropius and Berlin's Bauhaus school and the French master Le Corbusier, along with a few American practitioners, including Frank Lloyd Wright, Richard Neutra, and Raymond Hood. The exhibit and accompanying book would set the course for world architecture for the next forty years—above all, American adoption of modernism as the leading home and corporate building style.

Dashing, rich, precocious, the dazzling young Johnson—then a self-taught architect—dabbled in design and continued to pursue his role as a tastemaker in modern art. But, like a devouring flame, he longed for something greater, even more monumental. Devoted to his passions, body and soul, he had read deeply in the writings of the ancients and their nineteenth-century German interpreters, especially the works of his foremost philosophical inspiration, Friedrich Nietzsche. His notion of the superman, the hero able to fulfill his will without regard for modern society's conventions of right and wrong, fit Johnson's conception of the master builder, in architecture and perhaps more.

Not long after the MoMA exhibit upended American architectural thinking, Johnson traveled back to Europe. In the summer of 1932 he went to Berlin, where he stayed on into the fall during a period of revolutionary ferment and political struggle, an era when some of the same Nietzschean ideas that had obsessed Johnson took on a new currency within a nation upended by economic and social turmoil.

At a friend's urging, Johnson drove in early October to a Hitler Youth rally being held in a large field in Potsdam, outside Berlin. It would be the first time he saw Adolf Hitler, charismatic head of the insurgent National Socialist Party. That day, he experienced a revolution of the soul, a revelation he later described as "totally febrile." Decades later he recalled to his biographer, Franz Schulze, "You simply could not fail to be caught up in the excitement of it, by the marching songs, by the crescendo and climax of the whole thing, as Hitler came on at last to harangue the crowd." He could not separate the energy of the orchestrated frenzy from the day's sexual charge, either, feeling thrilled at the sight of "all those blond boys in black leather" marching past an ebullient Hitler.

Johnson returned home after that summer certain his life had been transformed in Potsdam. He found in fascism a new international ideal. The aesthetic power and exaltation he experienced in viewing modernist architecture found its complete national expression in the Hitler-centered fascist movement. But here was a way not merely to rebuild cities with a unified and monumental aesthetic vision for the machine age, but to spur a rebirth of mankind itself. He had never expressed any interest in politics before. After this, however, the Hitler-intoxicated Johnson was determined to "preach [the Führer's] the new gospel with new fanaticism" to Americans.

Over the next two years, he moved back and forth between Europe and New York City. At home, he mounted shows and promoted modernist artists whose works he considered the best of the new. All the while, he kept an eye on the Nazis as they consolidated power. Being gay, he had slept with his share of men in the sizzling demimonde of Weimar Berlin; now he turned a blind eye to Nazi restrictions on homosexual behavior, which brought imprisonment and even death sentences for homosexuals. He was taking a chance that his homosexuality would not surface.

Yet it was in modern art and architecture, the scene of his greatest personal triumphs, that he overlooked the most obvious discrepancies between Nazi policy and his own views. While arranging for Bauhaus friends to flee the increasingly dangerous attacks against their "degenerate" art by antimodernist Nazi forces, he saw the apparent contradiction in their plight only as a momentary falling back in order to leap that much farther ahead. "If in the arts," he wrote in an essay entitled "Architecture in the Third Reich" for an arts quarterly called *The Hound and the Horn*, "[Germany] sets the clock back now, it will run all the faster in the future."

Sharing the Protestant social elite's then-common disdain for Jews and fear of organized labor, he had no problem with the Nazi scapegoating of Jews or excoriation of communists. He wrote of a visit to Paris: "Lack of leadership and direction in the [French] state has let the one group get control who always gain power in a nation's time of weakness—the Jews." He added to that bigotry a personal snobbery toward mass democratic society. In an age of social collapse, Germany had figured out solutions he thought right for the crisis of democracy.

*Philip Johnson in January 1933,
photographed at his New York City
apartment by Carl Van Vechten.*

He was sure fascism could transform America, if perhaps occasioning some temporary dislocations for certain "alien" groups, much as it had Germany. As with his translation of European aesthetics into the American context, he felt ready to embark on an effort to import fascism to America.

To that end, he became a devoted follower of Lawrence Dennis, a Harvard graduate thirteen years his senior—and began to support him financially. A light-skinned African American who passed his life as white, Dennis was a former Foreign Service officer and brilliant economic analyst, and was deeply alienated from American society. He had attended Nuremberg Rallies and met with Italian fascist leader Benito Mussolini. He wrote several theoretical works on the decay of capitalism and on the fascist alternative, including *The Coming American Fascism* in 1936. Five years later *Life* magazine described him as "America's No. 1 intellectual Fascist." Johnson and longtime friend Alan Blackburn, a fellow MoMA official, were drawn to Dennis. The three gathered regularly at

Johnson's apartment to explore how, in practical terms, to bring about America's fascist future.

The press could not help but take notice of the prominent young men's switch from the art world to the political arena. *The New York Times* reported on their newfound mission in an article headlined "Two Forsake Art to Found a Party." Blackburn told the *Times*, "All we have is the strength of our convictions. . . . We feel that there are 20,000,000 to 25,000,000 people in this country who are suffering at present from the inefficiency of government. We feel that there is too much emphasis on theory and intellectualism. There ought to be more emotionalism in politics"—emotionalism, he meant, of the kind Hitler had tapped so successfully in Germany.

First, though, they needed their country's Hitler. They thought they might have found him in Huey Long, the Kingfish.

The populist former Louisiana governor and now United States senator was already famous, and among many notorious, for his rabble-rousing charisma and autocratic grip on his impoverished Southern state. The New York intellectuals thought Long was their man; Johnson said he needed only "a brain trust," like the one FDR brought with him to Washington, to win audiences throughout the land with his message. Johnson and Blackburn donned gray shirts—a restyled version of those worn by Hitler's brown-shirted paramilitary followers—placed pennons emblazoned with a flying wedge of Johnson's design on his Packard's fenders, and nosed the big car south to Baton Rouge.

Their footloose political convictions exuded a whimsy in venturing beyond society's norms. "I'm leaving . . . to be Huey Long's Minister of Fine Arts," Johnson said to friends, a risible version of Albert Speer's role as Hitler's personal architect in Berlin. Perhaps with tongue in cheek, the *New York Herald Tribune* article covering their planned escapade noted that the pair thought not only about politics, but about firearms: "Mr. Johnson favored a submachine gun, but Mr. Blackburn preferred one of the larger types of pistols." Blackburn was quoted as saying in earnest, "Of course we are interested in firearms. . . . I don't think it will do any of us here in the United States any harm in the next few years to know how to shoot straight." According to Johnson's friend Lincoln Kirstein, later a leading American cultural figure, he and Johnson stopped speaking for several years after he learned Johnson kept him and others on a list slated "for elimination in the coming revolution."

Johnson and Blackburn tried to meet with the Kingfish, who was considering a possible run for president. Before they could put their talents into his service, though, one of the Kingfish's many political enemies shot him dead.

Despite this setback, Johnson was not done with the possibility of bringing Nazism to America. He shifted his allegiance to a man even more in tune with his personal political agenda. In February of 1936, he moved briefly into Father Charles Edward Coughlin's Royal Oak, Michigan, parish house.

Every Sunday, the Roman Catholic "radio priest" preached a secular "mass" over the airwaves during his wildly popular *Golden Hour of the Shrine of the Little Flower*, broadcast from his parish house. At its peak, Coughlin's listenership reached some thirty to forty million people each week over William Shirer's own CBS Radio network—about one third of the country's entire population, and the largest audience of any regular program on the planet. Eventually Coughlin forged his own sixty-eight-station, coast-to-coast network.

After church Sunday mornings, families tuned in afternoons to hear his weekly on-air sermon, a florid combination of religious homily, politics, storytelling, and economic theory—delivered in his honeyed brogue with musical interludes on the organ and appeals for donations. Drawing on scriptural revelation and sensational secret sources placed deep within the enemy camp, he offered answers to the causes of his listeners' struggles and solace for their misery—together with a wrathful finger of blame pointing at elites, bosses of all kinds, and anti-Christian and communistic culprits. As the Depression deepened into a seemingly bottomless pit and federal intervention in the economy broadened, he accused FDR of having turned his back on the little man and aggrandizing his own powers, driving the nation toward ruin, dictatorship, and enslavement.

Coughlin excoriated Wall Street bankers and the Federal Reserve, men he called "the international money changers in the temple," for fleecing millions of average Americans. As the years went on, he honed in on a single Janus-faced culprit he called the "international conspiracy of Jewish bankers" and, without seeing any contradiction, the "closely interwoven relationship between Communism and Jewry." Listeners who might never have met a Communist or a Jew understood that there were stateless, conspiratorial, hook-nosed, money-grubbing villains working their evil designs upon the nation—and plotting worse.

Audiences worshipped Coughlin as prophet and celebrity. At his frequent public appearances, men and women fought to touch the hem of his cassock. A special post office had to be set up in Royal Oak for letters, often carrying listeners' precious dimes and dollars. These letters arrived at the rate of as many as one million weekly.

The money and popularity encouraged ambitions that grew beyond preaching to his national flock. Out of the Little Flower parish house, Coughlin launched a political organization he called the National Union for Social Justice, which backed candidates for office in several elections. *Social Justice*, the National Union's weekly news and opinion broadsheet, published his sermons, long disquisitions by theologians about evil loosed upon the world, texts of speeches by sympathetic politicians, articles about economics and world events, other news that would matter to Coughlin followers, and even sports coverage.

Almost every issue, though, contained articles about the "Jewish conspiracy" or about destructive economic forces led by figures with Jewish names. Coughlin personally possessed a large library of anti-Semitic works, and the pages of *Social Justice* became a widely read compendium of support for readers' anti-Semitic beliefs. *Social Justice* serialized "The Protocols of the Elders of Zion," a well-known nineteenth-century forgery about a Jewish conspiracy to take over the world through control of the media and finance and then use that power to weaken and enslave Christians. Coughlin blamed Jews and their role in the Russian Revolution and European communism for fomenting the anti-Semitic hatred now crushing them in Germany. In March 1939, *Der Stürmer*, an even more crudely anti-Semitic, semiofficial U.S. National Socialist Party newspaper, declared, "Father Coughlin in Royal Oak in the State of Michigan has the courage to speak his convictions."

At Coughlin's behest, the National Union's Christian Front organized what he termed "platoons." He urged that "American Christians . . . aid their Jewish fellow-citizens in shaking off Communism before it is too late." Christian Front platoons sold *Social Justice* on the street and started a "Buy Christian" campaign. Roving bands picked out Jews in various cities to taunt and beat up.

Coughlin rallied his following with a call "for restoring America to the Americans." However, he did not pretend to be democratic. According to one reporter on hand the night before the 1936 vote, Coughlin, who threw his weight behind a third-party right-wing candidate for the presidency, predicted, "America was seeing its last Presidential election." He declared, "We are at the crossroads. One road leads to Communism, the other to fascism." His own road was clear: "I take the road to fascism." Germany took notice. Although his prediction fell far short as his candidate lost badly, the German press denoted him as a leading voice in what it called America's "Front of Reason."

Although not religious, Philip Johnson believed Coughlin could emerge as an American fascist leader. He relished the fascistic message underlying Father Coughlin's movement, and shared the commonly held view that, wrote a reporter, "Coughlinism is the thread on which American fascism has been strung." Drawing upon his many talents and

In the 1930s Father Charles Coughlin built a national radio and publishing network. His public appearances, such as this 1936 rally in Cleveland, drew thousands.

ties to fascist Germany, Johnson was ready to bind those threads into a noose with which to hang American democracy.

A reported 80,000 paying supporters (*Social Justice* claimed "150,000 crusaders for Christian social justice") turned out for a September 1936 rally at Chicago's Riverview Park. Clad in white clerical collar and priestly black cassock, Coughlin stood alone before the vast throng high atop a stark white rostrum towering some twenty feet over the heads of his listeners. Directly behind him rose a five-story white wall topped by a row of enormous American flags fluttering from black posts. Silhou-etted against the white, Coughlin bobbed like a shadow boxer fending off blows while punching back with his fists and raising his hands in slashing gestures toward the blue sky.

His voice blasted out of immense speakers at the base of the tribune through the cheering crowd. He commanded his thousands to "form your battalions, take up the shield of your defense, unsheathe the sword of your truth, and carry on . . . so that the Communists on the one hand cannot scourge us and that the modern Capitalists on the other cannot plague us."

Some on hand that day may have already seen photographs or newsreel footage of a monumental white stage similar to one from which Coughlin spoke that day. The *Chicago Tribune* described the "special stand" with its "glaring white background . . . for the solitary figure of the priest" as "bordering on the modern." Johnson had modeled his design for the Chicago rally platform on the already famous one from which Hitler spoke each year at the giant Nazi Party Rally on Zeppelin Field in Nuremberg.

Convinced that fascism would govern America's future, Johnson returned to Germany in the summer of 1938. Fiery words and war tensions had been coursing through the Continent ever since Hitler's annexation of Austria the previous March. Johnson arrived with twinned goals of taking a special course offered by the German government for foreigners interested in Nazism—during which he seems to have made contacts with German agents in the United States—and attending the Nazi Party weeklong rally in Nuremberg.

Shirer's hell in Nuremberg was Johnson's Olympus.

Like Shirer, Johnson found in the party rally much of the spectacle of Wagnerian opera—an artistic performance encompassing all the audience's senses and beyond its power to resist being swept away by its orchestrated passion and grandeur. "Like the [Wagner opera cycle] *Ring*," Johnson recollected to his biographer, "even if you were at first indifferent, you were at last overcome, and if you were a believer to begin with, the effect was even more staggering." Here was a vision combining aesthetics, eroticism, and war, forces capable of sweeping away the past and building a new world. It was not lost on him that Hitler was trained in the visual arts and was obsessed with architecture and with constructing monumental works and carrying out gargantuan urban redevelopment plans for all the great cities of Europe to serve his vision of the Thousand-Year Reich.

Johnson believed, and hoped, that the tide of the future presently sweeping European democracies away might one day roll like a tsunami across the Atlantic Ocean.

On September 1, 1939, Johnson needed to pinch himself to be sure he was not dreaming. Sitting at a pleasant outdoor café in Munich, he kept repeating, "This is the first day of war." Three weeks later, he went as *Social Justice*'s correspondent on the German Propaganda Ministry road trip to see the war close up in Poland. Sticking beside Shirer, Johnson kept grilling him. Shirer thought it odd that Johnson was the lone American reporter invited along on the press trip not affiliated with a major news outlet. Shirer noted that Johnson kept "posing as anti-Nazi," but Johnson's reputation preceded him and Shirer tagged his traveling companion "an American fascist." He grumbled that Johnson kept trying "to pump me for my attitude" for more than an hour. He fended the importunate Johnson off with "a few bored grunts." Shirer assumed Johnson would report back anything he heard to the German Propaganda Ministry.

Johnson's views on the German invasion would soon appear in his articles for *Social Justice*. Johnson had visited the Polish Corridor, the Baltic seacoast, and Danzig in the last days of peace in August. At the time he described it as "the region of some awful plague. The fields were nothing but stone, there were no trees, mere paths instead of roads. In the towns there were no shops, no automobiles, no pavements and again no trees. There were not even any Poles to be seen in the streets, only Jews!" He found that "the longer I am here, the more I have to struggle to grasp once more what could possibly be the reason for Danzig's not being part of Germany."

One thing was clear to him: The resolution of Danzig's and the Polish Corridor's status, he wrote for *Social Justice*, would "not be solved by courts of law, on who has what right, where and for how long, but will be solved by the play of power politics." The arbiter of Poland's fate lay in the war for dominance among the powerful nations of Europe. Right and wrong meant nothing—only power did, in all its manifestations.

In his final report from his Polish trip on behalf of *Social Justice*, Johnson declared that the German victory amounted to an unmitigated triumph for the Polish people and that nothing in the war's outcome need concern Americans. He termed press representations of the Nazis' handling of the Poles "misinformed." German forces had inflicted scant harm on the country's civilian life, he wrote, noting that ". . . 99 percent of the towns I visited since the war are not only intact but full of Polish peasants and Jewish shopkeepers." However, his private letters about the same visit indicate he witnessed a very different reality.

Not long after his articles from Europe ran in *Social Justice*, he sent off a chatty letter to a friend with whom he had toured Poland in August, the German wife of a Luftwaffe ministry official. He reminded her of their previous visit shortly before the war started, to "the country that we had motored through, the towns north of Warsaw." A month later, he wrote, "it was unrecognizable." Venturing into the very same towns he'd found previously blighted as if by "some awful plague," he was delighted to report, "The German green uniforms made the place look gay and happy. There were not many Jews to be seen." Moving on from there, he watched the Nazi coup de grace in its decimation of Poland: "We saw Warsaw burn and Modlin being bombed. It was a stirring spectacle."

"By the play of power politics," Johnson wrote for *Social Justice*, Hitler was on his way to solving both the issues of race and the lingering international questions that had for so long plagued Europe. He concluded that Germany's triumph in this "minor war" proved the "truth" of Hitler's racial idea for Europe. In Philip Johnson's eyes, which saw a "stirring spectacle" where only weeks earlier he had found "no shops, no automobiles, no pavements . . . no trees . . . only Jews," the crushing of Poland was a triumph of a leader and his nation's will, proving its truth.

Shirer was back in Berlin a month when he met with another American reporter who had just come from Poland. Shirer noted in his private diary that the unnamed reporter told him of seeing thousands of Jews in Warsaw being forced at gunpoint from their homes and then barricaded into a walled-off sector of the city. That was part of planning for the war. A week into the invasion of Poland, on September 8, SS general and chief of the Reich Main Security Office Reinhard Heydrich was heard to say that "we want to protect the little people, but the aristocrats, the Poles and Jews must be killed." The day after the start of the invasion, an SS regiment captured the first 150 Polish citizens, penning them into a specially constructed concentration camp about twenty miles east of Danzig in the town of Stutthof (Sztutowo), which of course the Propaganda Ministry did not include in Shirer and Johnson's tour of the Baltic front. It was the first camp the Nazis built outside Germany.

The reporter who told Shirer about what he had seen in Warsaw said that "the Nazi policy is simply to exterminate the Polish Jews." He had also observed thousands of additional German Jews being expelled from Germany and "sent to eastern Poland to die." While stationed in Germany, Shirer could never get a report about the murder of Jews, or even their plight as a persecuted minority, past censors.

The world was again at war. "A new world," Shirer realized, had arrived.

Back from witnessing the destruction of Poland. Shirer scratched out his notes and hid them in his room in the Adlon Hotel in Berlin. The war barely a month old, he despaired for the world as he penned in his secret diary: "Black-out, bombs, slaughter, Nazism. Now the night and the shrieks and barbarism."

3

"That Prophecy Comes True"

Europe, 1939–1940

Back in the United States by the end of fall 1939, Philip Johnson was confident that the war would end soon. At the time, Johnson wrote in *Social Justice* that while London rattled its tin sabers and Paris shivered within its reinforced bunkers along the Maginot Line, Germany had raced forward, but the race was no longer to war. "[Berlin's] war aims are already attained, which is consistent with her inaction in the military sphere and her peace offensive in the 'talk' sphere," wrote Johnson. After Poland, Germany was intent on ultimate victory in "the moral war," he insisted. That was a war Berlin was also on the verge of winning, he opined. Hitler wished only to conclude peace with the rest of the world, in particular England. England's far more aggressive aims, on the other hand, could only be pursued through total war, according to Johnson. Who then, he asked, was guilty of fomenting war in Europe?

Johnson asserted that imperial London was unwilling to accept a rival power's dominating Europe and responded by insisting upon "the destruction of Hitlerism." To Johnson's mind, Germany's success was a fait accompli. He scoffed at the Allies' bellicose gestures. England's social and economic decay and moral decadence appeared in stark relief, he wrote, through this hollow chatter about her intention to wage "an extremely aggressive war against the best armed nation in the world . . . an aggressive war which she is not waging." The windbags of England, according to Johnson, had nothing but their ability to bluff in the face of a virile Germany's demonstrated willingness to fight.

Bellicose threats backed by inaction, Johnson wrote, offered ample evidence of the pitiful state into which the world's most powerful democracy and history's greatest empire had slumped. The wheels of history had been driven forward by Hitler. Facing no threat from Germany, America, he intimated, should support the formation of a new Europe dominated by the Third Reich.

However, Johnson overlooked a much larger, perhaps less widely reported battleground where war was already well under way and where England seemingly had the upper hand. Unlike the twilight war—soon known as the "Phony War"—on land, a shooting war between the two great powers began almost instantly at sea with the declaration of hostilities. England still ruled the waves. The Royal Navy, the world's most powerful surface fleet and enduring symbol of the globe-straddling British Empire, offered London its swiftest way to slap down Germany. London's preponderant naval strength provided the military basis for its vast colonial empire. Great Britain oxygenated its economy and sustained its domination of the United Kingdom entirely through maritime trade—and protected it with the vaunted Royal Navy.

At any given moment more than two thousand in- and outbound English merchants ranged global waterways, several hundred oceangoing vessels called in the nation's ports each week, and thousands more traders plied British coastal waters. England possessed a naval fleet of 375 oceangoing warships, including 7 aircraft carriers, 15 battleships, and 184 destroyers. Most of her ships were modern and well equipped, and of post–World War I vintage, except the battleships. The Admiralty also could call upon more than 20 additional naval vessels from Commonwealth allies.

Germany set sail with what amounted to a bathtub navy by comparison. At first the commanders of the German navy, the *Kriegsmarine,* trembled at the prospect of a naval war with England. Told by Hitler not to expect sea war with the Royal Navy before 1944 at the earliest, *Großadmiral* Dr. Erich Raeder, the fleet's commander in chief since 1928, despaired when the naval war came *five* years ahead of schedule. In a memorandum written at the start of the war, he laid out his assets. He noted that his fleet consisted of fifty-seven U-boats, only twenty-six of them suitable for duties in the heavy North Atlantic seas. He had no aircraft carriers, just two battleships (though two more, impressively advanced battleships, including the *Bismarck*, were being readied for service) and three heavy cruisers, and only twenty-two destroyers—less than a quarter of the enemy fleet. Raeder regarded his fleet as "so inferior in number and strength to those of the British Fleet that even at full strength, they can do no more than show that they know how to die gallantly," he warned Hitler. One day his grim words would prove brutally portentous, but to his surprise, the first weeks of fighting at sea showed that the relatively low-cost and quick-to-build U-boat force could inflict terrible damage on even the mighty Royal Navy's greatest ships.

On the same day he expressed his initial forebodings, *U-30*, part of the submarine fleet sent to sea in anticipation of war, waited two hundred miles northwest of Ireland. When the submarine's captain learned that war had been declared, he torpedoed a passing U.S.-bound liner, the *Athenia*. One hundred seventeen people died in the attack. More shocking to the British, who thought themselves secure behind their islands' moats, two weeks later two of their greatest warships were sunk—one within the shelter of the Royal Navy's principal base in Scapa Flow amid the Orkney Islands.

The world expected the mighty Royal Navy to come quickly to grips with the U-boat menace. The day after the *Athenia*'s sinking, a sixty-four-year-old Winston Churchill, a largely ignored Conservative Party backbencher for ten long years, heartened his stunned nation by accepting appointment as First Lord of the Admiralty. He would return to the helm of the Royal Navy he headed in the Great War. The Board of Admiralty famously signaled a lion's roar to all ships and naval bases: "WINSTON IS BACK."

Despite his florid and what some wags described as cuddly appearance, Churchill was a man of war to the soles of his zippered (to save time lacing) oxfords. Ever vigilant and ready to defend King and Empire, he was never at a loss for words and deployed armies of them in his nearly twenty multivolume histories, personal narratives, and speech collections published to date. The rotund Churchill stood only five feet six inches tall, yet he was rhetorically head and shoulders above any other European in his ability to counter Hitler's bombast about democratic Europe's demise. Churchill had famously scolded Prime Minister Neville Chamberlain in Parliament for choosing "dishonor" rather than "war" after he returned home with the 1938 Munich Agreement. He wrathfully intoned that the English people "have sustained a defeat without a war. . . . This is only the first sip, the first foretaste of a bitter cup which will be proffered to us. . . ," he warned.

Victory at sea was fundamental to Britain's fate in the war. "Never for one moment," Churchill later wrote of the war at sea, "could we forget that everything happening elsewhere, on land, at sea, or in the air, depended ultimately on its outcome. . . ." Despite a flurry of shipbuilding begun with the approach of war, Britain's navy remained preeminent, but Germany, too, had expanded its naval construction program, with a goal of building as many as thirty new, larger, longer-range, and more lethal submarines each month. Germany's underwater fleet would trump Britain's surface predominance.

Destroyers—swift, quick-turning, long-range—were Britain's most effective counter to the submarine. But Great Britain did not have near enough of them to protect her shores, screen her fleet, and patrol her global shipping lanes—not by a long shot. Almost immediately, the new First Lord of the Admiralty urged the government "to purchase destroyers from the United States," despite the "dollar stringency" the cash-strapped Empire faced, to remedy the "shortage of destroyers from which we [are] suffering." Churchill, though, knew something of the restrictions that might encumber even a sympathetic American government in selling warships to a belligerent power. And he could only hope for its benevolent intervention to find a way to pay for them.

He had little idea just how distant the fruition of that hope remained. Most people in the U.S. understood that the Nazi juggernaut endangered democratic ideals at home and abroad, and realized British defeat might jeopardize America's hemispheric security, but the nation had dug in its heels against intervening in another European war. President Franklin Delano Roosevelt was a conflicted leader of an isolationist nation. Whereas Germany and Italy chose or were forced to accept autocratic leaders and state control to contend with economic depression and civil strife, Americans voted by large margins for a leader committed to democratic ideals and liberal economic policies to pull their nation out of similar conditions. Those ideals and policies might wither and die in the heat of a world overwhelmed by fascism.

FDR had expressed his opposition to "those nations which are dominated by the twin spirits of autocracy and aggression" as early as 1935, in his State of the Union address. With Germany and Japan clearly in mind, he condemned them for having "reverted to the old belief in the law of the sword, or to the fantastic conception that they, and they alone, are chosen to fulfill a mission and that all the others among the billion and a half of human beings in the world must and shall learn from and be subject to them."

In that same speech, he espoused his nation's traditional commitment to neutrality in the affairs of other nations. "The United States and the rest of the Americas," he declared, "can play but one role: through a well-ordered neutrality to do naught to encourage the contest, through adequate defense to save ourselves from embroilment and attack, and through example and all legitimate encouragement and assistance to persuade other nations to return to the ways of peace and good-will." However, in a globalized world of wars of high-speed movement, could continental defense alone save America from attack? How could the U.S., isolated within the safety of its moated Western Hemisphere, persuade other nations to stop fighting, especially once war had begun?

As war loomed, FDR began to formulate a strategy he called "aggressive nonbelligerence" as his country's response to the ongoing world crisis. In his January 1939 State of the Union address, he pointed out that the U.S. possessed "many methods short of war" to assist victims of autocratic regimes and combat further threats of aggression. At his March 7, 1939, press conference, he expanded this view that, particularly at sea, the nation possessed powers to defend itself that did not amount to declared war. "This business of carrying on a war without declaring a war, that we think is new, it is not new," he told reporters. As president, he said, he had "a Constitutional duty to defend [the United States] . . . without the declaring of war." However, congressional antiwar factions, fearing just such a move, claimed that existing neutrality legislation required the president to seek authorization before sending American forces into even the possibility of armed conflict.

Roosevelt kept America's security foremost in his mind. He believed that defense considerations allowed him to respond in a warlike way without his formally declaring war. However, whatever Europe's fate, he would not abandon America's traditional role as a neutral nation by sending U.S. soldiers to war there again—unless America were first attacked.

FDR barely knew Churchill, and what he knew he did not particularly like. He was not comfortable with Prime Minister Chamberlain's previous appeasement of Hitler at Munich, but he doubted that Churchill would emerge as a leader to save democratic Europe—or even someone likely to prove America's enduring friend. The U.S. president may have risen from patrician and Anglophile roots, but he was a thoroughly modern American. The florid and bibulous Churchill was Victorian by birth and mind-set and second to none in his devotion to Empire, Crown, and class. Roosevelt was no friend of colonial empires and the rivalries and economic distortions they produced, leading, he thought, to the Great War. He also resented the way the British treated America as a junior partner in international affairs.

That distrust of Churchill was also tied to a lingering personal resentment. Sometimes thin-skinned, FDR still smarted from the snub he felt when the two men, both high naval officials at the time, had sat together at a London banquet during the First World War. The president described the First Lord of the Admiralty to his ambassador to London, Joseph P. Kennedy—no friend of the English himself—as "one of the few men in public life who was rude to me." Not one to forget a slight, he recalled that Churchill "acted like a stinker . . . lording it all over us. . . ."

He nonetheless could not miss their common interests and the need for their leadership talents in the present crisis. FDR appreciated Churchill's foresight on world affairs and, like Churchill, he felt it his rightful role to guide his nation in a time of crisis. He had indicated as much in 1936 when he told the Democratic Convention that his American generation faced "a rendezvous with destiny." Before then, the fight had been solely for national economic revitalization. Now, America, he told the party assembly, was "waging a great and successful war . . . to save a great and precious form of government for ourselves and for the world." By the time of his 1939 State of the Union speech two and a half years later, he could say to the American people: "That prophecy comes true."

Perhaps Roosevelt and Churchill's closest kinship lay in the great ocean that separated their two nations. Each felt a lifelong passion for the sea, the navy, and all aspects of maritime affairs. Until stricken by polio, Roosevelt had expertly sailed pleasure craft. Among his many collecting passions, he gathered an array of naval prints and historical ship models. Despite his physical limitations, he still felt at his best on the water. He frequently took the helm of the presidential yacht, a 165-foot former coast guard cutter, *Potomac*, for excursions with friends and official guests.

He had begun his political ascent as an ambitious assistant secretary of the navy during the 1914–1918 war. His boss at the time, Secretary of the Navy Josephus Daniels, a newspaperman with little interest in naval affairs, allowed the young Franklin enormous sway over the Navy Department. In part through Roosevelt's administrative drive, the U.S. Navy successfully transported two million troops and their supplies to Europe with relatively little loss of life. However, FDR could also attest to the Herculean efforts this undertaking demanded, along with embarrassing inefficiencies, outrageous cost overruns, and galling and egregious corruption among the ranks of contractors.

Roosevelt also learned political lessons from President Woodrow Wilson's successful reelection in 1916, when he ran as an isolationist, refusing to involve the nation in the Great War. Wilson campaigned in 1916 on the slogan, "He kept us out of war." With the advent of a second pan-European war and the spread of the world crisis, Roosevelt reconsidered his previously professed desire to leave office. In late 1939, he began leaning toward a historically unprecedented run for a third term in the coming year. With the 1940 election in sight, FDR understood that America was historically and by geographical isolation predisposed to keep out of wars outside its hemisphere. American attitudes toward Europe had hardened in the interwar period. A presidential campaign riding the rails toward war in Europe would jump the tracks.

Unlike Wilson, though, Roosevelt was a realist, and grasped well the geopolitical and military hurdles facing the nation should war come. His strategic acumen and global outlook were second to none within his administration. Describing himself as a man with "a map mind," he delighted in exploring the interplay of nations, geography, and history. He knew the world intimately, even if politics and polio restricted his ability to move about it any longer at his leisure. Three quarters of the planet was covered by water. Maritime affairs, naval history, and strategy obsessed him even as a boy; he had, he claimed, "practically memorized" the bible of American naval strategy, U.S. Navy admiral Alfred Thayer

Mahan's classic *The Influence of Sea Power upon History*. Roosevelt the president embraced the fundamental Mahanian concept that America's first line of defense lay at sea and that defense of the continent was best mounted as far as possible from its coasts.

But just how far from shore did that most defensible line of hemispheric defense lie? FDR reportedly quipped in early 1939, "The American frontier is on the Rhine." At his February 17, 1939, press conference, Roosevelt denied that U.S. defenses ran physically all the way to the Rhine. But after a reporter asked him point blank, "Just where are our borders?" FDR pointedly refused to say.

Potential enemies' military capabilities had leaped far ahead, most importantly becoming far more mobile and airborne, in the time since Mahan wrote about the projection of naval power at the turn of the century. Yet few Americans had fully grasped the direct impact these changes could have on their lives. FDR's capacity to lead his nation in a world at war depended on his ability to educate his people at home about threats that emanated far from home. From now on almost every public talk he gave aimed to persuade Americans that their security no longer ended at their nation's borders.

In his 1940 State of the Union address, Roosevelt called upon Americans to consider the warring nations' arsenals of modern weaponry—he was thinking particularly of Germany's large, advanced fighter-bomber air force—and mobile armies. Their capacity to attack swiftly, unexpectedly, and suddenly made wishful thinking of the belief that "the United States of America as a self-contained unit can live happily and prosperously, its future secure, inside a high wall of isolation while, outside, the rest of Civilization and the commerce and culture of mankind are shattered." Modern aircraft and long-range warships put U.S. shores that oceans had once made beyond reach without weeks of travel—giving defenders time to prepare—within reach of an overseas enemy within days, or even hours. He called for the country to pursue what he termed a "common sense" approach to "the danger to which we in America must begin to be more alert."

*   *   *

America's best hope for avoiding another war—and thus its first line of defense—lay in England's pursuing war against Germany to victory. The possibility existed, however, that London might be forced by arms, or by internal pro-appeasement factions, to reach terms with the odious and dangerous dictator Hitler. FDR might not like Churchill, but he could rely upon him to fight. Developing a personal relationship with the new First Lord of the Admiralty could only enhance American security along its Atlantic frontier and its Pacific bases, primarily the Philippines, near English colonial possessions in East Asia. And so Roosevelt set out to get to know Winston Churchill.

A week after the start of the war, FDR reached out to Churchill with a brief yet characteristically personal note. The president began: "It is because you and I occupied similar positions in the World War that I want you to know how glad I am that you are back again in the Admiralty. Your problems are, I realize, complicated by new factors, but the essential is not very different." It was most unusual in the annals of international relations that a head of state should pen such a letter directly to a cabinet minister of a foreign government. (And not atypical for FDR to inflate his prior post.) However, Roosevelt was not one to deal with important international questions through normal diplomatic channels—the "boys in striped pants," he disdainfully called his own State Department diplomats—nor did he have much use for existing governmental hierarchies. He trusted people, not organizational structures, and openly distrusted the cultures of bureaucracies.

Roosevelt invited Churchill to "keep in touch personally with anything you want me to know about." In his initial message to the new First Lord of the Admiralty, FDR sought to make clear that he wanted a direct and personal relationship and anticipated that the two would remain close. The president's message also presciently implied his expectations of Churchill's determinative role in the war against the autocratic forces now loosed upon Europe and the world.

* * *

Churchill's reply was equally epoch-making in intimating the strategic course of an unspoken alliance that both men intended their nations to pursue yet dared not make public. As a cabinet minister, Churchill's answering message went through redrafting by others within the government and required the cabinet's permission to send. In his original, Churchill hinted at his own feelings, calling it "a most unusual experience to occupy the same post fighting the same enemy 25 years later," but other Admiralty officials scratched that personal touch. Instead they redrafted the First Lord's reply to rest on more statesmanlike suggestions for ways to keep war away from the Americas. They knew exactly what the president wanted to hear, because he had already told them.

In June 1939, three months before Germany's invasion of Poland, FDR invited King George VI and his wife to visit the U.S. Nobody missed the point in seeing the British royals, the first royal visit since the American colonials had rebelled against English rule, motoring down the Potomac River aboard the presidential yacht to George Washington's home at Mount Vernon. Sitting with the king at the Roosevelt family estate in Hyde Park a few days later, FDR suggested to him that, should war come, America might consider delineating a neutrality zone extending far out to sea from which all belligerent activities would be excluded. "But can it be done without a declaration of war?" the king asked him.

With war declared in Europe, at the September 23, 1939, Inter-American Conference, the twenty-one Western Hemisphere nations adopted a unified approach to the war, accepting the president's proposal—though not publicly acknowledged as his—for a coastal zone throughout which all belligerent activity would be banned. The zone would extend out three hundred miles from the national mainlands into the Atlantic, far beyond the currently recognized three-mile territorial limit. Only the U.S. had the fleet and diplomatic heft remotely powerful enough to compel warring nations not to shoot at one another within such a large swath of ocean.

*   *   *

Churchill understood the president's thinking about U.S. defense and
endorsed the proposed "safety belt" in his first message to FDR. Given
the great imbalance in naval power between the European enemies, such
a broad safety belt would work entirely to London's advantage. Ship
traffic in and out of Germany now faced a tight blockade on the Baltic
approaches, and few vessels dared sail for Germany. With German shipping throttled in port, the "safety belt," or "neutrality zone" in American
parlance, effectively immunized from attack British, Commonwealth,
and neutral merchant traffic moving among American hemisphere ports.
They could assemble safely into convoys off Canada or South America
before making the dash across the Atlantic. Churchill did not have to add
that many of those ships would be carrying American-made weapons,
munitions, and aircraft bound for Allied forces.

Thus began an exchange that would eventually amount to 788
written messages and telegrams flowing from Roosevelt to Churchill and
1,161 missives from the Englishman to the American—the many more
messages from Churchill showing who was the needier correspondent.

Churchill's initial telegram ended: "We wish to help you in every
way in keeping the war out of American waters." To do so would take
an American willingness to keep German warships out of those waters.
But that, Churchill and FDR both knew, got awfully close to war itself.
Kept from putting his own characteristic flourishes on the message,
Churchill signed his first correspondence in a coded manner he knew
would appeal to Roosevelt: "Naval Person."

4

Unneutral Acts

In September 1938, as Britain's prime minister, Neville Chamberlain, was exiting his meeting with Adolf Hitler in Munich with a declaration that he and the German chancellor had reached an agreement assuring "peace in our time," FDR found himself doubting that the sops of appeasement would satisfy Hitler. He promptly directed the U.S. Navy to take its fleet of around fifty Great War–vintage destroyers out of mothballs and ready them for action.

For two decades the four-stackers had moldered against the Philadelphia Navy Yard piers and in other ports. After the invasion of Poland, the president ordered that the destroyers be detached to a newly operational "Atlantic Squadron." The initial mission was the limited three-mile patrol off the Eastern seaboard. Even this slender range heavily taxed the peacetime navy—poorly trained and undermanned, stretched for officers, inadequately armed, reliant on outmoded technology, and dependent on a small number of logistically limited bases. Thousands of reservists were rushed to duty to fill out crews on the destroyers. Many had never even seen a ship's gun fired. To fill out the thinned officer corps, the Naval Academy was eventually ordered to speed up graduation. Officer and crew alike would have to learn on the job.

FDR continued to push the navy to its limits. A year later, with the war in its first days, the president invited his newly appointed chief of naval operations, Admiral Harold R. Stark, to the White House. Roosevelt addressed the admiral as "Betty," a nickname which the good-natured officer was said to have accepted as a Naval Academy plebe. The two men first met when Stark, then a young lieutenant, had helmed the navy cruiser ferrying then-Assistant Secretary of the Navy Roosevelt to his summer home on Campobello Island. Twenty-five years later, in an unprecedented move, Roosevelt jumped Stark ahead of fifty more senior officers in line for the Navy's highest-ranking post. With the demeanor of a friendly bishop, the now white-haired, pink-cheeked, and reticent Stark had won favor for his diplomatic skills in working with the British on the navy's London staff in the previous war. He shared the president's conviction that British victory was essential to American security. In Stark's view, "If Britain wins decisively against Germany we could win everywhere; but . . . if she loses the problem confronting us would be very great; and, while we might not *lose everywhere*, we might, possibly, not *win anywhere*." That was an outcome to be avoided at all costs.

Sitting at his desk in the Oval Office, FDR motioned Stark over to a wall chart of the Atlantic he now kept nearby. The admiral knew his commander in chief's map mind. Roosevelt's command of geography transformed two-dimensional depictions of the earth into a multidimensional vision teeming with men and their doings, past, present, and future. "He could sit and plot all the towns that could be passed on a flight down Brazil and over to India," said Stark. He knew "the height of the mountains, depths of the oceans, the plains they watered and the tides." Roosevelt used maps to realize his geopolitical vision the way a great painter deployed brush and paint on canvas.

Roosevelt picked up a pencil and made a sweeping line along the sixty degrees west longitude meridian running from Newfoundland and reaching out nearly three hundred miles west of Bermuda, all the way to British Guiana on the shoulder of South America. The president's eyes alight, he excitedly asked Stark, "How would the navy like to patrol such a neutrality zone?" The admiral's pale blue eyes peered through rimless eyeglasses at the chart. He thought the president, known for his practical jokes, must be kidding, and explained that the Atlantic Squadron was already stretched beyond its limits in patrolling the Inter-American conference's new three-hundred-mile coastal zone. At a pencil stroke, FDR would effectively more than double the neutrality patrol zone, especially in the North Atlantic through which most American goods traveled to Europe. Roosevelt seemed to accept Stark's reply. The admiral returned to the Navy Department thinking the matter was at an end.

He would soon discover it was not.

Not long after, an inquiring State Department official sought out Stark. He asked about the challenges the navy faced in monitoring the newly greatly enlarged neutrality zone. Stark scoffed at the idea of patrolling such an impossibly vast tract of ocean and gulf. He explained that to cover the neutrality zone out to sixty degrees west would take the navy's entire 290-ship fleet (counting subs and auxiliary vessels) and would require triple the number of seaplanes it currently possessed. And then nothing would be left over for training or for operations in the Pacific, where the navy faced plenty of other troubles. The navy continued its limited patrols in place.

In early October, though, perhaps thanks to the arrival of Churchill's reply to the president's first message, Roosevelt's patience wore thin. He wrote a bristling memo to the secretary of the navy, intending, he told him, "to make the following orders clear": From now on the Atlantic Squadron would, he laid out point by point, one, "follow any suspicious craft of any nationality"; two, "remain in contact as long as possible . . . day and night"; and, three, on an open channel, "report the sighting . . . in plain English. . . ." The enlarged neutrality zone was a real operation, not just a fantasy FDR scratched out on the map. The effect of the order did not take long to be felt—especially the last point.

In the war's merciless open season on shipping, England, too, targeted passenger ships. A few days after the Europeans went to war, the German liner *Columbus*—among the world's most luxurious passenger ships—off-loaded her passengers in Havana and turned for home. Royal Navy ships spotted and chased her into the harbor off Veracruz. British navy patrols in the Atlantic also scared scores of other German and Italian ships into various Southern Hemisphere ports and continued to prowl in international waters like cats at mouse holes, daring the ships to show themselves.

For three long months *Columbus* remained anchored in Mexican coastal waters. On December 13, repainted completely black, fully fueled, she steamed out with her company of six hundred crewmen and a handful of women. A German freighter, the *Arauca*, slipped to sea shortly after that. Both ran dark and silent within the security zone of the North American coast until the *Arauca* headed into open water. Picked up by a British cruiser, she promptly raced back into the protection of American waters, finally finding refuge in Florida's Port Everglades. She would remain anchored there, a swastika flag flying from her mast like a pin pricking FDR's side.

The blacked-out *Columbus* continued on. Two American destroyers picked her up and shadowed her so tightly as she churned northward through U.S. coastal waters that the German captain felt, he said, like a "dog on a leash." Dropping away, the captain of one of the destroyers flashed out departing good wishes to the German ship, knowing, he said, that his signals were like "the kiss of death." Off New Jersey, *Columbus* built a full head of steam and then dashed for open waters. As she steamed to sea, the Atlantic Squadron's flagship *Tuscaloosa* pulled in behind her, sticking a few hundred yards off her stern. The skipper of the fully illuminated American ship flashed out greetings to the blacked-out German ship's captain, like a beacon to the horizon. "What the devil does this all mean?" the German captain sputtered. He wondered, "Is he protecting us or shadowing us?" He soon had an answer.

Running night and day, every few hours the *Tuscaloosa* broadcast its position near an unidentified ship. Two hundred miles northwest of Bermuda, a British warship picked up the radio signals. When the Royal Navy destroyer rose into sight, the *Tuscaloosa* dropped back a mile off the *Columbus*.

The British destroyer signaled the German ship to stop. When the German captain ignored the order, the destroyer fired twice across her bow. The *Columbus* shut off her screws; the captain sent his crew to their practiced tasks. They set fire to the ship, smashed the skylights, and opened her seacocks. The entire ship's company slipped over the side into the lifeboats. and the *Tuscaloosa* picked them up. On the American and British decks, the forlorn faces of thousands of seamen of three nations—two at war, one ostensibly at peace—watched as flames erupted and black smoke billowed over the once glorious liner. The Atlantic Ocean boiled up around her. Then she was gone.

Word of the great German liner's demise got out immediately. In a three-column front-page story the following morning, *The New York Times* reported that the *Columbus* had sunk during an incident with a British destroyer. According to the article, U.S. Navy Department officials claimed the *Tuscaloosa* was on "routine neutrality patrol" when it approached the *Columbus* in distress. Officials insisted that "no unneutral action has taken place." The White House press secretary, Stephen Early, emphasized that the *Tuscaloosa* had arrived on the scene only after the *Columbus* started to sink. Admiral Stark ordered the *Tuscaloosa* captain to remain silent about the circumstances of the German liner's sinking, explaining that "we do not desire . . . to make public the details of our . . . patrol."

With around eighty-five other German and Italian ships in Western Hemisphere waters at the start of the war, the Atlantic Squadron and

American harbormasters managed to alert the Royal Navy to the presence of most of them. About half of them remained stranded in U.S. and South American harbors. After barely four months of war, a pattern was emerging of neutral American ships seeking out and identifying German craft, helping out the British navy without firing a shot.

The Royal Navy took the tacit American cooperation as a sign that the New World would ignore even an obvious violation of its neutral status in the war. Shots, albeit between the belligerents, were soon fired elsewhere in the Americas. On December 13, an Allied squadron of three cruisers spotted the German heavy cruiser *Graf Spee*. The German ship had been on the hunt for Allied cargo ships in the South Atlantic since the start of the war. A sleek, gray, seagoing tank bristling with the latest in armaments and radar, *Graf Spee* could cruise ten thousand miles without refueling; some naval analysts thought she was "indestructible." Her captain, an affable aristocrat, Hans Langsdorff, had known his ship's famed namesake, a navy hero, as a child. He could proudly boast of having bagged ten Allied-destined merchant ships and oilers on his warship's maiden privateering cruise. Three enemy cruisers presented inviting targets, not serious threats, to Langsdorff. He closed upon his pursuers off the coast of Uruguay and Argentina. A sea dogfight ensued.

Graf Spee's eleven-inch guns could fire shells almost twenty miles, easily outdistancing her adversaries' six- and eight-inch guns' ranges. German rapid-fire shells burst into the HMS *Exeter*'s superstructure, killing nearly everyone on the bridge and temporarily knocking out her controls and communications. Langsdorff moved in for the kill, but the other two ships used the *Graf Spee*'s distraction to get close enough to score as many as seventy hits on her, forcing her off the final kill of the *Exeter*.

Langsdorff's ship suffered a hole at the bow waterline. Laying down a smoke screen, she made for shelter in Montevideo's harbor inside the mouth of the Río de la Plata. The two British cruisers tailed her as far as the river's wide mouth.

With the German vessel momentarily in protective harbor, Hitler met with his admirals to determine what the trapped and battered *Graf Spee* should do. In the meantime, the Admiralty in London radioed out false reports on channels known to be monitored by the Germans that a more powerful battle fleet was nearing the area. Langsdorff received word from Berlin that the Führer expected him to fight his way out rather than let the ship fall into British hands. His ship was in no shape to confront the Royal Navy flotilla he believed awaited her. Langsdorff weighed his options.

Early on the evening of December 18, the *Graf Spee* motored out with just a skeleton crew to the mouth of the de la Plata. Some twenty thousand people watched from shore as Langsdorff stopped the ship. The few sailors aboard went over the sides into a waiting tug. The last man off, Langsdorff stood in the tug's bow as it backed away from his great man-of-war. A long wire unspooled back to his ship. He turned, raised his hand in salute, and then pressed a button at the end of the wire. Explosions ripped through the enormous ship. The burning *Graf Spee* split below the waterline. Her swastika war flag visible through the billowing smoke, her twisted and fractured hulk settled into the river murk.

After he got back to Montevideo, Langsdorff was reportedly in a jovial mood, talking with reporters about his now dead ship's success in sinking merchants at sea. He went to his hotel room and wrote out a letter to the Führer. He told Hitler that he feared his decision not to attempt to fight it out might be "misconstrued" as a wish to save his own skin. He wanted him to know that "the fighting services of the Third Reich are ready to die for the honor of the flag." He sent off the letter and then put a bullet into his brain.

Several South American nations hotly protested the British violation of the newly declared three-hundred-mile combat-free zone. Proud of his cruisers' pluck and ultimate victory, Churchill cabled FDR on Christmas Day urging that he let the matter "die down."

The Admiralty's success in compelling the *Graf Spee*'s suicide seemed a small victory in the balance: In the first four months of the war, the Allies had lost more than 330,000 tons of shipping, some 220 ships of all kinds. How, Churchill asked, would the British survive, with the onslaught against the Allies anticipated to increase dramatically in the coming months? He looked longingly at America's Atlantic Squadron and began, in his messages to the president, to inquire about the possibility of their ships being handed over to the Royal Navy.

For now, the scuttlings of the *Columbus* and *Graf Spee* were just the sort of actions FDR intended in defining the Atlantic Neutrality Zone well out to sea and sending the Atlantic Squadron to patrol it. Nobody could accuse him of having acted in a manner favoring one or the other belligerent by pushing warfare far away from his hemisphere's shores. He had stood his ground as a neutral party to the war and protected his nation. If that happened to serve the English in their war, halting privateering fit well as a strategy for a nation committed to freedom of the seas since its founding.

In Berlin, Germany's rulers understood precisely FDR's game. Chief Admiral Raeder denounced the Americans for using their neutrality zone patrols to tip off British warships. "Nobody can expect a German warship to look on while an American warship communicates . . . to the British Admiralty," he warned several months later, after a number of similar incidents. "Such procedure must be regarded as an act of war . . . ."

An enraged Raeder was convinced that prolonging the war by restraining his forces served only the Allies. For the first time, but far from the last, he pleaded with Hitler to permit all-out submarine warfare, including against American naval and merchant ships, to halt aid from reaching the British Isles and to end U.S. naval collusion with the Royal Navy. Nothing should hold Germany's navy back, he told the Führer, not even the near certainty that sinking American ships would precipitate war with the United States, as it had a generation ago. "The earlier and the more ruthlessly we commence," he insisted barely a month into the war, "the sooner the effect and the shorter the duration of the war." Hitler demurred. He warned Raeder that "the psychological effect that any such step might have in the United States" could provoke the presently dormant power before he had pursued his war strategy to con-clusion in Europe. Despite the outrages of using ostensibly neutral naval patrols to alert the Allies, he insisted that American ships be permitted to sail unmolested. Raeder protested, but the Führer was adamant. Hitler's strategic outlook was clear: "Even if we are convinced that, should the war be of long duration, the USA will enter it in any case," he dictated in an army command memorandum coming out of a meeting that took place at the start of the war, "it must be our object to delay this event so long that American help would come too late." He warned his navy to turn away from American provocations and to distance combat from Western Hemisphere shores. "Nothing," the Führer dictated, should be done to budge Americans from their support for neutrality, "a shackle for the most war-loving of American Presidents, one which presumably cannot be shaken off so long as we do not provide him with the excuse to breach this shackle and thus fulfill the dearest wish of the British!"

Hitler's grand Western Atlantic strategic mission was to avoid arousing America into altering its status as a neutral. He was ready to accept even the most brazenly unneutral American acts and FDR's de-clared policy of providing aid short of war to the Third Reich's enemies. He fully expected victory before U.S. armed forces could intervene to influence the outcome of the war. He had good evidence for this. In Washington, the German Embassy's military and air attaché, Lieutenant General Friedrich von Bötticher, and Chargé d'Affaires Hans Thomsen reported observations made during two weeks of American army training exercises in mid-August 1939. They assured the Führer that what they observed during the maneuvers made clear "the United States' Army's lack of preparedness for war." And they were right.

The U.S. Army was the world's eighteenth largest in terms of man-power, with less than half a million regular army and reservists to call upon in total. Bulgaria had a larger army in the field. America's armed forces were sized and trained for hemispheric actions, border policing, gunboat diplomacy, and small-unit suppressive operations, and were woefully unprepared for the revolutionary blitzkrieg mobile warfare with which Germany had shocked the world. The sole assistance the U.S. would have the wherewithal to provide to its friends was matériel.

But before even that nonfighting aid could bolster the Allies enough to slow the Germans, the German Embassy attachés knew, the president would need "to create the necessary conditions" for changing U.S. laws restricting aid to belligerent nations. FDR's domestic opposition intended to block him from doing that.

5

Scooping Hitler

Europe, 1940

In mid-April 1940 Hitler snickered at "American arms production . . .
the biggest swindle on earth . . . simply a joke," but he knew that an
aroused America, with its massive resources and industrial capabilities,
could lengthen the war, leaving his country vulnerable and perhaps
shaking his power base. While public opinion and neutrality laws for
now stymied Roosevelt, time was not on Hitler's side. On May 3, Hitler wrote Mussolini that "the recurring undertone of threats in Mr.
Roosevelt's telegrams, notes, and inquiries is ample reason for seeing to
it that the war is brought to an end as soon as possible." The time to
attack was at hand.

In the early hours of May 10, 1940, Hitler's panzer forces and
accompanying troops and bombers swept into neutral Holland and
Belgium.

In London, his party's confidence in him lost, Prime Minister
Chamberlain resigned twenty-four frantic hours later. Parliament turned
to a man many in his own party still distrusted, Sir Winston Churchill.
The new prime minister acceded to a position he believed was his due:
to lead the United Kingdom in war. "I felt," he recalled after the war,
"as if I were walking with destiny, and that all my past life had been but
a preparation for this hour and this trial." His confidence unflagging,
he felt serene at finally having won authority "to give directions over

the whole scene." His first night as prime minister, Winston Churchill slept soundly.

The grim reality of his military's disaster, and the potential for total catastrophe, would become clear to him only over the following days.

On June 14, 1940, Paris fell. Hitler's army achieved in two weeks what Germany failed to accomplish in four years of fighting in the previous war. Only a sudden fit of anxious caution on Hitler's part brought his army to a halt before annihilating the British Expeditionary Force, which had been driven back against the Channel. Thousands of small craft in the "Dunkirk Miracle" rescued 338,000 men—minus all their precious heavy armaments.

The fall of Western Europe was the most spectacularly successful military encirclement in history, resulting in the capture of almost a million and a half prisoners. In Britain, the threat of German invasion appeared imminent. British troops had returned to their homeland with little but their uniforms. London had only its naval preponderance and the Royal Air Force to defend against the anticipated attack.

Churchill prepared his people for the onslaught to come. "We shall go on to the end," he intoned in a speech to Parliament which proved among the most celebrated in the English language. "We shall . . . fight on the seas and oceans," he declared, ". . . we shall never surrender, and if, which I do not for a moment believe, this island or a large part of it were subjugated and starving, then our Empire beyond the seas, armed and guarded by the British Fleet, would carry on the struggle, until, in God's good time, the New World, with all its power and might, steps forth to the rescue and the liberation of the old."

Discussions of Churchill's speech most often gloss over the last phrase of his long sentence. With Western Europe all but lost and England on the brink of catastrophe, Churchill looked across the ocean, to the scattered forces of Britain's imperial subjects, from where, should it prove necessary, salvation would come. But nobody could mistake just what nation he meant in calling upon "the New World, with all its power and might." If he expected his American cousins to come to the rescue and liberation of the English, however, their former colonial subjects had nothing of the sort in mind.

In the crisis, on May 16, 1940, President Roosevelt addressed a joint session of Congress. He sounded the alarm about "new powers of destruction, incredibly swift and deadly," and warned, ". . . those who wield them are ruthless and daring. No old defense is so strong that it requires no further strengthening, and no attack is so unlikely or impossible that it may be ignored." Stopping a modern enemy, he declared, "means military implements—not on paper—which are ready and available to meet any lightning offensive against our American interest. It means also that facilities for production must be ready to turn out munitions and equipment at top speed."

Congress had already increased peacetime defense expenditures following the start of the world war to their highest levels ever; Roosevelt now asked that it fund "great additional production capacity . . . [enough] for fifty thousand planes a year" to fly out of American factories. Despite many members' reluctance to back a president they opposed or to give more support for the warring nations, Congress boosted defense spending almost fourfold, from $1.66 billion in 1940 to $6.435 billion in fiscal 1941, accounting for 5 percent of the gross domestic product.

With France teetering shockingly on the brink of collapse just three weeks later, Roosevelt gave the June 10, 1940, commencement address at the University of Virginia. Fuming and righteous, the president excoriated Rome for joining with Berlin and now, like a latter-day Brutus, becoming "the hand that held the dagger . . . struck . . . into the back of its neighbor," by declaring war on a prostrated France. He assured the students that their nation was "overwhelmingly . . . convinced that military and naval victory for the gods of force and hate would endanger the institutions of democracy in the western world, and that equally, therefore, the whole of our sympathies lies with those nations that are giving their life blood in combat against those forces." Americans, he insisted, would not allow their nation "to become a lone island, a lone island in a world dominated by the philosophy of force." He pledged that the "material resources of this nation" would aid the democracies under attack. "We will not slow down or detour. Signs and signals call for speed: full speed ahead." *Time* magazine called this a "fighting speech," words "more powerful and more determined" than anything FDR had before then said about America and the war.

Words.

Near midnight in the Admiralty War Room in London, Churchill listened to a broadcast of the president's speech. He wrote him the next day praising "the grand scope of your declaration" and finding in his offer of aid "a strong encouragement to a dark hour . . . ."

FDR knew, however, that America did not possess enough weaponry for its own armed forces and that whatever sympathies Americans showed, the only opinion they "overwhelmingly" shared was that American forces should *not* fight to rescue the Old World once more. Regular scientific polling of public opinion had begun just five years earlier. Surveys remained unreliable, but FDR had latched on to them quickly. He followed Elmo Roper's column based on his *Fortune* magazine surveys in the *New York Herald Tribune*; tracked George Gallup's American Institute of Public Opinion polls; and regularly consulted with Hadley Cantril, who founded the Office of Public Opinion Research at Princeton in 1939. Roosevelt didn't blow with the winds of the poll results, but he did scrutinize trend lines. For anybody who wanted America to jump into the fight to save the Allies, the indicators could not have been worse.

Poll results made clear: Americans were adamantly opposed to sending troops to fight the autocratic nations. FDR may have been aroused to give a fighting speech by events in Europe, but just days prior to the University of Virginia speech, he was disheartened at

Gallup's poll results showing that just 7 percent of Americans supported entering the war against Germany. Almost as many Americans were willing to fight *for* Germany. Americans were entirely unwilling to stop Hitler's conquest, although a third of Americans now believed that Germany would win the war. Nearly half of all Americans despaired that no matter what the U.S. did, the country would not escape war. However large the possible threat posed by a German victory, two thirds of the population wanted the nation to "take no sides and stay out of the war entirely," and nearly a third of those surveyed wanted to "have nothing to do with any warring country—don't even trade with them. . . ," Cantril wrote.

FDR called for full speed ahead, but an anchor held him in place: "It's a terrible thing to look over your shoulder when you are trying to lead—and find no one there," he remarked to his longtime speechwriter Samuel Rosenman. His nation's people had made abundantly clear that they would not follow his lead if he led the way to war. With France near surrender and England likely next in line for attack, Americans indicated they were ready to send the Allies more assistance. But if that aid involved the sons of American mothers, he was far from having won the battle for such a sacrifice from his people.

Traveling out of Berlin, CBS Radio's correspondent William Shirer followed the German army through the Lowlands, France, and, three days after the city's fall, into Paris. "Poor Paris!" he cried. "I weep for her. For so many years it was my home—and I loved it as you love a woman." The City of Light had been snuffed out like a candle. He watched the first days of what he viewed as "the complete breakdown of French society—a collapse of the army, of government, of the morale of the people. It is almost too tremendous to believe."

The National Socialist Party newspaper, *Völkischer Beobachter*, described the conquest of Paris differently: "Paris," an article declared, "was a city of frivolity and corruption, of democracy and capitalism, where Jews had entry to the court, and niggers to the salons. That Paris will never rise again."

Two days after Shirer arrived in Paris, he drove fifty miles to one of the more nondescript yet most consequential sites of the twentieth century. Adolf Hitler would play out his final symbolic revenge for the Great War's humiliation of Germany on a dusty railroad siding in the Compiègne Forest. He ordered Marshal Ferdinand Foch's personal Pullman coach—the same railroad car in which Germany had been forced to submit to the French surrender terms twenty-two years before—blasted out of its museum display and rolled to the exact spot where the 1918 Armistice treaty was signed.

Hitler arrived on the scene and practically spat at the stone monument the French placed to mark the Armistice. In his years watching the volatile Führer, Shirer had never witnessed him so enraged, "afire with scorn, anger, hate, revenge, triumph." The terms of France's surrender were read out to the French generals. The next day, they would sign their nation over to her occupiers.

To gain maximum effect, Hitler decreed that he would personally release news of the French surrender the following day. This would be his greatest triumph. He sent the entire foreign news corps packing from Compiègne. Ignoring Hitler's order, Shirer never left.

Unnoticed, he slipped back to the Compiègne rail siding the following morning. Shirer watched Hitler arrive briefly to hear the surrender treaty's preamble read out and then speed away. Shirer used confusion among elements of the German Propaganda Ministry and the army to link his report of events through to Berlin and on to CBS Radio in America. For half an hour he reported on the signing of the treaty and described the scene to American listeners, eavesdropping on the signatories' conversation in the historic railroad car: the pens scratching, the tears being fought back. Like an execution, "It was all over in a few moments," he concluded. Americans in their homes thousands of miles away learned of the surrender several hours before the German people.

When Hitler learned that Shirer's scoop had "beat the world," he was furious. "Some of those who helped us get it are catching hell," Shirer noted. "My three German friends faced court-martial or worse." On the road back to Berlin, he scratched out notes in his diary. In doing so, he ran significant risks. Driving through Belgium, he noted that German army trucks and staff cars had Red Cross signs painted on their roofs. Using Red Cross symbols as a ruse was a clear violation of international accords. Driving into Dunkirk, he saw a worse sight: "the charred remains of a long line of British and French Red Cross ambulances." Stukas had bombed them while they were unloading the wounded onto transports bound for England. The burned corpses lay inside the scorched shells of the ambulances. Back at the Adlon Hotel, he made sure to place his notes carefully out of sight. "The Germans will shoot me . . . if [they] ever find these notes."

In Berlin, Shirer continued reporting for CBS. Over the next year and a half, by inflection, tone, notes of irony, he tried to indicate the menace of the German war machine and the violence and manufactured lies the Nazis used to impose obedience and to dupe their foreign enemies. Once British bombers began to raid the interior of Germany in earnest, censorship became so restrictive that he could no longer report any unofficial news. Foreign reporters were reduced to being readers of official Propaganda Ministry statements for broadcast.

By fall 1940, Shirer had reached his limit. He debated whether he could continue as the German Propaganda Ministry voice to America. Finally, in early November he cabled his CBS bosses in New York: "WE UNINTERESTED REMAIN HERE MERELY MOUTH OFFICIAL STATEMENTS. . . . ANYWAY PERSONALLY CANNOT REMAIN HERE AS MOUTHPIECE NAZI PROPAGANDA. . . ." A telegram came back announcing his bureau's dissolution.

"Like that I was jobless," he recorded despondently in his diary, "broke (except for the 2 weeks salary that would be forwarded)." His

wife had already left; she was pregnant, the baby due in a few weeks. A
month later, he followed her.

A few days before departing, Shirer went to see a German press bureau
officer. He asked that his broadcast manuscripts be approved for shipment home. Fortunately, the papers were "given a very routine inspection." He brought a small trunk and "packed the papers in with Gestapo
men looking on," he said later. He invited them to seal the trunk and
put their stamp of approval on it. He had interspersed throughout the
reams of papers the last handwritten pages from his illicit diaries. Instead
of taking the trunk to his room, he brought it straight to the Tempelhof
Airport's storage room.

On the day he readied to leave Berlin, German officials "went through
everything I owned," he later said. They confiscated every loose paper and
notebook. "They even took my expense accounts away from me because
the figures might have another meaning. I wasn't allowed one scrap of
paper that had writing on it." At Tempelhof, "at the very last moment," he
feigned "a private little ceremony of remembering the trunk." The airport
Gestapo men rushed up to keep him from loading it aboard the revving
airplane. He argued that the trunk had already gone through an inspection and pointed to the Gestapo stamp and unbroken seal. The airplane
was ready to take off, and "they let the trunk go through."

At Christmastime 1940, his trunk stowed safely away, Shirer started home
by ship to the United States out of Lisbon. Portugal remained neutral. As
the liner churned to sea in the darkness, he looked back at the last glim-
mer of receding lights. He pondered the world to come. "Civilization,
such as it was," he wrote, "had not yet been stamped out here by a Nazi
boot. But next week? Next month? The month after? Would not Hitler's
hordes take this too and extinguish the last lights?" For Shirer, the voyage
home after fifteen years of living in Europe was bittersweet. The Europe

that had lured him with its promise of personal freedom, ancient civilization and vibrant culture had succumbed to Nazi brutality. The world he loved so dearly had been destroyed. The thought brought him near tears.

His outlook, his life, everything about him had been utterly transformed in Europe. He "had been happy . . . and . . . [life] had had meaning and borne hope." Now, the world, and everyone in it, would never be the same. No longer forced to report the lies of the German Propaganda Ministry, no longer obligated to encode the secret truth when he spoke to Americans, he would do what he could to tell the full truth. He began to think about what he could do to fight "all the bombs blasting man's hope and decency."

Were Americans ready to face that truth? Plenty of people thought he was just wrong—or remained uncertain that what happened in Europe even mattered on the other side of the wide ocean.

6

Blitzkrieg Propaganda

America, 1940–1941

After his journey with Shirer to the Polish front, Philip Johnson returned home more convinced than ever of America's impending fascist future. He was filled with fighting energy to help bring it about. He immediately began writing about Hitler, Germany, and the war, rebutting press coverage he thought was on the wrong side of history. "Our 'neutral' press," he wrote in the pages of Father Coughlin's *Social Justice*, "gives only one side of the war." America was being fed a diet of falsehoods about the Nazis and about conditions in Poland and the nature of German war aims. The average American, he wrote, "knows too much about the war—90 percent of it wrong." He would use his multiple talents to try to correct this misinformation.

He embarked on a speaking tour through the following winter and into the spring, seeking out followers for fascism. These events were organized under the auspices of the American Fellowship Forum (AFF), which he helped to found in late 1939. Publicity for the AFF indicated no connection to Germany or Hitler, nor revealed any interest in promoting fascism. According to the AFF brochure, the organization served to bring "constructive-minded people together for united action . . . to form a powerful movement, the kind of active and determined group that can get things done under our American system."

The group's mission was to enable Americans to find "the solution of their domestic problems, make them recovery-minded, create a mental and emotional prerequisite to recovery . . . and prosperity." To pursue these goals and build membership, the AFF organized public meetings, provided speakers for other organizations' events, and published a magazine titled *Today's Challenge* (the name was later changed to the *Forum Observer*). The AFF proclaimed it would "combat every trend injurious to spiritual and material rejuvenation."

Never one to pull a punch, Dorothy Thompson, the most outspoken and prominent pro-interventionist newspaper columnist—and proud that, in 1934, she became the first American journalist expelled from Germany by the Nazis—did not mince words about the AFF. In October 1940, she warned her nationally syndicated column's ten million readers that the organizers behind the AFF had "long familiarity with the Nazi technique of the coup d'état." The AFF existed, she claimed, to apply in America "the strategy of insinuation into the political life of countries which the Nazis wish to undermine and paralyze. . . ." She excoriated the AFF's founder and leader, a German émigré and New York City college language instructor named Friedrich E. F. Auhagen, who she said had "conducted the most subtle and intelligent campaign to influence and direct American public opinion and American policy."

The mission of the AFF, she claimed, was the same as that of the so-called fifth column, the subversive supporters planted and abetted in cities and countries targeted for annexation or conquest. Using laws that protected individual liberties, the fifth column, a term that originated in the Spanish Civil War, hollowed out support for democracy in Europe, organized local sympathizers, and identified fascism's opponents for elimination, paving the way for eventual takeover of the country. The AFF did not aim to foster a mass movement, she explained. The AFF had a more insidious ambition to "reach the so-called realists and convert them to the idea that democracy needs considerable streamlining, discipline and authority, and that the economic interests of the United

States, its welfare and its peace can best be served by collaboration with the Germans, who are going to win the World War anyhow, and who represent, in a general pattern, the future form of civilization." According to Thompson, the AFF worked by undermining support for a messy democracy and an economy still struggling to revive—the very conditions that Hitler had exploited elsewhere to such advantage—seeding the country with Americans who welcomed fascism in Europe and perhaps one day at home.

Thompson labeled AFF leader Auhagen's agenda "Machiavellian," crediting his "leading brain trusters" for masterminding the AFF behind-the-scenes strategy. She pointed specifically to two men, long-standing intellectual collaborators in the promotion of American fascism: "Philip Johnson and Lawrence Dennis," the ex-diplomat turned author of books on fascism in America—"both," she wrote, "Harvard men and both brilliant."

Johnson wrote essays about Germany and fascism for the AFF house journal and lectured several times for the group. Among his talks were a December address in Philadelphia on "Facts and Fiction in the Present War," and, in January 1940, in Springfield, Massachusetts, where, according to advance publicity for the event, he would offer "both a vivid picture and an entirely new perspective on the great struggle in Europe."

The electorate had so far rejected the fascist vision Johnson promoted and the men—Huey Long, Father Coughlin, and himself—he backed as the nation's future leaders. But he had seen the future, a monumental worldwide future that was bound, like a great and irresistible wave, to sweep across the ocean from Europe and over America.

However, the AFF faced off against a formidable foe: The United States government was now secretly working hand in hand with U.S.-based British intelligence operatives. Together they intended to shine a bright light on fifth column activities and force German front organizations and agents out into the open. Johnson and the AFF had good reason to scurry out of sight. The British agents now slipping into the U.S. understood their Nazi enemies well and would employ some of the very same tricks and criminal tactics that fascist fifth columnists had employed so effectively in Europe.

In May 1940, the overseas British intelligence service, MI6, dispatched a shadowy, forty-four-year-old Canadian businessman to the U.S. William Stephenson traveled under false diplomatic passport designating him as a British passport control officer. He quickly contacted the White House about his role as liaison to American intelligence for its counter-espionage activities. To MI6's dismay, Stephenson learned that the U.S. government did not have anything of the kind, at least nothing concerned with uncovering and monitoring so-called fifth column activity under coordinated command. Before long, Britain's lone secret agent to the Americas became the unseen director of an American hemispheric intelligence and espionage empire and introduced the federal government to well-honed British methods of spying, counterintelligence, and destruction of enemy secret operatives.

Few men were ever so well equipped for such cloak-and-dagger work. Stephenson's life and lore were right out of a book—and before long would become one. Short, thickly muscled as befitted a former boxing champion, with cropped graying hair, hooded, penetrating eyes, and forward-thrusting chin, he dropped out of high school in Canada and before long joined the Royal Flying Corps in World War I. He was credited with twelve air combat kills. After being shot down, wounded, and captured, he made a daring escape from a German prison camp.

Following the war he returned to Canada, where he made a fortune in the hardware business and then, thanks to his invention of a wireless photographic transmission system, added to that wealth. He supplemented his income through ownership of a long list of other industrial, construction, radio, and car manufacturing concerns, as well as partial ownership of London's famous Shepperton Studios, the largest film studio outside Hollywood. He was already a man of enormous wealth, with many friends in many walks of life, a fascination with gadgetry, a love for clandestine chicanery, and comfort with physical violence and killing enemies. He was the perfect spymaster.

Future author Ian Fleming came from England to work with Stephenson, who later would serve as a model for characters in Fleming's fictional superspy novels, the James Bond series. Fleming watched Stephenson in action both in the field and in his penthouse overlooking Central Park. Fleming found Stephenson to be "a man of few words . . . one of the great secret agents," who had "the quality of making anyone ready to follow him to the ends of the earth." The quiet, watchful Canadian pursued his counterintelligence war in the "American theater" with a vengeance.

Going by the cable code address INTREPID—few, even among those closest to him, knew his exact role at the time—Stephenson set up shop in a floor-through suite of offices on the thirty-sixth floor of Rockefeller Center's limestone-clad International Building North at 636 Fifth Avenue in the heart of Midtown Manhattan. The sign outside Room 3603 read, "British Passport Control Office." The White House knew about the Stephenson office even while denying its existence. If any unsettling questions were asked, Stephenson could draw on many high-level political contacts to smooth the waves.

His friends included Pulitzer Prize–winning playwright and Roosevelt speechwriter Robert Sherwood, heir and FDR confidant Vincent Astor, and even Wendell Willkie, who would run against the president in the 1940 election. Stephenson also enjoyed close ties with leading figures in the news business, among them columnist Walter Lippmann; Arthur Hays Sulzberger, president of *The New York Times*; and Henry Luce, publisher of *Time*, *Life*, and *Fortune*; and another Roosevelt friend, Helen Reid, wife of the publisher of the *New York Herald Tribune*, which she took over upon his death. All proved eager accomplices in generating "news" about the British war effort.

Federal Bureau of Investigation director J. Edgar Hoover initially protested against permitting a belligerent nation's intelligence service to

Sir William Stephenson in New York City in 1954.

operate in America, an obvious violation of the recently passed foreign espionage act. Not only did the president not object to clandestine British operations in the Western Hemisphere, he personally ordered Hoover to cooperate with Stephenson and instructed the rest of the Executive Branch to wink at his network's presence and hidden work.

Stephenson moved quickly to embed a British spy network throughout the Western Hemisphere. Its cooperation with him took the FBI into an entirely new area of national security—identifying and pursuing potentially subversive foreigners and tracking and infiltrating their domestic networks. Within weeks of opening the British Passport Control Office in Rockefeller Center, Stephenson launched a hemispheric intelligence service that far outstripped the FBI in pursuing extralegal operations. Stephenson's undercover agents, informants, and other operatives employed deception, planted information, devised dirty tricks, and even assassinated South American fifth columnists or abetted assassins to advance the British cause—and to bring the U.S. into the war.

For the British this was war on a different front; for Roosevelt this was yet another means short of war to keep actual fighting offshore. Hoover designated Stephenson's burgeoning network the British Security Coordination (BSC) and never revealed FDR's breach of neutrality laws, let alone the potentially impeachable offense of permitting and aiding foreign spies operating on U.S. soil. Over the next year, British and American intelligence activities became so intertwined that the aims and operations of the two nations were increasingly hard to distinguish.

The BSC grew like Topsy, as if from nowhere into an amorphous network quickly reaching at least six hundred paid staffers—some reports claim up to three thousand people eventually worked for Stephenson, but only he knew for sure—and an untold number of undercover associates. Room 3603 housed the British Information Service (BIS), which published pamphlets and other so-called white, or soft, propaganda publications distributed around the country, paid for radio broadcasts, and launched a shortwave radio station broadcasting multilingual programming around the world. The service staff also provided assistance and cash to the many Western organizations popping up in support of the Allies.

BIS personnel acted as intermediaries with a wide assortment of sympathetic journalists, many personal friends of Stephenson, among them columnists such as Lippmann, Walter Winchell, and Drew Pearson, and a who's who of other writers, editors, publishers, and radio executives. The BSC paid Hollywood studios to distribute British films and hired English writers to develop scripts for American movies and articles for magazines that supported the anti-Nazi cause. Numerous authors and intellectuals, from bon vivant wit, playwright, and trenchant social critic Noel Coward to philosopher and Oxford don Isaiah Berlin, crossed the Atlantic to help the BIS promote London's cause.

The arrival of the BSC in New York also coincided conveniently with the launch of the pro-interventionist Committee to Defend America by Aiding the Allies and that group's even more interventionist successor, the Fight for Freedom Committee, which, not by accident, operated out of neighboring International Building offices. To help interventionist organizations mobilize American public opinion, the BIS paid leading public relations, advertising, and opinion survey men—among them the future advertising wizard David Ogilvy, an English assistant director in George Gallup's polling organization—to drive propaganda against the Axis powers and for the British.

Through data collected by Gallup, Ogilvy tracked American public opinion, helping the BSC and London gauge how best to promote the British message. Sometimes, he skewed survey questions to encourage belief that public support for the Allies was growing faster than it was. A polling organization called Market Analysts, Inc., run by British intelligence, routinely provided polling data purportedly demonstrating increasing public support for interventionist policies and growing public fear of fifth column operatives in America. All the while, INTREPID's hand in the operations remained hidden.

The BSC's vine spread from its root in Rockefeller Center until it covered all North, Central, and South America, with satellite offices and operatives scattered throughout. Stephenson set up a clandestine operations training center across the New York State border in Ontario where BSC and American operatives learned to forge papers, open locks, tap phones, read mail, and plant bugs. Once in the field they employed those skills to steal papers, listen in on phone calls, intercept mail, and plant false documents.

In an operation that showed the full panoply of the BSC's domestic warfare at work, Stephenson's spies were onto Gerhard Alois Westrick's quiet arrival in New York. The German lawyer and businessman represented various American corporate interests in Europe and maintained close ties to the Nazi leadership. He moved with his family into a large house in Scarsdale, outside New York City, and set up offices in the posh Waldorf-Astoria Hotel in Midtown Manhattan. Out of that office, he cultivated contacts among German sympathizers in the business community, including Sosthenes Behn, founder of ITT, and Torkild Rieber, CEO of Texaco.

With those powerful friends, he hoped to encourage continued flow of Latin American oil through the British blockade and convince other corporate bosses that Germany was on the verge of victory in Europe. Should they hope to do business in Europe after the German victory, Westrick suggested, they would do well to support isolationist forces at home now. On the day after France's surrender, Texaco's Rieber sponsored a celebratory dinner for Westrick at the Waldorf-Astoria attended by executives from General Motors, Ford, Underwood, and other major U.S. corporations. Westrick promised that for businesses that proved friendly to Germany, golden opportunities awaited after the fall of Great Britain, which he forecast would come within three months.

BSC intermediaries tipped off *Herald Tribune* reporters about Westrick and his attempts to win over American business leaders to the Axis side. The newspaper's series of front-page articles about Westrick—one scandalized headline declared, "Hitler's Agent Ensconced in Westchester"—were picked up by other newspapers around the country. *Time* magazine headlined him the "German Tempter." Before long, reporters and anti-Nazi protesters had camped outside Westrick's Scarsdale house. Other writers, including Winchell and Pearson, claimed Westrick was not just setting up business ties, but plotting to set up a German-administered corporate takeover of America.

The bad press drove Texaco to fire Rieber. Other American businessmen now denied any connection to Westrick, while protesters threatened him and his family until they moved away late at night. BSC agents followed and passed information about his whereabouts to FBI agents,who arrested him for driving with an illegal driver's license. In the fall of 1940, Westrick and his family were forced to return to Germany.

Acts of White House cooperation with the BSC included presidential speechwriter Robert Sherwood's sending Roosevelt's foreign policy statements to the BSC prior to their public disclosure. Some people in the administration found the cozy relationship with the BSC dangerous. Assistant Secretary of State Adolf A. Berle was in charge of monitoring diplomatic activities in the U.S. for the department. He personally distrusted the Brits and disliked their imperialistic ways, though he supported aid for the country as advantageous for American interests.

After investigating the BSC's clandestine activities, Berle expressed alarm to Sumner Welles, number two at the State Department and a close friend of the Roosevelts and FDR's occasional special envoy. Berle wrote Welles that he was shocked to discover that "a full size secret police and intelligence service" with field offices in cities across the country "regularly employed secret agents and a much larger number of informers, etc . . . [to collect] information . . . [that] enters into the whole field of political, financial, industrial, and probably military intelligence . . . an obvious breach of diplomatic obligation." He feared that the State Department risked congressional sanction—and that FDR himself risked worse—should it not expose the illegal British operation.

Berle eventually complained directly to the president. "I do not see that any of us can safely take the position that we should grant blanket immunity for any foreign spy system, no matter whose it is," he wrote Roosevelt. FDR stopped him short. "By Roosevelt's order," stated Sherwood, "and despite State Department qualms, effectively close cooperation between Hoover and the FBI and British security services" in the U.S. continued without interruption. FDR made clear that he was ready to risk a great deal to keep England going.

Charged with increasing the flow of aid to the British and eventually bringing America into the war, the BSC's operations reached into the machinery of the democratic process. During the fall 1940 campaign for Congress and the presidency, BSC operatives waged a shadow fight to influence one of the most crucial elections in the nation's history. Among its covert activities, the Stephenson office mounted smear campaigns and provided funds in races against isolationist congressmen. These actions included a concerted effort to defeat Hamilton Fish, the Republican congressman who was a thorn in FDR's side in representing his Hudson River Valley home district. The dirty tricks included distributing a 1938 photo showing Fish together with Fritz Kuhn, leader of the German American Bund, an American Nazi organization. Though Kuhn had come uninvited to a Fish state committee meeting, photographers happened to shoot him standing near Fish.

BSC polling associates provided survey results for opposition candidates indicating that isolationist incumbents' constituents opposed their foreign policy stands. Despite those efforts, Fish and most other anti-intervention legislators held on to their seats. The BSC also sent operatives to Philadelphia, where the unlikely former Democrat Wendell Willkie mounted a successful dark horse campaign to garner the Republican presidential nomination at the party's convention there in the summer of 1940, despite Willkie's support for stepped-up aid to the British. Stephenson accepted few limits in waging war on the Western Hemisphere front.

7

Shadowed by the G-Men

America and Latin America, 1940–1941

Allowing a foreign intelligence service such as the British Security Coordination to operate with the encouragement of the U.S. federal government on American soil might seem implausible today, but the U.S. at the time had no formal counterespionage operations of its own. With the conquest of the Lowlands and France, Roosevelt realized he needed to fill the gap in his country's foreign intelligence gathering—and to counter fifth column operatives who, he now suspected, were surreptitiously inveigling their way into American society and elsewhere in the hemisphere.

He worried in particular about the politically unstable countries south of the U.S. border. Through his Good Neighbor Policy, FDR had sought to mend strained relations with Latin America, scene of many U.S. invasions and regularly forced to serve Uncle Sam's economic interests. He did succeed in improving ties, but even under FDR, America had shown little interest in its hemispheric neighbors except to exploit business opportunities there, particularly extraction of raw materials like tropical hardwoods, oil, rubber, and minerals and precious metals.

German industry relied on transatlantic trade for many of the same South American products and resources. Trade with the Axis nations had grown before the war to encompass a significant portion of several southern nations' economies, and the importance of that inflow of currency for the countries opened doors to Nazi sympathizers in government palaces. Moreover, unlike the U.S. and England, Germany under Hitler had invested heavily in cultural exchanges and deepened political ties with southern leaders. Hitler's speeches and German-produced Spanish- and Portuguese-language broadcasts and newsreels were regular fare from Mexico to Chile, often through the government-controlled press and radio. As the world crisis deepened, America lacked comparable ways to get favorable viewpoints out about life in the U.S. or government policy.

With Latin America's European trade disrupted by the war, British shipping threatened by German U-boats, and trade with Germany block- aded by the British, Roosevelt feared that the region's ailing economies made countries ripe for further political destabilization. He doubted the steadfastness of Latin American governments when it came to resisting the lures of Nazi Germany and its fascist allies. England relied on oil, rare metals, and other South American products for its own war economy. London viewed nations that permitted German agents to operate freely as a war threat, and FDR considered control of southern approaches to U.S. territory vital to its defense. After the fall of France, the possibility of a German invasion of the "bulge" of northeastern Brazil, jumping off from French West Africa or the Azores and Canary Islands, raised the terrifying specter of a Nazified South America and the vital Panama Canal falling into Axis hands.

In the late 1930s Nelson Rockefeller, the charismatic and ambi- tious grandson of America's first billionaire, Standard Oil tycoon John D. Rockefeller, embarked on a personal study of South and Central America. He learned Spanish, visited every country south of the border, and invested in several business ventures there. He also donated to art museums and commissioned Mexican mural artist Diego Rivera to decorate his family's iconic Rockefeller Center. When the European war threatened to spill into the Western Hemisphere, he wrote a memo with recommendations for shoring up "our soft underbelly," which he sent to the president via his aide and close confidant Harry Hopkins.

Sparked by the Rockefeller report, on August 16, 1940, Roosevelt issued an Executive Order creating the new Office for Coordination of

Commercial and Cultural Relations between the American Republics. That unwieldy name was changed a year later to the only slightly more felicitous Office of the Coordinator of Inter-American Affairs (generally known by the acronym "OCIAA"). He installed the thirty-two-year-old Rockefeller as its first "coordinator," and the new agency was quickly dubbed the "Rockefeller Shop." Determined to win a reputation for being more than just the cosseted heir to an outsized fortune, Rockefeller set out to make his mark in government service by building America's first homegrown foreign intelligence network.

He had followed Stephenson as he weaved his web at the BSC in the space his family rented to him (for a nominal cost). Rockefeller modeled the Shop on the BSC's dual track, with its "white" propaganda's friendly face and "black" ops' clandestine espionage and counterespionage. Rockefeller brought friends from among New York's most powerful public relations, advertising, publishing, and broadcast executives to Washington to head teams that crafted publications, radio programming, films, and other projects and developed Latin distribution networks for them. The Rockefeller Shop also sent numerous cultural ambassadors, high and low, south; they included crooner Bing Crosby, starlet Rita Hayworth, animator Walt Disney, and the American Ballet Theater.

At its height, the OCIAA's fourteen hundred staffers gave the country an official presence in every major population center below the Rio Grande for the first time. Though some might balk at such a comparison, in a glowing spring 1942 profile of Rockefeller, *Life* magazine lauded him for "accomplish[ing] more in a year and a half than Herr Goebbels [Joseph, chief of the German Propaganda Ministry] did in a decade." To pay for the Shop's operations, costly beyond his limited federal allocation, Rockefeller reached into his own pocket for cash when needed.

He also kept a fund for secret operations stashed within the OCIAA budget. Hemispheric intelligence was the OCIAA's first mission. For its first homegrown "black" operation, the Rockefeller Shop set out to establish a "Black List" of local business leaders and regional politicians "known to support objectives contrary to the best interests of the American Republics," with the intention of fencing them out of trade and political power, according to a later OCIAA report. Coming up with an accurate list from among the tens of thousands of individuals and offices doing business for American companies there would not be a simple task. In those days the U.S. government stationed few nonmilitary personnel in Latin countries and had almost no operatives there except for a handful of FBI agents looking for wanted American criminals on the lam. To find out quickly who the Nazi sympathizers, companies, and agents were in Latin America, and which American businesses were trading with them, Rockefeller turned to Stephenson's BSC for help.

The British had a head start in building an espionage network in Central and South America and identifying locals in cahoots with Germany. Stephenson made his agents' findings available to Rockefeller and offered up his own spy network to identify South American firms and individuals supportive of the Nazis. To keep the relationship at arm's length, as required by U.S. neutrality laws, Stephenson delivered reports via his FBI contacts—who were immunized by the president's verbal orders to assist him. The Bureau passed along the BSC reports to Rockefeller or congressional investigators when they took an interest in fifth columnists. The FBI reports on them labeled the information "from a confidential source believed to be reliable." A year after the establishment of the Rockefeller Shop, American companies had "voluntarily" ended contact and business with some two thousand South American firms and individuals believed to have Berlin connections. A few companies, such as General Motors, resisted shutting off their lucrative Latin agency contacts, but as the world crisis deepened the anti-Nazi blacklist became mandatory.

The success of the Rockefeller Shop's and, clandestinely, BSC's South American economic attack on German traders infuriated the Nazi government. William Shirer attended a late July 1940 press conference with the German economics minister, Walter Funk. He was, commented Shirer, "a shifty-looking little man" known to drink too much. Funk "belligerently attacked" what he called American "intervention" in German trade with South America. Shirer recorded afterward that the apoplectic Funk shouted, "'Either we will trade directly with the sovereign South American states or we won't trade at all'"—precisely the response Rockefeller and Stephenson had intended.

Stephenson wanted to defeat the German enemy and its collaborators in any way he could. He was not above using the FBI to dupe American officials. In June 1941, BSC forgers manufactured an official-looking German letter suggesting that a fascist plot was under way to topple the Bolivian government. Stephenson lied to the FBI that BSC agents had stolen an unidentified German courier's diplomatic pouch in Buenos Aires and found he carried "incriminating documents." Hoover took the "purloined" papers to the White House.

Roosevelt was by then pushing Congress to reduce restrictions on American naval activities in the Atlantic. He sought to bolster anti-Axis opinion by sounding frequent alarms about fifth column subversion. Whether he had been the victim of a trick or was just willing to accept without question the sort of evidence Stephenson's agents conveniently found, FDR personally forwarded information about a bogus coup plan to the Bolivian government. Bolivian leaders promptly booted the entire German Embassy staff out of the country and rounded up some 150 Nazi sympathizers named in the documents. Most were imprisoned, and many were shot by firing squads.

The BSC was not done. It planted tips about the plot with sympathetic American journalists. Their reports further inflamed fears that fifth column operatives were infiltrating the hemisphere. Not long after, FDR closed all Italian and German consular offices and ordered their staffs out of the country.

When Berle, the State Department's assistant secretary in charge of the diplomatic corps, learned of the alleged Bolivian coup plot and the source of the letter, his antennae went up. He warned Assistant Secretary of State Sumner Welles against being duped by British agents and urged suspicion about "'planted' documents of dubious authenticity." Stephenson learned that Berle was again interfering with BSC operations. Hoping to silence a critic, his shop began building a file on Berle in a smear campaign against him. When Hoover learned about the BSC's plot against the New Deal "brain truster," it backfired: The unidentified BSC operative behind the campaign was tossed out of the country.

In the wake of the quick fall of apparently powerful European nations, fear gripped Americans who increasingly suspected that people carrying on seemingly normal lives among them were secretly plotting their nation's downfall. While FDR at first focused his intelligence investment on the vulnerable Latin south, he genuinely feared saboteurs at home. For the sake of pushing public opinion more firmly behind aid to the Allies, though, he was not averse to ginning up citizens' anxieties. He repeatedly spoke out against what he called the "Trojan Horse" menace. In one of his famed "Fireside Chat" radio broadcasts, on May 26, 1940, FDR warned that America faced "new methods of attack. The Trojan Horse. The fifth column that betrays a nation unprepared for treachery. Spies, saboteurs and traitors are the actors in this new strategy. With all of these we must and will deal vigorously."

When reporters pressed FDR afterward at a news conference to point to any specific acts of sabotage, he sidestepped the question. Instead, he urged the newsmen to look carefully at the evidence being collected by congressional investigators from the House Un-American Activities Committee (HUAC). They had been charged with smoking out possible Nazi, Communist, and Japanese subversives hiding behind front organizations at home. Getting wind of this, the Republican senator Robert A. Taft of Ohio, a leading isolationist, scoffed, "There is a good deal more danger of infiltration of totalitarian ideas from the New

Deal circles in Washington than there ever will be from the activities of the . . . Nazis."

However, Hoover's FBI and Rockefeller's operatives, with INTREP-ID's close cooperation, had been working behind the scenes with the HUAC, then known as the Dies Committee for its chairman, Texas Democrat Martin Dies. The Rockefeller Shop "Black List" offered some of the best clues for where Dies's investigators should look for the Trojan Horse. Working back from known Nazi agents in Latin America, they soon found a trail leading to a number of suspected German operatives and front organizations in the U.S. Among the most prominent, the American Fellowship Forum, and Philip Johnson could not avoid being swept up in the nets the government was setting out to snare fifth column operatives.

On November 21, 1940, investigators armed with subpoena powers of the House Un-American Activities Committee pounced. With reporters in tow, they carried out raids in homes and organizations in eight cities across the country to seek further proof of what it charged was a widespread, interlinked network of propaganda, illicit trade, subversive operations, and espionage on behalf of Germany. A Dies Committee white paper published in conjunction with the raids reported that committee investigators, independent of FBI sleuthing, had, according to one newspaper account, "uncovered what it said was an ambitious plan for post-war German domination of a large section of the economic structure of America, and turned the spotlight on many of the leaders of the alleged propaganda agencies now carrying on activities here. . . ." The committee paper named Philip Johnson among those leading the American Fellowship Forum and tied AFF backers to a shell company involved in smuggling rare metals from South American needed for German weaponry. The principal figure in the operation, Ferdinand Kertess, a naturalized German citizen, was eventually found guilty of directing the secret operation. The Dies Committee report described him as the "chief angel" of the AFF.

*   *   *

As Americans debated what, if anything, their nation should do in the European war and anxieties mounted about fifth columnists, Johnson's pro-Nazi activities began to attract wider public notice. In September 1940, a lengthy *Harper's* magazine article featured him among leading American Nazis. The FBI followed him and reported to headquarters that Johnson enjoyed friendships with several German diplomatic officials and Americans whose activities on behalf of German interests were well known. According to FBI agents shadowing him, plus informant reports, Johnson developed extensive contacts with the German Propaganda and Foreign Ministries while in Germany and then returned to propagandize on the Nazis' behalf in the United States.

None of this was criminally damning or seditious at the time, Johnson having made clear like many other pro-Germans and American fascists his sympathies in the war. With his reputation as a Nazi cemented, though, Johnson's friends warned him about the risks he was running. He was growing increasingly uneasy, especially as the winds of public sentiment, always sympathetic to the beleaguered British Isles and distrusting of Hitler, blew increasingly against Germany.

At the president's behest, the Justice Department began to scrutinize groups advocating for Germany and against American intervention. On January 14, 1940, after a lengthy undercover operation, during which an informant was planted in the National Union for Social Justice's Christian Front, the Federal Bureau of Investigation arrested eighteen members of the New York City branch on charges of plotting to overthrow the U.S. government. The FBI claimed the men planned to bomb various Jewish and Communist organization offices, blow up theaters, bridges, banks, and other structures, assassinate government officials, and seize stores of arms, "so that," said FBI director J. Edgar Hoover, "a dictatorship could be set up here, similar to the Hitler dictatorship in Germany, seizing the reins of government in this country as Hitler did in Germany."

After initially turning his back on the accused Christian Front members, Coughlin changed his mind and issued a statement in which he declared, "I re-encourage the Christians of America to carry on in this crisis for the preservation of Christianity and Americanism, more vigorously than ever. . . ."

If the men were indeed out to take over the national government, they possessed only a small stockpile of guns and bombs, none of it likely to be enough to cause much more than a bit of mayhem. Eventually most of the group's members were acquitted, but anyone associated with Coughlin and his Union for Social Justice was now under watch as a possible subversive. By the summer of 1940, Johnson understood that included him. He grew increasingly anxious.

Finally, the G-men moved in.

Implicated in the Dies Committee investigation, AFF founder and head Friedrich Auhagen was apprehended trying to flee the country and arrested for, among other charges, failing to register as an agent of a foreign government. Auhagen would eventually go to prison for his activities as an unregistered foreign agent. Kertess received a six-year sentence for his South American smuggling activities. Lawrence Dennis, Johnson's intellectual guiding light and the man nationally syndicated columnist Dorothy Thompson called, along with Johnson, "the brains" behind the AFF, was also indicted and charged with sedition, along with twenty-eight others—acting to bring down the federal government. Their cases lingered on for nearly five years. Some of the charged men died before they could be brought to trial. One committed suicide.

Alone among those Dies Committee investigators implicated as possible foreign agents for their pro-German AFF activities, Johnson was never indicted. He slipped quietly from view in plain sight. Until William Shirer flushed him out.

8

The Roosevelt Brand

America, 1939–1940

As the world crisis escalated, retired Marine Corps major general Smedley Butler, twice winner of the Medal of Honor and one of the most decorated warriors in American history, joined the swelling chorus of those opposing American intervention. Many among those most loudly opposed to getting involved were veterans of the Great War. Butler delivered twelve hundred antiwar speeches in 1939 and 1940 alone, often including his trademark slogan, "War is a racket!"

As pressure to intervene in Europe built, Butler, formerly the Marine Corps' second highest ranking officer and at one time considered the likely commandant of the corps, grew increasingly emotional. In a national radio broadcast delivered a month after Germany's invasion of Poland, he warned "You mothers, particularly" not to be taken in by those who would call for America to send their sons to fight on foreign battlefields. "After you've heard one of those speeches," his voice deep and rumbling, "and your blood's all hot and you want to bite somebody like Hitler—go upstairs to where your boy's asleep. . . . Look at him. . . . Look at this splendid young creature who's part of yourself, then close your eyes for a moment and I'll tell you what can happen. . . ." He painted a lurid and graphic mental picture of battlefield violence, terror, and death. He ended, "There's a lot of tangled rusty barbed wires out there and a boy hanging over them—his stomach ripped out, and he's feebly calling for help and water. . . . He's in agony.

"There's your boy. The same boy who's lying in bed tonight."

He died shortly before France's surrender of what some said was exhaustion caused by his antiwar fight. Many others among America's most revered warriors followed behind him in proclaiming that their nation should never again bloody its hands trying to straighten out foreign squabbles. Among those who wanted to build an American fortress to keep foreign wars out were Eddie Rickenbacker, America's top Great War air ace, and General Hugh S. "Iron Pants" Johnson, a regular newspaper and magazine columnist who had headed the draft in that war. And the onetime conscientious objector who became a Medal of Honor winner, Sergeant Alvin York, touched many Americans when he said, "I believe in letting those fellows fight their own battles . . . [and] we should stop messing in their family fusses over there." He became a folksy spokesman for the Emergency Peace Campaign.

The voice of one First World War veteran opposed to intervention carried more weight than all others. His very name stood for making the world's wars his nation's business: Theodore Roosevelt, Jr. His father, Teddy Roosevelt, had made such a monumental and permanent imprint on America that his face had been freshly enshrined in granite on Mount Rushmore, dedicated just two months before the start of the Second World War. The Colonel had led the Great War campaign to abandon American neutrality and join the fight to defend the small nations of Europe.

Once again bullies were beating up democracies, but Teddy's son would have nothing to do with it. Ted wrote his first cousin, Eleanor Roosevelt, wife of their mutual distant cousin, President Franklin Roosevelt, "I myself am a convinced pacifist." The Colonel would have been horrified. But Ted, Jr., continued, "As I see it, the matter can be summed up in this fashion: A country always loses by a war." Ted's qualified pacifism was virtually an apostasy, a renunciation of all that his father's name—and he himself—had once stood for.

The eldest of Teddy's sons was America's boy. Ted had spent his teen years in and out of the White House, an eager cadet in his father's finishing school for the warrior spirit. Having a world-famous father brought real and psychic burdens. Ted got into scuffles, often in defense of his father's politics and the family name. Just five and a half feet tall and slight, the son of the Rough Rider would not back down. He couldn't. Playing football for Harvard, his nose was so badly smashed in after Yale ran play after play right at him, while he refused to come off the field, that it would remain flattened for life.

When the Great War started in August 1914, Colonel Roosevelt condemned Wilson and the rest of the "flub-dubs," "mollycoddles," and "flap-doodle pacifists" who turned their backs while Germany crushed "little Belgium" and then torpedoed unarmed vessels—most notoriously for Americans, the passenger ship *Lusitania*—plying the open seas. He could not abide those who watched acts of bullying and injustice with their arms folded and eyes averted. "Dante," he fumed, "reserved a special place of infamy in the inferno for those base angels who dared side neither with evil nor with good. . . . There can be no . . . peace until well-behaved, highly civilized small nations are protected from oppression and subjugation."

Colonel Roosevelt promised that his sons would enlist promptly, and when war was declared, they did. A French magazine joyously declared, "The Fighting Roosevelts had arrived." None left whole.

The youngest, most adored Roosevelt sibling, Quentin, was soon shot down and killed over France. Just days after Quentin's death, Ted was gassed and blinded temporarily. He recovered and quickly went back into the line, but a bullet that nearly tore off his leg finally knocked him out of combat.

Twenty-five years later, he still felt the tragedy of war in his bones and his heart, but he loved the army like a second family. He cofounded the American Legion veteran's organization in 1919 and retained his commission as a reserve colonel. Even two decades after the war ended, he confided to a wartime comrade who had stayed on in the military, "I feel exactly the same way that you do about service with troops. It is very soul-satisfying. Somehow you feel that it is a man's game. I have never been able to look at office work with a pen as more than something a man should do when he was not doing man's work." Man's work for now was stopping Franklin Roosevelt from taking the nation to war overseas again.

Ted Roosevelt, Jr., shared his siblings' view that Franklin, who modeled his own political rise on Teddy's, was an intellectual lightweight and, in their worst epithet, self-serving. He was an unworthy vessel to carry their father's legacy. The Long Island Roosevelts could not abide a TR simulacrum when in TR, Jr.—armed with his father's famously toothy grin, record of battlefield heroism, bully tone, and progressive Republicanism—America had the real thing.

The family rivalry broke into open war when Franklin ran as the 1920 vice presidential candidate on the Democratic ticket. The Oyster Bay Roosevelts campaigned for the Republican presidential nominee, Warren G. Harding. Ted took the lead in attacking FDR: "He is a maverick," Ted told reporters. "He does not have the brand of our family." The Democrats and FDR lost.

FDR got revenge in 1924, when TR, Jr., made a run for governor of New York, his father's stepping-stone to the vice presidency and from there to the White House. While assistant secretary of the Navy Department, Ted had avoided being directly implicated in the notorious Teapot Dome scandal over payments made to department officials in return for oil contracts. He might have escaped the taint had not the Hudson Valley Roosevelts made sure the scandal stayed in the headlines. Franklin spurred Eleanor to turn on her cousin and childhood friend. Traveling in an open car carrying a massive steaming papier-mâché teapot, she trailed Ted's campaign caravan around New York State. Wherever Ted went, there was Eleanor and her teapot-mobile. Ted, she said, was a "personally nice young man whose public service record shows him willing to do the bidding of his friends."

He lost badly in what was otherwise a national Republican landslide. His political career was finished. Not so Franklin's. Despite his affliction with polio, Franklin Roosevelt returned to triumph in politics unlike any other man in American history. To Ted and his siblings, a false Roosevelt usurped their rightful place in the White House. They refused to accept that Franklin was an exceptional, even uniquely gifted politician.

The fight over America's role in the Second World War brought the simmering family feud to a boil. On the very day the European war started, September 1, 1939, Ted wrote to Alice Roosevelt Longworth, his older half sister, "Like you I am bitterly fearful of Franklin. I am confident he is itching to get into the situation, partly as a means of bolstering himself and partly merely because of the megalomania that seems to possess most people who have wielded the powers of the Presidency." For his part, he was clear: America should take up arms, he told a University of Virginia audience, only in defense of "our free institutions and our representative democracy, our own territory, and the Monroe Doctrine." Stopping Franklin Roosevelt from going to war was a fight from which Teddy Roosevelt's namesake refused to back down.

TR, Jr., quickly became an officer in the antiwar army, taking to the airwaves and speaking at public gatherings across the land. He emerged as one of the most effective and energetic opponents of American intervention in Europe. He did not need to remind audiences that when the last war broke out, ". . . I went over to Europe with the first American troops to fight in Europe. We were told that it was the war to end wars, the war to make the world safe for democracy. We were told we had won." Now he asked, "Did we? Conditions in Europe today give the answer. Nobody wins a war."

While publicly battling against going to war, he remained a colonel in the Army Reserves, even spending a month in the summer of 1940 voluntarily attending a dreary and draining training camp with his reserve regiment.

When FDR finally accepted his party's nomination—despite a refusal to appear in person at the Democratic Convention—to run for a historic third term in 1940, the Oyster Bay Roosevelts' pent-up fury at Franklin exploded. "I'd rather vote for Hitler," the venomously funny elder half sister Alice Roosevelt Longworth said about the prospect of a third term. She claimed "FDR" stood for "Führer, Duce, Roosevelt." Ted dropped his business affairs and took to the hustings. He stumped tirelessly for Roosevelt's Republican opponent, Wendell Willkie, in his race against "my fifth cousin soon to be removed," as he laughingly taunted him.

He hammered at FDR at every turn for approaching the prospect of war much as he had his entire career: in a self-serving fashion. "Franklin Roosevelt," said Ted Roosevelt, Jr., ". . . has never stated to us in clear fashion just what the threats against us were and from whence they might be expected. He has told bogey man stories so vague that they are clearly designed merely to frighten us and to make us vote for him as the indispensable man." He campaigned *against* FDR more than *for* Willkie, with the type of inexhaustible energy normally exhibited by someone in search of vengeance—which was, in large measure, what he sought against the man who presumed to wear the family crown.

With two weeks to go until Election Day, he was going at a pace "beyond belief . . . making one night stands everywhere," he wrote his son Cornelius. In the then-short campaign season, he had already traversed a phenomenal sixteen thousand miles through twelve Western states, stopping to speak to any crowd he could find on Willkie's behalf. The push for Willkie had an effect—polls ticked over; suddenly FDR was looking vulnerable.

Ted had advice he was sure would push Willkie over the top. The former Democratic Party member and corporate lawyer Willkie had positioned himself on foreign affairs as an internationalist in support of aid for the British. Voters had trouble distinguishing the two presidential candidates on the most pressing foreign policy question. Ted cabled Willkie's wife: "Please tell your husband that I have finished each speech with the statement that under Roosevelt we will be drawn into war and that under your husband we will not. This has invariably been the high note in the appeal I have made." He wrote Willkie directly, asking him to tell Americans that a vote for FDR was a vote for war: ". . . the great issue is staying out of war. . . ," he insisted. "If we can prove to the satisfaction of the American public that Roosevelt will get us into war, the battle is won."

TR, Jr., was right. With just three weeks left before Election Day, Willkie surged in the polls. An increasingly confident Ted was making three and four speeches a day for Willkie. He wrote his son Cornelius a few days before the vote, "The campaign is now in its very last stages and I am too close to the picture to be really a good judge. I do feel, however, in spite of everything, that Willkie has the edge." The Republican Party knew it was in a horse race, and felt sure it would ride what looked like an insurgent winner in a sprint to the finish.

The day before the vote, the Republican Party ran a chilling radio ad addressed to the "mothers of America." An ominous, bloodcurdling voice, reminiscent of those heard in the popular horror dramas of the air, spoke as if from the grave. "When your boy is dying on some battlefield in Europe," said the announcer, "and he's crying out 'Mother! Mother!'—don't blame Franklin D. Roosevelt because he sent your boy to war—blame YOURSELF, because YOU sent Franklin D. Roosevelt back to the White House!" What mother would do that to her son?

As Willkie's candidacy caught fire and FDR's reelection chances seemed to wobble, the Democrat's aides convinced him that he *had* to respond to the Republicans' warmongering attacks. He answered in a way that would come to haunt him. In the heat of the tight race, he felt forced to declare in a nationally broadcast campaign speech just days before the vote, "I have said this before but I shall say it again and again and again: Your boys are not going to be sent into any foreign wars. . . ." He pounded the rostrum: "We will not send our army, navy or air forces to fight in foreign lands. . . ."

Those insistent, repeated, definitive words would stick to him with the discomfort of a perspiration-soaked shirt. His speechwriter, Robert Sherwood, believed "in yielding to the hysterical demands for sweeping reassurance," and the president did what he had to to win reelection, but in doing so he locked out the possibility of going up against Hitler short of a direct attack on American soil. If voters wanted a candidate who would join the fight against German aggression, neither party offered that possibility. The world would pay a terrible price for the rhetoric of American election politics.

As voters headed to the polls, some surveys indicated a dead heat.

9

Cassandra

At midday on a clear December 12, 1937, the USS *Panay* lay at anchor on a broad, fast-flowing stretch of China's Yangtze River about thirty miles above Nanking (Nanjing).

Japanese army forces had attacked Nanking two days before, unleashing a brutal siege of the city. Taking aboard the last remaining American Embassy personnel and a handful of foreign journalists, the *Panay* raced upriver, away from the fighting. Early in the afternoon, its skipper, Lieutenant Commander James J. Hughes, saw Japanese bombers and fighters approach up the river until almost directly overhead. Suddenly the bombers dropped their noses and came shrieking from the sky. Their bombs hit the *Panay*. Her top deck cracked open like a walnut shell, and soon she settled ablaze into the river. Fighters zoomed around and then flew in at masthead height to strafe the crew fleeing the burning ship.

The attack left two sailors dead and forty-three wounded. One of the newsmen died and five other civilians were hurt. *Panay*'s crew counted as the first uniformed Americans to exchange gunfire with the Japanese military in almost a century of relations between the two nations. She was the first American naval vessel sunk in combat since the Great War.

Some regard the *Panay* Incident as the first battle of the Second World War for the United States.

When word of the fatal attack reached the United States, President Roosevelt remarked at an emergency Cabinet meeting that not so long ago attacking and sinking an American warship would have automatically been considered an act of war. And Secretary of the Interior Harold L. Ickes thought immediate war was the answer, given the deteriorating situation in Asia. Japan was making clear that it would never step back from China and that its imperial ambitions would eventually require driving out the Western powers from their Asian colonial possessions. War seemed the likeliest future. "Certainly war with Japan is inevitable sooner or later," Ickes told the president. "If we have to fight her, isn't this the best possible time?"

Asian affairs analysts suggested that extremists within the Japanese army had ordered the attack to scare remaining foreigners out of China. They also suspected this was a test of America's stomach for war. If so, Japan learned that the U.S. was in no mood to fight. The stifled protest against the attack on the *Panay* barely registered. Except in Japan.

Keenly aware of his nation's isolationist temper, Roosevelt was reluctant to respond militarily, particularly given the extensive trade relations between the two countries, which favored the fragile American economy. Japan had the capital and freighters to buy and ship American scrap metal, oil, and refined fuels across the Pacific, where they were manufactured into the bombs, bullets, warships, and airplanes the country used to wage war on the politically split, mostly preindustrial China. Effectively, the U.S. supplied the raw materials that built Japan's military, and the aviation fuel that made possible the deadly attack on the *Panay*.

Congress and the vast majority of the American people desired to stay out of war, despite such a transparently provocative action. A national Gallup Poll of American voters found that 70 percent of those who had an opinion agreed the U.S. should bring fleets and marines, business, charitable activities, missionaries and indeed every American, home. As conflicts in Europe over German expansionism and in Asia over Japanese imperial ambitions sharpened, isolationist sentiment grew in the nation.

Japan and America pulled back from their first violent confrontation, but continued to eye each other from opposite sides of the Pacific, aware that they stood atop a rumbling volcano.

Former Secretary of State Henry L. Stimson detested the isolationists. He was normally unflappable, but their outcries over the *Panay* Incident made his moral fibers resonate like plucked piano wires. He was certain that the events under way in China marked a fearsome turning point for the West. "Unhappy [in the] temperamentally ill-fitting role of Cassandra," he later wrote, he felt he *must* speak out.

Seventy years old at the time of the *Panay* Incident, Stimson had been out of government for five years, but remained the nation's most respected statesman. "I held the great statesman in awe," wrote Joseph Alsop about Stimson. The normally voluble columnist and Washington power-elite chronicler of what he called the "WASP ascendancy" found himself tongue-tied in the presence of "the white-whiskered, straight-backed" Stimson, "an impossibly grand figure." Stimson's public service record, stretching back to Theodore Roosevelt's days in the White House, merited that reverence. He had served as a Cabinet officer in three administrations.

The Japanese attack on the *Panay* bore out earlier warnings he'd issued as secretary of state after Japan's 1931 invasion and swift occupation of Mongolia and northeastern China. At the time, President Herbert Hoover was unwilling to attempt to force Japan to roll back its invasion forces, despite the obvious violation of international collective security agreements made after the Great War. With the U.S. economy in free fall, he would not risk confronting Japan over what he called "scraps of paper, or paper treaties." Stimson responded that treaties were only worthless if other nations treated them as such by breaking them. Laws, he insisted, must govern the affairs of nations, and nations must enforce those laws. "If we lie down," he warned, "and treat them like scraps of paper nothing will happen, and in the future the peace movement will receive a blow that it will not recover from for a long time." His warning went unheeded.

Stimson remained ill at ease but undeterred. The high road was the only road Stimson took—often on horseback. He said of himself that he "preferred to choose his main objective and then charge ahead without worrying, confident that aggressive executive leadership would win followers." Stimson was a throwback to an earlier age, one in which he and his political mentor, Teddy Roosevelt, respected a man according to his resolve to risk much, even all, for the sake of a cause he knew to be right.

Certainly, Stimson firmly believed in his class's leadership role as stewards of civilization wherever they went: across the continent, around the globe. He embodied in full what would later become known as "the Establishment." These so-called "Wise Men" were sons of generational wealth and breeding whose sense of noblesse oblige comprehended service to country as a duty to detour from their moneyed lives and careers—as indeed a second career, made possible by their wealth. Nearly all were Republicans. However, they prided themselves on their independence from party machinations, particularly in their conviction that principle and national interest trumped party politics, above all in international relations. Most were of old New England stock and Ivy League–educated—for Stimson, Harvard Law School after Yale College, where, already picked out for future success, he was selected a member of the vaunted secret senior class society Skull & Bones.

After great success as a Wall Street banking lawyer and then as a crusading New York district attorney, Stimson was called to Washington to serve as secretary of war by Theodore Roosevelt's White House successor, William Howard Taft. Stimson took the reins of the nation's minuscule army, one intended for small-scale actions, not the international stage. When the U.S. entered the Great War in the spring of 1917, Stimson, ignoring his age—forty-nine at the time—and happy marriage, enlisted in the army. Given charge of an artillery regiment—making him one of just two nonregular army officers to hold that large a command in the war—he served nine months in wartime France.

Back in the Cabinet as Hoover's secretary of state, Stimson tried to run the nation's foreign affairs with the same gentlemanly code of honor he brought to his personal affairs. Upon learning of the department's secret operation to break foreign nations' codes to spy on their diplomatic correspondence, he promptly shut it down and purportedly famously declared, "Gentlemen don't read other gentlemen's mail."

After Franklin Roosevelt defeated Hoover, Stimson continued to spend part of each year in Washington and remained a welcome visitor to the FDR White House. Stimson was out of step with many men in his class, who despised the New Dealer-in-chief. No friend of the New Deal, Stimson nonetheless saw in FDR "a man [I] knew and liked, and not a bogey. . . ." Stimson approved of the Roosevelt administration's general rejection of isolationism, yet watched and worried as the nation, absorbed by its internal economic woes, turned a cold shoulder on Japan's war in China and the imperious German chancellor's bullying acts in Europe. Lawlessness in the international order did not confine itself to a few spots, he warned; if not contained, like fire it sparked and flared outward until it burned everything around it. Few were ready to heed his warnings.

As the world crisis worsened, Stimson felt he needed to speak out publicly. He went on radio, gave talks, and wrote opinion essays in *The New York Times* and other publications. He shared his conviction that the U.S. would eventually have to confront the menaces to civilized world order now loosed by Japan in Asia and Germany in Europe. Isolation, he said, was not just wrong for U.S. national interests, but a moral failure which in the long run would prove far more damaging to the nation than confronting global aggressors.

On March 7, 1939, a week before the Nazis completed their take-over of Czechoslovakia, Stimson wrote a long letter to the editor of *The New York Times*. "I believe that our foreign policy cannot with safety be geographically limited to a defense of this hemisphere," he wrote. "On the contrary, I think that if we should stand idly by until Britain, France and China are either conquered or forced to make terms with militaristic aggressors, our own hemisphere would neither be a safe nor a happy place to live in, for a people with American ideals of life."

The president seemed to listen to Stimson's and others' appeals for him to act. Roosevelt gave a blistering speech in Chicago on October 5, 1937, in which he likened war to a "contagion" and urged law-abiding nations to "quarantine" the "epidemic of world lawlessness." He called for, he said, "The peace-loving nations [to] make a concerted effort in opposition to those violations of treaties and those ignoring of humane instincts which today are creating a state of international anarchy and instability from which there is no escape through mere isolation or neutrality." However, the speech laid out no actual steps the U.S. would take—or any "concerted effort" his government would make in alliance with other nations—to "quarantine" lawlessness. The *Times* of London remarked that the American president had put forward "an attitude without a program." This would prove a leitmotif in Roosevelt's confrontation with the world crisis.

At his news conference the next day, Roosevelt spoke off the record about what he meant by "a concerted effort," which had sounded to most ears like a move toward some kind of alliance—impossible under current neutrality statutes and prevailing isolationist sentiment. He insisted that, while looking for a way ahead with other nations, he rejected the idea that the U.S. could not remain, as *Newsweek*'s respected foreign affairs writer Ernest Lindley said to him, "neutral if you are going to align yourself with one group of nations." To many, that sounded like the dictionary definition of "nonneutrality."

Roosevelt rejoined, "We are looking for some way to peace; and by no means is it necessary that that way be contrary to the exercise of neutrality." In fact, he said, "It may be an expansion" of neutrality. The implications of such an "expansion" were plain to everyone in the room except the dexterous president, who insisted there was no need to "overhaul" the neutrality statutes.

By the middle of the following year, he took his first steps toward an "expansion" of neutrality within his present powers. He issued a presidential proclamation declaring what he termed a "moral embargo" against certain exports to Japan, most important a nonbinding but nonetheless effective ban on the export of airplanes and airplane parts. Embargoing vital trade was a powerful weapon against Japan's warmaking capacity, which he would lean on going forward. He held out the possibility that he might even cut off American crude oil and petroleum products, a sword of Damocles that threatened Japan's ability to continue its multi-year war in China.

Chinese Nationalist officials came to Washington seeking help in their fight against Japan. As the Chinese industrial centers along the Yangtze River fell to the advancing Japanese army and air force, China needed to move scarce and vital industrial machinery and tools to secure sites a thousand miles inland. However, China lacked roads and trucks to carry them, instead employing Stone Age forms of transport—pole-and sailboat, donkey cart and human muscle. After meeting with a representative of the Chinese Nationalists' leader, General Chiang Kai-shek, FDR arranged a $25 million loan to the Chinese government on December 18, 1938. The loan was followed by a second for $20 million less than three months later and additional loans after that. Terms called for repayment not in cash but in shipments over the coming five years of tung oil, a Chinese tree oil useful in waterproofing industrial products. The Chinese used the loans to buy Chrysler and Ford trucks, tractors, and excavators, in addition to gasoline—and had money left over to purchase Soviet-made planes, tanks, and guns and British war goods, until that country faced off with Germany.

The barter loan deals skirted the spirit of the neutrality laws, which required full payment in cash—known as cash-and-carry—prior to delivery of American products into war zones. FDR would keep that model in mind.

Two years later, the U.S. still remained a neutral power in the world war. Roosevelt continued his public dance between the conflicting poles of maintaining official neutrality and seeking a way for an "expansion" of neutrality to defend a world under siege. In his 1940 State of the Union address, he insisted, "The first President of the United States warned us against entangling foreign alliances. The present President of the United States subscribes to and follows that precept." He acknowledged the polls and the isolationists: "I can understand the feelings of those who warn the nation that they will never again consent to the sending of American youth to fight on the soil of Europe," he told the nation. "But, as I remember, nobody has asked them to consent—for nobody expects such an undertaking."

But he did not say it would not happen. He proposed hefty upgrades to the peacetime army and navy forces and called for new taxes to pay for them.

Congress would go along only so far. Even many members of his own party resisted spending money the Treasury did not have, in the words of Colorado Democratic senator Alva B. Adams, "for a war which is not coming."

Less than six months later, on June 18, 1940, William Shirer stood in the Place de la Concorde in Paris amid a huge yet largely silent crowd of Parisians watched over by German soldiers. Loudspeakers blasted out news of France's surrender. Those around him, said Shirer, "were almost struck dead."

That same evening in New Haven, Henry Stimson delivered a national radio address from a mansion not far from his beloved Yale University campus, where he had met with Yale students earlier in the day. He told listeners that their nation faced "probably the greatest crisis of its history," threatening the world "based upon law and justice instead of force." The world was now almost fully divided between two fundamentally opposed camps. Echoing Abraham Lincoln, Stimson warned, "The world cannot endure permanently half slave and half free." In this crisis "which strikes at the very existence of all that our nation has cherished and fought for" throughout its history, the United States, he declared, faced a very real emergency for which it was ill-prepared—and worse, prevented from facing by neutrality laws.

He called for practical steps, including repeal of those statutes, "a shackle to our true interests for over five years." He also asked that America arm the British and open its ports to Royal Navy warships for repairs, refueling, and supplies. He called on Congress to speed up sending munitions and aircraft to the British, "if necessary in our own ships and under convoy." Most significantly for American families and the students he'd met with that day, he called for establishment of a compulsory military draft. That was a startlingly radical notion: In its 164-year history, America had never conscripted private citizens except in times of war. Not one.

Pushing for conscription was not something Stimson decided on alone. He had attended a widely reported May 22, 1940, "secret" meeting at the Harvard Club in New York City. The conclave was convened by Grenville Clark, a wealthy and influential Manhattan lawyer at the same firm where Stimson had started out and an intimate of Franklin Roosevelt since boyhood. The Harvard Club group hatched a plan to launch a campaign for creation of compulsory military training—and to replace the current isolationist secretary of war, Harry H. Woodring.

Constitutionally unwilling to deliver bad news, FDR loathed firing anyone, but Woodring had been dragging his feet on the president's insistence that he fulfill British purchasing requests for the first American-built B-17 bombers and other scarce advanced weapons. Even Roosevelt was reaching his limit with the recalcitrant Woodring as he sought to speed up industrial production and cargo shipments to the Allies.

Through Supreme Court associate justice Felix Frankfurter, Clark's friend and a confidant and adviser to Roosevelt, Clark took the lead in lobbying army brass and the White House to push legislation to create a conscript army. He also secretly lobbied to replace Woodring with Stimson.

Stimson thought Clark's "ridiculous idea" would never fly, but the interlocking wheels of power moved. The week before Stimson's radio speech, *The New York Times* editorialized in favor of a peacetime draft. America's elder statesman threw his weight on the scale. "I believe," he concluded his June 18 Yale radio talk, "we should find our people ready to take their proper part in this threatened world and to carry through to victory, freedom, and reconstruction."

Many of the young people listening over their radios and with whom Stimson had met earlier in the day at Yale asked, Victory? Reconstruction? In what war? Rather than fight another war, they chose to follow somebody else. They were hell-bent on staying out of the war.

10

A Rising Sun

Washington and London, 1940

FDR had read the transcript of Henry Stimson's interventionist Yale radio talk. Nothing Stimson said dissuaded him from bringing the arch-interventionist into the government. On June 3, Felix Frankfurter met with the president to raise the idea of having Stimson replace the obstinately neutralist Woodring as secretary of war. A happy Frankfurter reported back to Grenville Clark that his idea had "struck fire." FDR had already been floating the notion of creating a national unity government. Forever moving about the weights on the political balance, Roosevelt also knew that bringing Republicans into his administration would defang some of his potential Republican opposition should he make a run for a third term in office, as seemed increasingly likely. Appointing a man of Stimson's stature would signal that FDR's focus on the world crisis rose above party or private cause.

He called Stimson the day after his radio address to invite him to join his Cabinet as secretary of war. Stimson had not expected Roosevelt would go through with it. The president told him that "everybody was running around at loose ends in Washington and he thought I would be a stabilizing factor," Stimson recorded a few days after. Roosevelt told him he "was in full accord with" his recent speech; he too wanted to commence compulsory military training. Stimson knew the president was not for war, but that short of war he was ready to help the Allies—and Stimson had made his views about the wars in Europe and China clear.

Roosevelt sealed the deal for Stimson by pairing his appointment with that of another Republican Party stalwart and anti–New Dealer, *Chicago Daily News* publisher Frank Knox. Knox had been the vice presidential candidate on Alf Landon's ticket in his 1936 run against FDR. In the midst of the campaign, he had charged Roosevelt with taking a "path [that] leads straight into Communism, Nazism, Fascism, or whatever 'ism' the fancy of the moment dictates it be called." But in the world crisis, Knox's cutting words and distrust of FDR evaporated. With France about to capitulate, Colonel Knox—he retained his military commission—said that in this new crisis, "I would do anything the President wanted me to do, from putting a gun on my shoulder up."

At age seventy-three, Stimson accepted Roosevelt's offer to return to the same position he'd last held twenty-seven years and a world of differences ago. He immediately called Clark to congratulate *him*. He said, "Your ridiculous plot has succeeded."

His former Republican friends would not make the hoary patrician feel welcomed in returning to the Cabinet. Stimson had last served as secretary of war in Senator Robert A. Taft's father's administration. The son now charged Stimson with a "concealment of the real purpose" in his mind, which he claimed was to draw out public opinion "to support a war policy," something few Americans favored. The reality, Taft contended, was that should the U.S. become involved in the war, "I see no reason to think we will ever see any real peace during our lifetime." Perpetual war would inevitably lead America to "become a totalitarian state," no different from the militarized tyrannies Stimson found so unconscionable in Germany and Japan. Stung by Taft's harsh words, Stimson let him know that he felt betrayed by the "unfair" questions and accusations of "warmongering" from "you of all people."

In objecting to Stimson, fellow committee member Republican senator Arthur H. Vandenberg asserted that permitting British naval vessels to utilize American port facilities for fueling and repair "would be a direct invitation to bring war to all our ports. . . . We should become belligerents then and there—we would be in the war." Stimson conceded it would be "an act of un-neutrality."

With an election coming up in November, Stimson's congressional support was at best tepid, even among the administration's friends. Only two senators spoke in his favor on the Senate floor. The nation's most respected and longest-serving public servant won confirmation, but no commander in chief's nominee to head the War Department had faced such stiff opposition since before the Civil War. The isolationists in FDR's own party, as well as twelve out of twenty-two Republicans, cast votes against him.

FDR charged Stimson with the task of giving "the British all we could," Stimson said. He arrived at his War Department office and soon realized that there wasn't much to give. The situation was even worse than he feared. The U.S. Army had nowhere near enough arms stockpiled or in near-term production to fill its own needs. A May 1940 War Department assessment found the regular (nonreserve) army personnel stood at 14,000 officers and 227,000 men, of whom only 80,000 were combat-ready, with equipment on hand for fewer than 500,000 men—not the millions envisioned for the new draft army. The air force had only 1,350 planes and, at the current production pace, would have just 3,000 by the following summer. Both Japan and Germany had armed forces many times larger and far better equipped. Stimson realized that, as far as helping out the British went, "We have so little that we can give them."

In London, Churchill disagreed. Two weeks before Stimson's nomination as secretary of war, the last men of the British Expeditionary Force were valiantly plucked out of the fire at Dunkirk. Behind the scenes, a grave Churchill admitted that this had been "the greatest British military defeat for many centuries." On stage, Churchill insisted his people would "outlive the menace of tyranny." He roared, "We shall never surrender!" However, with France on the verge of capitulating, he warned Roosevelt in a June 11 letter "that the voice and force of the United States may count for nothing if they are withheld too long."

The president had given his widely lauded "fighting speech" at the University of Virginia commencement the day before, during which he had sounded the ringing call to push aid "full speed ahead." He pledged to provide the "material resources of this nation" rather than allow America "to become . . . a lone island in a world dominated by the philosophy of force." For the first time, Churchill believed that England was fighting "for what we may now indeed call a common cause" with America. The prime minister fully expected, he told FDR, that "Hitler . . . will turn upon us and we are preparing to resist his fury and defend our Island," and applauded FDR's offer to provide his nation's full resources to help the last standing democracies.

Churchill had specific items "so needful to us in the impending struggle for the life of Great Britain." Knowing that Roosevelt had reconditioned his large fleet of Great War–vintage four-pipers for the Atlantic Neutrality Zone patrols, Churchill asked that, in the present emergency, FDR instead transfer the aging ships to London. "Nothing," he said, "is so important as for us to have thirty or forty old destroyers. . . . Not a day should be lost."

Those destroyers were not only for blocking the German amphibious invasion London now expected; they offered a desperately needed addition to the overstretched force protecting the convoy lifelines bringing food, fighting men, and war supplies from around the world to England. Battleships and heavy cruisers provided almost no defense against nimble submarines. Designed for antisubmarine operations, fast, quick-turning destroyers and other smaller warships carried sonar detection equipment, low-firing guns, and depth charges, making them powerful sub chaser-killers. When a U-boat was spotted near a convoy, the escorts could peel off to attack. With aircraft presently lacking the range to fly out to mid-ocean, convoy escorts provided lifesaving protection for slow-running merchantmen.

At present, Hitler's cross-Channel invasion plans, called Operation *Seelöwe* (Sealion), projected a September 15, 1940, D-day. Churchill could call on just sixty-eight destroyers, he informed FDR, with ten more due for completion over the coming four months—not enough to defend Britain's coast from invasion and protect its convoys.

Just three days later, with French resistance having crumbled, he repeated his plea, this time with an unwonted hint of desperation. The enemy would shortly possess the entire English-facing coast and, in all likelihood, the French fleet. Churchill insisted his nation would fight on whatever happened. In his celebrated "Finest Hour" speech of June 18, he had proclaimed his confidence in his people's will to resist, but warned Washington, "If we fail, then the whole world, including the United States, and all that we have known and cared for, will sink into the abyss of a new dark age made more sinister, and perhaps more protracted, by the lights of a perverted science." Darkness was now visible on the eastern horizon.

Invasion was not by any means the prime minister's sole worry: England still ruled the waves, but with Europe's major ports in German hands, together with those of the North Sea, Baltic, and much of Scandinavia, and with Italy and French North Africa providing safe havens in the Mediterranean, Germany had in effect doubled the number of submarines prowling continuously in search of prey. Allied shipping losses, which had previously been significant, but fitful and sustainable, suddenly proved devastating as the German navy added a deadly efficiency to its U-boat operations. Between June and October 1940, more than 270 merchant ships went under in U-boat attacks.

Even that horrific toll paled when the German Admiralty accumulated sufficient numbers of U-boats to commence so-called "wolfpack" operations. The subs lurked in lines spread like a net along the major convoy routes, waiting to sight ship silhouettes or smoke smudges on the horizon. At a signal upon spotting a flotilla, the U-boats converged on the approaching ships. As the convoy neared, they submerged like crocodiles awaiting a fat meal. The prey rarely knew they were in danger until it was too late.

Starting on September 21, 1940, over two nights of carnage a pack of four U-boats mauled a convoy of forty-two merchantmen, sinking eleven ships and damaging two. Overnight on October 18–19, five subs made a concerted attack on a slow convoy of thirty-five merchantmen. As terror began, the escorts searched frantically for the marauders, but never realized the U-boats were moving about *inside* the convoy formation, killing ship after ship. Before the attack ended, twenty ships had gone down and two more were badly damaged and barely able to limp home. The vessels that made it home survived only because the wolfpack turned away to attack another rich school of merchant ships steaming in the other direction. The subs bagged twelve more cargo ships the next night.

U-boats were not the lone ship hunters: Coasting ships and naval vessels laid up in ports made easy targets for aerial bombardment. On June 27 alone, separate German air raids demolished two destroyers and heavily damaged three others.

That marked barely the start of the German aerial attacks on England. Hitler expected his Messerschmitt fighters—superior in numbers, equipment, and experience—to make quick work of the British defenders and their Spitfires. Massive nightly bombing raids sought to knock out English defenses, destroy airfields, and reduce fighting morale. The Blitz, as the English called the raids on London and other urban centers, intensified, with thirty-five large-scale raids—eighteen on London alone—involving two hundred or more bombers per sortie between September 7 and October 5, 1940. Thousands of civilians died in those raids.

Projecting command of the Channel skies, merchant convoys disrupted, coastal defenses reduced, and civilian morale blasted to bits,
the Führer expected that Operation Sealion's invading forces would
encounter little more than English ladies swinging their handbags to
slow them on their drive into Trafalgar Square. When the massive bombing campaign against England began, Luftwaffe chief Hermann Göring
promised Hitler, "The defense of Southern England will last four days
and the Royal Air Force four weeks. We can guarantee invasion for the
Führer within a month."

Trusting his air force to bring the English to their knees, Hitler
made ready: He ordered every available barge, specially built landing
craft, portable loading dock, and logistical support moved into position
on the French and Belgian coasts. Paratroopers, aircraft, and landing
armies assembled behind them, where they practiced storming beaches
under fire—with film crews recording the action for posterity—rehears-
ing the assault on landing sites spread across the south coast of England.

British losses were not sustainable, certainly not in the face of an impending invasion. In mid-June Churchill pressed upon the American
president the unsettling prospect of Germany's forcing England to
"becom[e] a vassal state of the Hitler empire," as was taking place
in Vichy France. At that point, he warned, "long before the United
States would be able to prepare against it . . . you may have a United
States of Europe under the Nazi command far more numerous, far
stronger, far better armed than the new [world]." Speaking to a fellow
naval man, Churchill knew that FDR understood the significance
of the "overwhelming sea power [that] would be in Hitler's hands."
All would surely be lost. "We must ask as a matter of life or death to
be reinforced with these destroyers." The English would not give in
without a fight, but that fight "may well be beyond our resources . . .
[without] . . . this reinforcement on the sea."

As France capitulated a week later, he cabled Canada's prime minister, Mackenzie King, "I shall myself never enter into any peace negotiations with Hitler, but obviously I cannot bind a future government, which, if we were deserted by the United States and beaten down here, might very easily be a kind of Quisling affair ready to accept German overlordship and protection." The British government prepared contingency plans for moving the Royal Family, Parliament, critical civilian and military leaders, and the entire fleet across the Atlantic to its commonwealth land, Canada. Churchill urged King, who was about to meet with FDR, to "impress the danger upon the President."

Whatever sympathies FDR may have had for England, his foremost concern was the grave risk his own country faced should Germany capture the British, along with the French, fleet. He had already received a sobering report from his military planners. FDR charged a joint military planning board with coming up with a defense strategy should England fall. The planners projected that the nation would have just months to mobilize its forces. They concluded that even a U.S. defense force combined with its presumed Western Hemisphere allies, above all Canada, could not hope to defeat the united forces of Germany, Italy, and conquered England and Europe. Instead, the most optimistic outcome would be to reach "favorable" terms "in the eventual peace settlement." The planners did not consider the nightmare possibility of the country having to fight a second war simultaneously in the Pacific.

Roosevelt wanted to act quickly. He moved to make twenty torpedo boats and several sub-chasers being constructed for the U.S. Navy and Coast Guard available for London's purchase. Senator David Walsh of Massachusetts, an isolationist and Boston Irishman who had no truck with the English, chaired the powerful Senate Naval Affairs Committee. After he learned of Roosevelt's transfer plan, he stopped him cold by adding a proviso to a big navy appropriation bill that prohibited transfer of military supplies unless the chief of naval operations, now Admiral Betty Stark, and his army chief of staff counterpart, General George Marshall, certified them "not essential to the United States." Thus, the English might not even get their hands on the aircraft and ships they had already contracted for.

Roosevelt succeeded in persuading Marshall and Stark to interpret the question of "surplus" of various stockpiles of Great War weapons generously. They were sold to private manufacturers for resale to the British. Twelve ships loaded with seventy thousand tons of "surplus" bomber planes, rifles, tanks, machine guns, and ammunition sailed for Britain, where they restocked much of the munitions left behind in Dunkirk.

However, the life-or-death disposition of the aged destroyers appeared to be out of the question. Admiral Stark could not walk back his recent testimony on Capitol Hill that the navy was speeding up reconditioning of one hundred four-pipers to serve its overstretched fleet's extended neutrality patrol needs. Senator Walsh warned the White House not to send them overseas. FDR risked impeachment should he negotiate their sale. The British purchasing agent in the U.S., Arthur Purvis, reported home that Roosevelt had determined, "to his regret," that as far as destroyers were concerned, "the United States could not spare any."

Churchill refused to concede, given that those ships, rather than sailing unchallenged through largely empty seas, could save Great Britain from imminent destruction. With Britain losing a destroyer every day on average to enemy action, Churchill warned FDR on July 31, "We could not keep up the present rate of casualties for long." He practically got down on his knees to beg: "Mr. President," he concluded, "with great respect I must tell you that in the long history of the world, this is a thing to do now."

A frustrated and moved Roosevelt read out the PM's depressing letter to a glum Cabinet at the August 2 meeting. Attending his first meeting since winning Senate approval, Navy Secretary Knox raised a point for discussion. Well before being approached by FDR to join the administration, Knox had pushed for the U.S. to acquire bases in the

Caribbean to shield the Panama Canal and other crucial Atlantic approaches to the hemisphere. The night before, Knox told the Cabinet, he and British ambassador Lord Lothian had discussed the idea of London selling some of its Atlantic and Caribbean possessions.

Unknown to Knox, Lothian had cabled London to inquire about the sale of colonies as a ready source of cash. The proud imperialist Churchill would not willingly stoop to dickering in a territorial fire sale. He would consider *leasing* basing rights on the dominions to the Americans if, he cabled, "It is understood that this will enable us to secure destroyers and flying-boats at once."

After hearing from Lothian, FDR realized he might have found a way to thread the needle of supplying the British with the life-or-death destroyers without getting jabbed by Congress. A bases-for-destroyers swap would strengthen the protective chain of hemispheric bases and send the vital destroyers and other presently embargoed vessels and airplanes to Churchill without an obvious violation of the neutrality laws. In the current political situation the U.S. government could not sell or give away the prized ships and aircraft outright, but by mid-August FDR had concluded he could do some "Yankee trading," bartering base leases for the destroyers. Roosevelt knew, he commented, that "Congress is going to raise hell about this but even another day's delay may mean the end of civilization. . . . If Britain is to survive, we must act."

It was a big political risk, but leaving Congress to debate the matter would almost certainly put German troops in London before any destroyers sailed. A series of consultations among various constitutional authorities led Attorney General Robert Jackson to conclude that, like the Louisiana Purchase, it was "an opportunity that entails no obligation" and that therefore an executive decision, not a treaty requiring Senate consent, would be sufficient to do the deal.

FDR and Stimson traveled by train on August 17 to Ogdensburg, New York, on the Canadian border—ostensibly to observe army training

maneuvers. That evening they gathered in the presidential railcar's par-
lor with Canadian prime minister Mackenzie King, who had rushed to
meet them there. Roosevelt told the reporters on hand that their hastily arranged summit was designed to create hemispheric cooperative
defense arrangements. Stimson said the president's personal initiative
in establishing the Permanent Joint Board on Defense—a precursor to
today's North Atlantic Treaty Organization (NATO)—to secure North
Atlantic approaches to the West so moved King that he "almost [had]
tears in his eyes" over the tremendous morale boost this would give the
Canadian and the British people.

No mention was made in the release following the parlay of the
other major topic the men discussed that night: effecting transfer of
fifty destroyers to the British. Ever the naval authority, FDR detailed
to the others how the transfer would take place, what weaponry the
ships carried, even the size of crew needed to ferry them over the ocean.

That night, Stimson felt, "was very possibly the turning point in
the tide of the war, and that from now on we could hope for better
things." Although this was a wildly overoptimistic appraisal, the trade
would keep Britain's convoys running for months more, saved an island
nation utterly reliant upon sea traffic from drowning for at least the next
several months, and meant that Hitler could not send an amphibious
force over the Channel unmolested.

On September 2, the deal was officially done, and the U.S. agreed
to provide fifty four-pipers in an exchange for long-term leases of British
bases in the Bahamas, Antigua, St. Lucia, Trinidad, Jamaica, and British
Guiana. To make the "bargain" appear that much sharper on the U.S.'s
part, and thus more politically palatable, London added basing rights
in Bermuda and Argentia, Newfoundland, as a "gift" to the American
people—which would also bring American ships, airplanes and military
personnel that much closer to Europe. U.S. Navy ships and flying boats
began shifting into these bases over the next few months, providing
much more logistical support, air coverage, and harbors for the most
crucial of the Atlantic Squadron's patrol zones.

Isolationists howled. "Mr. Roosevelt today committed an act of war," declared the *St. Louis Post-Dispatch*. "He also became America's first dictator. Secretly, [he] entered into an agreement . . . that amounts to a military and naval alliance with Great Britain. . . . If this secretly negotiated deal goes through, the fat is in the fire and we may as well get ready for a full-dress participation in the European war. If Roosevelt gets away with this, we may as well say good-by to our liberties and make up our mind that henceforth we live under a dictatorship." A few House members called for bringing impeachment proceedings against FDR.

Even the most ardent isolationists softened quickly after realizing that the deal for the quarter-century-old ships worked so lopsidedly in America's favor. Critics left off altogether when Republican presidential candidate Wendell Willkie voiced solid support for the bases-for-destroyers trade.

While the deal did not yet indicate a willingness on the Americans' part to aid the defenders without some tangible benefit in return, it did establish the notion in the public's mind and among political officials that the quid in any deal with the United States need not be cash. For the Roosevelt administration, a precedent for the deal existed in the loans made to the Chinese government, enabling it to purchase American-made trucks and other products in return for future deliveries of tung oil. The question of whether the nation could loan and barter its military might, making deals with difficult-to-decipher repayment terms, terms that need not include actual cash, would soon become the center of the most fractious debate in modern American history.

For the English, who were living through a thunderstorm of German bombs, fear of invasion, and daily rationing, the belief that they had an American partner, even if not fully an ally, made tea-less afternoons and sugar-free biscuits, nights in bomb shelters, days clearing rubble and burying the dead, and constant armed watch more bearable.

A beaming Churchill went to Parliament to discuss the arrangements he would soon consummate. He claimed that he had not dealt away the colonial lands, but made a magnanimous gesture on Britain's part to assuage mounting "anxiety" about the war among the country's American friends. "We had therefore decided spontaneously," he told Parliament, "and without being asked or offered any inducement, to inform the Government of the United States that we would be glad to place such defense facilities at their disposal by leasing suitable sites in our Transatlantic possessions for their greater security against the unmeasured dangers of the future."

As a result of the basing of Americans among the dominions' people, Churchill continued, "these two great organizations of the English-speaking democracies . . . will have to be somewhat mixed up together in some of their affairs. . . ." Looking over the ocean horizon, he saw that an inevitable process had begun, bringing the two nations closer. "Like the Mississippi, it just keeps rolling along," he intoned. "Let it roll. Let it roll on—full flood, inexorable, irresistible, benignant, to broader lands and better days."

Later, he would call the American transfer of fifty destroyers into the Royal Navy a "decidedly un-neutral act" that might have "justified the German Government declaring war upon [the United States]."

Churchill was right. And he was pleased.

Rumors—or spy reports—of a deal in the works reached German Embassy chargé d'affaires Hans Thomsen in mid-August in Washington. He dashed off a cable to Berlin. "Although the transfer of the destroyers would hardly have the importance of an act indicating a decision for war," he wrote, it would prove decisive in another way: ". . . it would finally eliminate the United States from the status of a neutral power." Mussolini told German foreign minister Joachim von Ribbentrop later that month in Rome, "America's intervention in the conflict on the side of England" was "already a fait accompli."

The Duce was largely blasé about the possibility of deepening U.S. intervention, feeling "not too much worried by the situation," he commented to Ribbentrop. He told the German visitor that he did not envision any scenario in which the American army joined the fight, so, he asked himself with a shrug, "what more could America really do" to influence the outcome of the war.

Clouds on the Western Hemisphere did not darken Ribbentrop's outlook, either. He was certain that England would fall swiftly once Operation Sealion slammed its shores. "English territorial defense is nonexistent," he confidently told Italian foreign minister Galeazzo Ciano, Mussolini's son-in-law. "A single German division will suffice to bring about a complete collapse." Ciano was not as sure about Germany's success. He'd heard that even Ribbentrop's aides disagreed with his fantastic optimism. They just couldn't risk upsetting him by telling him so.

In Berlin, though, Grand Admiral Raeder was furious. His U-boats had been striking blows against the British supply line that might prove lethal if his force's full potential power were unleashed. The arrival of those fifty destroyers amounted to "an openly hostile act against Germany" by the Americans, he groused, and would weigh heavily against his navy. Given what he now took to be a near certainty that America would officially enter the war before long, he urged the Führer to permit unlimited warfare, right into U.S. ports.

Hitler refused. Less than two weeks after the bases-for-destroyers deal was announced, Hitler told his military commanders he had decided to postpone the start of Operation Sealion. He blamed bad weather, but the Luftwaffe had failed to gain command of the skies and had not reduced the Royal Navy's heavy ships sufficiently, while barely touching her fast patrol boats. He could not be certain of a safe passage for German amphibious forces over the Channel. A failed invasion would derail all of Hitler's European plans and undermine Germans' confidence at home, so strong after the long string of sweeping, lightning-speed conquests to date. He decided on waging a bombing campaign, primarily against

London to force English capitulation. He kept invasion facilities in readiness for the spring to keep British forces off balance.

Hitler resisted the grand admiral's pleas to open war on the Americans. He did not want to provoke the sleeping giant for now. He had another trap to spring on Roosevelt. He was sure now he could thwart any further American moves to intervene in the war, a war soon to experience a complete change in direction. He saw his European—and possibly his global—endgame in formation.

11

Prairie Fire

Germany and Japan, Summer–Fall 1940

Ribbentrop could barely contain his excitement on September 19, 1940, as the German foreign minister drove with Italian foreign minister Ciano into Rome from the airport. He had arrived with what he called a "surprise in his bag." Tokyo and Berlin would shortly conclude negotiations for a military alliance of his creation. Ribbentrop came to win Mussolini's agreement that Rome would join to form the Tripartite Pact, the Berlin-Rome Pact of Steel extended to Tokyo to enchain the world. A few days later, Ciano went to Berlin. At a theatrical, internationally broadcast ceremony on September 27, 1940, he joined Japan's ambassador Saburō Kurusu at the gilded table before Hitler strode into the hall with a grandiose flourish to oversee signing the Berlin-Rome-Tokyo Axis agreement. The Tripartite Pact recognized that Germany and Italy would establish a new order in Europe and that Japan would have similar freedom to establish its hegemony in East Asia.

The agreement made clear that its signatory powers aimed their new alliance at Washington. The nations contracted to "assist one another with all political, economic and military means if one of the Contracting Powers is attacked by a Power at present not involved in the European War or in the Japanese-Chinese conflict." Ribbentrop told Ciano that the global Axis would effectively box in the U.S. fleet, "which," he said, "under the threat of the Japanese fleet will not dare move."

On hand in Berlin, CBS reporter William Shirer immediately saw
that Hitler's outward triumph actually signaled his failure to pull off the
widely expected invasion of England—opening the door to increased
American intervention. Britain, he reflected, "might still be fighting
next spring . . . [when] American aid . . . would begin to make itself felt
rather seriously." Hitler could no longer ignore the Americans. Shirer
went through Hitler's thought process in concluding the Tripartite Pact.
"Something," he jotted down in his journal, "must be done after all about
the United States. What?" With this ironbound agreement to deploy
Axis war powers against any enemy of its signatories, Hitler thought he
could boost U.S. internal opposition to intervention: "Something to
scare her and to set the American isolationists loose again with a new
cry about the danger of war."

The Tripartite Pact aimed to burden Americans with worry about
the potential cost of increasing their support for the English. Hitler
had declared "war" on the FDR administration: the prize would be the
vacillating will of the American people.

The Tripartite Pact worked as Hitler had hoped to bolster isolationists'
dismal regard for Roosevelt's short-of-war aid policy, which had, they
contended, now greatly increased the likelihood of war not just in Europe
but in Asia. "Our policy has succeeded in driving Japan into the arms
of those who were the last ones we wanted her associated with," North
Dakota senator Gerald Nye said in reaction to news of the Axis treaty.
Montana senator Burton Wheeler called for "a cessation of attacks on
every other nation" to keep from risking "a two-ocean war with our
one-ocean navy." A month after the pact was signed the man emerging
as the anti-interventionist movement's foremost spokesman, aviation
hero Charles Lindbergh, charged that the U.S. government's "blunder-
ing diplomacy . . . forced Japan to turn toward Germany." He warned
that aid to Great Britain had left the U.S. with "no forces to spare for

an Oriental war." Rather than fight wars everywhere, he said, the U.S. should seek conflict nowhere.

However, Stimson thought the Axis alliance had done much good "in waking our people up" to the reality that the isolationists had, in fact, achieved their goal: "The U.S. is isolated except for one great power. . . ." Stimson was increasingly worried that the time was fast approaching for "beginning to think about the future when Great Britain can no longer be saved by 'help less than war.'"

The pact had increased the possibility of war for America—not one war, but two. The United States could now easily confront its worst international scenario: a two-front, two-ocean war against a unified Axis. For Japan, the turn to Germany against America represented a break with long-standing peaceful, if sometimes uneasy, ties. Prince Fumimaro Konoe, Japan's prime minister, was typical among Japan's elites in both his admiration for the U.S.—he sent his son to prep school in New Jersey—and his resentment of Western racism, slights to his country's status as a great power, and imperialistic affronts to what he considered Japan's natural role as the dominant power in the region. He rarely opposed the increasing belligerence of his country's military, and was at the head of the government in 1937 when the China war began with a small incident. He then oversaw its escalation and now its long and increasingly painful duration.

He blamed the Western colonial powers for the dogged Chinese resistance. As the war dragged on, he had eliminated multiparty rule in the Diet, Japan's parliament, and set up imperial council structures that encouraged Japan's independent army and navy heads to take strategic leadership away from civilian authorities. Now, he pushed for Japan to join the Axis with Germany and Italy.

The alliance, he expected, would put the U.S. on notice about Japan's willingness to resort to force to gain a free hand in Asia. He was frank about the danger of the situation in an October 4 press conference following the Tripartite Pact's signing: "I believe it is better for the United States if it tries to understand Japan's intention and actively participate in the building of the world's new order," he contended. "If the United States continues to deliberately misunderstand the true intentions of Japan, Germany, and Italy . . . and continues its provocative acts, there won't be any other options left to us but to go to war." He thought the Americans, faced with the threat of war in both the Pacific and the Atlantic, would quietly back down.

Hitler, too, thought he had FDR in check. The following week Hitler met Mussolini in the Alpine Brenner Pass. Hitler smiled with delight: "America has been warned," he boasted. He told the Duce that he was confident that "the possibility of a two-front war would have quite a dampening effect on America."

The Duce's son-in-law Ciano did not share either leader's certainty. He thought the pact might instead provoke the U.S. to greater interference in Europe. While in Berlin for the treaty signing, Ciano observed that war had started to hit German domestic life. Once plentiful food had grown scarce, and store shelves were bare of products. Berliners now spent four or five sleepless hours a night crammed into cellars and underground shelters, escaping the clockwork British air raids. "Bomb damage is slight," the Italian minister noted, but the effects on morale were devastating: "Nervousness is very high." Amid the high-strung atmosphere of the Third Reich's capital, he met twice with Hitler: "No more invasion of England. No more blitz destruction of England," he realized. He found that even the foolishly overconfident Ribbentrop "is more nervous."

Ciano knew things were taking a turn for the worse, and noted, ". . . we must avoid conflict with America at all costs. . . ." In the midst of the German Führer's triumphalism, Ciano left for home convinced, "Only one thing is certain: that it will be a long war."

Across the Atlantic, the Tripartite Pact led Roosevelt to tell his Cabinet that "Japan has already begun to checkmate." Emboldened by German conquests in Europe and deeply worried by the American threat to embargo oil and aviation fuel, Japan's military leaders had determined that their hard-pressed nation had to secure Asian sources of tin, rubber, oil, and rice. That summer of 1940, thirty thousand Japanese troops occupied northern French Indochina, ostensibly at the invitation of the French colonial government, effectively positioning Japan to interdict movement of supplies into China via the Burma Road and to threaten remaining French, British, and Dutch territories.

Treasury Secretary Henry Morgenthau pushed for a total ban on export of American goods and raw materials to Japan, but now it was Roosevelt's turn to back down: He feared a total embargo would push Japan to move south immediately into the Dutch East Indies and Singapore, and likely the U.S. commonwealth in the Philippines, precipitating a war for which his country was not presently prepared.

FDR limited the American response to Japan's aggressive moves to extension of another $50 million credit line to China. He ratcheted up pressure on Japan by adding scrap steel and iron, vital to Japanese industrial production, to his list of embargoed exports.

The newspaper mouthpiece of the Japanese ruling circle, *Asahi Shimbun*, viewed the reprisals as another step making "inevitable that a collision should occur between Japan, determined to establish a sphere of influence in East Asia, including the Southwest Pacific, and the United States, which is determined to meddle in affairs on the other side of a vast ocean by every means short of war." The day after the widened American embargo was announced, Japan signed the Tripartite Pact.

With the formation of the Axis, war between Japan and the Western colonial powers (most of which were in exile from their German-occupied homelands) appeared suddenly likely to explode throughout Asia that fall. Japan moved its occupation forces deeper into Indochina, threatening Britain's vital port in Singapore. Britain and Australia moved to reinforce Singapore. In expectation of an attack, orders were issued to most American personnel stationed in Southeast Asia to return home. The U.S. sent more aircraft and submarines to the region.

Ambassador to Tokyo Joseph Grew, long experienced in Japan and like Roosevelt a Groton and Harvard graduate, wrote his army head, General Marshall, questioning "whether getting into war with Japan would so handicap our help to Britain in Europe as to make the difference to Britain between victory and defeat," adding that "the principal point at issue . . . is not whether we must call a halt to the [southward expansion] but when." Grew felt that war would likely come, but that America's Atlantic priorities should be put first.

The president's military leaders also cautioned him against risking war in Asia. "Every day that we are able to maintain peace and still support the British is valuable time gained," insisted Admiral Stark, urging the President to contain Japan as long as possible without provoking a military confrontation. Even appeasement, a dirty word since Munich, appeared better than going to war prematurely. Hitler seemed to have won this round.

But FDR would not go quietly. Along with beefed-up naval support, the White House offered firm words, moved the Pacific Fleet from its long-standing San Diego home port to Pearl Harbor, deployed additional marines, and earmarked fighter aircraft and bombers slated to be produced in the new assembly plants for basing in the Philippines, Wake Island, and Midway Atoll. He also took his domestically most difficult step.

FDR determined upon pushing to create the nation's first-ever peacetime draft army. With the election coming soon, he ran a major political risk.

Unlike the secretly consummated bases-for-destroyers deal, the debate over compulsory military training of young American men brought the poisonous fight over intervention out into the open. The aroused opposition moved forcefully against the legislation. However, the start of Germany's savage air war on Britain shifted public support decidedly toward aiding the British. Fear of German attack spread. Radio broadcasts from London, particularly those made by CBS's Edward R. Murrow, moved Americans, as did the newsreels and photographs showing the toll the bombing took upon civilian life. In July a possibly BSC-tainted Gallup survey found that two-thirds of voters favored compulsory military service. Still, isolationists held out. In a national radio broadcast, Senator Burton Wheeler argued, "If this [draft] bill passes, it will slit the throat of the last Democracy still living—it will accord to Hitler his greatest and cheapest victory."

In his testimony to the House Military Affairs Committee, War Department secretary Stimson spoke soberly of the danger he foresaw should the U.S. continue watching without preparing while "the forces of lawlessness gather like prairie fire growing nearer and nearer to our country." He admonished the committee members, "The successive experiences of Norway, Denmark, Holland, Belgium, France and Britain teach the lesson of the danger of not preparing before war actually arrives." He warned the committee members not to ignore "a very grave danger" of attack. "Hitler," he intoned ominously, "doesn't wait."

The powerful North Dakota Republican isolationist, Senator Gerald Nye, who had led passage of the neutrality acts that Stimson so detested, responded that a peacetime draft amounted to "a move to shanghai American youth into totalitarianism and militarism." West Virginia's youthful Democratic senator Rush Holt was even less respectful of the hoary secretary of war. He pointed at the "warmongering" Stimson and shouted, "Show me a dictatorship and I'll show you conscription!" Answering cries broke out in the hearing room. An outraged Great War veteran rushed the rostrum, where he scuffled with Senate committee members.

The shouts and fighting in the committee room drew loud echoes among protesters gathered outside the Capitol Building. Pacifist groups, an organized "mothers' movement," the Young Communist League, the German-American Bund, and thousands of unaffiliated citizens marched on Washington, confronting congressional supporters of the draft wherever they found them. A colonially garbed "Pauline Revere" rode on a white horse up the Capitol steps, brandishing a sign that read, "Mobilize for Peace and Defeat Conscription." Others hung pro-draft congressmen in effigy. Meantime, Father Coughlin told his followers that compulsory conscription was part of a "communist plot" hatched by "a Hitlerized president and his American Gestapo."

Anger over conscription turned to fisticuffs on the House floor. Anti-conscription Democrat Martin Sweeney, a red-faced Cleveland Irishman and Coughlin follower, charged FDR with steering the nation into a foreign war that was none of its business. Roosevelt was acting no differently, he declared, than when Wilson had betrayed his promises and taken the country to war in 1917. Representative Beverly Vincent of Kentucky, a First World War veteran, sat steaming next to him. He muttered about "the son of a bitch" Sweeney and huffed that he would not "sit by a traitor." The affronted Sweeney launched a roundhouse at Vincent, but missed. Vincent didn't, and his return punch staggered Sweeney. Upon hearing the punch land, the House's ancient doorkeeper declared Vincent had thrown "the best blow he had heard" in his half century in the Capitol.

Only after Republican Party nominee Willkie came out for the draft—a "godsend," exhaled Stimson—did the tide of support swing in favor of the selective service legislation. Many congressmen simply voted "Present" rather than go on record with an election coming. Even then, passage was not assured until riders were attached to the bill to handcuff the president. The new Selective Service Act limited the draft to a maximum of nine hundred thousand conscripts, whose terms would expire a year after induction. Not a single draftee was allowed to be deployed outside United States territory.

As Election Day drew near, the fight for the presidency had become a vote not for the next president but for or against coming to grips with the threat Hitler posed to the country. Speaking from his campaign train on October 12, Columbus Day, Roosevelt gave a ringing rebuke to the message Hitler, Mussolini, and Konoe thought they had sent him. He declared, "We will continue to help those who resist aggression, and who now hold the oppressors far from our shores. . . . The people of the United States, the people of all the Americas, reject the doctrine of appeasement. They recognize it for what it is—a major weapon of the aggressor nation." He could not count on his nation's willingness to stand up to the new Axis alliance; only the vote would tell how far Americans were ready to go along with him. And his Republican opponent, Wendell Willkie, on the advice of Ted Roosevelt, Jr., and others had veered sharply into the isolationist camp, pushing him into a dead heat or even ahead according to some polls as Election Day neared.

President Roosevelt looks on as Secretary of War Henry Stimson, blindfolded, draws the first number in the draft lottery at the War Department auditorium on October 29, 1940.

Just one week before the election, with FDR on hand to witness the selection of the lottery numbers of the initial conscripts, the first American men to ever learn they had to report for army duty during peacetime. In his remarks at the ceremony, Roosevelt never uttered the word "draft"; instead, drawing on a precedent dating back to the Revolutionary War, he referred to the moment as a "muster" to "achieve . . . independence and to establish certain fundamental rights for all men." A woman in the hall screamed out in anguish when her son's number was called.

12

"Aviation, Geography, and Race"

America and Germany, November 1940–January 1941

Americans were nervous about the impact of Roosevelt's policy of all aid short of war, shaken up as the first draftees were called up, and frightened by the implications of the Axis formation's being squarely aimed at them. The final outcome of the FDR-Willkie presidential race would not come clear until the second wave of state vote counts were released on election night, Tuesday, November 5, 1940. Even the preternaturally confident FDR thought he might lose the presidency as the first tallies came in on the ticker tape set up at his home in Hyde Park. Before the evening was through, though, he had won handily—albeit by his closest-to-date victory margin.

The Oyster Bay Roosevelts had fallen short once again against the Hudson Valley brand. Downcast, Ted Roosevelt, Jr., took heart. "Well, the election is over," he wrote his son Cornelius, "and we have been beaten, but the defeat was not an overwhelming defeat—not by any means. There is now in the United States a convinced and active minority group which knows what it is about and knows it is fighting. . . ."

He could not remove this impostor from the White House any more than he could the arthritic pain in his knee, but the Herculean effort to defeat Franklin had not been all in vain. On the biggest question of all, war or peace, the president knew he now faced a powerful, well-organized opposition. Ted saw this "bright side." He wrote to Cornelius,

". . . I believe that the majority of the American people . . . have made up their minds they do not want to be involved in war, and that they do not intend, if they can help it, to let this country be shoved in."

Charles Lindbergh and his wife, Anne Morrow Lindbergh, passed the evening of the election at some friends' Upper East Side apartment in New York. As the state-by-state tallies came in, the increasingly despondent gathering resolved on the need for changing *who* should have the right to vote. "'Democracy' as we have known it is a thing of the past," Charles reflected later that evening. He told his friends "that . . . a political system based on universal franchise would not work in the United States. . . ." Who, then, should vote? "I said that I felt one of the first steps must be to disenfranchise the Negro. Everyone agreed to this. . . ."

From there, conversation veered toward the country's other, even more vexing minority, what Lindbergh called "the Jewish problem and how it could be handled in this country. . . ." Jews were much on Lindbergh's mind of late. He was convinced that Jews exercised outsized influence relative to their numbers. He particularly worried about what he believed to be their control of newspapers, newsreels, and advertising—although outside of *The New York Times* and most of the prominent Hollywood motion picture studios, Jews had virtually no measurable media ownership. Lindbergh blamed Jews, Anglophile British descendants, and Wall Street bankers for pushing the country into a war most people did not want. Above all others in his reckoning, Jews—often not even visible—pushed the nation like a crosswind against its natural heading: "Were it not for the Jews in America," he penned, "we would not be on the verge of war today."

American society, Lindbergh believed, had gone out of balance as a result of Jewish agitation against Hitler. The resulting dangerous spiral, he anticipated, pointed to a dark end for Jews, and not Hitler: "The more feeling there is against the Jews," he wrote, "the closer they band together; and the more they band together, the more the feeling rises against them." As a result, he feared for their fate in America: "We are not a moderate people, once we get started, and an anti-Jewish movement might be considerably worse here than in Germany." During two extended visits and other shorter stays in Germany, he had witnessed, at least on the streets, some of what that might mean.

The Lindberghs had made their first visit to Germany almost four and a half years earlier, in the summer of 1936. The U.S. Army was eager to get an expert look at the much-ballyhooed German aviation industry, believed to have grown dramatically in size and to have leaped ahead in engineering since Hitler came to power. At the instigation of the American military attaché in the Berlin Embassy, Army Major Truman Smith, German air minister and Luftwaffe field marshal Hermann Göring arranged a guided inspection tour of his commercial and military facilities for the celebrated aviator. Lindbergh was eager to visit Germany, a country, he wrote his mother beforehand, that "has taken a leading part in a number of aviation developments." For Germany, a visit by the aviation hero promised to bring positive news coverage worldwide and an opportunity to show off their military aviation prowess and associate their national advances with the great man.

Arriving on July 22, Lindbergh set off on a week of inspections and appearances that took him to sites around the country. The week's tour included a day in the company of the Luftwaffe's elite Richtofen fighter group, a tour of two Heinkel factories where medium-range bombers and transports were rolling through the assembly line, and a full day exploring bomber and fighter production and the engineering center at the Junkers plant. He started at Berlin's impressively rebuilt Tempelhof Airport, where he piloted a massive four-engine Junkers-built airplane, named the *Field Marshal von Hindenburg*.

CBS reporter William Shirer flew along with the press contingent in the rear of the *Hindenburg*. He had been at Le Bourget in 1927 when Lindbergh completed the historic flight that catapulted him to worldwide fame. Shirer was surprised to find "how little he had changed, except that he seemed more self-confident." Lindbergh put the *Hindenburg* through some steep banks and other acrobatic maneuvers, "which," Shirer said, "terrified most of the passengers." Lindbergh may have done that with them in mind. He still hated reporters.

By the end of the week, Lindbergh, a man who rarely offered compliments, disclosed that he was "greatly impressed by the German development" in aviation. The large-scale assembly lines, he reported, are "now able to produce military aircraft faster than any European country[,] [p]ossibly even faster than we could in the States. . . ." In all aspects of flight, the Germans had raced ahead of the rest of the world. "A person would have to be blind not to realize that they have already built up tremendous strength," he told a friend in the U.S.

The ultimate significance of all that manufacturing, training, and engineering came home to him in Göring's company at the field marshal's lavish official residence. Göring brought out a photo album to show his guest. He thumbed through page after page of pictures taken at bases around the country. "Here are our first seventy," Göring said triumphantly. More were being constructed. Lindbergh was convinced that Germany would shortly fill those fields with bombers and fighters, an air force on a scale and with technological capabilities beyond anything previously conceived. No other Western nation came close to matching German airpower.

Lindbergh and Smith were swept up by Göring's descriptions of the Luftwaffe's unassailable power and the German Air Ministry's claims for the present size of the German air force. In their report to the army, they claimed German factories were turning out eight hundred new airplanes per month, with ten thousand already flying—virtually all of them among the world's most technologically advanced. Over the next four years, this Smith and Lindbergh report would serve as the Allies' standard force estimate documenting the seemingly unmatched might of the German war machine.

In reality, even four years later, according to archived German reports, the Luftwaffe possessed less than half that number of aircraft. As it pounded English targets in preparation for Operation Sealion, Germany could count on only 1,711 bombers, 424 dive bombers, 354 escort fighters, 1,356 pursuit planes, and 830 reconnaissance and other planes—more than any one of Germany's enemies, but by no means a swarming force able to darken the sky and through overwhelming numbers vanquish a modern military foe. When the Battle of Britain turned in the Royal Air Force's favor in the summer of 1940, despite the smaller number of British fighters, the Luftwaffe discovered that English aviation engineering more than matched up to its vaunted technology.

At the time of his visit, Lindbergh was sure that few people fully grasped the revolution modern airpower had wrought. At a luncheon in his honor at the Berlin Air Club, he spoke about aviation's radical transformation of the world. He told his audience that airplanes had bridged time and space and made previous ways of making war obsolete. Nations now faced sudden attack for which they could not prepare, he said. "It is no longer possible to shield the heart of a country with its army," he contended. "Armies can no more stop an air attack than a suit of mail can stop a rifle bullet . . . ." Sitting in the audience, a proud and grinning Göring could not have agreed more.

On the last day of their 1936 visit, August 1, the high-profile American visitors ended their German stay on a high note, attending the spectacular opening ceremonies of the Berlin Olympics as Göring's special guests. From their seats among the dignitaries on the Olympic Stadium dais, the Lindberghs saw the hundred thousand spectators screaming for their Führer, chanting in unison, saluting as one.

Shirer was there, too. He had covered previous games, but nothing like these. The Berlin Olympics were "on a lavish scale never before experienced." He had seen it all before, though, at the Nuremberg Rallies.

Among those whom Nazi leaders most wanted to impress with the day's spectacle were their special guests, the Lindberghs. "I'm afraid," Shirer lamented, "the Nazis have succeeded with their propaganda." He heard that Charles and Anne "have been favorably impressed by what the Nazis have shown them."

The next day, as they were getting ready to leave, Charles Lindbergh told reporters that he was, indeed, "intensely pleased" by all he had seen of Germany. His praise was even more unstinting in a letter to Göring three weeks later. He wrote, "I have never been more impressed than I was with the aviation organizations I saw in Germany." Almost forty years later, he still recalled the intensity of his experience there: "The organized vitality of Germany was what most impressed me," he found, "the unceasing activity of the people, and the convinced dictatorial direction to create the new factories, airfields, and research laboratories. . . ."

Shortly after leaving, he wrote U.S. Embassy attaché Truman Smith that the visit "leaves me the impression that Hitler must have far more character and vision than I thought existed in the German leader who has been painted in so many ways by the accounts in America and England." If Hitler was a "fanatic in many ways," he wrote another friend not long after the visit, then he was putting it to productive use, for he "has accomplished results (good in addition to bad), which could hardly have been accomplished without some fanaticism." He concluded, "He is undoubtedly a great man."

Anne was, if anything, even more smitten as a result of her guided tours through a resplendent Berlin, from which most anti-Semitic signs—and Jews on the streets—had been effaced for the Olympic Games. ". . . I have never in my life been so conscious of such a directed force," she recorded in her diary. "It is thrilling when seen manifested in the energy, pride, and morale of the people—especially the young people." She, too, saw the good in the Germans' fanaticism, despite "their treatment of the Jews, their brute-force manner, their stupidity, their rudeness. . . ." Tyranny and the devotion it elicited, and the will to construct a new state among the Germans, she decided, "could be a force for good in the world," if only the world worked to turn "the power, unity and purposefulness of Germany . . . in the right direction." She hoped she might help Americans understand Nazi Germany better. By 1938, the Lindberghs began looking for a house to move to in Berlin.

On November 9, 1938, still feeling the afterglow of their week in Olympian Berlin, Charles wrote the American ambassador in London, Joseph Kennedy, to tell him they were "extremely anxious to learn more about Germany." Lindbergh shared his findings with Kennedy about the immense air force Germany had already mustered. Hearing Lindbergh's impressions and reading his and Major Smith's Final Report, Kennedy was convinced that, should war come, Great Britain would lose. When war broke out, he felt London should reach an accommodation with Hitler rather than face aerial devastation and invasion. He urged FDR not to waste American resources on a losing cause. Some later said that the inflated figures Lindbergh reported back about German airpower from his earlier visit not only convinced Kennedy that Germany was unbeatable, but influenced Neville Chamberlain to appease Hitler at Munich. Certainly the airpower Lindbergh observed fed into Kennedy's conviction that the U.S. risked its destiny as a great nation if it intervened in the European war.

Charles and Anne returned for another lengthy visit to Germany in October 1938. There, he accepted as factual claims that German engineers had developed a fighter plane able to fly at speeds in excess of five hundred miles an hour—though in reality the most advanced Luftwaffe aircraft flew at little more than half that speed. After a dinner at Göring's estate, the field marshal surprised Lindbergh with a special German honorary medal. "By order of the Führer," the air minister trumpeted as he draped the Service Cross of the German Eagle, decorated with four swastikas hanging off a ribbon, around Lindbergh's neck. A photographer snapped his picture. Lindbergh thought little of it at the time, but that Nazi medal and the image of him next to a plump and glistening Göring would come to weigh heavily on him as Americans considered his attitudes about the Nazis.

On the night that Lindbergh wrote Kennedy to say they were thinking about moving to Berlin, November 9, 1938, Germany started two days of organized attacks on Jews. The *Kristallnacht* pogrom sent SS troops and enlisted civilian mobs streaming into the streets to destroy Jewish businesses, homes, and places of worship. Hundreds of Jews were murdered, and thousands more herded into concentration camps. "My admiration for the Germans is constantly being dashed against some such rock such as this," admitted Charles in his diary. Worried about "embarrassing" the U.S. government, he and Anne determined the timing was not right for a move to Germany.

The following year, with war on the horizon, Charles and Anne returned to the United States. They eventually settled on an estate in Lloyd Neck on the North Shore of Long Island. As Europe collapsed into conflict, Lindbergh wrote and spoke against America's embroiling itself in Europe's "fratricidal war." What began hesitantly soon became a steady stream of articles, speeches, and public appearances.

Millions of American ears tuned in or turned out at public events to hear him speak on the subject. Tall, lanky, winsomely sandy blond and blue-eyed, with a deeply cleft chin, Lindbergh looked like a streamlined airplane ready to take flight. His lonely, previously seemingly impossible feat in flying in a single nonstop leap over the ocean made him an instant American icon. He was also among the first truly global celebrities. Deeply shy, Lindbergh, rarely smiling in public, almost never meeting the eye of the cameras that dogged him, did little to court fame, but public adulation and unblinking attention—with its horrific cost in the kidnapping and death of his and Anne's toddler son—followed his every step after the transatlantic flight. For the first time, he saw an advantage to exploit in his otherwise distasteful celebrity.

He thought America had little to fear from Hitler's Germany and saw no threat to American interests or its hemisphere. A far greater danger, he felt, lay in intervening in a war that, with the advent of aviation, almost certainly would surpass the 1914–1918 war in its cataclysmic casualties and devastation of European and, should the U.S. intervene, American civilization. Lindbergh feared the West was on the verge of what he called "race suicide."

He tried to explain his fears in the portentously titled "Aviation, Geography, and Race," an article read by millions in the November 1939 issue of *Reader's Digest*.

America had no "vital need" in Europe "to decide who is at fault . . . or to argue over our concepts of right or wrong." There was nothing America could gain by choosing sides in Europe; the war would eventually be over. In the end, though, no matter which nations emerged from the carnage the "winners," both sides would have lost their civilizations.

If Europe chose war, so be it. America alone should remain aloof, building up its ramparts to defend Western civilization's last, best hope for survival. By succumbing to the momentary distraction of a transitory battle for European dominance, America risked the very existence of what Lindbergh termed "the White race"—Western civilization, that cultural and biological heritage which emanated from ancient Greece and Rome. The true threat to America and the White race came not from national squabbles for power and profit but from "a pressing sea of Yellow, Black, and Brown" on Euro-American borders.

In postwar years, Lindbergh claimed he was repulsed by the Nazis' autocratic methods and violent repression, but he justified Nazism as a response to the threat of race suicide. ". . . I was seeing in Germany," he wrote, "despite the crudeness of its form, the inevitable alternative to decline—a challenge based more on the drive to achieve success despite established 'right' and law." As Philip Johnson had defended "Hitler's 'racism,'" Lindbergh endorsed what Johnson called "the myth of 'we, the best,' which we find, more or less fully developed, in all vigorous cultures."

Lindbergh asked Americans "to turn from our quarrels and to build our White ramparts again," to eschew involvement in these fleeting conflicts among European nations. The fate of the West was at stake: "With all the world around our borders, let us not commit racial suicide by internal conflict," he concluded.

Lindbergh was as determined, disciplined, and skilled in his drive to keep the U.S. from going to war in Europe as he once was to fly solo between the continents. Even before the German invasion of Poland, Lindbergh had taken the lead in opposing intervention. In the first year and a half of war, he made five nationwide radio broadcasts, addressed two large public meetings, published three articles in popular magazines, testified twice before congressional committees, and consulted with many leaders in the growing movement to block intervention. Wife Anne Morrow Lindbergh, a popular author in her own right, came to the defense of German fascism in her number one best-selling 1940 testament, *The Wave of the Future: A Confession of Faith*. Hitler's Nazism and other movements crushing human freedom, she wrote, were just "scum on the surface of the wave" as civilization moved into a new "highly scientific, mechanized and material era."

A week after Germany's May 10, 1940, invasion of the Low Countries, Charles Lindbergh told a national radio audience that America had nothing to gain and everything to lose by intervening. "We are in danger of war today," he declared, "not because European people have attempted to interfere with the internal affairs of America, but because American people have attempted to interfere with the internal affairs of Europe." He urged the nation to get its own house in order and secure its borders, which in any foreseeable scenario, he felt, remained beyond invasion. "If we desire peace," he said, "we need only stop asking for war. No one wishes to attack us, and no one is in a position to do so."

He warned that certain unspecified groups within society were behind the drive to join forces with the British against Hitler and the fascists. He spoke to millions of receptive listeners: "The only reason that we are in danger of becoming involved in this war is because there are powerful elements in America who desire us to take part. They represent a small minority of the American people, but they control much of the machinery of influence and propaganda. They seize every opportunity to push us closer to the edge." Ultimately, he contended, America's spiritual rebirth, a change in outlook adequate to a revolutionary age of technology and social organization, was the key to its future: "It is time," he declared, "for the underlying character of this country to rise and assert itself, to strike down these elements of personal profit and foreign interest." Nearly all his listeners realized he was speaking primarily about the Jews.

Reverend Coughlin, notorious for his own concerns about racial and religious threats to "true" Americans, thought enough of Lindbergh's writings and talks to proclaim, "It is too bad that Col. Lindbergh is not a politician: he might even be President of the United States."

The day after Lindbergh's broadcast, FDR confided to Secretary of the Treasury Henry Morgenthau, Jr., "If I should die tomorrow, I want you to know this: I am absolutely convinced Lindbergh is a Nazi." The following day he wrote to Henry Stimson, soon to be his secretary of war, "When I read Lindbergh's speech I felt that it could not have been better put if it had been written by Goebbels himself. What a pity that this youngster has completely abandoned his belief in our form of government and has accepted Nazi methods because apparently they are efficient." Given Lindbergh's apparent devotion to antidemocratic ideals and indifference to Hitler's conquest of European states, the president began to see him as a threat to his nation. The more effectively Lindbergh fought against intervention, the more Roosevelt felt the need to use the great power at his disposal to fight back to save democracy—sometimes without regard to the legality of the means the government employed.

*   *   *

For R. Douglas "Bob" Stuart, a Yale law student when he helped found
the America First Committee (AFC) on campus earlier in the summer
of 1940, and now leader in organizing its national antiwar campaign,
Lindbergh's views about the war meshed with his own. The aviator's
heroic past made him an American ideal and role model, and his articulate and knowledgeable opposition to intervention made him an
ideal spokesman for the nascent group. He immediately targeted Lindbergh to become America First's national chairman. Stuart attended
an August 4, 1940, dinner at the Chicago home of *Chicago Tribune*
publisher Colonel Robert McCormick for Lindbergh following an anti-
intervention rally where the aviator spoke that day. Afterward Stuart
had a long talk with Lindbergh, and the following day he dashed off
a letter to him asking that he and Anne help the movement "give sane
national leadership to the unexpressed conviction of the majority of
American people that this is not our war. 'Defend America First' will
be our theme."

That theme, of course, resonated with the Lindberghs, and America First's appeals, sent to mailing lists provided by Senators Taft and
Wheeler, repeated many of the very words Charles Lindbergh had already written and spoken. Lindbergh liked the young man's idealism
and appreciated the nonpartisan spirit America First encouraged. He
would remain unaffiliated for the time being, but a few months later he
officially joined the America First Committee's executive board. With
Lindbergh as its leading spokesman, the AFC became the country's most
effective, and by far the largest, organization campaigning to stop FDR
and intervention in the war.

By mid-October the organization had a national board composed
of prominent people expressing a wide range of political viewpoints, but
all of them committed to blocking intervention. With funds coming in
from national chairman and Sears, Roebuck president General Robert
Wood, Colonel McCormick, and Stuart's Chicago family friends, the

AFC grew its staff to build and operate a national organization that ran massive events, placed ads in every daily newspaper in the country, sent speakers to meetings across the land, and eventually claimed more than eight hundred thousand members.

Yale University, where America First began, proved a welcoming venue for Lindbergh to express his views. On October 30, 1940, he addressed the Yale community in Woolsey Hall, a gilded concert space as big as a city train station.

Lindbergh before his October 30, 1940, talk at Yale, flanked by students Kingman Brewster (left), chairman of the Yale Daily News *and a leading anti-interventionist, and Richard M. Bissell (right), chairman of the event sponsored by the campus chapter of the America First Committee.*

In one of those coincidences of the presidential election campaign season, on the day Lindbergh was scheduled to speak at Yale, FDR made a whistle-stop at New Haven's *actual* train station. He was heading north to Boston, where he was to give a major speech that night at almost the same time Lindbergh would speak at Yale. Many voters in New Haven and around the country were deeply troubled by the draft. As rain showered onto the platform and tracks, the president reassured the drenched crowd that just because men were being called into the army did not mean that America was on the way to war. "We have started to train more men," he proclaimed, "not because we expect to use them, but for the same reason your umbrellas are up today—to keep from getting wet." He continued on to Boston.

Few students showed up to greet FDR. Twenty-five years earlier, Woolsey Hall had been the scene of raucously pro-war student rallies even before America declared war and sent those students to Europe to fight in the Great War. As Lindbergh took the stage, some three thousand people packed the hall. "Every seat was taken, and people were standing along the walls," Lindbergh observed. "You could feel the electricity," recalled Richard Ketchum, then a Yale student looking at "our boyhood hero, the most famous American of our childhood . . . the personification of the air age that was shaping the destiny of our generation." Decades later, Ketchum recalled how students reacted to "the sheer magnetism of his presence." They took him seriously, aware "that he probably knew more about the strengths and weaknesses of the air forces now locked in combat in Europe . . . than any man alive."

Lindbergh reprised many of the same themes and phrases of his previous talks and writings, telling the students that no nation on earth could attack America from across the ocean. America should pursue its "independent destiny," he said, or expect "to control the affairs of the rest of the world" forever. The decision Americans faced had enduring consequences for the future. As if his audience might forget, he reminded the students that, thanks to the draft, which had begun the previous week, they would be called to fight should their nation go to war.

* * *

The students applauded wildly for Lindbergh, who found his evening at Yale "by far the most successful and satisfying meeting of this kind in which I have ever taken part." FDR received a far more tepid reception that same night in Boston. He was chasing voters among the city's heavily Irish Catholic population, who had little sympathy for the English plight. With Willkie gaining, he repeated his "assurance": "Your boys are not going to be sent into any foreign wars." That line drew his loudest applause of the night from an otherwise listless crowd.

Learning about the success of Lindbergh's Yale speech and FDR's flat-out noninterventionist statements on the same evening, General Wood congratulated Lindbergh: "We have forced the Administration in power to come out with some very strong statements which it will be hard for them to repudiate after the election even in the event they are successful." Indeed, the man who wrote many of FDR's words in those campaign speeches agreed. Robert Sherwood wrote later that ". . . the isolationists' long and savage campaign against the President . . . exerted an important effect on Roosevelt himself: Whatever the peril, he was not going to lead the country into war—he was going to wait to be pushed in." The campaign cost him the freedom to act against Hitler outside the shadows.

It seemed that everyone in Washington understood what had happened. While Germany had been eager to see FDR go down to defeat, they were assuaged, as the German Embassy's chargé d'affaires Thomsen cabled Berlin, that the president "had assured the American people that he would not lead them into the war and he intended to keep his word."

13

Indictments

America, January–Spring 1941

The campaign to defeat Roosevelt at the polls failed, but it succeeded in galvanizing opposition to the war. After Franklin won reelection, Ted Roosevelt, Jr., followed his half sister Alice's and brother Archie's lead in joining the America First Committee's leadership committee, putting his powerful name on its banners and mailings. He spoke to groups, went on the radio, and wrote articles, campaigning as if he might still bring Franklin down—"working," he wrote his son Cornelius, "like beavers to get America First going. . . ."

Unlike some within the anti-intervention organization, Ted was no political reactionary. He admired the socialistic Scandinavians and criticized what he called his father's generation's "empire complex." And unlike his friend Charles Lindbergh, he had no sympathies for fascism or German "vitality." He criticized his own country for failing to live up to its ideals. No matter what the First World War actually accomplished, he came home thinking that his wounds, the death of his brother, the whole bloody fight, would have been worthwhile if the war had succeeded in building enduring bonds among all Americans, whatever their background, whatever their wealth, religion, or color. He told his closest friend, the Algonquin Roundtable wit and *New Yorker* writer Alexander Woollcott, "[After the war] I felt when I came back that no matter what we might have failed in doing, at least we stamped out intolerance in the United States, for our common service, shoulder to shoulder for the common cause, could not help but accomplish this." He was sorely disappointed that America failed to live up to the armed forces' ideal. "The [actual result]," he lamented, "was the Ku Klux Klan and bigotry, hooded and rampant."

Since then he had supported civil rights for Jews and African-Americans, serving on the boards of the NAACP, the National Council of Christians and Jews, and an American Zionist committee. His advocacy for tolerance brought him hate mail by the bagful. Patiently answering a letter blaming Jews for the discrimination they faced, he insisted, "If we persecute any racial or religious group we are committing a grave offense against our concept of government."

Ted saw Franklin's push for war as another form of elitism putting American democracy to the test. "No small group of men," he told an audience at the University of Virginia, "should have the right to decide for the American people questions of this sort in secret." That his distant Roosevelt cousin—a man who had never taken up arms—stood at the head of that warmongering cabal made it that much more insidious.

Ted took refuge at Old Orchard, the handsome brick Georgian home he and his wife—like his first cousin and Franklin's wife also named Eleanor—built in a former orchard down the hill from his parents' Sagamore Hill house in Oyster Bay. Their many visitors reflected Roosevelt's democratic outlook and eclectic business, cultural, and military life. They spent joyous hours singing around the piano while Harpo Marx of the famous Marx Brothers played. Along with Woollcott, Ted and Eleanor knew many other leading literary lights, among them H. G. Wells and Edith Wharton. Popular novelist and playwright Thornton Wilder was a friend, though the interventionist-leaning Wilder felt tested by Ted's isolationism. On the sporting side, he knew the boxer Gene Tunney and home run king Babe Ruth. As high as those circles ran, he never lost touch with his men and fellow officers from his beloved World War I First Infantry Regiment and continued to promote the American Legion, which he helped found.

Still, rarely had weekends in a row brought guests with such wildly conflicting viewpoints as the two men who stopped by Old Orchard in early January 1941.

On Friday night, January 10, 1941, Charles and Anne Lindbergh came over for what Roosevelt called a particularly "delightful" visit. Ted wished his son Cornelius, an MIT grad and mining engineer in Mexico, could have been there. "Undoubtedly," he wrote him, "you would have a bond with him on the mechanical side of his character, on which I do not touch at all." Roosevelt admired the man who embodied so much of what his father had described as an American ideal, a man of action and a man of thought, and now a man who did not shy from the public arena. Ted valued his ability to articulate the anti-intervention position so much that two months later he paid out of his own pocket to reprint and distribute one hundred thousand copies of an antiwar article Lindbergh wrote for *Collier's* magazine.

The weekend after the Lindberghs came to Old Orchard another guest with a very different take on the war visited the Roosevelts, William Shirer, "the CBS Berlin man," Ted wrote Cornelius, ". . . just returned to the United States."

Shirer, who had come back a few weeks ago from Europe, had a new child and was broke. He was about to embark on a series of lectures, "largely to see the country," he said, following his long sojourn abroad, though he needed the money from his speaking fees. He was also slated to make occasional broadcasts for CBS Radio. Shirer knew Ted Roosevelt's isolationist stance. He had no reason to fear censors any longer and almost certainly—neither man seems to have documented the evening—attempted to enlighten him about the reality of life under Hitler. He had already started to formulate his lectures and very likely shared with Roosevelt the stories and analysis of Germany he intended to tell audiences on his upcoming lecture tour.

When Shirer embarked on his speaking tour, Americans listened raptly to what he had to say. Four months after his visit to the Roosevelt place, sixty-five hundred people paid to hear him speak in Kansas City, one of the largest paying crowds ever for a public lecture there. Shirer said that they should indeed take heed of the cruelties inflicted by the Nazis, which involved a barbarism unseen in modern times. The Germans, he said, were systematically engaged in what they called "mercy killings" of "mental defectives." Many Americans simply refused to believe such barbarity possible—though castration and lobotomies were common practices on U.S. mentally ill patients. Fewer still were willing to accept his report that a policy of genocide aimed at Poland's Jews had begun.

Most were eager to get his opinion about Hitler's threat to America. Don't expect Germany to stop with Europe, he warned. In his famous even-toned voice, he told one of the largest audiences ever to turn out for a lecture in Memphis that Hitler "would try to invade Britain and then, if successful, this hemisphere." Don't trust what Hitler says, he repeated in dozens of talks: "Hitler breaks his promises." Once Germany conquered Britain and acquired her navy and gained possession of her colonies, he would never permit the U.S. to live on in peace as a last bastion of freedom.

"Naturally," Shirer explained in Oregon, "Hitler wishes us to believe he considers war against us as 'fantastic.'" The German leader had made similar assurances many times before. "He does not believe in winning a race by running faster than his competitor," he asserted. "He believes in shooting or poisoning the other fellow, while pretending friendship. The fantastic thinkers are they who think Hitler has no ambitions for the conquest of the Western Hemisphere." He urged the nation to wake up.

He told a huge audience in Cedar Rapids, his hometown, that he disagreed with Lindbergh that it was "too late to aid the British." He saw a nation vacillating over what to do. He worried that continuing "our present half-hearted policy. . . " would mean "the United States will have Hitler to fight alone in five years."

After witnessing the military might of the Nazis in action, he had been shocked to come home to a nation mired in uncertainty about the war. "What strikes a person coming back here after being in Europe," he said, "is that the American people have not made up their minds what they want to do. They've got to decide, and right now." At a talk in Syracuse, New York, he asked the question on everyone's mind: "Will Hitler finally be stopped?" He closed on a dark note: "He may be; but it will take a Britain far more powerful than we see her now; it will take much more help from the United States than we are giving now."

He told audiences, "I, too, dislike war, but, from a selfish standpoint, we must make certain that Britain wins, even if it means shooting. . . ." In Memphis, a questioner asked: "What do we face if Germany wins?" Shirer replied: "We face a pretty black future. . . ."

Ted Roosevelt, Jr., disagreed. "You know my position. I believe it is sound, and unassailable," he reiterated to his son, Cornelius, the month before Shirer's visit. ". . . I do not believe the United States should permit herself to be drawn into this war. I have preached this all over the United States." Like Lindbergh, he coupled his stand against intervention with his view that an adequately prepared America could defend itself against invasion. His speeches for America First always followed up his antiwar message with a call for preparedness. He would do his part, he told audiences. ". . . I not only believe in preparedness," he said, "but . . . I took my active duty this summer, and . . . I stand ready to be called whenever the United States may need me."

He was Teddy Roosevelt's son. He would never shirk his duty. He would not leave off the struggle to keep his country out of war, but if called up by the United States Army, he would go. "I think that every American should always stand ready to serve the country in time of national need," he told Cornelius, "even if it has embarked on a course of which he did not approve." He did not say so in the midst of the fight, but he seemed to know that before too long he would have to live up to his word.

Shirer soon received a mammoth advance payment for a book based on the secret journal he kept during seven years in Nazi Germany. His money troubles were over. After his *Berlin Diary* appeared the following June, it remained at the top of the best-seller lists for months. Americans were desperate for firsthand accounts of a now almost completely closed German society and for Shirer's expert insights into Hitler's mind and the almost mythically disciplined fascist nation and army. His book became practically required reading in literate homes. President Roosevelt's wife Eleanor told readers of her hugely popular "My Day" newspaper column that in the White House, "In the evening we read aloud from William Shirer's *War Diary*. The book is a wonderful piece of vivid writing."

Shirer's book was everywhere, much to architecture student Philip Johnson's dismay. He thought he had found an academic refuge from his recently abandoned Nazi past. Publication of Shirer's book assured that his time as a Nazi would not go away.

After the Dies Committee investigation into fifth column activities led to the arrests and indictments of nearly all his American fascist friends and associates in the spring of 1940, the thirty-four-year-old Johnson knew he had to change his skin. He enrolled as a full-time student in Harvard University's Graduate School of Design's architecture program. He stopped in twice in September 1940 at the German Embassy in Washington for reasons FBI informants could not explain, but after that his life as an evangelist for fascism came to an abrupt end.

He went to class and soon became Harvard's enfant terrible of modernism. He designed and built a glass-walled modernist pavilion as his residence in Cambridge. Not surprisingly, his lively, sharply opinionated presence and prodigious spending made his house the center for forward-looking aesthetics in town. He was back to arguing about principles of art, design, and architecture, matters of aesthetic taste that launched his precocious youthful career. The ghost of his past, though, refused to go away. *Berlin Diary* ensured it would haunt his life. The CBS man pulled no punches in his description of Johnson, the "American fascist" who covered the Polish front with him at the start of the Second World War and wrote pro-Hitler screeds for Father Coughlin's *Social Justice*. He let millions of American readers—most of whom were already jumpy and hypervigilant about hidden saboteurs, subversives, and secret agents in their midst—know that the foreign press corps could not "stand" Johnson and suspected he was "spying . . . for the Nazis."

Johnson seemed to panic. He went to absurd lengths to show that he was not the man Shirer depicted. Harvard undergraduate Carter H. Manny, Jr., who became a Johnson intimate that year (though not a lover), wrote that the older graduate student, until the previous year a Nazi supporter, had flipped entirely and "has now become publicly interventionist. . . ." Johnson even organized a campus *anti*fascist group. But he was no better at that beard of a political effort than he'd been at launching an American fascist movement. Johnson was dissembling, hoping to remake himself, and "doing this," Manny was sure, "to save his shirt. His long experience in Germany and his naturally dogmatic manner have given him unsavory fascist reputations." Shirer's book, "none too kind to him," Manny said, had put a bull's-eye on his back. Johnson joined a Harvard campus civil defense unit, but Manny said people were "constantly calling up" to tip off authorities "that one of its heads is a fascist."

Johnson knew that FBI agents were still stalking him, looking into his current activities and questioning his associates. The investigators reported back to Bureau headquarters in Washington, "In some quarters [it is] believed that [Johnson] has reformed and is attempting to convince people of his sincerity while others feel that his present position is covering up his real feelings." Whatever Johnson's shape-shifting and his neighbors' doubts about him at this point, he continued on at

Harvard and avoided being swept up in government crackdowns on fifth columnists. Nonetheless, a year later, when questions arose about a possible government intelligence analyst position for Johnson, an FBI agent sent a memo to J. Edgar Hoover warning him, "I can think of no more dangerous man to have working in an agency which possesses so many military secrets. . . ."

In an atmosphere of increasing fear and suppression of anyone with suspect loyalties, Johnson's continued freedom from indictment, virtually alone among his past associates, may have been thanks to powerful friends from the period before he turned to Nazi ideology and the pursuit of visions of an all-conquering Third Reich. One friend in particular may have been influential on his behalf: Washington's powerful Latin American intelligence and propaganda czar, Nelson Rockefeller. He knew Johnson well from his New York days, when he lit up the salons of Manhattan's Upper East Side. Rockefeller regarded himself as a connoisseur of art, particularly architecture, and had helped his father in developing the monumental Rockefeller Center. He was also a leading patron of modern art in America and served as president of the Museum of Modern Art, where he had taken a particular interest in Johnson's Department of Architecture.

Two years younger than Johnson, Rockefeller was reportedly present when, in the last days of 1934, Johnson announced his grandiose plan to leave the museum and become "Huey Long's Minister of Fine Arts." While neither man ever discussed the matter publicly, Rockefeller may have asked FBI director Hoover and Justice Department officials, who were hauling in AFF leaders and Coughlinites, to back off Johnson. Rockefeller's mother, Abby Aldrich Rockefeller, had been the driving force in founding the Museum of Modern Art and worked closely with Johnson during his time there. She reportedly said about his long dalliance with fascism, Hitler, and the Third Reich, "Every young man should be allowed to make one large mistake." Arresting MoMA's precocious and celebrated architectural leading light for being a German agent spreading fascism's gospel to Americans would almost certainly have cast an embarrassing shadow upon his friends in the Rockefeller family.

In any case, Johnson remained free to pursue his Harvard studies. He seemed determined to leave the world of politics behind him. He intended to make himself anew as an architect and tastemaker for a world that was on the verge of the American Century, not the Thousand-Year Reich.

Shirer seems to have been unaware of the impact his book was having on Johnson—though an FBI special agent sought him out to interview him about the architect—but his influence on American politics was beginning to be felt. A week after he went to see the Roosevelts on Long Island, the House Foreign Affairs Committee invited him to testify. Shirer figured the committee's interventionist leaders wanted him to respond to what he called "Lindbergh's silly statement earlier in the week that it was America's promise of aid to Brit[ain] and France which caused the war, a piece of sheer Nazi nonsense." Shirer fell ill with flu before he could testify, but he knew about and supported an improbable plan, Franklin Roosevelt's most audacious to date, to speed aid to the Allies.

14

The Garden Hose

America, December 1940–March 1941

The outlines of that plan came to FDR, as did many of his ideas, at sea. After the down-to-the-wire race to hold on to his job, the sixty-year-old Roosevelt had needed a break. He went fishing aboard the USS *Tuscaloosa*. The Navy's heavy cruiser was moving through the blue waters near the Bahamas on December 9 when a Navy seaplane splashed down with the day's sack of White House mail. FDR was expecting a letter from Winston Churchill, who would later say that the four-thousand-word missive was "one of the most important I ever wrote."

Many in England wrongly assumed that the reelection of the president meant America would join the war in a matter of weeks. Churchill knew that was not in the cards, but in the letter he asserted "that the vast majority of American citizens have recorded their conviction" that their nation's safety and the future of civilization "are bound up with the survival and independence" of Great Britain. Invasion dangers had receded for now, though most analysts still expected Germany would try again in the spring; meanwhile the bombing campaign continued. Replacing that immediate threat was a "less spectacular, but equally deadly" peril. Britain could withstand the Blitz, but her fate lay "in shipping and in the power to transport across the oceans, particularly the Atlantic Ocean. . . ." It was in the continued control of the seas "that in 1941 the crunch of the whole war will be found."

Despite the weight of the additional American destroyers now coming into play, German subs—operating in their new, lethally effective wolfpack formations, which converged to torpedo unsuspecting cargo and naval ships—were sinking ships at a rate far faster than replacements could be built. In the face of these losses, Churchill told the president in his letter, "the decision for 1941 lies upon the seas." He called upon Roosevelt to push for revision of the Neutrality Acts, and to permit American ships to enter the combat zone and begin convoying across the ocean and using bases in Ireland as their ports. This "decisive act of constructive nonbelligerency by the United States," he claimed, ". . . would make it certain that British resistance could be effectively prolonged for the desired period and victory gained." He was asking far more than the president could hope to give.

In terms of actual war munitions, Churchill asked specifically for a massive increase in American shipbuilding capacity, sufficient to construct an additional three million tons of shipping. He also wished to place "an immediate order" for two thousand more combat aircraft a month, twelve thousand in all, particularly heavy bombers, "the weapons on which, above all others, we depend to shatter the foundations of German military power." The U.S. was still not close to possessing the capacity to manufacture ships or aircraft in such numbers, though shipyards were expanding from Bath, Maine, to Mobile, Alabama, from Brooklyn, New York, to Richmond, California, and vast new aircraft and airplane engine plants were coming on line from Los Angeles to Detroit and from Long Island to St. Louis to Seattle.

Money was now the big drawback. Britain had reached the end of the line in its ability to pay for American goods and manufactures. London's cash reserves were nearly exhausted. Under the neutrality legislation's cash-and-carry provision, England, as a belligerent, was forced to pay in full before delivery of armaments (though not of raw materials). By spending down the last of its currency reserves and selling off public assets for cash to fight the war, Churchill stated, Britain would shortly "stand stripped to the bone": its finances ruined, its morale sapped, its future ashen whether in victory or defeat. "If, at the height of this struggle, Great Britain were to be divested of all saleable assets," Churchill wrote, "[it] would be wrong in principle and mutually disadvantageous in effect" upon British morale and American willingness to continue supporting them in the war and future economic trade.

Before FDR returned from his fishing trip, the U.K. Exchequer and the U.S. Treasury had worked out Britain's current payments deficit: London would have a bill due on September 5, 1941, for an amount already equaling almost a third of the UK's annual economic output, and growing exponentially.

The prime minister of the United Kingdom would not beg, but he told the president that Americans would not want to limit their help "only to such munitions of war and commodities as could be immediately paid for." He concluded: "The rest we leave with confidence to you and your people, being sure that ways and means will be found which future generations on both sides of the Atlantic will approve and admire." His plea to Roosevelt was to ensure England's and civilization's survival so that this letter might not prove to be its epitaph.

FDR had already indicated he would do everything in his executive power "short of war" for the last nations and democratic governments-in-exile fighting against Hitler and Japan, but his hands were tied by the Neutrality Acts, which required full payment in cash for any American war matériel. He had for now no "ways and means" and little chance of amending them. Amid what Morgenthau called "this blue fog here in Washington, that Britain is licked," Congress was not disposed to amend the cash-and-carry law nor to send aid that would end up either on the bottom of the ocean or in Hitler's hands.

Churchill's appeal struck Roosevelt with the force intended. For the rest of day at sea, he sat alone on deck rereading Churchill's letter, and then saw no one at all the next. "Then one evening," said Harry Hopkins, his closest aide and confidant, "he suddenly came out with it—the whole program. He didn't seem to have any clear idea how it could be done legally. But there wasn't a doubt in his mind that he'd find a way to do it." He returned with vigor to his fishing knowing what needed to be done. He would get the British their aid, and do it without breaking their bank.

The germination of FDR's thinking on the matter stretched back months, in some regards years. A month earlier, at the November 8 Cabinet meeting, the first since the election, the president had raised the possibility of leasing the Allies "ships or any other property that was loanable, returnable or insurable," according to Interior Secretary Ickes's notes from the meeting. Most of the discussion that day involved look-ing for ways to make an end run around congressional cash-and-carry provisions. Subterfuge seemed the only recourse in defeatist and isola-tionist Washington. Morgenthau thought the U.S. should simply make a gift of the armaments outright to the English, a move of questionable legality. But FDR had *won* the election; that freed him up to consider longer-term ways to aid the Allies. He could not hope to break the lock of the Neutrality Acts, but he did have precedents for alternative ways to provide aid: He had exchanged destroyers for bases, with no cash; he had sent government loans to the Chinese in return for future repay-ment in kind, not in cash.

He was intent on keeping the British Isles afloat through expanded national output, without being blocked by the need for immediate pay-ment. The British were doing all the fighting, but under the Neutrality Acts they could not fight with an American-made bomb, let alone the American-made airplane in which to carry it to its target, unless they first paid for the privilege of defending Americans. Washington and London impatiently awaited FDR's return from the Caribbean to see what he had up his sleeve to enable Britain to keep the flow of contracted ships, bombers, American iron, food and grain, oil and oil products, and more steaming across the dangerous Atlantic waters.

On his first day back from his vacation, December 17, 1940, relaxed, tan, and seemingly recharged, Roosevelt met with an overflow crowd of reporters jammed into his office. He opened his press conference by echoing Churchill, telling them that "a very overwhelming number of Americans" agreed that "the best immediate defense of the United States is the success of Britain in defending itself." He added that "from a selfish point of view of American defense . . . we should do everything to help the British Empire to defend itself."

He quickly turned to the British and other munitions purchasers' money problems. "Nonsense . . . about finances" during wartime, he declared, was clouding many minds. He recalled bets he overheard being made at the start of the First World War that Britain would not last three months. The figuring was that war fighting was "absolutely dependent on money in the bank. Well, you know what happened," he said with a twinkle in his eye: The British fought on for four years. Despite that experience, he said, many remained fixed on "banal" ways of thinking about financing the present British war effort. For the last few weeks, he went on, he had been considering other pathways to continue sending U.S. output to the cash-strapped English.

Then he suggested to the reporters a notion he'd been thinking about to help Britain while also meeting America's own defensive goals: British and other Allied contracts could be taken over by the U.S. government, and then terms could be crafted to lease the output to the British. But he went beyond setting up credit vehicles. The lease terms could be repaid in many forms—including simply returning the goods in usable condition. "Now," he said, "what I am trying to do is eliminate the dollar sign. That is something brand new in the thoughts of everybody in this room, I think—get rid of the silly, foolish, old dollar sign."

From there he turned to an analogy every American could immediately grasp. Holding his cigarette holder aloft, he said, "Let me give you an illustration. Suppose my neighbor's house catches fire, and I have a length of garden hose." He would not ask his neighbor to pay for it, but would loan it immediately. "I want my garden hose back after the fire is over," he said, adding that he expected it back in good condition. FDR then expanded the analogy to munitions: If American ships and airplanes came back from the Allies more or less intact or repaired to an operable condition after the war, things would be square. If they were so damaged as to require replacement, "it seems to me you come out pretty well if you have them replaced by the fellow you have lent them to." FDR knew that driving a good bargain would appeal to Americans. And he insisted as well that lending ships, bombers, and guns to the British in their hour of need would not put the U.S. any deeper into the war.

Robert Sherwood, one of the president's aides who helped mount the White House's campaign to gain congressional approval for what quickly became known as Lend-Lease, gave all credit to FDR's easily grasped and moving comparison. "With that neighborly analogy," he remarked later, "Roosevelt won the fight for Lend-Lease."

Another evocative slogan also contributed to the victory. Ten days later, FDR gave his first radio "Fireside Chat" from the White House in more than six months—and the first one ever to focus solely on foreign affairs. He struck a note at once of alarm and hope. Recasting New Deal themes, he urged Americans to oppose "an unholy alliance of power and pelf to dominate and to enslave the human race."

To keep those forces of tyranny far from America, he told his listeners, "We must be the great arsenal of democracy."

Harry Hopkins may have suggested the use of that memorable phrase. It stuck. More and more over the past year, Roosevelt had come to value Hopkins's judgment. FDR had entrusted him with high governmental responsibilities since his days as New York governor, but in recent months the president had come to value him in more profound ways. He had come to feel that unlike any other person in Washington, even his wife, Eleanor, Harry Hopkins was there solely for him. Before Roosevelt determined upon running for a third term, the two even discussed building a Florida fishing shack to share in retirement. Hopkins was an unlikely candidate for Roosevelt's highest esteem and deepest friendship.

Lanky, bright-eyed, caustic, profane, the fifty-year-old son of an Iowa harness maker, Hopkins was educated as a social worker and rose to become FDR's chief apostle of the New Deal and head of the eight-million-man Works Progress Administration (WPA). He was a suspected Communist and even a Soviet mole, according to embittered enemies of the New Deal. He was also a hero to the common man for his willingness to cut through the bureaucratic fog and put the unemployed to work. He employed more people and spent more taxpayer money than any American in history before him. In late 1938 FDR tapped him as his secretary of commerce, a post sometimes viewed as a stepping-stone to the White House itself. He seemed destined to take the liberal wing of the Democratic Party and, predicted some, succeed Roosevelt in office.

Any ambition for the Oval Office he had ended late the following year, when a surgeon removed a hefty chunk of stomach plus a lengthy hose of intestine to relieve a cancerous condition (though the diagnosis was never "positive"). Unable to absorb sufficient nutrition after that, he became a ghostly walking skeleton, wan, long-faced, and wasted. His overcoat and hat seemed to swallow him up. He required regular injections of nutrients and frequent hospitalizations to restore his flagging vigor. After a White House dinner at which Hopkins took ill in May 1940, Roosevelt insisted he stay the night in what was known as the Lincoln Study, the small second-floor suite where Lincoln had worked. It was just down the hall from FDR's own rooms. A widower, Hopkins stayed on at the White House, and his daughter moved into a room on the third floor. Except when he went on missions for the president or for hospital stays, they would not leave again until Hopkins remarried three and a half years later.

Once he arrived as "the man who came to dinner," at the end of most days Hopkins, in his tattered bathrobe, would pad down the hall to the president's study. There, he and Roosevelt, in silk pajamas and robe, would sit together before the fireplace or at the president's desk.

They'd discuss the day's events, read briefing papers, work on speeches, wisecrack, smoke nonstop, play cards; often, Roosevelt would rearrange his enormous stamp collection in binders, all the while sharing his perspective with Hopkins. The Iowan was a congenial listener, with an antenna tuned to Roosevelt's shifting moods. For FDR—the greatest political actor in generations—Hopkins served as an ideal audience with whom to rehearse ideas and work on speeches.

Hopkins was not passive: He knew how to push Roosevelt in ways others did not dare. He also knew when to let him be. Through sheer force of a muted will, exceptional organizational talents, ease with men of high rank and grand birth, undivided loyalty to Roosevelt and comfort with his complicated needs, he filled a unique position in the administration, perhaps unique in American history. Other personal advisers and emissaries outside appointed posts had served presidents—Colonel Edward House under Woodrow Wilson and Franklin's wife Eleanor during the New Deal period being among the closest comparisons—but nobody had sat at the president's elbow, served as the president's alter ego in foreign affairs, administered national programs, attended Cabinet meetings, or guided policy, politics, and speechmaking to this degree without having had any official post at the White House. For almost a year he went without title or salary—though he had no accumulated wealth—yet he could act and speak with the implicit authority of the president behind him. Reporters took to pegging Hopkins "Deputy President."

Some within the White House resented Hopkins's extraordinary access to the president. Some were openly jealous, Interior secretary Harold Ickes among them. "I do not like him," he noted through gritted teeth, "and I do not like the influence that he has with the president." Ickes had once stood in similar good graces with Roosevelt, though never possessing comparable trust and power. He saw Hopkins as a parvenu, eager to hobnob with the "fleshpots," swept like a moth to the flame of wealth, fame, aristocracy, and power—and a guard dog who kept him away from the president.

But FDR knew better what he had in his live-in adviser. Shortly after the 1940 election defeated Republican opponent Wendell Willkie (who would after the election become an ally in the interventionist cause) came to see him at the White House. Roosevelt explained more clearly than on any other occasion why he needed this one unorthodox and sickly man by his side. Willkie felt contemptuous of Hopkins. But FDR would not have it. "I can understand that you wonder why I need that half-man around me," Roosevelt reflected. He said that Willkie may have failed this time, but that one day he might be sitting at the president's desk. "And when you are, you'll be looking at that door over there and knowing that practically everybody who walks through it wants something out of you. You'll learn what a lonely job this is, and you'll discover the need for somebody like Harry Hopkins, who asks for nothing except to serve you."

FDR clasped ultimate authority firmly in his own hands, and as arms production ramped up, he designed administrative structures to make sure that even more minor decisions passed through him personally. Granting authority to Hopkins thus served him well, for he served at the president's behest in any way he asked. He made sure "the Boss," as he called him, was always in control: Whatever Hopkins's fingers touched, Roosevelt felt.

For many, Roosevelt's style of dealing with state matters through personal channels that he alone opened and controlled could be infuriating. He held his cards close to his vest, out of sight of those even most loyal to him. Secretary of War Stimson had been brought into the administration in part to help unblock the bottlenecked defense procurement process. He often found himself at loggerheads with FDR and exasperated by his management. The hierarchical and linear-thinking Stimson found dealing with the president's seemingly disparate and loose-ended thinking frustrating and worse. The straightforward and sometimes wooden Stimson could be blind to the more subtle intentions and political genius behind an ever-calculating Roosevelt's obfuscations.

After a particularly inconclusive meeting, Stimson fumed that FDR was simply an empty-headed, almost incoherent fellow: "His mind," a frustrated Stimson recorded in his diary, "does not follow easily a consecutive chain of thought but he is full of stories and incidents and hops about in his discussions from suggestion to suggestion and it is very much like chasing a vagrant beam of sunshine around a vacant room." Stimson the lawyer and statesman believed in the purpose behind maintaining and following order, rules, and chains of command. FDR didn't live or work that way.

Though at first Stimson did not appreciate the value Hopkins as a Cabinet officer without portfolio brought to the president, gradually he came to realize just how essential his role was, particularly in cutting through the clutter and organizational rivalries that Roosevelt deliberately created, thus allowing the president to retain his decisive authority in all matters of consequence. In this administration, Hopkins's unique character and abilities were indispensable. "It is a Godsend," Stimson exhaled at one point, "that Harry Hopkins is at the White House."

As the English financial crisis deepened, Hopkins helped the president think through the issue of getting help to a penniless friend and unofficial ally in mortal danger. Hopkins had put the nation to work through the New Deal; now plowshares would become swords: America would become the Arsenal of Democracy through Lend-Lease, as the program would be known. Lend-Lease amounted to the most programmatically concentrated power ever invested in the White House, and Harry Hopkins was the man who would make it work for the president.

In late December 1940, FDR called on Congress to grant him the authority to "loan" ships, trucks, aircraft, and munitions to London without requiring specified repayment. They were not gifts and they were not bought on credit, nor would repayment terms determine the amount and type of aid made available to Great Britain; thus, Lend-Lease would not endanger the United States' status as a neutral.

Two weeks later, in his State of the Union address, the president called for switching the national economy from production of "implements of peace" to "implements of war . . . no small task." He also reiterated the need for a program of deferred return for the increased output of American weapons for loan to the fighting democracies. He couched his reasoning in what he called the "Four Essential Human Freedoms" for the postwar era: freedom of expression, freedom of worship, freedom from want, and, most famously, freedom from fear of armed aggression. Each freedom, he said, should hold true "everywhere in the world." He asserted, "That kind of world is the very antithesis of the so-called new order of tyranny which the dictators seek to create with the crash of a bomb." FDR articulated foreign affairs as an extension of the moral ideals that had previously motivated his domestic New Deal policies. To speak of human freedom was an audacious gesture in the darkest hours of its collapse before the dictatorial armies' onslaught. The Lend-Lease bill— symbolically labeled House Resolution No. 1776, formally titled "An Act to Further Promote the Defense of the United States"—permitted the president to "sell, transfer title to, exchange, lease, lend, or otherwise dispose of, to any such government [whose defense the president deems vital to the defense of the United States] any defense article." Effectively, Roosevelt would hold absolute power to provide military equipment to any foreign nation in any way he deemed fit.

The isolationists, of course, jumped to block Lend-Lease. The proposed legislation began more than two months of public discussion, argument, and verbal jousting across the land. Historians have labeled it "the Great Debate." Even before legislation reached the Hill, Senator Wheeler claimed, "We are doing Great Britain a great disservice in urging her to go on and fight until she is exhausted. . . . As much as we hate Hitler, as much as we may doubt his word, it seems to me better for the British people and the United States to work out a peace which at least will save the British Empire and save American boys from being slaughtered upon foreign battlefields." Wheeler shared many isolationists' conviction that Lend-Lease amounted to "the warmongers get[ting] us into the war, as it looks now they will," via the good neighbor's garden hose. He condemned Lend-Lease "as [a new version of] the New Deal's Triple A [a reference to the Agricultural Adjustment Act, which paid farmers not to harvest crops and to kill off excess livestock, until it was ruled unconstitutional]; it will plow under every fourth American boy."

On college campuses, the debate over Lend-Lease drove students into ever-hardening ideological camps, much as it did in the rest of the country. German conquest of Europe, the Blitz, and the U-boat campaign had moved many to reconsider their neutrality and anti-interventionist position on the war. A large majority of Yale students, when asked before the previous summer, had indicated little willingness to risk war. A poll of Yale students taken during the Great Debate found that that 75 percent of students now favored aid to England, though student respondents were almost evenly split on their willingness to push intervention to the point of risking war. (About 20 percent of the students favored continued aid to the English on a strictly cash-and-carry basis, effectively eventually ensuring the exhaustion of their means to stave off German attack.) Yale history professor and First War veteran Arnold Whitridge, who had previously charged undergraduates in the pages of *The Atlantic* with indifference to the fate of democracy and freedom, found "there has been a definite change in undergraduate sentiment since last spring. Isolationism is a dead issue."

A vocal, well-organized minority among students disagreed. On February 7, 1941, Kingman Brewster, chairman of the *Yale Daily News* and leader of the campus's America First Committee chapter of the organization he helped found, testified against Lend-Lease before the Senate Foreign Relations Committee. He was the first from his youthful generation to speak about the bill before Congress. Every student now faced the possibility of being drafted into the army upon graduation.

The twenty-two-year-old college senior insisted his generation would do its duty if called, but, he said, "Fundamentally we believe that the peace of this hemisphere has more to offer the world of tomorrow than any possible outcome of a devastating transoceanic war." War would destroy democracy: "Nazism," he proclaimed, "can only be defeated by making Democracy *work* as an alternative."

The proposed Lend-Lease bill would grant the president unlimited power to determine allotment of American defense production. Said Brewster, "Unless you want to go to war—in which case dictatorship seems inevitable—I can see no justification for such a sweeping grant to any one man." He pounded on Roosevelt and said that isolationists among the young "resent the intention to make intervention seem a good and easy bargain. We resent the effort to hide from the American people tomorrow's consequences of what we do today."

Scores of other witnesses went to testify on Capitol Hill. Reflecting public sentiment that a successful defense of England might keep the U.S. out of the war, on February 8, 1941, the House passed Lend-Lease. Opposition to the "war measure" ran deeper in the Senate. America First mobilized a massive petition and letter-writing campaign. The Chicago chapter alone gathered 700,000 signatures demanding defeat of "the dictator bill." Hill staffers counted 328,000 protest telephone calls.

In London, Winston Churchill, learning from the White House that organized resistance might still drag the bill down, delivered a radio address the night following House passage. He spoke to the British people about recent military successes in North Africa and offered his firm belief that "the fate of this war is going to be settled by what happens on the oceans, in the air, and—above all—in this Island." He was confident "that the Government and people of the United States intend to supply us with all that is necessary for victory." He then spoke to American listeners, assuring them that Lend-Lease would keep them from having to send troops to war. He understood their worries, but they were based, he explained, on a misconception. "In the last war," he said, "the United States sent two million men across the Atlantic. But this is not a war of vast armies, firing immense masses of shells at one another. We do not need the gallant armies which are forming throughout the American Union. We do not need them this year, nor next year; nor any year that I can foresee."

He promised the American people: "Give us the tools, and we will finish the job"—with no American troops.

Unwilling to wait on passage of Lend-Lease in the urgent rush to arm Britain against an anticipated invasion, the White House covertly arranged to send more than a quarter million more rifles and fifty million rounds of ammunition.

Wheeler threatened to filibuster in the Senate if the leadership tried to move the bill through without full debate. Along with Kingman Brewster, a train of witnesses testified, from Lindbergh—who declared, "I want neither side to win"—and Socialist Party leader Norman Thomas in strong opposition, to General George Marshall and Admiral Harold (Betty) Stark in support.

Wendell Willkie again proved the interventionists' most valuable friend. Debate raged over the constitutional powers the president held to defend the country "short of war." In the world crisis, Willkie testified, "extraordinary powers must be granted to the elected executive. Democracy cannot hope to defend itself in any other way." Willkie had just returned from a trip to London, where, as the president's emissary, he met with Churchill and others in the government. He returned home convinced that England would endure the terrible pounding it was taking, but that the country needed more immediate assistance to repel the Germans.

He agreed with Roosevelt that Britain provided America's first line of defense. As long as Britain stood in its way, Germany was unlikely to move against America. Without Britain, who knew what Hitler would do next? He excused his own prior criticism of Roosevelt's foreign policy as "campaign oratory." Roosevelt was now "his President." The *Chicago Tribune* labeled Willkie a "Republican Quisling."

Moved by his testimony, several wavering senators came out in support of Lend-Lease. FDR understood the importance of Willkie's support and the courage he showed in bucking his party's stalwart opposition to anything put forward by a Democratic White House—courage that had likely cost him any possibility of a second shot at the presidency. "We might not have had Lend-Lease or Selective Service or a lot of other things if it hadn't been for Wendell Willkie," FDR speechwriter Robert Sherwood heard him remark. "He was a godsend to this country when we needed him most."

To win final Senate passage, though, the White House was forced to accept several amendments, including a statement added to the bill that nothing in the act could be construed as conferring on the president power to send U.S. Navy units to escort merchant ships. Outside of a vocal dozen, Senate Democrats fell in behind the president. As in the House, a large majority among the minority party Republicans voted against Lend-Lease, but not enough to stop its enactment. His famous grin shining as photographers' flashbulbs popped, President Roosevelt signed Lend-Lease into law on March 11, 1941. In effect, Secretary Stimson explained to the War Department's supply officers, Lend-Lease made "the warring democracies an expeditionary force of our country of which we were the base and the supply of munitions."

Shortly after the big victory for Lend-Lease, Stimson watched a series of German-made combat films, and "the impression upon me was very intense—somber," he recorded afterward. The films showed bombing raids on cities as well as armored units moving to attack. He found the air raids "very impressive." The "tremendously well trained" soldiers "moved to their objectives with superb efficiency." He worried, "They seemed to be the very personification of deviltry." A few days later, Stimson's gloomy outlook darkened further. Lend-Lease was important, but American aid might not get to Britain at all if the British could not safely ferry cargo over the ocean. Germany was winning the Battle of the Atlantic. Ships were going under at an unprecedented pace. In the first six months of 1941, Germany sunk 756 merchant ships and damaged another 1,450, losses that, if they continued at that rate, would reach seven million tons for the year. Stimson predicted that a crisis was just around the corner, and that "convoying is the only solution and . . . it must come practically at once."

The president seemed unwilling to take that next big step without direct provocation. He was unwilling to get out ahead of the American people. He admitted to Ickes that he would not fire the first shot. But he would fire back: "Probably we would have to wait for a German 'incident' before taking action," FDR told him. Those around the president knew he had begun to think about the next step: how to make such an "incident" happen.

In the first days of the Great Debate over Lend-Lease, on January 3, 1941, presidential press secretary Steve Early, fresh from Roosevelt's first press conference of the year, rang Harry Hopkins upstairs in the White House. He was in his room at the time, working on what became the Four Freedoms speech. "Congratulations!" Early said.

"On what?" Hopkins asked.

"Your trip!" said Early. Might this be one of FDR's practical jokes? He took wicked glee in playing tricks on his friends.

"What trip?" Hopkins asked.

"Your trip to England," said Early. "The president just announced it at his conference."

15

How Do You Do?

Following enactment of Lend-Lease, Roosevelt tapped Hopkins to "advise and assist me in carrying out the responsibilities placed upon me." Such a vague job description gave Hopkins nearly complete oversight of the immense effort to ramp up war production. "Under my new responsibilities," Hopkins wrote to Churchill, "all British purchasing requests are now routed through me." He meant that quite literally. While Hopkins ran it, Lend-Lease purchase and delivery orders emanated from his small study or, when he was feeling ill, from a table piled high with briefing books next to his bed. He served as secretary to the four-member War Production Board charged with carrying out the Lend-Lease purchase orders. Many hurdles and bottlenecks remained to be overcome, but thanks to a massive 400 percent increase in the national defense budget for 1941, to nearly 7 billion dollars (for purchases that would cost approximately 435 billion in today's dollars), war production hopped, stumbled, and surged ahead.

In mid-February, confident he would win Lend-Lease's passage, Roosevelt sent another personal envoy, W. Averell Harriman, a fellow Grotonian son of power and privilege, to London. He would manage the receiving end of Lend-Lease, and also serve as another pair of eyes and ears reporting solely to the White House. Roosevelt tasked Harriman "to go over to London and recommend everything that we can do, short of war, to keep the British Isles afloat." He would in effect be FDR's personal man on the scene, in direct coordination with Churchill and his government. Harriman was to be "defense expediter," FDR said at a press conference. "There's a new one for you," he quipped, much to his own amusement. "I believe it is not in the diplomatic list or any other." As the demands of war extended the range of Lend-Lease recipients, Hopkins, Harriman, and a small coterie of other scattered "defense expediters" dispatched to meet with foreign leaders—including Deputy Secretary of State Sumner Welles (sometimes without Secretary of State Cordell Hull even knowing), Colonel William Donovan, and, the most prominent among them, Wendell Willkie—came to be called "Roosevelt's own personal foreign office."

Many of those opposed to the president now centered their ire and their criticisms on Harry Hopkins. His many enemies howled at seeing the New Dealer, who had mostly slipped from public view since his illness, reloaded with such unrestricted purchasing and disbursement authority and with practically limitless money to carry out his duties. "The mere thought of Harry the Hop as Defense Production Manager is enough to send shivers down the spine," opined the tiny *Lynchburg* (Virginia) *News*. The massive *Chicago Tribune* reminded its readers, Hopkins "is . . . remembered for his reputation as the world's greatest spender in pouring 12 billion dollars down the WPA drain and on other relief projects."

Senator Wheeler could not resist painting Hopkins as so sickly that he could barely lift himself up, let alone shoulder the burden of running the buildup of the nation's massive new defense industry and disbursing its products. Deriding him for spending "most of his time in bed," he added, "Both the United States and Great Britain are in pretty bad shape if they are dependent upon Harry Hopkins to tell them what they have to do."

Some of FDR's own Cabinet members had their doubts. Interior Secretary Harold Ickes, cranky and jealous, shared this view of Hopkins:

"Harry has not successfully operated any government enterprise since he came to Washington," he grumbled after learning Hopkins would have charge over Lend-Lease and war production. "People have no confidence in him and, I believe, justly so. And yet the President is relying upon him increasingly." Winning few friends, he made sure that his singular influence within the White House remained unassailable.

But Hopkins's enemies and Janus-faced friends badly underestimated him. The former social worker, charged with carrying out the largest global military industrialization and direct foreign aid program in history, drew on bedrocks of personal strength and confidence that he credited in part to his simple Middle American origins. He had also served steadily in public administration roles during the initial development of large-scale government programs. Indeed, before this he had run the largest domestic investment program in U.S. history—the Works Progress Administration, better known as the WPA—and thus already knew how to build and lead on a diffuse, continent-wide scale: Thousands of park pavilions, seawalls, art projects, roads, bridges, and public buildings scattered from coast to coast remain monuments to the work of the eight million employed by the WPA.

And although he sometimes had a chip on his shoulder about his humble origins in a White House crammed with bluebloods, he learned to hold his own socially. He could be entirely charming and mixed easily with the cocktail lounge swirl around the president; his delight in lewd and practical jokes, his cursing like a sailor, tickled not just Roosevelt but many of the refined but jocular men who formed a tight circle around the president and upon whom FDR relied for fun and relaxation.

Hopkins had another quality that kept him true: an unflinching commitment to lifting up the downtrodden. Unlike some men of great wealth and privilege, Hopkins never lost his fervor for the mission of assisting the underdog and his commitment to wage democracy's messy and at times vicious fights to help the unemployed, sick, and aged during the Depression. And he had sharp elbows and skin thick enough for the political grapple up the "greasy pole," as Victorian Britain's prime

minister, Benjamin Disraeli, famously denoted it. He knew how power
worked in Washington and in the wider nation as a result of his WPA
experience, during which program expenditures at their height reached
nearly 7 percent of the nation's gross domestic product.

Roosevelt's Thomas Cromwell was absolutely loyal and ruthless
in achieving FDR's ends—and never mistook his own needs for the
president's. Comfortable in his now sallow skin, Harry the Hop, as
his fans referred to him, had no compunctions about speaking his
mind to and using his untitled authority over the industrial giants,
princes, and redoubtable intellects he bent to the president's will.
These personal attributes, and the occasional injection of vitamins
and other more powerful supplements, kept the iron hot in him to
carry out his gargantuan duties from his cramped, overstuffed White
House rooms.

He had shown practical ability to fight the Great Depression
previously; now his task had grown global in dimensions. He shared
Roosevelt's conviction that Hitler threatened America directly and that
he would have to be stopped. "Our people," he wrote a few months
later in an article he authored for the then widely circulated *American
Magazine*, "know full well that the success of Germany over Europe
and Africa would have far greater implications than merely the defeat
of Britain. It would mean that Nazi power would spread throughout
the world. . . . And, with these vast powers, Germany could so squeeze
the American hemisphere on economic frontiers that we never could
withstand the inroads of Nazi philosophy—a philosophy which is
already espoused, consciously or unconsciously, by a small minority
in this country.

"This conflict is a conflict to the bitter end for the control of the
world." He was quite certain that sooner or later war would come and
that the U.S. must prepare to win it. But nobody had ever prepared to
fight a war of comparable scale in human history.

*   *   *

Hopkins knew America, not the world. Unlike most White House officials, his experiences beyond American shores barely equaled those of a typical prep school boy. One reason he hadn't traveled: He was scared of flying. But he was about to embark on a very long flight—the first of many over the course of which this "half-man" working behind the scenes would alter history.

At his January 3 press conference, FDR made a seemingly off-the-cuff remark that he would be sending Harry Hopkins over to England. The two had actually discussed the idea in December, but the president made no further mention of it to him after that. The defeatist Joseph Kennedy had resigned as London ambassador, much to FDR's satisfaction—though he dared not say it to his face; he reputedly shouted to Eleanor, who happened to be standing there after the office door closed behind Kennedy, "I never want to see that son of a bitch again as long as I live. Take his resignation and get him out of here!"

Some questioned if Hopkins might not be in line to replace him as ambassador to London. No, FDR insisted, Hopkins was going "as my personal representative," with no title, "for a very short trip—a couple of weeks." He went with "no powers," not even a salary, though the government might, said Roosevelt with a big grin, provide "a per diem—not very large. . . ." The reporters laughed and then laughed again when he added, "He's just going over to say 'How do you do?' to a lot of my friends."

The president needed to know the kind of man he was dealing with in Churchill. Churchill pushed for a summit, but as much as Roosevelt expressed his own desire for a face-to-face meeting, he worried that his opponents would string him up should the two meet in the midst of the Lend-Lease debate. He thought Hopkins's personal candor, indifference to title, and practicality in getting what mattered done would be just the thing to send the president's messages to London. He wrote to tell Ickes that he was "sending over to London Harry Hopkins for two or three weeks so that he can talk to Churchill like an Iowa farmer." The idea, though, was a daring venture in personal diplomacy, a deeply risky bet given the potential for disastrous fallout in relations between the two countries should the royalist English prime minister and the no-title Middle American democrat dislike each other.

Some in government, particularly in the State Department and the army, still questioned Churchill's reliability as an ally and the power of his people to withstand the Blitz, the grinding sea war, and a probable invasion. The legacy of appeasement, prognostication of English defeat by Lindbergh, Kennedy, and other American diplomats based in Europe, and recent battlefield losses raised American fears that the prime minister's political coalition might crack. The national leaders were also both widely known for their need to dominate the room, and nobody dared predict how two such headstrong personalities so famed for their stage charisma and rhetorical powers might get along at close quarters.

The morning of Roosevelt's January 6 State of the Union address to Congress, Harry Hopkins boarded the Pan American *Yankee Clipper* out of New York's LaGuardia marine terminal bound for Lisbon by way of Newfoundland, and from there to England. When Churchill heard, the puzzled British leader sputtered, "Who?"

Hopkins arrived in England after five long days of flying—torture for his frail frame and flight-terrified soul. Whisked off his seaplane in Poole on the southern coast, he immediately saw the blasted remnants of structures leveled by German bombers. As his train started, an air raid held him up on his way to London. This was no longer the world at peace he'd left behind in Washington. He arrived ready to measure the man Churchill and his nation's vital signs. One of his first stops was a visit with CBS London chief Edward R. Murrow. Over the five hours they were together, Murrow bolstered his confidence in the endurance of the English and the fighting spunk of their leader. Asked just what he hoped to accomplish there, Hopkins told the newsman he came on a mission "to be a catalytic agent between two prima donnas."

An aide to Churchill had filled him in on Hopkins's background as a New Dealer. Thinking he perhaps made the long journey to study social conditions in wartime, when the two men first met the prime

Presidential envoy Harry Hopkins boards an airplane on January 6, 1941, on his way to meet Prime Minister Churchill for the first time.

minister started prattling on about the programs his government pro-vided for the poor. Finally Hopkins could bear it no longer. "Mr. Churchill," he broke in, "I don't give a damn about your cottagers. I've come over here to find out how we can help you beat this fellow Hitler." Churchill's round face reddened. Then his eyes lit up, and the two got down to business.

The president, Hopkins told the prime minister at their first meeting, "is determined that we shall win the war together . . . and sent me here to tell you that at all costs and by all means he will carry you through . . . ." Before long, Churchill had become smitten with Hopkins, entirely taken, like FDR, by his forthright manner and good-humored insistence on cut-ting through smoke, mirrors, and red tape. He found his "sardonic humor" and "his company, especially when things went ill," welcome. "He could also be very disagreeable and say hard and sour things."

After this first meeting Hopkins jotted down his impressions in a long handwritten letter to FDR. In essence, American international policy in the midst of the world crisis was being formulated in personal epistles between a president bound to the Oval Office and a White House official without portfolio, some penned by Hopkins on creamy stationery from his Claridge's hotel room. This would by no means mark the last time Hopkins would connect entire nations bound on disparate courses with his willingness to listen and speak up in a straightforward manner and then communicate the essence of life-and-death matters between prickly and emotionally complex national leaders.

The answer to one question mattered most to the president, and Hopkins assured his boss, "*Churchill* is the gov't in every sense of the word." He controlled both his empire's grand strategy and the tactical pursuit of its goals. This was just what FDR needed to know. When the two met—and Churchill absolutely wanted to meet Roosevelt, and "the sooner the better," Hopkins wrote—they would meet as nations.

Churchill in turn quickly realized that Hopkins's worth was more than his slender frame's weight in gold to the United Kingdom. At the end of a series of grandiloquent statements about British principles in the war at a large dinner held in Hopkins's honor, the American's turn to speak arrived. In black tie, he stood and turned to Churchill and intoned in an exaggerated American drawl, "Mr. Prime Minister, I don't think the President will give a damn for all that." The air sucked out of the room. After a pause, Hopkins said, "You see, we're only interested in beating that son of a bitch in Berlin." Before long, Churchill promised to have him knighted, dubbing him "Lord Root of the Matter."

Extending his originally intended two- or three-week stay to six, Hopkins traveled across Britain, inspecting cities, ports, and others important sites, as well as military bases, from Scapa Flow in the north to the southern air bases and shipyards, in the company of Churchill or his close aides nearly the entire time. He toured the devastation from the Nazi bombing, seeing leveled neighborhoods in Liverpool and the remnants of Coventry and other ruined cities and meeting with locals on the rubble-strewn streets. Hopkins was moved by what he saw and by the unwavering readiness of the people he met to fight off an expected German invasion

Hopkins with Churchill and Vice Admiral Gordon Ramsey at Scapa Flow in January 1941.

to the end. Hopkins wrote the president, "This Island needs our help now, with everything we can give them." Without American aid—"and soon"—Hitler would crush this last resister. He urged the president to take whatever steps he could, on his own if need be, "for the battering continues and Hitler does not wait for Congress. . . ."

Reading Hopkins's letters, Roosevelt took this message to heart. He was delighted, said Ickes, "that his friend from Iowa was just the right kind of human being who would make the greatest impression on Winston Churchill, son of a duke, English gentleman, etc. And, according to the President, the deeply laid plot had worked out even better than he had anticipated. Apparently the first thing that Churchill asks for when he gets awake in the morning is Harry Hopkins, and Harry is the last one he sees at night." Despite Ickes's disdain for him, the two nations were fortunate to have such a man as their first diplomatic bridge.

After Hopkins's return to the White House, Stimson met with him. The War Department head and longtime statesman disliked the president's reliance on personal diplomacy and initially questioned whether the "amateur" Hopkins had been overawed by Churchill and blinded by his pity for the plight of the English under the Blitz. But Stimson quickly realized Hopkins's political realism, mastery of strategic issues and the importance of the intimacy being established between Roosevelt and Churchill through him. "It's a real connection that helps," Stimson recorded after meeting with Hopkins, "and Hopkins himself is a man that I have grown to appreciate and respect more and more the more I see him." Stimson did not say so directly, but he understood that Hopkins "knew exactly what we are going to do in the situation that I see and what everybody ought to see if they'd look." What both saw was war. The question remained whether the president would take the nation into the fight and whether that war would come in time to save the English.

On March 15, emboldened by his new authority and congressional affirmation of his all-aid-short-of-war policy, Roosevelt seemed to confirm that Lend-Lease was, in fact, a step toward war. The annual White House Correspondents' Association dinner at the Gridiron Club was usually a lighthearted affair, but he chose the gathering to make clear that Lend-Lease amounted to a decision to defeat the dictators. "The big news story of this week is this," he told the reporters and editors at the banquet. "The world has been told that we, as a united nation, realize the danger that confronts us—and that to meet that danger our democracy has gone into action." Americans had fought against "Prussian autocracy [which] was bad enough in the first war," he said. "Nazism is far worse in this."

The nation was "just now engaged in a great debate . . . and it was finally settled and decided by the American people themselves. . . . This decision is the end of any attempts at appeasement in our land; the end of urging us to get along with dictators; the end of compromise with tyranny and the forces of oppression." He lauded "the magnificent morale" of the British people under the Blitz and sea war and their "brilliant and great leader in Winston Churchill."

He listed the many ways in which the United States, "the arsenal of democracy[,] . . . is going to play its full part." Several times, he brandished words that unambiguously declared that the time was at hand for the nation to do its share for the approaching day "when—no, I didn't say 'if,' I said 'when'—dictatorships disintegrate." To that end, he called upon all Americans to make sacrifices and "to put aside all personal differences until the victory is won." For the first time, FDR made clear that America in its role as the Arsenal of Democracy intended to defeat the fascist powers and rid all of Europe and Asia of the Axis.

Intentions for a day to come were one thing; war was wholly another. The pathways to Axis defeat ran over the Atlantic sea-lanes through which millions of tons of Lend-Lease aid sailed. Like a hydra-headed monster, surface raiders and submarines lurked, ready to send every vulnerable ton of shipping to the bottom of the ocean. Slogans did not win wars.

Berlin knew this, and maintained a steady silence about the reelection and postelection developments. Berlin's official policy, according to a Foreign Office memorandum following the election, would be one of "cool reserve," indicating "that the [election] outcome was expected by us and we have reckoned with it for a long time." Behind the scenes, the implications of FDR's victory and Lend-Lease weighed heavily on Germany. The armed forces general staff thought they meant "prolongation of the war," and sent orders out "to begin making the preparations necessary for a long war. . . ."

Hitler realized that the longer the war lasted, the more meaningful American intervention would be. In public he showed nothing but disdain for America, depicting Lend-Lease as a way to make England Washington's "paid vassal." America posed no threat to Germany's European plans for now, but FDR's Gridiron Club speech, according to the German Armed Forces High Command, "may be regarded as a declaration of war on Germany." The official Nazi newspaper *Völkischer Beobachter* wrote the day after FDR signed Lend-Lease into law that the U.S. was fully allied with the Third Reich's enemies: "We now know what and against whom we are fighting, and the final struggle has begun."

Where previously he'd sought merely to limit U.S. interference in Europe, Hitler now calculated his grand strategy with a view toward waging the war in a way that precluded American intervention. Used to swift low-cost victory and frustrated by his military's failure to invade England in the fall, he determined that he must pursue an alternative path to bring the continental war to an end before the close of 1941. This was necessary, he told his *Wehrmacht* chief of operations General Alfred Jodl, "because in 1942 the United States will be ready to intervene."

At a military High Command conference at his Bavarian Alps Berghof retreat on January 8 and 9, 1941, Hitler conceded that until he had "complete air supremacy," invasion of England would remain out of the question. Germany could rest secure within its European fortress indefinitely and might yet win a settlement with London, but, he told his military generals, this was not possible so long as "Britain is sustained in her struggle by hopes placed in the U.S.A. and Russia." He needed to crush those hopes definitively to force London to accept terms.

Hitler was certain that London was seeking "to set Russian strength in motion against us," and despite the 1939 German-Soviet nonaggression pact, he completely distrusted Stalin, who he suspected would turn on Germany "at any time." Were Russia and the United States to join the war, "the situation," he remarked, "would become very complicated." Germany's most pressing strategic need was to eliminate that potentially catastrophic prospect from ever being realized. "If the Russian threat were nonexistent," he reasoned to his commanders, "we should wage war on Britain indefinitely. If Russia collapsed, Japan would be greatly relieved; this in turn would mean increased danger to the U.S.A."

A swift conquest of Russia would bring complete resolution to the problem of likely U.S. intervention, while ridding him of Stalin's knife at his back and bringing London to its knees. The Japanese were eager to gain control of southeastern Asia and its natural resources. He would give them "a free hand even if this may entail the risk that the U.S.A. is thus forced to take drastic steps," meaning war in Asia. He thought a quick and decisive Japanese move against British and Dutch colonial possessions there would blunt U.S. will to mount a military response—particularly while Germany threatened from the Atlantic.

In early March, he announced his desire "to bring Japan into active operations in the Far East as soon as possible. This will tie down strong English forces and the focal point of the interests of the United States of America will be diverted to the Pacific" and away from the European war. That would free him to move against Russia. A two-ocean war would be the worst American nightmare. And faced with that prospect, he was sure the U.S. would withdraw into its traditional neutral carapace.

During a summit at the Brenner Pass shortly after signing the September 1940 Tripartite Pact with Japan, Hitler and Benito Mussolini discussed expectations for the war. As always, the imperious Führer took the lead. The Axis pact allowed him to move against the Bolsheviks, his highest priority. Indeed, Russia had been a focus of Hitler's ambition and racial animus at least since he wrote his 1925–1926 autobiographical *Mein Kampf*, in which he called for the taking of *Lebensraum*: living space and production of foodstuffs and raw materials for Germans from the Slavic residents to the east. The Communist government in power there bolstered his view that reducing the Slavic population to slaves and eventually murdering them in history's largest genocidal war served his Aryan nation's rightful ends. "Bolshevism," he said to the Duce, "is the doctrine of people who are lowest on the scale of civilization." The Anglo-Saxons of the British Isles, he admitted, had proved "a hard nut to crack" so far, but the Soviet Union would succumb quickly to his racially superior forces. "The Russians are inferior," Hitler sniffed to his commanders in December 1940. Stalin's purges of the officer corps had chopped off the head and left "the army . . . leaderless."

That month he ordered his forces to prepare for a spring blitzkrieg invasion of the Soviet Union. "You have only to kick in the door," Hitler growled to Field Marshal Gerd von Rundstedt, who would take charge of the southern army among Germany's three invading forces, "and the whole rotten structure will come crashing down."

He expected the war's endgame to follow quickly after. In January 1941, he told Field Marshal Fedor von Bock, "The gentlemen in England aren't stupid, you know. They'll realize there's no purpose for them carrying on the war when Russia has been beaten and eliminated from it."

Hitler personally code-named the invasion Operation Barbarossa, in honor of a medieval Holy Roman emperor who conquered a vast European empire and to whom the Germanic people ascribed godlike powers. "When Barbarossa begins," he intoned to his generals, "the world will hold its breath."

On January 30, draft plans for Operation Barbarossa were submitted to Hitler. The German war machine secretly began redirecting troops and equipment away from the coast of France and Belgium east toward the border with the Soviet Union.

16

Intolerance

America, Spring 1941

Despite President Roosevelt's big Lend-Lease win—which polls indicated about half of Americans supported—opposition to intervention remained strong. Americans were not simply divided about the war—their thinking about it was rife with self-contradiction, wishful for peace, certain of war, and muddled about the implications for the country. Results from Gallup Polls in the spring of 1941 showed that a steadily increasing percentage of Americans wanted to get more aid to Britain even at the risk of war, some 68 percent, and by even larger numbers, 73 percent, they were convinced that an Axis conquest of England would pose a "serious danger," even a military threat, to the U.S. By May 1941, 85 percent of those polled thought the U.S. would have to get into the war before it ended. Yet those same polls found that almost the same number of Americans opposed U.S. entry into the war, even at risk of a British defeat.

Into that yawning gulf between anxious outlook and willingness to act, opposition to intervention grew more emboldened and radical, voices of protest more strident, and calls for action against the "warmongers" more extreme. America First rallies drew crowds *Time* described as increasingly made up of "Jew-haters, Roosevelt-haters, England-haters, Coughlinites, politicians, and demagogues." Not to be outdone, interventionist organizations took to labeling all who opposed the war as

"Nazis," "anti-Semites," and "appeasers"—and while Moscow and Berlin remained in uneasy truce, "Commies" and "Bolsheviks."

In early April, the America First Committee, which began as an attempt to unify the anti-interventionist factions, formally identified itself with its most popular, if most controversial, symbolic leader: Its directors asked Charles Lindbergh to join its national committee. Bob Stuart, the organization's national director, knew that attaching Lindbergh's name to America First would "give the Committee a big lift throughout the country." But Lindbergh's concerns about "race suicide" and his ties to Germany and positive remarks about Nazi achievements there made him an easy target, and Stuart expected "the smearing to start."

Lindbergh immediately proved by far America First's most popular speaker and opposition leader. After his identification with the AFC, money poured in to the Chicago headquarters, many letters and checks addressed personally to Lindbergh. Membership surged to, the organization claimed, more than eight hundred thousand across some 450 chapters. The AFC announced his official role at an April 17 rally at the Chicago Arena, where more than ten thousand people packed inside the hall; another four thousand stood outside and cheered. He told the fevered crowd that America First was "a purely American organization founded to give voice to the hundred odd million people in our country who oppose sending our soldiers to Europe again."

In the next eight months he spoke at thirteen more America First rallies across the country. Tens of thousands turned out to hear him speak. Chapters vied among each other to get him to appear at rallies in their towns. Stuart wrote him, "If you can arrange to divide yourself into 118 equal parts, the America First representatives will be happy."

At a May 23, 1941, New York City AFC rally, twenty-two thousand people packed the flag-draped Madison Square Garden. An estimated fourteen thousand more could not get in. Not everyone there was antiwar. Interventionists were on hand, ready for a fight. At an isolationist

rally held just the previous month, running street fights had broken
out between pro- and anti-interventionist groups. The British Security
Coordination sent rabble-rousers to hand out leaflets calling Lindbergh
an "American Hitler." Christian Front platoon members hawked copies of *Social Justice* and heckled pro-British forces. Fearing a riot, eight
hundred police officers set up barriers to hold the shouting factions
apart; inside the arena officers lined the stage and seats.

Even before the rally began, the mood turned sour. Introducing
the evening, *The New Republic's* well-known liberal antiwar columnist,
John T. Flynn, chairman of New York's America First chapter, spotted
Joe McWilliams, the self-styled "Führer of the Christian Mobilizers"
and head of a Coughlin-associated movement known for its violent
attacks on Jews and Jewish businesses. Rather than let the press depict
the rally as a gathering welcoming McWilliams's anti-Semitic and pro-
Hitler rhetoric, Flynn called for him to be thrown out. When others in
the crowd tried to get at McWilliams, police moved in to protect him.
He refused to leave.

After that, the crowd was raring for a fight. Speaker after speaker
derided the White House's push for aid—and what they viewed as the
back door to war. The crowd hissed at each mention of Great Britain or
the names of the White House "warmongers." The loudest boos were
of course reserved for Roosevelt. Shouts of "Impeach Roosevelt!" and
"Hang him!" could be heard.

The crowd went wild when Charles Lindbergh stepped to the microphone. Calls of "Lindbergh for president" rang out. He warned that
American democracy was being endangered by "intolerance" at home
and said that "democracy, tolerance, and our American way of life"
would not survive if the nation were forced into a war it did not want.
He declared, "We deplore the fact that the German people cannot vote
on the policies of their government—that Hitler led his nation into war
without asking their consent. But have we been given the opportunity
to vote on the policy our government has followed? No, we have been
led toward war against the opposition of four-fifths of our people. We

had no more chance to vote on the issue of peace and war last November than if we had been in a totalitarian state ourselves. We in America were given just about as much chance to express our beliefs at the election last fall as the German would have been given if Hitler had run against Göring." He called on Americans everywhere to join America First to "create the leadership necessary" to halt the warmongers. The crowd gave Lindbergh a four-minute standing ovation.

Among those standing and cheering loudest were several Oyster Bay Roosevelts, together on the Madison Square Garden stage with the rest of the America First dignitaries and leaders. However, Ted Roosevelt, Jr., and his wife Eleanor were not among them. The previous month, on April 14, they had helped to organize what proved to be their last antiwar event—a women's unity rally at New York's august Carnegie Hall. Eleanor served as the evening's honorary chairperson. North Carolina's virulently antiforeign, rabble-rousing senator, Robert Reynolds, the South's sole isolationist, told the three thousand people attending that they were there to oppose "warmongers and those swept away by cunning propaganda." With American ships being permitted to convoy supplies now being openly considered, he declared himself unwilling to "lose one single American life" to get Lend-Lease aid safely to England. "This," he declared, "is not our war."

Another Senate Democrat, Missouri's Bennett Champ Clark, told the audience that the idea of the president's Four Freedoms existing everywhere in the world was meaningless if they did not apply at home. "Certainly as to freedom from want and freedom from fear," he said, "we have as yet made only a sorry start at home. It will be an ill-omened start if we set out to reform the world by surrendering the most prized of those prized freedoms at home." A dignified Eleanor agreed, urging the gathering to join in fighting against "the mounting wave of anti-Semitism," which she blamed the push toward war for setting off.

Ted Roosevelt, Jr., was also perturbed by the growing intolerance among Americans of all political stripes. "I have an abiding fear that democracy will be slain in the name of democracy," he said. He had paid a heavy price for his public isolationist stance. Despite his earlier war record and long advocacy of tolerance, civil rights, and justice for all, now, he complained to a friend, "My mail is full of abusive letters." "Fascist," "Nazi," "Communist," "coward," "appeaser"—every low name had been pinned on him.

He worried, he wrote Alexander Woollcott, about "the intolerance that is seething below the surface here in this country. Fuel is being added to the fire by the people of the ilk of Dorothy Thompson, Bob Sherwood, et al, who accuse all who do not share their views on foreign policy of being appeasers, pro-Nazis, etc., and at the same time, by others who share my views and who brand all of the opposing faith war-mongers. There is nothing so infectious as intolerance. Once you start it, God knows where it finishes." Like Eleanor, Ted worried that mounting anti-Semitism in particular would spiral into violence. He told Woollcott that "all of us [should] take up the battle [against anti-Semitism] ourselves and get other prominent Christians to do it. It is folly to wait. If we wait we may find the fire has gained such proportions that we cannot put it out."

The Carnegie Hall rally would prove to be the last time the best known of the Oyster Bay Roosevelts would publicly show his support for anti-intervention views or express his concerns about growing intolerance.

During the Great Debate, Ted stood firmly against Franklin's Lend-Lease program. But he also opposed the notion that American aid to the British should substitute for fighting the war against Hitler. He told his son, Cornelius, that he was ". . . fed up with the mass of speeches which are to the effect that England is fighting our battles and that therefore we must furnish her with weapons, but on no account men."

A *real* Roosevelt fought his country's wars and did not leave the fighting to others. "If England is fighting our battles, to my way of thinking it is cowardly not to go the whole-hog in backing her," he said.

Once Lend-Lease passed through the House of Representatives, he told Cornelius America had gone to war in all but name. "In the days when old procedure governed," he wrote, "we undoubtedly would have been considered at war with Germany and Italy now." With the nation standing on the brink of war, even an undeclared one, he found himself increasingly uneasy. He did not believe that this was America's war to fight, but remained certain that refusing to fight for his country was wrong. Many among his isolationist friends disagreed.

Shortly before the Carnegie Hall rally, he wrote to his brother Archie, part of the AFC national committee. "Being as strong as I am against entering the war" placed him in an increasingly awkward position, Ted felt. "I have to be exceptionally careful that I don't find myself yoked up with people whose views I do not share. For example, last night at a small meeting of the directing board of America First here, I found that three out of four with whom I was sitting at the table were all for everyone refusing to cooperate, enlist or fight in case we did get into war. That in no way represents my feeling. I have fought and will fight our entrance, but if and when we are committed, then I feel that every last one of us has got to do all he can to bring the war to a successful conclusion."

According to family members, Ted took steps at that point to end his ties to America First. Before he formally resigned from the organization, the decision to end his campaign against the war was made for him.

Franklin Roosevelt could not ignore the Oyster Bay Roosevelts standing out front at rallies, putting the Roosevelt name on antiwar statements, and sounding off against his policies. The children of Teddy Roosevelt were, like the Rough Rider himself, implacable fighters, and they dogged the president's every step. Ted was in some circles a more persuasive antiwar voice even than Lindbergh. Lindbergh's well-known Darwinian racial views and cozy relations with Nazi Germany made him an easy target for critics. Theodore Roosevelt's namesake's opposition confounded and confused many Americans. Franklin knew this. Ted's troubled younger brother Kermit volunteered to fight with the British army for a period and cabled FDR to say that he was disavowing membership in the isolationist Republican Party. FDR made sure that his press secretary, Steve Early, spread the word among reporters.

President Roosevelt could not win over the rest of the Oyster Bay Roosevelts. He could as commander in chief silence the best known and most respected among them. A week after the Carnegie Hall event, the U.S. Army called up Reserve Colonel Theodore Roosevelt, Jr., for active duty.

Ted was fifty-four years old, his knee so bum and arthritic as a result of his Great War wound that he needed a cane to walk, and afflicted with as-yet-undiagnosed heart disease. He had a wife and four—albeit grown—children, and was the prominent patriarch of a large and emotionally complicated family. He maintained a costly property which he could ill afford without a business income. His opposition to the president's all-aid-short-of-war policy and personal distrust of the man were widely known. He might have sought, and in all likelihood would have received, a deferment. But he could not have been happier to report for duty. He was leaving Old Orchard, his job and the incomplete life he led to retake command of his beloved 26th Infantry Regiment.

Eleanor tagged along with her husband to his first posting at Fort Devens in Massachusetts and then followed him when his regiment transferred to North Carolina for more training. She wrote Woollcott that Ted "is very well and far happier than he has been for some years. He has got his teeth into something he knows he can do supremely well." Ted's war with Franklin was over; he was getting ready to fight his country's enemies as his father would have expected of him. He may not have believed he was preparing for America's war, but going on active duty, according to his nephew, Archie Roosevelt, Jr., felt like an "emotional homecoming."

Passage of Lend-Lease brought other leaders of America First to reconsider their positions within the organization and their own plans going forward. Some isolationists felt themselves, like Ted Roosevelt, Jr., forced to accept a national policy that effectively fully aligned their country with Great Britain in the war. Yale student Kingman Brewster, America's most prominent student-activist in the isolationist movement, opted to resign from the organization he cofounded. He wrote to Bob Stuart, his fellow founder who remained the national director of America First, "Whether we like it or not, America has decided what its ends are. . . . A national pressure group therefore is not aiming to determine policy, it is seeking to obstruct it. I cannot be part of that effort." Trying to explain his decision to another America First founder, Yale law student and future Supreme Court justice Potter Stewart, he wrote that he "still believe[d] it outrageous to commit this country to the outcome of the war abroad," but, he felt, "the question from now on is not one of principle, it is one of military strategy and administrative policy."

The time for dissent had ended for Brewster and Roosevelt. Most isolationists felt the time to rouse the nation's fiercest resistance had come.

17

Good Americanism

FDR would not lead the country into war, at least not without the country's pushing him to fight. His quandary remained how to provoke that popular national push. To do so required that he stop Lindbergh and the America First Committee—or turned them into national pariahs and representatives of an alien power. With the world's fate at stake, Roosevelt would not allow Lindbergh and the AFC to win this fight. He would defend democracy against those who were ready to accept and, in some cases, even embrace the totalitarian tide, and he would push aid to the British, increasingly America's first line of defense against that wave. He saw in the AFC's extremist fringe and in Lindbergh's own ideology and taint from his many trips to Germany levers to swing the fractious and vacillating country away from the isolationist camp.

Roosevelt regularly criticized the isolationists as "ostriches," but held off from calling out Lindbergh or other private citizens for encouraging Americans to bury their heads in the sand. He let others do his talking. They did not hold their verbal punches. Speechwriter Sherwood accused Lindbergh of being a spokesman for "Nazi propaganda," a "poisoned mind," even an out-and-out traitor. Interior Secretary Harold Ickes took particular pleasure in taunting Lindbergh. At a widely reported speech to a Chicago Jewish organization, Ickes excoriated him as "the first American to raise aloft the standard of pro-Nazism," and dubbed him the nation's "No. 1 Nazi fellow traveler." Reminding the audience that Lindbergh received a swastika-adorned medal from Göring, Ickes denounced the Lone Eagle—unfairly, given that Lindbergh hadn't been forewarned about the medal presentation—as "the proud possessor of a Nazi decoration which has already been well earned." Nor did he spare Anne Morrow Lindbergh and her poetic celebration of fascism, *The Wave of the Future*, which he called "the bible of every American Nazi, Fascist, Bundist, and appeaser."

Behind these attacks was the awareness that Lindbergh was proving to be a dauntingly hard-nosed and effective fighter for his cause. Despite his hatred of the press and crowds, he had matured as a speaker and accepted his leadership in arousing war opposition. Even the Pulitzer Prize–winner Sherwood admitted that Lindbergh's "forcible and persuasive" ability to move audiences was holding the White House back. He was, he said, "a violent and extremely eloquent crusader for the cause of isolationism . . . undoubtedly Roosevelt's most formidable competitor on the radio."

FBI director J. Edgar Hoover started to keep a file on him in 1939. He assigned investigators to identify possible subversive connections he made in Germany and to check on foreign backing for his appearances. Before long field agents had him under steady surveillance.

At the president's urging, Hoover looked for dirt on Lindbergh, but failed in all efforts to besmirch him. Still, in his commitment to saving the West from tyrant regimes, FDR could not resist criticizing his most recognized domestic opponent.

FDR's personal animus finally came to a head in late April of 1941. Shortly after the Chicago Arena rally where Lindbergh declared his formal affiliation with America First, Roosevelt asked a friendly journalist to do a little historical digging for him into the Civil War Copperheads. That was the name given by critics to Northerners espousing pro-Southern sympathies during the Civil War. The most notable Copperhead was the leader of the congressional antiwar faction, Representative Clement L. Vallandigham of Ohio.

The newsman's report on the Copperheads reached the president on April 22. At his press conference three days later, Roosevelt spent a few minutes lambasting unnamed people in the country "who say out of one side of their mouth, 'No, I don't like it, I don't like dictatorship,' and then out of the other side of the mouth, 'Well, it's going to beat Democracy, it's going to defeat Democracy, therefore, I might just as well accept it.'" He added: "Now, I don't call that good Americanism." That tantalizing remark sparked a reporter to question why, when the army needed experienced pilots, Lindbergh, a reserve colonel with more flying know-how than almost any other man in the country, had not been called back into service. Roosevelt did not answer the question directly, but like a cat playing with a mouse, he batted it about before he pounced.

As he often did, he gave a seemingly off-the-cuff history lesson about present-day matters before the nation. He recalled how during the Civil War both sides had "Vallandighams. . . . Well, Vallandigham, as you know, was an 'appeaser.'" Vallandigham wanted to make peace in the war "because," FDR said, he thought that "the North 'couldn't win.'" He went back even further, to the "appeasers" at Valley Forge who told General Washington to quit "because he couldn't win." When another reporter asked if he was still talking here about Lindbergh, the president, with a mischievous look in his eyes, replied, "Yes," setting off a round of derisive laughter.

When Lindbergh read about Roosevelt's "Copperhead" remarks later that day, he confided bitterly in his journal that he would gladly fight an "intelligent war. . . . Here I am stumping the country with pacifists and considering resigning as a colonel in the Army Air Corps when there is no philosophy I disagree with more than that of the pacifist, and nothing I would rather be doing than flying in the Air Corps." He dashed off an angry public letter to the White House declaring that the commander in chief had made clear "that I am no longer of use to this country as a reserve officer." Knowing "no honorable alternative," he resigned his army officer's commission.

Freed from official ties to his nation's military and spurned by a president he distrusted, he no longer felt impeded in the isolationist fight from saying what was on his mind. Knowing the trouble that might bring to the isolationist cause, President Herbert Hoover privately urged him "not . . . [to] say things just because they are true." Lindbergh would have none of that. "I would rather say what I believe when I want to say it," he answered, "than to measure every statement I make by its probable popularity." In the coming summer, he thought about ways to bring the war agitators to heel—or at least to make the public record clear about the culprits who were driving the country to war. The time had come to name names.

Lindbergh met on July 11, 1941, with two America First New York chapter heads at the Commodore Hotel. He noted later that day that the three shared their worries about the "danger" of an "anti-Semitic movement in this country. We believe that if such a movement can be prevented, or held in check, it can best be done by frank and open discussion. To refuse to recognize the Jewish problem, or to discuss the Jewish war activities which are now going on, is to build higher and higher a dam that has no outlet, and which must eventually give way before the rising waters beyond. The higher the dam is built, the worse the flood when it comes." He was thinking of ways to use his privileged platform to release the water before the deluge came. He was convinced that he had a responsibility to make clear to Americans that Jews were a central, foreign, and largely subterranean force driving resisting Americans to war.

18

Living in a Nightmare

America and the Atlantic, March–May 1941

The passage of Lend-Lease permitted the White House to open the spigot wide for the flow of cargo, men, and information running between the U.S. and Great Britain. By the spring of 1941, the ring of convoys, intelligence exchanges, and unofficial joint planning circled back and forth so freely that Robert Sherwood described it, perhaps overly optimistically, as a "common law marriage." Isolationists suspected as much. Were they informed of the full extent of the developing relationship between the two nations, they might have protested even louder.

The exchanges that overflowed into Lend-Lease ran not just from New World to Old but both ways over the Atlantic. Scientific knowledge exchanges in particular brought new technologies to America. British scientists had spent more than two years advancing research in military technology. They had far outpaced their American counterparts.

Sir Henry Tizard, chief scientific adviser to the Air Ministry, traveled to the U.S. on an ultrasecret, 1940 technology-sharing mission. The British expected nothing in return for what some called the greatest gift of the war. Tizard flew with a case containing plans and some prototypes for British state-of-the-art war technologies that included-high performance engines, bomb fuses, and details of early progress in purifying uranium, at that time intended for use as a possible energy source.

Tizard also carried a small top-secret device considered so valuable that Churchill alone made the decision to give it to the Americans: a high-power microwave tube called a cavity magnetron. The technology was the heart of a miniaturized radar system that could be installed in aircraft and escort ships for submarine and airplane detection. War secretary Henry Stimson recorded after learning about the radar-enabling technology's being handed over to America for development, "We were getting infinitely more from the British than we could give them." By early 1941 cavity magnetrons were in production in the U.S. and Canada, though not yet in use.

During his visit to London in January, presidential emissary Harry Hopkins had urged increased transatlantic scientific collaboration. Back in Washington, he had already set up an organization to promote U.S. scientific research with potential military applications—the National Defense Research Committee—under the direction of Vannevar Bush, an engineer who was most recently president of the Carnegie Institution of Washington, a respected research center with university and government ties.

In July of 1941 Bush and his associate, Harvard president James Conant, received a copy of a draft report from the NDRC's liaison office in London. A British scientific group named the MAUD (Military Application of Uranium Detonation) Committee had studied the feasibility of developing an atomic weapon. The MAUD report laid out calculations showing that when sufficiently purified, highly radioactive uranium 235 could provide the fuel for a nuclear chain reaction. This as-yet-theoretical fission reaction held the potential to unleash unimaginable explosive force—an atomic bomb. Many steps lay between theory and an actual atomic bomb, but the MAUD report provided the blueprint for its creation. Bush and Conant went to work laying the foundations for an atomic weapons program that would later be designated the Manhattan Project.

In the late fall of 1941, Bush presented his committee's findings to the president and a very small group privy to what Stimson called "an extremely secret statement." After meeting with Bush, an evidently shaken Stimson described its potential as "a most terrible thing." He would one day make the recommendation to use it.

The U.S. paid a high price in going to war in April 1917 with virtually no prior contacts between its armed forces and the Allies. FDR hoped to get a head start this time around, should war come. Even before Lend-Lease passed, war planning talks began in Washington on January 29, 1941, among British, Canadian, and American military staff planners. Roosevelt wanted no confusion about the meetings' significance as far as any U.S. intention to go to war. FDR insisted that the planning chairman, Admiral Betty Stark, refer to the British delegates as "associates," never "allies." The president instructed the planners that their task was to develop strategic approaches solely with contingencies in mind "should the United States be compelled to resort to war." Over the next two months, the Americans, British, and Canadians produced a joint Anglo-American grand strategy, known as ABC-1, for fighting a war against the Axis.

Winning a European war, according to ABC-1 planners, would require "a sustained air offensive against German military power," defeat or separation of Rome from Berlin, and support for resistance forces on the Continent, while building up forces in England and elsewhere on the periphery of Europe, leading to "the capture of a position from which to launch the eventual offensive" against Germany. The ABC-1 plan proved remarkably close to the strategy that would unfold in the years ahead.

Churchill pleaded with Roosevelt for more direct help. He asked him to seize the seventy or so Axis and Danish ships—some six hundred thousand tons of shipping—that had been idled, boxed into American and South American harbors, since the start of the war, and make them available through Lend-Lease. FDR considered his request, but hesitated to act in such an openly unneutral way without some defensible reason for doing so.

On March 19, the English leader asked Roosevelt to begin patrolling as far out from the U.S. Eastern Seaboard as the 30th meridian—fully halfway across the ocean at most points. Everything west of the 30th meridian lay outside Germany's declared combat zone and, as such, the U.S. Navy could patrol there, Churchill pointed out, "without any prejudice to neutrality"—though German vessels regularly sailed beyond the boundary of the combat zone. Churchill hoped that the American warships and aircraft "might report what they saw and we could then dispatch an adequate force to try to engage them." What he actually hoped was that American ships would come into contact and conflict with a German vessel.

The Atlantic Fleet had begun training in convoy escort and antisubmarine operations. Secretary of the Navy Frank Knox felt confident enough about his navy to present the president with a plan for Anglo-American escort cooperation in the Atlantic; he wrote him on March 21 that U.S. naval convoy operations were "the only adequate answer" to save the British. A few days later, Admiral Betty Stark agreed that "if England is to be saved, we will have to get in and quickly." He went on to admit that, to stop the Germans, there were things the United States would have to do "which may cause war." Secretary of War Stimson agreed: If Britain was to be saved without direct American intervention, "convoying is the only solution and . . . it must come practically at once."

FDR stayed in bed many days through the winter and into the spring. He complained of a terrible flu and cold. But visitors who came to his bedside found him in surprisingly good health. As he had previously explained to his friend Admiral Stark, "When I don't know how to move I stay put." He finally fled the White House on a fishing trip aboard the *Potomac* in late March with Hopkins, Ickes, and a handful of others from his administration. But the sea would not cooperate to provide them relief from their war woes. The Gulf of Mexico proved so rough that even hands of poker proved impossible. The men became seasick. After a particularly stormy night, according to Ickes, the president emerged from his cabin "looking like a boiled owl."

The trip was anything but relaxing. The news from overseas remained unremittingly grim. In these "ominous days," confided Ickes, "no one can be entirely carefree even for a brief period." Ever optimistic, Roosevelt told his coterie of friends on board that "things are coming to a head; Germany will be making a blunder soon" that would provide an excuse for him to at least gain authority to begin convoying American supplies to Great Britain. But Ickes had his doubts: "I suspect that the Germans will avoid at all possible costs any such incident as the President would like to take advantage of."

Finally defeated by rough seas and the stormy international climate, the would-be vacationers steamed back to Port Everglades, Florida. Tied to the docks there was the German cargo ship *Arauca*, where it had remained after being chased to harbor by a British cruiser more than a year before. As if in a personal affront to the president, the German swastika still flew over her.

In early March, an Army Intelligence report warned that fifth column saboteurs planned to sink a German ship stranded at the Atlantic end of the Panama Canal to block passage through the vital artery. The possibility then emerged that other German, Italian, and Danish ships stuck in American and South American ports might be scuttled to bottle up harbors. Rumors of impending sabotage spread. When the FBI questioned Italian crews from a vessel in Boston Harbor, they found the stranded ship had been trashed. Sitting aboard the *Potomac*, Roosevelt considered that cause to order all Axis and Danish ships in U.S. ports seized.

On March 30, 1941, the last day of his miserable vacation, Roosevelt watched as coastguardsmen boarded the *Arauca* and hauled down the Nazi flag. The Axis and Danish vessels stuck in South America were grabbed at the same time as those in U.S. ports. Here, finally, was action of a sort. Most of the seized ships were turned over to the British when Congress authorized their transfer in June. "Piracy!" Berlin screamed. *Life* magazine acknowledged the dubious legality of the seizures, but declared, "In the Battle of the Atlantic, the U.S. had won a bloodless victory."

Seizing ships in U.S. ports posed little danger; Roosevelt vacillated through April and beyond about exposing American lives to real shooting enemies. Polls showed a large majority still opposed entry into the war. Concerned that FDR was not getting the message, on March 31 Senator Charles W. Tobey of New Hampshire and Wisconsin representative Harry Sauthoff introduced a joint resolution in Congress prohibiting American merchant vessels from transporting cargo to belligerents and American warships from escorting them. That threat convinced Roosevelt, he told Morgenthau on April 2, "that public opinion was not yet ready for the United States to convoy ships." The Treasury secretary found the president "to be still waiting and not ready to go ahead on 'all out aid for England.'" The American people had not pushed him far enough to convoy, a step almost certain to lead to direct clashes with German seagoing forces, and thus a step too far toward risking open warfare.

America First knew this as well. Their letter-writing campaigns, advertisements, public talks, and rallies were stymieing the White House. Writing to Lindbergh in late April, Bob Stuart said, "The only thing that is preventing convoys is public opinion. And the President knows it is becoming more articulate every day. We must continue to hit hard!" A couple weeks later, he shared a "pep" letter with Lindbergh for his review before sending it out to the membership: "There can be absolutely no doubt," the letter read, "that the President is profoundly disturbed by his inability to swing opinion around. He is genuinely frightened at the consequences of taking an unwilling country into war."

* * *

Admitting he felt "discouraged by the war news," Stimson blamed the president for not taking the country in hand to end the national state of uncertainty. He accused Roosevelt in private of failing to convince Americans about the gravity of the situation and thought the president's naturally optimistic and jocular character ill-served the nation in the present crisis. Stimson "found that complaint quite universal—that he had not taken a serious enough note with the people and they consequently think that they are not being given the full facts." He judged FDR harshly because he "doesn't seem to be keeping his leadership" in facing up to the horrific state of the war.

While Roosevelt's tone may have not measured up to the gravity of the world situation, he could not lose sight of American interests—and present limitations—in entering into a globalized war. His strategic outlook comprehended far more than Stimson acknowledged. FDR summarized his strategic viewpoint in a long telegram to Ambassador Joseph Grew in Tokyo: "I believe," he wrote, "that the fundamental proposition is that we must recognize that the hostilities in Europe, in Africa, and in Asia are all parts of a single world conflict. We must, consequently, recognize that our interests are menaced both in Europe and in the Far East . . . . Our strategy of self-defense must be a global strategy which takes account of every front and takes advantage of every opportunity to contribute to our total security."

Roosevelt had concluded that every move he made affected some other part in the world conflict and came at a cost, especially given the present limits of American military power, some of which could not be fully calculated. "The problems which we face are so vast and so interrelated that any attempt even to state them compels one to think in terms of five continents and seven seas," he told Grew. No president had ever confronted such a multidimensional chessboard, in which war threatened the nation and its interests anywhere and everywhere, and all at once—and his means were already so overstretched that to assert American power in one part of the world created vulnerabilities in another.

Roosevelt's caution was understandable, given the country's paucity of military resources. In January, American assembly lines produced 159 bombers of various types. Seven went to the army, 52 to the navy, and the rest to Britain. Out of 248 fighters turned out, 8 went to the Army Air Corps, the navy received just 25, and the British got the others. Naval shipyards were not moving any faster. So far the keel of just one new aircraft carrier had been laid in the past three years. No additional destroyers would be ready for duty until mid-May; a battleship and an aircraft carrier in the Atlantic Fleet were laid up for three months of repairs. In April the Atlantic Fleet could count on less than 160 ships, including only 78 destroyers ready for escort duty. Most of the ships were old and their sailors new. In the present state of national peace, FDR's cajoling had accomplished little to date to get the nation's peacetime economy on a world war footing.

Stimson urged the president to enlarge the Atlantic Fleet with ships taken from the Pacific Fleet. However, that might be robbing Peter to pay Paul: The Atlantic Fleet desperately needed bolstering, but reducing forces in the Pacific carried its own risks. Signals from Japan remained confusing. Discussions within the State Department indicated the Konoe government might be willing to pursue a settlement of disputes with the U.S., but other channels indicated that its military was preparing to move south into European colonial possessions. A recently signed nonaggression pact between the Japanese and the Russians seemed to increase the likelihood that Japan, now freed of long-standing fears of a Red Army attack from the north, would concentrate to the south. A Japanese southern operation would likely thrust the U.S. into war with Japan—and very possibly into a global war with Japan's Axis treaty partners: a two-ocean war for which the U.S. was entirely unprepared. FDR feared encouraging further Japanese aggression by transferring ships out of the Pacific into the Atlantic.

* * *

Short of convoying aid, though, Roosevelt still possessed ways to enlarge his encouragement and support for the British. With Churchill's
plea for help in enlarging the U.S. presence in the Western Atlantic in
mind, on April 10 FDR gathered a group that had become his War
Council, the six men he now kept closest to the Oval Office: Secretary
of War Henry Stimson; Secretary of State Cordell Hull; the secretary of
the navy, Admiral Frank Knox; the navy chief of operations, Admiral
Harold Stark; the army chief of staff, General George Marshall; and the
ubiquitous Harry Hopkins.

Sitting at his desk, FDR opened an atlas to a map of the Atlantic.
He had a proposal: He drew a line midway between the bulges of Brazil
and Africa, at about twenty-five degrees west longitude, and said he was
considering patrolling everywhere west of the line; U.S. Navy warships
and airplanes would patrol the zone, and they would notify convoys "of
any German raiders or German submarines that we may see. . . ." That
would place American warships just shy of Iceland in the North Atlantic
and the Azores in the mid-Atlantic. Hazy American intelligence indicated
the Germans intended to occupy both island territories before long,
and this extended patrol might stall that move. A somewhat mollified
Stimson described it as "a rather important step forward."

Still, the push was on to begin U.S. convoy escorts. At a Cabinet
meeting on April 25, several at the table spoke up for ignoring the isolationists and beginning to convoy. Instead FDR laid out his plan for
stretching the neutrality patrol eastward. The limited approach drew a
tepid response. "Well," he shrugged, looking around the room, "it's a
step forward." Stimson quipped, "Well, I hope you will keep on walking,
Mr. President. Keep on walking." The other members of the Cabinet
burst out laughing. FDR soon joined in.

A few days later, though, he seemed to walk back even this step.
On April 29 Admiral Stark gave a speech in which he indicated that

American patrols would soon range out fully two thousand miles from American shores. At his press conference later that day, Roosevelt said that the idea of an outermost eastern limit misrepresented the patrol's purpose. "You could draw a map on this easily," he insisted, "in words of one syllable and one sentence—that it would be extended out as far as necessary for the protection of this hemisphere. Now is that clear? Now, how can you draw a line on that statement, I ask you?"

Later on he warned, "Don't try to put that on paper with a line, because it will be different every single day that this patrol is going on, as it has been for a year and a half. Now is that clear? Any more geographical questions?" He was trying to push away from the idea that anything limited the patrols other than a conception of hemispheric defense which he—and Germany and Japan—alone would determine.

Before long, on May 21, the inevitable occurred: Germany made its first attack on American shipping. A U-boat in the South Atlantic stopped an American-flagged freighter, *Robin Moor*, sailing to South Africa. The U-boat's skipper ordered the *Robin Moor* crew into lifeboats and then sunk her. Left with a small amount of food and water, the men in the lifeboats drifted for nearly three weeks before being rescued.

Roosevelt condemned this "piracy" as the "act of an international outlaw." In reprisal he ordered all Axis consular and German propaganda offices closed and their officials sent home. However, when his special emergency message to Congress was read out, many members did not even bother to stay on the floor to listen. With the president proposing no military response to the attack, whatever ire the legislators felt mattered little.

Asked now to beef up his patrols, Admiral Ernest J. King, commander of the Atlantic Fleet, complained, per Stimson, that "he did not have butter enough to spread over the bread that he was supposed to cover. It was too thin." Stimson campaigned to transfer part of the Pacific Fleet over to the Atlantic, America's principal theater of operations.

Hoping to demonstrate that some ships might, with little risk, be detached from the Pacific Fleet, Stimson asked General Marshall to look into Hawaii's defenses. Marshall came back convinced that "Hawaii was impregnable whether there were any ships left there or not. . . ." Land and air defenses, he said, were "amply sufficient . . . to keep off the Japanese." Knox seconded Marshall's assessment, telling the president "that Hawaii was impregnable so far as keeping vessels there was concerned. . . ."

Still FDR hesitated. He wanted to hold back enough ships to deter the Japanese from making an aggressive move. He also insisted that the Atlantic Fleet's mission remained to spot and track possible threats to American ships and territory. Stimson refused to accept the equivocation and told the president as much: "I wanted him to be honest with himself," he reflected. The beefed-up and expanded patrol was a "clearly hostile act to the Germans." With a smile on his face, he said to Roosevelt, "You are not going to report the presence of the German fleet to the Americas. You are going to report it to the British fleet."

FDR finally relented, ordering transfer of a quarter of the Pacific Fleet—among the capital ships an aircraft carrier and three battleships—to the Atlantic. The Pacific Fleet commanders and Secretary of State Cordell Hull strongly opposed the decision. Nobody could realize this, but the decision would prove a great stroke of luck before the end of the year.

FDR had long planned and often postponed a speech now scheduled for May 27. On May 24, Stimson sent the president a daring draft resolution to present to Congress as part of his speech. Stimson proposed calling on Congress to authorize "use of force" to maintain "control of the sea," to "secure" delivery of Lend-Lease supplies to Europe, and "to take all steps necessary to keep away . . . aggressor nations" from the Western Hemisphere—effectively sending a declaration of war to the president. In his accompanying letter, he urged Roosevelt to get out in front and to stop leaving it to the American people to make the

"momentous decision of opposing forcefully the actions of the evil leaders . . . because by some accident or mistake American ships or men have
been fired upon by soldiers of the other camp. They must be brought
to that momentous resolution by your leadership. . . ." Three days later,
Roosevelt had Stimson believing that he was ready to incorporate his
virtual declaration of war into his speech.

That day he did tell the American people that "what started as a
European war has developed, as the Nazis always intended it should develop, into a world war for world domination." That war, he continued,
was now becoming an American war. For, ". . . unless the advance of
Hitlerism is forcibly checked now," he warned, "the Western Hemisphere
will be within range of the Nazi weapons of destruction." This was not
a drill, he said. "Attacks on shipping off the very shores of land which
we are determined to protect present an actual military danger to the
Americas." Even that very day, he added, without naming the *Bismarck*,
"a Nazi battleship of great striking power," had steamed into "Western
Hemisphere waters." He discussed the history of escorting merchant
convoys to assure the freedom of the seas and informed listeners that
the Atlantic Fleet had been strengthened and its patrols extended to
"warn of the presence of attacking raiders. . . ." However, he did not
say he would start escorting or what U.S. Navy ships would do when
they identified raiders. He concluded by issuing a "Proclamation of
Unlimited National Emergency."

Issuing a formal proclamation seemed to fall just short of declaring
war, placing the nation's defenses "on the basis of readiness to repel any
and all acts or threats of aggression. . . ." While less than he hoped for,
Stimson felt the speech committed the nation to ensuring the freedom
of the seas and getting American weapons to the British, ends that were,
he said, "all right and very praiseworthy."

Ickes's response was more blasé, calling the president's address just
more words without action: ". . . we really are in the same status quo. . . ,"
he remarked a few days after the speech.

* * *

The German Embassy chargé d'affaires Hans Thomsen thought something had in fact changed with the declaration of a state of emergency. The president had declared emergency powers, particularly to prevent strikes which had disrupted the pace of production at some defense plants. Thomsen felt that the "negative character" of the speech left much in doubt and added that it "abounds in insults, insinuations and lies." The German press at the command of the Propaganda Ministry described it as "a typical product of Roosevelt's Jewish prompters."

In Rome, Italy's foreign minister, Galeazzo Ciano, thought Roosevelt's speech "a very strong document, even though it is unclear as to plans to action." His boss and father-in-law, the Duce, fumed in response and "thundered against Roosevelt." Mussolini roared that "never in the course of history has a nation been led by a paralytic. There have been bald kings, fat kings, handsome and even stupid kings, but never kings who, in order to go to the bathroom and the dinner table, had to be carried by other men." Ciano noted unnecessarily that "clearly Roosevelt is the individual against whom the Duce directs his greatest hostility." But however great his loathing of the man, Mussolini told Hitler when they met again shortly afterward at the Brenner Pass that making a formal reply to FDR's taunts would only serve to arouse U.S. war fervor and, by paralleling arguments being made by the isolationists, give more fodder to those who claimed they were acting on Axis orders.

With America watching, the world seemed daily to darken, with only bad outcomes seemingly likely. Averell Harriman had arrived in London as a special envoy for the Lend-Lease program at the receiving end of the supply line. He was stunned by the devastation from the continuous German bombing campaign (fifty-seven straight days of the Blitz in London) and U-boat attacks (more than sixty ships sunk in May alone, fourteen hits credited to a single U-boat on one patrol), now coupled with withering losses in Greece, Crete in the Mediterranean, and in colonial North Africa. Hitler appeared destined soon to straddle the Mediterranean Sea, potentially controlling sea access to North Africa, Central Europe, the Middle East, and the canal route through to the Indian Ocean, and from there Asia.

"It has been as if living in a nightmare," Harriman wrote Hopkins from London, "with some calamity hanging constantly over one's head." Even some officials within the Roosevelt administration worried that Britain was licked or would be if the U.S. did not intervene directly soon. "England's strength is bleeding," Harriman warned Roosevelt. "In our own interest, I trust that our Navy can be directly employed before our partner is too weak." Symbolic of the nadir of British fortunes, on May 11 German bombs reduced the House of Commons to a stone shell.

In response to the crisis, FDR's emergency proclamation speech seemed both bellicose and weak, further signs of vacillation on his part. American commentators viewed the president's address as an emergency declaration that raised alarms, not arms. Pundit Joseph Alsop, widely considered to have almost free access to the administration, described the speech and its aftermath as a Hamletian failure to act: "He says that he means to act, yet he does not act, and in the next breath even seems to foreclose important avenues of action," he wrote. "The contradiction is easy to explain, however, once it is understood that the immediate future depends on the answer to a simple question. Will the President continue [to be] determined to force the Germans to fire the first shot? . . . In the past weeks, he has been repeatedly urged to order immediate action. He has been warned that to delay was to court disaster. He has been able to act, for all necessary preparations for meeting the German threat in the Battle of the Atlantic have at last been completed. Yet he has not acted, because he hopes to drive the Germans into shooting first. . . . No one can doubt the German high command will do everything possible to avoid shooting first. The President's plan leaves the initiative to Germany, which is a mode of procedure that has cursed the democracies since the start of the war." Was America in 1941 doomed to repeat the experience of England in 1939?

Everybody following closely understood that a strange dance, a global martial arts demonstration, was under way. FDR rattled sabers, stuck his chin forth, and dared Hitler to strike; Hitler and Mussolini stamped and cursed and held their punch.

Three days after Roosevelt spoke, Lindbergh addressed an America First gathering in Philadelphia. Some interventionists in the city thought that the president's "Unlimited National Emergency" should result in immediately banning the famous aviator from bringing together "subversive elements" for a rally in the city. One large hall refused to hold the event; radio stations wouldn't broadcast announcements about the rally; and local buses and trolleys refused to display ads for it. Isolationists were up in arms. Kansas Republican representative William P. Lambertson warned, "The very first evidence of Nazism is censorship such as this."

Despite the limits on the AFC's getting the word out, the 9,300 seats in the arena the AFC could get were filled to capacity and another 5,000 people stood outside—a far greater turnout than at a pro-intervention rally held just the day before. Lindbergh said that Roosevelt had gone beyond "even Hitler" in claiming that islands (the Azores) in the "Eastern Hemisphere" lay within the American defense perimeter. If Germany made similar claims to islands off South America, he said, "Obviously this country would go to war."

Lindbergh battled FDR over the definition of American hemispheric geography: "If we say that our frontier lies on the Rhine," he proclaimed, "they [the Germans] can say that theirs lies on the Mississippi." He asserted that "Roosevelt himself advocates world domination" by mixing American interests into European and Asian wars. The loudest cheers came when he said the time had come for the nation "to turn to new policies and to a new leadership . . . [to] create a leadership for our nation that places

America first." Some, including Roosevelt, questioned afterward whether Lindbergh was not edging toward advocating subversion, even rebellion.

Lindbergh noticed during his speech that the arena became insufferably hot, not surprising given the boisterous, standing-room-only crowd. Still, he wondered about possible sabotage: "There has been considerable opposition to us here—mostly Jewish inspired—and it is quite possible that the ventilators were turned off intentionally," he penned in his diary that evening.

Two days later in New York City, he met with former president Herbert Hoover at his apartment. While not on the America First board, Hoover was actively working against intervention. The British, the ex-president growled, "cannot win the war!" Lindbergh thought he was saying the obvious and wondered why it had taken him so long to come around to that conclusion. Lindbergh thought that like most people, Hoover failed to understand the significance of Germany's air superiority. "But," thought Lindbergh, "in addition to that, I do not believe he recognized the decadence in England or the virility in Germany." He fully expected virility would win because, he reflected a few days later: "Personally, I have enough faith, and enough optimism to believe that 'right' *will* win at the end. But possibly this is because whatever wins out in the end is 'right.'"

Roosevelt read the newspaper reports about the America First rally in Philadelphia and the pallid pro-British gathering there the day before. He looked over the weekly polling numbers and considered the present limitations of American forces, especially with the increasing possibility of war with Japan. He was boxed in by his own words and by a world situation in flux. He could not drive an unwilling nation into war, and resignedly confessed to Morgenthau on May 17, "I am waiting to be pushed into this situation." He admitted to his entire Cabinet three days later that he remained adamant: "I am not willing to fire the first shot." Hitler was equally unwilling to confront American intrusions into the Atlantic. FDR would need to aggravate the Führer again and again, waiting for "an incident." Rather than push events faster than his nation would follow, Roosevelt deemed it best to continue movements he termed "sidewise."

As if to underscore the toothless nature of his emergency proclamation, three days after his speech, nine U-boats attacked a convoy due south of Cape Farewell, southernmost tip of Greenland, sinking nine ships carrying Lend-Lease cargo bound for Britain.

Discouraged by his predicament, Roosevelt returned to bed with unnamed gastrointestinal ailments.

19

Volunteers

Great Britain and China, April–June 1941

Roosevelt had long wrestled with how to assist the Chinese in their war with Japan without provoking open hostilities between the U.S. and Japan. He pushed forward loans that enabled China to acquire U.S. goods and Soviet-made weapons and other supplies. Although FDR aimed to thwart Japan, few people in the administration trusted the corrupt Chinese Nationalist leadership under Chiang Kai-shek. The country was badly split between Nationalist and Communist forces fighting in an uneasy alliance against the Japanese. The possibility of civil war remained ever-present. FDR dispatched a White House assistant, economist Lauchlin Currie, as his envoy to the Chinese. Currie reported to Roosevelt that an infusion of American advisers and economic and military aid would promote Nationalist forces and encourage future stability. Roosevelt was determined to keep Chiang fighting.

A number of Americans were advising Chiang's army in China. The president asked another assistant, Thomas Corcoran, to meet with one of them, a former U.S. Army Air Corps colonel, Claire Chennault, who had been advising the Chinese army leadership since the war began in 1937. He came to Washington over the winter of 1940 to promote sending American aerial aid to the Chinese.

Chennault made a strong impression wherever he went. Arrogant, brash, a bare-knuckle Louisiana Bayou brawler, Chennault had a chiseled, leathery face with hawklike features befitting the fighter pilot he was. He had been raised on tales of the Confederate cavalry dashing out on raids, wrecking the Union forces and depots, and then getting away scot-free before the enemy knew what had hit them. He would update Stonewall Jackson's cavalry assaults for the modern battlefield.

Corcoran heard out Chennault's seemingly fantastic plan to create an *aerial* guerrilla warfare squadron. Corcoran's eyes grew wide as the flinty Chennault described his idea to operate American-flown fighters out of bases hidden in the forests along the Burma border, launching surprise raids behind Japanese lines against bombers on the ground and ships in ports. Corcoran decided after the meeting that he was "dealing with something original, whether it was genius or madness" he could not be sure; but he found Chennault "irresistible."

Roosevelt was immediately taken with the idea of an aviation Stonewall Jackson. The president wanted to keep the Japanese pinned down in China, to slow their movement south into Indochina. With White House encouragement and help, in early January Chennault developed plans for the American Volunteer Group, the AVG—later renamed the Flying Tigers. Chennault wanted airplanes, and experienced pilots to fly them in combat. Since neither China nor Japan had declared war, Americans could travel and American warplanes were permitted to be sold into the war zone, but the plan clearly skirted the intent of the neutrality laws.

To get around any questions, the Chinese government set up an American corporation as a front to purchase and deliver one hundred P-40 fighter planes. The company packed them up and, under U.S. Navy escort, shipped them to Burma for the hop from there into China, where they would serve as aircraft for a noncombatant "flight school."

Getting the skilled pilots to fly them represented another level of complexity. Chennault wanted to bring flight "instructors" who would go "prepared to defend the school property and personnel," of course expecting to get quickly into combat. Currie lobbied Knox and Stimson for pilots. They finally agreed to let Chennault recruit active-duty army

and navy pilots willing to resign their commissions in return for employ-
ment and higher pay to fly for China against the Japanese. Chennault
began to tour U.S. air bases, looking for his first hundred pilots and
ground support personnel. Chennault succeeded in hiring hard-boiled
adventurers and mercenaries eager for air war.

Chennault's U.S. preparations for the AVG were complete by June.
Over the summer, with a passport listing his occupation as "Executive," he sailed for Burma. As his ship left port, "For the first time in
my battle against the Japanese" he felt he would command "everything
I needed to defeat them." Most of the pilots for the soon-to-be-called
Flying Tigers were traveling under a variety of civilian disguises at sea
on December 7, 1941.

Before those American military pilots volunteered for foreign war,
others found themselves "volunteered." When Knox wrote to Roosevelt
in late March in a failed bid to persuade him to begin convoy operations, he also sought permission to send some naval aviators to operate
the PBY-5 Catalina aircraft being sent over for coastal convoy escort
duty under Lend-Lease. "I don't expect them to fly our planes in actual
combat," he wrote the president, "but I presume that some of them may
see active service in the guise of observers." Having watched the English
in patrol operations, they could help other American aviators prepare for
the realities of warfare. FDR agreed that "volunteers" should be recruited
to ferry the patrol flying boats and act as "observers."

Shortly thereafter, Navy lieutenant Leonard B. "Tuck" Smith
received orders along with sixteen other pilots to "volunteer." They
reported to Washington on a mid-April day in 1941, where Rear
Admiral John Towers, chief of naval aviation, briefed Smith and the
others on their mission. He said they would soon be happy for the
experience of observing actual war theater service. "It's not a question
if we go to war," he told Smith and his fellow pilots. "We just haven't
selected the date yet."

Smith and three other pilots arrived on May 15 at an RAF Coastal
Command base in Lough Erne, North Ireland. The other Americans

were scattered around Scotland and England. Within hours of their arrival at Lough Erne, Smith and his fellow volunteers began flying America's first unofficial war patrol missions. The American trainers for the British pilots would teach them quickly at the controls; the Brits would school the Americans for a longer period on convoy escort and coastal patrol duties.

Ten days before that, on May 5 in Kiel, Adolf Hitler and his High Command entourage made a lengthy inspection of the newly commissioned *Bismarck*, the pride of the German navy. What they saw was awe-inspiring: The *Bismarck*'s big guns included eight monstrous fifteen-inch fast-firing forward turrets that could shoot a shell almost thirty-five miles. Nearly impenetrable curved armor plating, as much as fourteen inches thick, protected the ship. She could make a top speed of better than thirty knots. Forty-four antiaircraft guns could spray out a storm of iron hail at any aircraft daring to approach.

She was the most dangerous warship ever built, potentially unstoppable. Britain knew that and had desperately sought to destroy her with raid after raid while she was under construction, without success. German forces pulverized the British Mediterranean fleet a few days earlier in the battle at Crete, encouraging German grand admiral Raeder to hope "additional severe damage might be inflicted on British sea power." He was keen to get the most formidable seagoing weapon ever launched out on the main before British navy forces, reinforced by the Americans, completely closed off the Atlantic approaches. "The inevitable entry of the United States into the war," he observed, ". . . was staring at us in the face."

Five days after Smith and the rest of the Americans went aloft with their British counterparts for the first time, the monstrous new battleship *Bismarck* and her sleek and powerful heavy cruiser cousin, *Prinz Eugen*, slipped out under cover of night, fog, and stormy weather through Swedish waters, and into the Denmark Strait between Iceland and Greenland. Hungry for battle, *Bismarck*, with her company of more than twenty-two hundred officers and men, churned toward the North Atlantic hunting grounds.

The Royal Navy knew the German capital ships had broken loose. The cruisers *Suffolk* and *Norfolk* kept out of range of the two vessels as they followed them between Iceland and Greenland. The battleship *Prince of Wales* and battle cruiser *Hood*, the latter among the most advanced ships in the Royal Navy, scrambled out of Scapa Flow, on a course to intercept the German raiders where the strait emptied into the North Atlantic.

Eager as a player waiting for the big game to begin, Churchill alerted the White House about the chase on May 23. His nervous energy was palpable: "Should we fail to catch them going out your Navy should surely be able to mark them down for us." British warships would then close on them. "Give us the news," he cabled, "and we will finish the job."

On the morning of May 24, *Prince of Wales* and *Hood* met the German warships to the west of Iceland—within the American Atlantic Fleet's patrol zone. As the British squadron closed range, from about ten miles off *Bismarck* and *Prinz Eugen* concentrated their fire on *Hood*. A German salvo ranged over the battle cruiser, followed quickly by a shell that struck the Royal Navy man-of-war amidships. The monstrous bullet blew through the deck armor and into the powder magazine. *Hood* returned fire for a few seconds, until a massive explosion rocked the ocean to the horizon; flame and a mushroom of smoke rocketed hundreds of feet into the air. Like an exploding volcano blowing its top, sections of funnels, masts, and other pieces of the ship rose into the sky, some falling back on the *Hood*'s blasted superstructure. After less than four minutes, she disappeared into the ocean depths. From out of her company of 95 officers and 1,324 men, just three survived. German shells turned on the outgunned *Prince of Wales*, which, badly mauled, broke off the battle under a smoke screen.

Herbert Manthey, a seaman aboard the *Bismarck*, stood on deck to watch the battle unfold. After the second salvo at the *Hood*, the ship's loudspeaker announced, "Enemy is burning," and with the third,

"Enemy is exploding." Cheers erupted from all corners of the ship. The two German battle machines sailed on.

Desperate to keep track of them, torpedo planes from the carrier HMS *Victorious* raced out. "Electrified" U.S. sailors aboard the coast guard cutter USS *Modoc* were picking up survivors from a wrecked convoy south of Greenland when suddenly the monstrous German battleship hoved into view on a fast southerly heading, then just as quickly slipped out of sight. They were less happy when bi-wing torpedo bombers from *Victorious* buzzed the *Modoc*, thinking in the enveloping twilight that she might be their German prey. They broke off when they realized their mistake.

As the sea battle unfolded, Washington was wilting in an early heat wave. Bulletins came in from the Admiralty in London all the previous day reporting on the fight with the *Bismarck* and then her disappearance. Word came to President Roosevelt, sitting in his shirtsleeves at his Oval Office desk, that *Bismarck* was now making a southerly course. Questions flew about the *Bismarck's* intentions. Some thought she might attack Halifax, or maybe put on a display of power by sailing right into a South American port. She might possibly even intend to shell an American city.

The U.S. would not be able to stop her if she showed up on the nation's seaboard. The Navy's most modern battleship at sea was twenty years old and carried no guns or armor thick enough to trade punches with the likes of the *Bismarck*. Speechwriter Robert Sherwood wrote that Roosevelt was convinced Hitler had sent the battleship out "primarily to scare the U.S. with a tremendous display of Nazi might right on our doorstep." The president had announced plans to give his May 27 "state of emergency" speech, and he was sure the dueling German leader wanted "to kill the effect."

Eleven American PBY Catalina flying boats scrambled in Argentia, Newfoundland, to search for the German battleship, but had no chance of finding her in the darkness and fog. Sherwood recollected that though an "oppressive calm" surrounded the president at the White House, all there were caught up in events that were "inexpressibly thrilling."

FDR wondered whether *Bismarck* might make for the Caribbean, where she could capture Martinique or some other strategic outpost: "Suppose she does show up in the Caribbean," he remarked. "We have some submarines down there. Suppose we order them to attack her and attempt to sink her? Do you think the people would demand to have me impeached?" Somebody quipped, "Only if the Navy misses."

In reality, the German battle engine had set its course away from North America. Before the wounded *Prince of Wales* broke off the fight, two of her shells had stung the *Bismarck*. A resulting oil tank leak forced her to turn off from her mission. Trailing oil, the massive ship made hard southeast through heavy seas for German-occupied France for repairs. *Prinz Eugen* also broke away to the southwest; she escaped in the night before making a course for the African coast. In the early-morning darkness of May 25, the Royal Navy ships lost contact with the *Bismarck*.

Despite the *Hood* catastrophe, Churchill went to bed confident the *Bismarck* would be sunk by morning. Upon awakening he learned that she had vanished into the North Atlantic night and storms. An all-out order declared, "SINK THE BISMARCK!" The Royal Navy sent out a veritable armada—six battleships and battle cruisers, two aircraft carriers, thirteen cruisers, and twenty-one destroyers—to find the *Bismarck* and kill her.

For the entire following day, high winds, squalls, and low clouds shrouded *Bismarck* as she steamed unseen toward France, safety, repairs, and refueling. The two shots the ship had taken slowed her, but a temporary repair at sea allowed her to make steady headway. The British were desperate to find the *Bismarck* on the increasingly high running seas. Royal Navy scouts assumed wrongly that she would turn north back through the Denmark Strait for home. Many warships were closing on the area and long-range patrols flew out of Britain and Iceland. Storms made conditions treacherous for the searchers. *Bismarck* vanished like smoke into the fog, clouds, and night.

Anxious hours passed. RAF Coastal Command scrambled every available patrol plane for the hunt. Although not officially a pilot, Tuck Smith took the controls of a Lend-Lease Catalina with a British copilot and crew, getting off the water at three-thirty in the morning on May 26. He drove the big flying boat into a strong wind until, at ten-thirty, the aircraft reached its search area. Banking just beneath low, dense clouds, Smith was stunned: Almost immediately, he spotted a gray form moving through heavy seas about five miles ahead, "maybe less," he recalled. He and his British copilot shouted at the same instant, "There she is!"

Smith flew in for a closer look while the sighting was called in. Smith passed in and out of the cloud cover at less than three thousand feet. He approached close enough to see the swell boiling up around the bow of the big gray ship. A couple puffs of smoke opened like dark flower blossoms past the cockpit window, followed by loud popcorn pops and metallic pings. Then thick brownish black smoke surrounded the cockpit windshield. They were under fire. Shrapnel dinged off the forward hull, and the airplane bounced about. Smith realized he was a "red-assed ensign on his first game for keeps."

He could see her directly below him, the dark ship entirely "aglow in red AA [antiaircraft] fire," all those guns firing at him. He thought, "Hell . . . I could spit on you!" With no time for second thoughts, he jettisoned his depth charges and banked steeply. Not waiting to see the results, he pulled the throttles back and climbed as fast as the lumbering seabird could make for the clouds.

Out of sight, he checked out his PBY-5. He saw light through "quite a few shrapnel holes" in the hull, but with no fuel leak, the aircraft ran on in flying condition. He stuck on the *Bismarck* for four more hours, until another Catalina and later a third relieved him. Those two planes also had American "volunteer" pilots at the controls. By the time Smith put down in Lough Erne, he had been aloft for eighteen hours straight. He was the first American in uniform to face Second World War combat.

The other flying boats continued to shadow the *Bismarck*, evading her antiaircraft fire. Although she was now just 670 miles northwest of her destination in Brest, she was still too far for German air cover or destroyer relief to reach her. The aircraft carrier *Ark Royal*, patrolling southeast of *Bismarck*'s reported location, headed directly to cut off her path to Brest. The undergunned cruiser *Sheffield* took up a shadowing position. Other Royal Navy ships, including the battleship *George V*, moved to seal off her escape.

As *Bismarck* continued on, the Nazi fleet commander addressed the entire crew: "We shall win or die." The deadliness of the battle she was now in came home to everyone on board. Seaman Manthey noted how the crew's previously lighthearted spirit grew "serious."

Fifteen Swordfish torpedo bombers took off from the carrier *Ark Royal* in the evening twilight. Over the next hour or so, in conditions of low clouds, strong winds, and fading daylight, the aircraft ran in on the German battleship, releasing torpedo after torpedo. Only two hit home—but one was enough: A lucky strike jammed her rudder. Unable to make a straight course, *Bismarck* could no longer outrun her converging pursuers. She carouseled, her turrets blasting at distant British ships, all the while her guns blazing at torpedo bombers running at her like pecking birds. She swatted several out of the sky, but could not rid herself of attackers.

At first light on May 27, British warships moved in for the kill. A steady bombardment thundered. The encircling British rained down more than twenty-eight hundred shells on *Bismarck*, scoring more than four hundred hits. The relentless shellfire exploded off the armor. *Bismarck* steamed on, seemingly impervious to mortal shot. But on board the German ship, the situation grew increasingly chaotic. Sections of the main deck were obliterated, guns blown out. Fear spread among the crew. "We had the impression that we were fired at from all sides," recalled Manthey. The ship began to list. In the heavy seas, waves swept over the upper deck. An explosion near Manthey's armored shield blew him into the water.

As the battle raged, Churchill came to the House of Commons, then meeting in temporary quarters. He reported that an epic sea battle with the big German warship was under way. "I do not know the results of the bombardment," he admitted to a grim Parliament, shaken by the loss of the *Hood*, the fleet's pride. Just as the scowling prime minister sat down, an aide handed him a slip of paper. He rose again. A big smile lit up his round and florid face: "The *Bismarck* is sunk!" The roar that followed echoed across the British Isles and far beyond her shores.

On the other side of the Atlantic, "we were electrified," Ickes recorded. When word of the *Bismarck*'s death arrived at the White House at the end of four tense days, he could sense, "even as far away as we are . . . there is no doubt that British morale fully recovered from the severe shock that had been sustained when the *Hood* sunk." He remarked, "It is gratifying that some of our latest American airplanes played a prominent part in this great drama of the air." He thought only American aircraft took part; even he did not know the essential role that Smith and the other American pilots played in sinking the *Bismarck*.

Few people outside the navy's top brass and the tightest circle around the president knew about that. Although in his May 27 speech FDR mentioned that a powerful German ship had approached North America, he never spoke of American pilots' participation in sinking her. Smith received a Distinguished Flying Cross for his service in finding the *Bismarck*. No public announcement was made of the prestigious award. Smith continued to fly for the British Coastal Command on through the summer and into the fall, totaling almost two hundred hours of flying time with the RAF, most of them as pilot. He and the other U.S. Navy pilots fought the Battle of the Atlantic under British command, while America debated whether it would go to war. Finally, in October, Smith flew away from the U.K. He passed through Pearl Harbor before continuing on to Wake Island, the Pacific air base closest to Japan.

After the *Bismarck*'s sinking, the embittered Raeder redoubled his insistence on confronting American intervention. He likely didn't know about the American role, but in an interview with the Japanese news service Domei that took place in the midst of the *Bismarck*'s fatal battle, he directed comments to Americans: "I can only confirm President Roosevelt's opinion that convoying means 'shooting' . . . a plain act of war and unprovoked aggression." He warned the United States not to extend patrols farther into the Atlantic. In fact, he already considered the navy's Atlantic Fleet patrols' tipping off of the British "an act of war." At the next

Lieutenant Smith, on right, being awarded the Distinguished Flying Cross for his secret role in finding and sinking the Bismarck.

High Command meeting, he renewed his request to Hitler to end the shadow war and begin to "wage warfare against U.S. merchant shipping." With Operation Barbarossa set to launch in less than a month, though, the Führer's mind was now firmly fixed. Victory would come quickly in Russia, he assured Raeder. After that, "America will have less inclination to enter the war, due to the threat from Japan which will then increase." The Führer was determined not to provoke the Americans. Although Raeder told Hitler he couldn't guarantee that an accidental attack on American patrol ships intruding into the combat zone wouldn't happen, Hitler directed that a firm order go out to the *Kriegsmarine* "so that incidents are eliminated as far as possible." As if he could read Roosevelt's thoughts, Hitler, mulling his war strategy in the sparkling air of his Alpine retreat, the Berghof, refused to give his American enemy his incident.

20

The Strongest Fortress in the World

Tokyo, Washington, and Pearl Harbor, March–July 1941

Japan made no secret of its intention to drive Western powers out of their Southeast Asia colonies—the U.S. Philippines, French Indochina, Dutch Indonesia, British Malaya and Hong Kong, and the many Pacific island territories held by the West. Less than a month after Pearl Harbor became home to the American Pacific Fleet in May 1940, Japan's Ministry of Foreign Affairs declared the country's hegemony over a regional "Greater East Asia Co-Prosperity Sphere," Pacific Asia to be ruled from Tokyo, in effect Japan's version of the Third Reich. Japanese army leaders steadily beat the drum for war—with slogans echoing Germany's in Europe, including "Asia for Asiatics." Popular books depicted Japan emerging victorious following a quick war with the U.S. and British.

Feeling emboldened by the fall of Paris in June 1940, Japan moved to occupy northern French Indochina (today's Vietnam and Laos, primarily). After America responded by further boosting its support for Nationalist forces in China and embargoing shipments of scrap metal to Japan, Japan answered by signing onto the Tripartite Pact in September with Germany and Italy. Dealing with this roiling political environment and gathering information through the veil of Magic—the unreliable intercepts, decryptions and translations of Japanese radio cable transmissions—the White House struggled through diplomacy, threat of military force, tightened trade sanctions, and aid to the Chinese to "quarantine" Japanese imperial aggression.

Not everyone in Japan's leadership oligarchy favored war, but extremists held sway within the military, and few officers and government leaders would dare to show weakness in confronting the West. Those who merely questioned Japan's outward imperialism were "berated as 'pro-Western,'" remarked a Japanese admiral in later years. "People got away with the most irrational nonsense," he found, "so long as it was in the name of the 'Way of the Gods.'" Among Japanese naval officers, he said, "those men with any sense who couldn't go along with all this god stuff . . . tended to keep quiet." Those who didn't risked assassination. Surprisingly in the dangerous and often violent atmosphere of military extremism and feeble civil authority, one of the Japanese navy's earliest and loudest critics of possible war with the West became its chief architect: Admiral Isoroku Yamamoto.

As deputy naval ministry chief in 1939, Yamamoto voiced his opposition to aligning with Berlin. He thought such an alliance would prove a definitive step toward war with the United States and Great Britain, rather than a way to frighten the colonial powers out of Asia. And war, he stated, "would be a major calamity for the world, and for Japan it would mean, after several years of war [in China] already, acquiring yet another powerful enemy. . . . It is necessary therefore that both Japan and America should seek every means to avoid a direct clash, and Japan should under no circumstances conclude an alliance with Germany." He had plenty of experience with the Westerners on which to base his views.

Yamamoto knew the United States and its navy better than almost any other Japanese navy officer. Fluent in English, he had studied for two years in the U.S. and served two terms in the 1920s as naval attaché at the Washington Embassy. He was also an adviser to the 1930 London Naval Conference, and understood the intermeshing of American and

British naval power. Vivacious and charismatic, he was a rising star, at one point considered likely to be the next head of the powerful Navy Ministry.

Alarmed by his antiwar views, though, extremists set out to bring Yamamoto down. The self-proclaimed League of Diet Members Supporting the Prosecution of the Holy War, a clandestine cell known for dealing mercilessly with its opponents, warned him to resign or face death. Fearing for the life of his protégé, the then–navy minister, Admiral Mitsumasa Yonai, sent Yamamoto to sea and safety in late August 1939. Yamamoto took command of the Combined Fleet, the Imperial Japanese Navy's main fighting force. Fifty-five at the time, Admiral Yamamoto was relieved to escape the political machinations and violent rivalries that roiled Tokyo.

Subject to "direction" and "instruction" from the Navy Ministry, answerable only to the emperor, Admiral Yamamoto stood at the navy's operational pinnacle. He delighted in writing exultant poetry in praise of emperor, nature, and navy. On New Year's Day 1940, aboard his flagship, *Nagato*, he rhapsodized:

> *Today, as chief*
> *Of the guardians of the seas*
> *Of the land of the dawn,*
> *I gaze up with awe*
> *At the rising sun!*

Japan's rising sun now shone on a diminutive, round-faced, boyish-looking fleet commander in chief. Yamamoto had two great weaknesses: sweets and gambling. Once insistent that all navy officers remain in top physical shape, he allowed himself to go plump gorging on the *Nagato* pastry chef's concoctions—the navy facing few of the severe food shortages afflicting ordinary citizens. Gambling was an even more persistent vice for the admiral. He could not resist a bet and played poker, bridge, whatever game of chance he could bet on, even when aboard the *Nagato*.

But Admiral Yamamoto was the son of a samurai and a proud, self-made graduate of the august Etajima, the Imperial Naval Academy. While studying at Etajima, he was inducted into the fanatical Black Dragon Society. The *Kokuryūkai* prided themselves as latter-day samurais, ultranationalists who cut a fingertip off as proof of lifelong fealty, under penalty of death, to the emperor's unassailable divinity. His dedication to the emperor was total, and like all Japanese military officers, he longed for death to defend the glory of Tennō (the holy emperor). Tennō's position placed him in the role of chief planner for a war he did not favor. But expected to lead the fight, he thought he understood his enemy's vulnerability. The gambler now waged the greatest bet in his imperial land's history, a recklessly all-in bet that he believed was the sole hand a weaker Japan held that could trump the U.S.'s overwhelming military and economic strength.

Yamamoto specialized in naval aviation. Japan traditionally prepared its navy for massed battle between great armadas close to its island home ports. He did not think that strategy would prevail in a war with the Western powers. Japan lacked the industrial capacity, the manpower, and the oil reserves necessary to draw the British and Americans into a war close enough to the island nation's strengths for total victory. He proposed a radical change in military strategy: The country needed to project force into the enemies' strongholds, firepower sufficient to cripple them at one blow. Only through stealth and surprise would such a strike be possible. On January 7, 1941, in his *Nagato* quarters, he wrote out on nine sheets of naval stationery his "Opinions on War Preparations." Addressed to the current navy minister, Admiral Koshiro Oikawa, Yamamoto set an audacious target for the main surprise attack: the very heart of American power in the Pacific Ocean, four thousand miles from Tokyo—Pearl Harbor, home of the Pacific Fleet.

A single devastatingly cataclysmic blow would, he explained, destroy much of America's Pacific Fleet and render its principal base inoperable, stopping the enemy from projecting force against Japan while the country solidified control over conquered territory, building an Asian fortress as impregnable as Germany's in Europe. Most important, he wrote, if successful, the attack would deplete American will to fight a remote enemy "to such an extent that it cannot be recovered." He admitted, "The operation is a gamble," but he was a gambler who understood the value of preparation, bluffing, secrecy, shockingly unexpected tactics. Like all Etajima graduates, he studied closely Japan's celebrated surprise assault on the Russian fleet, resulting in decisive victory at Port Arthur in 1904 and in the war. He knew his American enemy's propensity to ignore danger, to underestimate the East, to lack discipline and resolve. A surprise attack, he wrote, "will be the most effective way of holding the U.S. Fleet in check because this is what they will least expect."

He laid out plans for a combined massive aircraft carrier task force and submarine assault on Pearl Harbor, launched with simultaneous attacks on American and British forces and occupations of the Philippines, Singapore, and other Asia Pacific strongholds. "We should do our very best at the outset of a war with the U.S., and we should have a firm determination of deciding the fate of the war on its first day." He planned for the war to be won before the enemy even knew it was at war. While Germany held U.S. and U.K. forces in check in the Atlantic, Japan could consolidate its sway over East Asia.

He concluded his long memorandum on preparations for the war with the request that when his responsibilities for organizing the attack were complete, he be relieved of overall command and placed in charge of an air fleet for the actual attack. He desired "to attack Pearl Harbor so that I may personally command that force . . . [and] so that I may be able to devote myself exclusively to my last duty to country." He knew the attack was potentially a suicidal gamble for his nation. If that bet failed, he would die happily for Tennō, his emperor, his nation, and people's gods.

The wheels of war began to grind forward. After initial resistance, Japan's military set in motion planning, training, force assembly, weaponry development, and operational organization for the never-before-attempted task of sending an air, sea, and underwater armada in secrecy nearly four thousand miles across the open ocean to within two hundred miles of the enemy's island citadel. On X-Day, the designation for the as-yet-not-finalized date for the attack on Pearl Harbor, Japan would launch a spectacular and devastating surprise aerial attack on the enemy fleet and its aerial defense forces, supplemented by submarine attacks carried out inside the enemy harbor.

Although only the top navy heads knew about Yamamoto's audacious plan, "rumors of war" were bouncing about Tokyo, according to U.S. ambassador Joseph Grew. He heard them "from many quarters, including a Japanese one." He learned from another country's diplomat that "the Japanese, in case of a break with the United States, are planning to go all out in a surprise mass attack at Pearl Harbor." He scoffed at the notion: In his diary, Grew discounted the plausibility of such an attack plan, which, he noted, "seemed fantastic." He sent word about the rumor to Secretary of State Cordell Hull, who in turn asked War secretary Stimson about the possibility.

Stimson consulted with George Marshall, the army chief of staff. Five thousand miles in the other direction from Pearl Harbor, Marshall worried about the risk of some kind of attack on Hawaii, but anticipated an attempted landing. He wrote his commanding general there, "if no serious harm is done us during the first six hours of known hostilities, thereafter the existing defenses would discourage an enemy against the hazard of an attack." Hawaii, he concluded, could readily defend itself against amphibious assault. And he did not concern himself with aerial vulnerability, not against a military installation protected by three major airfields and hundreds of fighter aircraft.

Some two months later, he again reviewed Hawaii's vulnerability to attack with a view toward possibly transferring Pacific Fleet warships over to Atlantic operations. Marshall remained adamant that the Pearl

Harbor defenses were "impregnable." In a memorandum prepared for
Stimson, he insisted, "due to its fortification, its garrison, and its physical
characteristics . . . [Oahu is] the strongest fortress in the world." Plans
were moving forward to bolster the island's air strength with additional
new and technologically advanced fighters, patrol planes, and B-17
bombers. Stimson showed Marshall's memo to the president. Marshall
concluded: "With this force available a major attack against Oahu is
considered impracticable." He was as overconfident about Pearl Harbor's
defenses as Yamamoto was about a single devastating blow depriving
America of the means and will to fight back.

The pilots of those attacking fighters and bombers would need to know
their target intimately when X-Day came. Already in December 1940,
Magic intercepts indicated that the Japanese Consulate in Honolulu
was "a hotbed of espionage," according to Major General Charles D.
Herron, army commanding general in charge of the Hawaiian district.
Report after report went out from there to Tokyo identifying schedules
and routines for the Pacific Fleet. With planning for the attack on Pearl
Harbor moving ahead fast, the Japanese navy needed a more capable and
expert eye on the scene in Oahu. In March 1941, Takeo Yoshikawa departed Japan. As he watched Mount Fuji fade into the distance, emotion
welled up inside him. "I did not expect to return alive. . . ," Yoshikawa
thought. His life had been spent in preparation for this one mission.
    Takeo Yoshikawa grew up the son of a small town police chief on
the island of Shikoku, southeast of Tokyo. He recalled his childhood in
a proud age of "manly virtues" when "the death of a young man in battle
was still likened to the fall of the cherry blossom, which alone among
the flowers drops to its death at the height of its vigor and beauty. . . ."
He was a devotee of Bushido, "the unquestioning and absolute loyalty
of the samurai" to the emperor. He swam miles daily offshore, practiced
martial arts, enriched his mind, all in expectation of serving his emperor.
He, too, joined the *Kokuryūkai*, chopping away a finger digit.

Graduating at the top of his Etajima class in 1933, Yoshikawa thought himself "the envy of my classmates" and "squarely on the road to professional advancement." He served on ships, trained in submarine warfare, and flew with the elite naval aviation service. Then disaster struck. A stomach ailment forced him from active duty. Finally, in 1936, he retired. Within a year, the navy, knowing he had been learning English, asked him to return, to develop U.S. Navy fleet expertise on the American Desk in the Third Division of the Navy General Staff, the Imperial Navy's intelligence service. Even then he believed that war with America was "inevitable."

He pursued what he called "hard and thankless" work, a scholar's toil, learning everything he could about the U.S. Navy. Yoshikawa scoured every article, news report, book, and briefing by Japanese diplomats and intelligence officers from all over the world—anything that could give him information about the U.S. Navy. "I knew," he claimed, ". . . every U.S. man-of-war and aircraft by name, hull number, configuration, and technical characteristics. I knew, too, a great deal of information about the U.S. naval bases at Manila, Guam, and Pearl Harbor." He could identify a ship in silhouette much the way a father could pick out his son from behind. He read *The New York Times* and other American publications' military correspondents' reports and every book by Admiral Alfred Thayer Mahan. "It is all there," he said of American naval strategy and facts, "if you will only take the trouble to dig for it." He pursued his intelligence studies for three long years on the American Desk "with single-minded determination," until he was the Navy General Staff's acknowledged American expert.

At the end of 1939, his chief called him into his office. "Yoshikawa," he intoned, "you are ready now." Hearing those words, he bowed—"and in my heart I rejoiced." Before long he would be sent out as a field agent, a spy. He was appointed a junior diplomat in the foreign ministry and worked there each morning to establish his professional identity, then continued his U.S. Navy studies in the afternoon. Finally, his orders came. He would go to Honolulu, where he would spy on the American fleet and bases and report back what he learned there. His mission, said the chief at Naval Intelligence in dispatching him to Pearl Harbor, was to "report on the daily readiness of the American fleet and bases." He said gravely, "I do not have to tell you the importance of the mission."

"*Hai*," Yoshikawa answered. His assent was "unquestioning. . . . My whole being was dedicated to the mission."

Even as Yoshikawa's liner steamed into Honolulu Harbor on March 27, 1941, details of Admiral Yamamoto's attack plan were still being formulated. Yoshikawa didn't know when or where the first attack would occur, but his training and experience told him that his assignment presaged war—likely before the end of the year.

His diplomatic passport gave his name as "Tadashi Morimura," posted as vice consul general at the large Japanese Consulate in Honolulu. The twenty-seven-year-old chancellor met immediately with the forty-six-year-old consul general, Nagao Kita, who had arrived earlier that same month from Japan. The senior diplomat had close ties to the navy and knew about his new chancellor's spy mission. Yoshikawa took immediately to the bluff Kita, a friendly widower who enjoyed golf, drinking, and carousing. Kita gave his young deputy plenty of cash and freedom to come and go as he pleased. As time went on and tensions mounted, the brash young spy's presence seemed to unnerve him, but he made sure nothing held Yoshikawa back.

Almost from the moment he took up his Honolulu diplomatic post, Yoshikawa effaced the hardened graduate of Etajima and samurai to become somebody he would not have recognized as himself, an alter ego he sometimes referred to as "Bobby Make-Believe." He no longer walked with the sharp stride of the Japanese naval officer. He showed up late for work or not at all. Sometimes he staggered back to the consulate compound drunk. Women spent the night in his quarters. At times he spoke so freely with the consul general that many among the shocked

staffers questioned just who this "Morimura" was. But with Kita's blessing, the hard-drinking, lazy, geisha-escorting vice consul went about his
business largely unsuspected.

He moved quickly to his task. "Of most importance," he was sure,
"would be the number of ships present at Pearl Harbor at any given
time; the number of aircraft present at the airports in the main Hawaiian islands and their dispersal patterns; naval sortie and movement
patterns from Pearl; air defense readiness; and reconnaissance activities
and security measures mounted against attack."

His diplomatic status amid the large Japanese and Japanese-
American population—eighty-three thousand in Oahu alone and nearly
that many more scattered among the other islands—made it easy for him
to move about unnoticed. Most days he walked in from his apartment
on the grounds to spend a couple hours scribbling notes at his desk
outside the consul general's office. He listened to the local radio and read
the newspapers, which reported daily on ships in port and other local
military activities. Then he strolled out to the taxi he kept on call. The
driver pulled up, sometimes with one or two tittering geishas seated in
back. And Deputy Consul Morimura disappeared.

He worked strictly alone. Never able to "find anyone whom I could
trust sufficiently," he shared nothing about his mission with others,
except for Kita.

He rented small planes to fly over the islands and from a distance
could make out the hangar and airstrip configurations at Hickam and
Wheeler army airfields. He walked nearly every day through Pearl City
to the end of the peninsula. From there he could survey the Pearl Harbor basin and ship moorings, berths for the hundred-vessel Pacific Fleet
scattered among the lochs, Battleship Row and docks, as well as the
dry docks, munitions house, oil tanks, and other facilities. He could
watch Ford Island, the naval air installation in the middle of the Pearl
Harbor basin.

Buzzing off Ford Island's airstrip and the Pearl Harbor waters were reconnaissance planes of Patrol Wing 2, mostly PBY flying boats that pushed off the aprons for water takeoffs. Inland the Army's Wheeler and Hickam airfields together were home bases to 233 fighter planes, P-36s and P-40s, with 21 new B-17 bombers scheduled to arrive soon from Boeing's assembly plant in Seattle. These aircraft formed a daunting Pacific Ocean spearhead of the American military more than two thousand miles from the nation's West Coast. Who would dare approach such a massed force?

From vantage points around Oahu, Yoshikawa watched the incoming and outgoing reconnaissance flights pass overhead and noticed that they almost never flew north. Later stories about Japan's master spy on Oahu claimed he even swam at night into Pearl Harbor itself, using a breathing straw to avoid detection while passing among the carriers and battleships of the Pacific Fleet, testing the basin bottom, searching for torpedo screens. Seeing that Ford Island protected Battleship Row from torpedo attack, he sent word that bombs and torpedoes would both be necessary to hit ships at Pearl. He noted the regularity with which the ships moved in and out of port and how most boats in the fleet tied in routinely for the weekend. Routine left the ships vulnerable.

Yoshikawa went on long ocean swims. His Shikoku Island boyhood came in handy as he swam for miles outside the breakers beyond Oahu's rugged shoreline. A speck rising and falling on the shimmering swell, he observed the shore batteries and watch posts otherwise not visible to him. He made note of underwater obstructions, tracked tides, measured how far out the shelf around the island dropped away. He took glass-bottom boat tours of Kāne'ohe Bay on the other side of Oahu to determine whether the U.S. might use it as a secondary anchorage; it was, he saw, not deep enough.

Asked by Tokyo to find out whether the navy blocked the entrance to Pearl Harbor with antisubmarine nets, he disguised himself as a laborer—unshaven, barefoot, and in an Aloha shirt—and tried to walk out to the harbor entrance. Sentries turned him back, one even leveling a gun at him, but looking from afar he guessed, wrongly, that the Americans left the mouth wide open. He tried to have his taxi driver enter Hickham Field but, lacking proper identification on the car, they were turned back. He never photographed and rarely sketched what he saw, storing details safely in memory to write out when he got back to the consulate.

"The key information" Yoshikawa wanted were potential targets, "always the number and type of ships present at Pearl Harbor and the number and type of aircraft present at the various island airfields. . . ." That information provided a valuable supplement, confirming information gathered by Tokyo's many listening posts, which picked up nearly all American radio traffic in the Pacific.

Each week he hiked the Aiea Heights and Tantalus Mountain above Honolulu. From those high vantage points he could spend hours watching the fleet ships sortie from Pearl Harbor, like fish in a bowl, and see how aircraft flew in and out of Ford Island and the timing of their reconnaissance flights. Most days ended at the Shuncho-Ro Teahouse in Alewa Heights below Aiea. He insisted on the upstairs room with the owner's convenient telescope that gave him a view of the brightly illuminated harbor. The geishas who worked there entertained American military personnel regularly and, with his clever prodding, would unknowingly gossip about the men they met, accidentally dropping bits of useful information.

Many nights, the friendly Japanese owner would let her regular patron simply stretch out on a mat to sleep off the evening's effects. Left alone in his watchtower, he thought the blazing lights of the harbor "a magnificent sight indeed." At dawn he watched first-light sorties, gathering "much useful information on ships present and deployment patterns," he later commented.

Back at the consulate the walking encyclopedia of the Pacific Fleet crafted his observations into reports. Week after week the code clerk prepared the cables in J-19 cipher, which went out under Kita's diplomatic imprimatur through a commercial radio operator in town to Tokyo. They were confident that their elaborate and changing codes kept their messages secret.

One U.S. Army intelligence official later lamented that "all hands knew that espionage was going on" through the consulate. Military watchers assigned to the consulate even knew about Morimura's daily taxi excursions. The officer later complained, "He went all over the goddamn place." He could do nothing about it. His orders were *not* to stop him. The War Department expressly forbade anything that might further poison already toxic relations with the Japanese. Nobody wanted to strike the match that lit the bonfire of war.

The FBI Honolulu bureau chief, Robert L. Shivers, did not face such strictures. He considered the two-hundred-plus consular agents "definitely a source of potential danger." Bureau headquarters in Washington sent him instructions "to conduct very thorough, complete investigations of all the Japanese consular agents." He assigned five field agents to the task. He personally questioned Kita and Morimura several times at the consulate.

"Go ahead, Mr. Kita, cruise around the island and see what you can see," Shivers mocked after hours on a visit to the consul general's office.

"Oh, no," Kita replied with a Cheshire cat grin. "Then you would follow me and chase me." Shivers did not know that Kita was not the one whose cruising around the island he should have stopped.

Spies and war warnings were far from the mind of an eight-year-old tomboy living smack in the middle of Pearl Harbor. Charlotte Coe, her five-year-old brother, Chuckie, and about a dozen other "Navy Juniors" made the northern end of Ford Island their seaside playground. "We felt free as birds," she said. Charlotte's family had lived on Ford Island since November 1940. Her father, Lieutenant Commander Charles F. Coe, a navy pilot, served as operations and plans officer, number three in the chain of command for the Naval Air Station's flight group, Patrol Wing 2. He came to Ford Island as part of the previous year's transfer of the Pacific Fleet to Honolulu. The commanding officer, Admiral Patrick N. L. Bellinger, lived next door to the Coes' house, one of the nineteen plantation-style bungalows in the loop of married officers' housing known as Nob Hill.

Charlotte and Chuckie went to school on Ford Island, took a ferry to shop in town, and otherwise ran free—outside the restricted airstrip in the center of the island. From their house's water-facing veranda, the Coes overlooked the East and Southeast Lochs toward the pineapple groves and cane fields around Pearl City and up the lush green flanks of the Aiea Heights beyond. Closer across the lochs' oily green waters was the Navy Yard, with its piers and dry docks and prehistoric bird-like cranes, storage yards, munitions house, and oil tank farm. Mostly what they saw were ships: Less than two hundred yards away, the hulls of the USS *Arizona*, *Nevada*, and *Oklahoma* rose up high and pitched like gray cliff faces out of the still water. The children lived so near those ships that evenings while lying in bed, Charlotte could hear voices from movies the sailors were watching on the main decks.

When officers off the ships ferried by gig to shore, Charlotte and her flock of friends rushed out the long pier off Nob Hill to meet them. Walking onto Ford Island often represented the officers' first steps on dry land, sometimes after weeks at sea—and often after months away from their mainland homes and families. The children swarmed them like raucous seabirds.

"They missed their own families," the skinny, freckled Charlotte realized. The long-serving officers delighted to hear the laughter of children again. When he returned from cruises, Rear Admiral Isaac C. Kidd, commander of the Pacific Fleet battleship force, had his steward hand out matchbooks with covers emblazoned with his flagship *Arizona*'s insignia to the waiting children. With his lantern jaw, cleft chin, and steely look, Kidd appeared intimidating, but when he stopped in to see Charlotte's father at their house, his face lit up at the sight of Charlotte and Chuckie. The little girl kept the *Arizona* matches he gave her with the other "ships" in her "fleet."

Then the children raced off. One of their favorite places to play lay beneath Admiral Bellinger's house, Quarters K, at the head of the loop. Built on a small rise, the commandant's house next door to the Coes' place sat atop a former artillery battery emplacement dug into the rise. The big underground chamber had a wide opening facing the harbor and concrete-lined interior rooms where shells and gunpowder had once been kept behind barred gates. Charlotte and her friends tried to scare each other inside the cool, dark fortification they called "Our Dungeon." The "Dungeon" would one day save Charlotte's life.

From Admiral Bellinger's front door, they might spy the top of the USS *Utah*'s birdcage conning tower rising along the northwestern shore of the island. That was where the *Utah* moored when the big carriers were at sea. Her resident sailors did not think they were living in anything like an Aloha paradise. The *Utah* was once the pride of the U.S. Navy; today she was the butt of other gobs' jokes. Her life began as the greatest of the Great White Fleet, one of the last dreadnoughts President Teddy Roosevelt had ordered up for his "Big Stick" Navy. Little more than a decade later, she was outmoded; then she became dispensable. The navy ordered her bombardment guns removed, turrets fixed in place; her once gleaming white hull was repainted in standard dark gray. With her former four stacks piped into a single funnel, outmoded birdcage conning tower, and untidy timber-shielded deck, she was not a pretty or tight ship.

The recommissioned *Utah* was now a floating bull's-eye, a target under steam. Pilots and gunners for aircraft operating off carrier decks practiced bombing runs against her. Sandbags stuffed into the air vents and gangways shielded the 521 seamen when the heavy water and smoke bombs burst against the decks. When she wasn't taking hits in target practice, antiaircraft trainees from other ships came on board to fire back blanks at the Douglas TBD Devastator torpedo planes and PBY seaplanes zooming in on her. While the sparring went on, belowdecks the sailor's life was steamy, smelly, tedious, noisy, potentially dangerous, yet entirely routine aboard the superannuated battleship turned seagoing shooting range.

The crew was almost as motley as the ship. Most were reservists, barely having set their sea legs. Twenty-two-year-old Don Green of Burlington, Iowa, described himself as "a man of the land at sea by dislocation." He had started at college and joined the navy reserves to supplement his income until his call-up. His darkly ironic sense of humor at finding himself in the middle of the Pacific sometimes went over the heads of what he called "the men of the sea by profession." Green as Green was at sea; happily for him he was a former semipro baseball player and had been recruited to play first base for the USS *Utah*'s baseball team almost as soon as he stepped on board. The ball field on Ford Island was a relief from life aboard a floating dartboard.

Berthed close by, twenty-five-year-old John Vaessen was a shipyard worker and electrician from Sonoma, California, who joined the reserves, sending most of what he made home to his mother. When he was called up, several regulars assured him that a posting aboard the *Utah* was like winning the lottery. The ship never steamed too far from shore and never in foul weather, and people around the country paid to vacation in its Honolulu home port.

Reality fell well short of the imagined prize. With little money in their pockets, Vaessen and his shipmate friends found themselves unwelcome anywhere beyond Honolulu's raucous and beery Hotel Street, with its bars, shooting galleries, and whorehouses. Sometimes the managers of the hotel bars and better restaurants would take one look at their navy whites and not even let them through the door. "People weren't looking to serve you," he found; "they were looking to turn you away." And liberty ashore wasn't so free in any case. The MPs were always ready to haul in men caught out late, too drunk to stagger back to base or ship, or too rowdy in uniform.

Pete Tomich, like most regulars aboard the *Utah*, wanted as little as possible to do with reservists like Vaessen and Green who now filled out the majority of the crew, just as they did on all the other ships scattered around Pearl. They were poorly trained, given too much responsibility too quickly, and had little sense of what it meant to be part of the United States Navy. At age forty-eight, Tomich was the ship's chief water tender—its head plumber—in charge of the steaming, hissing hell of the boiler room, the ship's fiery powerhouse. With no children and no kin in his adopted land, Austro-Hungarian immigrant Tomich called the navy his family, the *Utah* his home. The sweltering steel chamber encased deep in the *Utah*'s bowels that others saw as an inferno worthy of Dante was his life.

21

Geographers

Through the spring the Third Reich had gathered the largest army in history—an army well equipped, practiced, war-hardened, confident that they were on the verge of one of the greatest victory in European military annals, one exceeded only by their conquest of Western Europe. As early as April 9, the mobilization along the eastern border of Germany's conquered European territories led Churchill to tell the House of Commons that "many signs" pointed to "a Nazi attempt to secure the granary of the Ukraine and the oil fields of the Caucasus"—resources Hitler wanted, the prime minister said, "to wear down the English-speaking world." Soviet leader Joseph Stalin refused to heed warnings from the American Embassy in Moscow and questioned the veracity of shared English decryptions of German radio traffic indicating a coming German attack.

The Kremlin received more than one hundred separate reports on the German mobilization and Hitler's intention to attack. Believing the two-year-old Molotov-Ribbentrop Pact would hold, the Communist news service Tass denounced the "clumsily cooked up propaganda." Internally, the Kremlin viewed Hitler's massed forces as an effort to squeeze more grain and raw materials out of the Soviet Union for the blockaded Third Reich. War with Germany, Moscow figured, while inevitable, was entirely unlikely at the moment, not while Germany was embroiled in a life-or-death struggle with England. "Hitler," Stalin scoffed on June 12, "is not such an idiot."

On June 21 a German soldier deserted and swam across a river into a Red Army camp. He insisted that his unit would attack in the morning. Stalin sent word to have him shot for spreading "disinformation."

According to some accounts, the next day, a warm Sunday, the Soviet ruler was fishing from a boat on the Black Sea near his dacha in Sochi. Word was passed to him as he fished that three million Axis troops were at that very instant bursting across a front eighteen hundred miles long in three concentrated wedges, north, south and central. The three Nazi armies moved together with 600,000 motor vehicles—among them 3,350 tanks—and 750,000 horses. The *Luftwaffe* put 2,770 planes into the air. Upon learning of the attack Stalin supposedly tipped his line up from the water and said, "Who would have thought now?" He disappeared from sight for several days while the Russian front lit up in flame and turned to ash like newsprint before a raging fire.

In the first two days of fighting, Russia lost more than two thousand aircraft. Within a week, the German Northern Army group was halfway to Leningrad and the Central Army drove one third of the way to Moscow. The Southern Army crushed a thousand-tank Soviet mechanized counterattack in the Ukraine. The army was racing ahead so fast, advancing more than thirty miles a day, that General Gotthard Heinrici half-complained and half-rejoiced to his wife, we're "running, running until our tongues hang out, always running, running, running."

In the first week of war, six hundred thousand Red Army soldiers were taken prisoner. The vast majority were sent back behind the German lines to concentration camps, where they were systematically shot. Processing prisoners and sending them back for "special treatment" proved onerous, given the breakneck pace of the German advance. Orders changed, and Red Army prisoners were shot where they surrendered.

"We are only taking very few prisoners now," a soldier wrote to his wife, "and you can imagine what that means."

The bloodthirsty juggernaut pushed on. Panicked residents in the vital industrial centers of Stalingrad (Volgograd) and Kiev could hear the spiteful crackle of gunfire from the fighting. German foreign minister Ribbentrop bragged to his Italian counterpart Ciano, "The Russia of Stalin will be erased from the map within eight weeks." Within two weeks of the invasion, Mussolini spoke proudly to his Council of Ministers of their German allies' rapid solidifying of the political and military situation. The outcome would bring clarity to Europe: "The United States will intervene," he said, "but its intervention is already taken into account. Russia will be defeated in short order, and this may persuade Great Britain to yield."

"But," the ever-skeptical Ciano asked himself, "what if this should not be the case? If the Soviet armies should show the world a power of resistance . . . what results would this have. . . ?"

Hitler's ambitions were territorial, but his deeper mission to expand the Third Reich's German empire included elimination of "the lesser races" in conquered lands. "This is a war of annihilation," Hitler declared to his generals on March 30 during a planning session for Operation Barbarossa. As the troops moved into place, guidelines issued to them on May 19 called for "ruthless and energetic action against Bolshevik agitators, irregulars, saboteurs, Jews and total elimination of all active and passive resistance" in occupied cities and towns.

Along with the military invasion, the Nazis unleashed special military squadrons of the SS elite corps, *Einsatzgruppen*, who recruited sympathetic local civilian and fifth columnists already in place to join them in identifying and rounding up Communist Party officials, Jews, and other undesirables for mass murder. A brand of barbarism and sadism was unleashed even beyond that inflicted on the Poles. The effort to eliminate the Jewish population accelerated: Soon orders that initially called for killing all adult male Jews were extended to include women and children. By December some half a million Jews had been murdered by bullet.

Death by bullet proved too slow for the advancing Germans. In late July, Hitler's military chief and principal deputy, Hermann Göring, ordered subordinates to develop a comprehensive plan for "carrying out the desired final solution of the Jewish question." In September, the first experiments were undertaken releasing cyanide gas into a sealed chamber into which masses of people had been herded at a camp in Auschwitz, Poland.

Word of unfathomably vast massacres of civilians reached the British quickly. By the summer of 1941, British Military Intelligence was regularly decrypting intercepted German radio orders about *Einsatzgruppen* shootings in the Soviet Union. Weekly summaries of those intercepts went to Prime Minister Churchill. He acknowledged the unprecedentedly monstrous scale of the murders in an August 24 radio broadcast: "Whole districts are being exterminated," he said. "Scores of thousands— literally scores of thousands—of executions in cold blood are being perpetrated by the German police-troops upon the Russian patriots who defend their native soil. Since the Mongol invasions of Europe . . . , there has never been methodical, merciless butchery on such a scale, or approaching such a scale." Churchill went on to say, "We are in the presence of a crime without a name."

He made no mention at the time that most of those being murdered, other than Soviet prisoners of war, were Jews. However, in November he sent a public letter to a British newspaper, the *Jewish Chronicle*, acknowledging the terrible plight of the Jews before the Nazi onslaught: "None has suffered more cruelly than the Jew, the unspeakable evils wrought on the bodies and spirits of men by Hitler and his vile regime."

Although very likely aware of the ongoing slaughter of the Jews, so-called "mercy killings" of "mental defectives," and other Nazi mass murders, the U.S. government leadership did not speak publicly about these things. Questions remain in terms of how fully informed the White House was about the situation, but reliable reports filtered into the U.S. In November a regular Army Military Intelligence (G-2) briefing bulletin reached the White House that confirmed stories of systematic mass murders being carried out by the German forces and their henchmen. Based on an SS informant's statement, the G-2 report stated, with certainty, that Jews were being singled out for wholesale systematic slaughter as part of Nazi occupation plans for conquered Soviet territory: "There is no question," read the briefing, "but that the SS units are killing the Jews in many of the localities which are occupied in Russia. The normal procedure on taking over a city is to establish local commandos, check over the inhabitants, segregate the Jews, shoot them." U.S. officials may have deliberately avoided public acknowledgment of the Jewish genocide because isolationists often painted those who favored intervention most strongly as Jews and organizations supported by Jews. Others in the FDR administration, particularly in the State Department, made clear their anti-Semitism and indifference to the Jews' plight.

The American public got their first intimations about the extent of Nazi barbarism in the East from CBS journalist William Shirer. He spoke out on his lecture tour, which continued through 1941, about Nazi "mercy killings" of mentally handicapped people and efforts to annihilate the Jews and Poles. In early November 1941, speaking in Milwaukee at the Grand Avenue Congregational Church before sixteen hundred people, he said that "Germany . . . was trying to exterminate the Polish people." He went on to predict "that the Nazis would slaughter the 4,000,000 to 5,000,000 Polish Jews there and reduce the others to beaten, hungry, diseased slaves." Few people were ready to accept that sadism, inhumanity, and murder on such a scale was even possible.

*   *   *

Churchill was staying at Chequers, his weekend estate, the night of June 21. At the time nobody could be certain of Germany's true intentions or whether all was a bluff to force Russia to surrender more resources. An attack appeared imminent and Churchill told his dinner companions that should Germany invade, "Hitler is counting on enlisting capitalists and right wing sympathizers in this country and the U.S." to turn a cold shoulder to the Russians' fate. Hitler, he intoned, "is wrong." The prime minister told his guests that he intended to "go all out to help Russia" and thought America would do the same.

After dinner one of those on hand asked if "the arch anti-Communist" was not prostrating himself before a false god. Only a few weeks earlier, Churchill had condemned Stalin as "an amoral crocodile lurking in the depths." In light of the new turn of events, retorted Churchill, "Not at all. I have only one purpose, the destruction of Hitler, and my life is much simplified thereby. If Hitler invaded Hell I would make at least a favorable reference to the Devil!" However, he added, "Russia will assuredly be defeated."

He slept soundly, with his usual order that only invasion of England merited waking him early. Informed late on the morning of June 22 that the German invasion of Russia had begun, he promptly sent his valet to the room of his overnight guest, friend and fellow Conservative politician Anthony Eden. The valet presented Eden a large cigar on a silver tray and said, "The Prime Minister's compliments and the German armies have invaded Russia."

A new, vastly enlarged war had begun. Nearly everyone expected the war in the East would last no more than a few months before Hitler would ride triumphantly into Moscow as he had Paris.

The realization that the world war had entered an entirely new phase was shared on the other side of the Atlantic. When word reached Roosevelt about the Nazi drive to the east, his eyes grew wide behind his glasses. He broke into a grin. Hitler's attack on his former ally—even the West's most enduring ideological foe, Stalin—was "his first big political miscalculation," FDR reasoned. Should the invasion of Russia prove more than a brief diversion, "It will mean the liberation of Europe from Nazi domination," he wrote Admiral William Leahy, his ambassador to Vichy France. And that was his singular goal. Hitler had given him an opportunity to implement the next and perhaps most crucial step in his "sidewise" move into the Atlantic and toward the war.

Stimson, too, thought that the German invasion "offers to us and Great Britain a great chance, provided we use it promptly." He wrote the president on June 23 that the country should "push with the utmost vigor our movements in the Atlantic theater of operations . . . before Germany gets her legs disentangled from the Russian mire." He double-teamed the president with Knox, who wrote Roosevelt on the same day, "The best opinion I can get is that it will take anywhere from six weeks to two months for Hitler to clean up on Russia." That was a small window of opportunity, but Knox insisted, ". . . we must not let three months go by without striking hard—the sooner the better." Normally cautious, Admiral Stark called for FDR to "immediately seize the psychological opportunity presented by the Russian-German clash and announce and start escorting immediately. . . ."

Like most of the world outside the Kremlin, Washington anticipated the Red Army's quick collapse, in all likelihood by the end of August. Early intelligence reports depicted the worst: A U.S. military attaché in the Moscow Embassy predicted, based on a "confidential British informant," that the "Germans will reach Moscow in five days." At best, Harry Hopkins figured, Hitler had given Britain "a temporary breather." The "German Moloch," Stimson grimly foresaw, would defeat Russia in a maximum of three months and then fasten an iron hold over most of the industry, oil fields, mines, breadbaskets, and population centers of Eastern Europe. For Great Britain, a Russian collapse would be catastrophic. Almost certainly, German possession of Russia west of the Urals would unleash Japan to move north into Siberia or south into U.S., French, Dutch, and British territories. Churchill warned that "the lives and happiness of a thousand million additional people are now menaced with brutal Nazi violence." He, too, didn't think Russia would last three months.

Roosevelt was not sure how long the Red Army might endure—but he was certain that Hitler had given him an opening. He was not willing to move so hastily as his advisers wished, either by beginning convoy escorts or by extending Lend-Lease aid to the Soviets immediately. He would do what he felt he could to make Hitler's eastward turn as costly as possible, but with his characteristic caution about overstepping Americans' willingness to join the shooting war.

The opening of the Eastern Front raised complex issues for the United States. Even after FDR established diplomatic ties with the Soviet Union in 1933, the two great powers stood as ideological polestars. Capturing Americans' general dislike for both Hitler and Stalin, Missouri's junior senator, Democrat Harry S. Truman, suggested that the president provide aid to whichever side appeared to be losing, "and that way let them kill as many as possible."

Even *The New York Times* questioned the wisdom of providing American Lend-Lease aid to the Red Army. "Stalin is on our side today," an editorial read. "Where will he be tomorrow? In light of his record, no one can say that he will not switch sides again, make a sudden treacherous peace with Germany and become, in effect, Hitler's *Gauleiter* [regional leader] in the East. We should be in a fine state of affairs if we succeeded in landing a hundred bombers on Russian soil just in time for this reconciliation."

However, the *Times* did not expect reconciliation, but capitulation: "A tremendous victory for the legions of National Socialist Germany, sealing the fate of Soviet Russia, is confidently forecast," the *Times* reported after less than four weeks of fighting. "The Russians are officially reported to be throwing in 'their last reserves' in an attempt to stem the German drive along a front from the Arctic Ocean to the Black Sea."

Whatever Russia's fate, Germany's drive to the east represented an opportunity to ramp up America's presence in the Atlantic. U.S. forces were already based along Newfoundland's and Greenland's coasts. For months FDR and his closest advisers had considered the possibility of a far more brazen intrusion into the war zone, by occupying the eastern Atlantic islands that stood closest to the Western Hemisphere—the Azores, Cape Verde, and most significantly Iceland. Iceland was the most strategically important among them. As the Vikings realized a millennium ago, Iceland provided a mid-Atlantic stepping-stone between Northern Europe and North America. Hitler knew that, and toyed with the idea of taking it himself in 1940. Twenty thousand British and Canadian troops got there first, occupying the tiny nation on May 10, 1940. Those U.K. soldiers stranded in the Icelandic cold and darkness were now badly needed on the front lines in North Africa. An American takeover of Iceland would relieve the British garrison—and push U.S. forces more than two-thirds of the way toward the world at war.

In April 1941, Stimson and Knox had dispatched a team of navy planners to Iceland, eyeing port facilities and aircraft-basing sites for future American escort operations. That led to the first U.S. "combat" operation of the war. On April 10, the destroyer *Niblack*, with the team of military planners bound for Iceland, lay by while her crew took aboard sixty shivering survivors off a Dutch freighter torpedoed six hundred miles southwest of Iceland. Watches were posted in the U-boat-infested waters. The sonar ping rang through the bridge. The sound man heard a tinny return sound. A large object was fourteen hundred yards off and closing fast. "Full speed ahead!" called the commanding officer, confronting the attacker rather than risking turning broadside to a torpedo. As the ship veered away from the approaching object, the commander realized he might be starting a war, but unwilling to risk his ship, ordered an attack. Depth charges dropped astern, unleashing rumbling underwater explosions and roaring spouts of spray. No sign of wreckage or oil boiled up. The sonar lost contact. The commander felt what he termed "a curious mixture of disappointment and relief" as the *Niblack* steamed on to Reykjavik Harbor. Whether *Niblack* had dropped depth charges at a sub, a whale, cold currents, or an anxious sonar operator's case of nerves was never clear, but Germany had no record of a U-boat in the vicinity.

The *Niblack* incident happened to occur on the same day President Roosevelt decided to extend the neutrality patrol to the middle of the Atlantic, roughly out to the 26th meridian. Two days later, Oscar Cox, Harry Hopkins's legal aide, provided him with a brief contending that U.S. vessels could be used to transport men and material to the American bases recently acquired in the Atlantic—or islands that might be occupied in the future. In fact, Cox claimed, nothing in the Neutrality Act of 1939 prohibited public vessels from going anywhere with anything. Public opinion remained the key roadblock. The president wasn't ready to go all the way to the British Isles, but the German-Russian war opened a window of opportunity, and he intended to stick his head through it.

In early June, in the wake of FDR's "Unlimited National Emergency" speech, Knox and Stimson came together to urge the president to provide military "protection" for neutral Iceland. He agreed, and on July 1 the U.S. reached an agreement with the government of Iceland for the U.S. to provide for its defense. A first contingent of marines landed there a few days later. On July 8 Roosevelt told the public about the occupation, portraying it as the hemisphere's forward line of defense.

But he had now stationed American ground troops, navy ships, and aircraft on the turntable of the Atlantic, astride the main convoy routes to Britain—and possibly the Soviet Union—though also beyond the Denmark Strait, through which German U-boats regularly passed on their way to attack convoys in the mid-Atlantic Gap. The Atlantic

Fleet and naval supply ships and accompanying warships no longer strayed along the western margins of U-boat operations, but now cruised along the broad avenues beneath which they prowled. Churchill told the House of Commons that this extension of America's self-defense zone amounted to "one of the most important things that have happened since the war began."

That same day, Roosevelt secretly ordered the navy to prepare for convoy escort duty. This marked a direct attack on the Neutrality Act and prohibitions on convoys contained in the Lend-Lease bill Congress had passed. American contractors also began building military port facilities in Northern Ireland where American naval vessels and airplanes could base in event of war. The sidewise steps by the president took him and his nation to Iceland and to within a short stride of the United Kingdom and war.

When Roosevelt formally announced the occupation of Iceland, Ohio's leading senator, Robert Taft, declared, "The landing of troops in Iceland is an act exactly equivalent to aggressive war. . . . Historically and geographically, Iceland is part of Europe and we are now intervening in Europe." The fight over intervention had become an argument about geography. With his "map mind" Roosevelt knew exactly where every feature in the Atlantic lay, and with his political mind he understood the malleability of lines on a map.

At his July 8 press conference in the Oval Office, FDR again made light of the idea that some firm boundary existed in the ocean—ironically, he himself had previously declared the 26th meridian that—past which Americans could not sail in defense of their country. "Mr. President," a reporter queried, "the last time you gave us the imaginary line [demarcating the Western and Eastern Hemispheres], it ran between Iceland and Greenland. Has there been a shift in that location?" There had, indeed, been a shift in the hemispheric boundary lines, but Roosevelt dissembled.

With laugh lines spreading around his glinting eyes, Roosevelt quipped that nobody could exactly say where such a line could be found. "That is," he said to much laughter among the men crowded into the room, "as I say, depending on the geographer I had seen the previous night." He continued, "I tried very hard for a week to see if it was possible to draw a line of demarcation. Well, I gave it up." He pointed out that what actually lay inside some geographical concept of the Western Hemisphere mattered less than what actually served national security needs. "That is why you can't draw an imaginary line and put a buoy on it," he concluded.

But others were not willing to accept his rhetorical fog about geographers' meridians within which he sought to envelop the move. Moving the line, they felt, amounted to undeclared war.

Berlin reacted with fury to the U.S. takeover of Iceland. The Nazi Party's official *Völkischer Beobachter* newspaper took pity on the Icelanders: "Roosevelt has occupied Iceland, a defenseless European people, quoting as an excuse the insane fable that Germany intends to attack America." Germany understood well the game: "The truth of the matter is that Roosevelt is seeking some means of getting into the European war against the wishes of the American people and contrary to his pre-election promises. He has made this dagger thrust at Europe at a time when all Europe is uniting in ridding the world of the Bolshevik menace."

In his diary, Lindbergh considered it ". . . the most serious step we have yet taken. . . .Will Germany pick up the gauntlet we have thrown down? We have now entered her declared war zone for the avowed purpose of getting war supplies to England. It is now Hitler's move—or will he pass?" The percipient former public affairs director for America First, Sidney Hertzberg, writing in the influential pages of his "Uncensored," a mimeographed antiwar newsletter that went to isolationist editors and reporters around the country, pointed out the obvious: Reykjavik lay 2,834 miles from New York and only 670 miles from Scotland and 600 miles from Norway. ". . . Obviously," he wrote, "the occupation of Iceland is one more shortcut around the convoy issue. By keeping open the sea route to Iceland, the U.S. Navy will, in effect, be convoying British shipping as far as Iceland. . . ." Hertzberg was clear-eyed about the president's plan: "A move involving such dangers means that the President has decided to go to war now if it were necessary to protect British merchantmen. Such is the present status of aid to Britain 'short of war.'"

National polls continued to show strong opposition to American entry into the war, unless attacked. However, the same surveys showed a marked rise in support for increasing aid to Great Britain, and also to Russia and China. And the vast majority of Americans, 80 percent in a Gallup Poll, now thought America would sooner or later go to war. At the same time, just as many said now was not the time to fight. Americans seemed ready to accept the president's "sidewise" steps into the Atlantic, but they were not ready to push him all the way to war.

Infuriated by the White House's brazen move to occupy Iceland, Lindbergh now believed that war was "practically inevitable." He could no longer hold back in confronting what he'd previously referred to as the "powerful elements" pushing an unwilling nation into war. Three days after the announcement that marines were on their way to Iceland, he recorded in his diary: ". . . it is . . . essential to combat the pressure the Jews are bringing on this country to enter the war. This Jewish influence is subtle, dangerous, and very difficult to expose. . . ." He thought about ways to combat it.

At an America First rally on June 20 at the Hollywood Bowl, he drew an overflow audience of more than twenty thousand people, which organizers claimed was the largest rally of its kind in California history. Fidgeting from foot to foot, Lindbergh prophesied, "Someday in the not too distant future, the men who are responsible for this [deliberate attempt to misinform and confuse our people] will be called to account by an aroused and enlightened nation. The attempt to involve our country in the war by subterfuge and propaganda is not a crime to be passed over lightly. Public opinion will bring the charges, and history will be the judge." He was beginning to think the time had come to lay out the charges before the court of public opinion.

The war tango continued at sea. If Roosevelt hoped to entrap Hitler into firing the first shot, Hitler was unwilling to oblige his undeclared enemy. Preoccupied in the East, Hitler was not yet ready to precipitate war with the U.S.—at least not for the next month or so, until his army had Russia firmly in control. On July 9, he again ordered Admiral Raeder to restrain his navy from attacking American ships. Fear of causing an incident with the Americans brought a respite from U-boat attacks. North Atlantic convoys began to pass unmolested. Not a single ship was sunk for the rest of the summer.

The need to establish an integrated convoy escort system and, should war come, for the U.S. and Great Britain to identify common peace aims necessitated high-level conversations. FDR turned again to his straight talker and alter ego to get the conversation going. Hopkins and Roosevelt huddled for hours after dinner on Friday, July 11. They discussed the logistical challenges of supplying the Soviets; the continued threat to the Atlantic convoys; and Lend-Lease snarls in Washington and London. The president also made clear he wanted to meet "in some lonely bay or other" with Churchill to "talk over the problem of the defeat of Germany," but he insisted to Hopkins he was not going to meet the prime minister to discuss going to war.

He did have a present for his envoy to bring Churchill. FDR pulled out a copy of *National Geographic*, from which he tore out a small map of the Atlantic Ocean. He drew a pencil line on it, dotted at the top of Greenland, running south in a semicircle bulging out to about two hundred miles east of Iceland, then hooking around Iceland's southern coast. From there the line ran straight down, south through the Azores

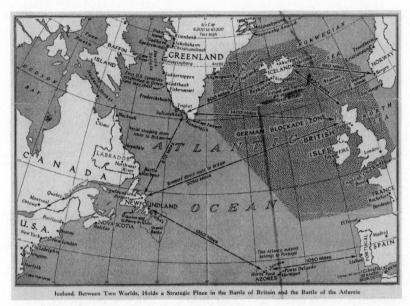

Iceland, Between Two Worlds, Holds a Strategic Place in the Battle of Britain and the Battle of the Atlantic

President Roosevelt penciled the line indicating the easternmost line of U.S. Atlantic patrols on this map from National Geographic *brought by Hopkins to his second meeting with Churchill, on July 17, 1941.*

and on to the page's edge. The Atlantic Fleet would police everything west of the line—virtually the entire Atlantic Ocean would henceforth compose the U.S. Neutrality Zone. The British could focus on escorting the most treacherous seas immediately around the British Isles—the Bay of Biscay south to Gibraltar and the Mediterranean Sea—as well as protection of ships now trafficking north on the "Murmansk Run" to Russia. Hopkins took the map and went off to pack.

In the early morning of July 13, with so little fanfare that almost nobody else in the White House knew he was gone, Hopkins climbed aboard a B-17 Flying Fortress. The big bomber stopped in Gander, Newfoundland. From there he flew in the cold, noisy, airless belly of a twin-tail B-24 Liberator, one in a formation of twenty Lend-Lease bombers droning nonstop through the white northern night to England.

22

Son of a Harness Maker

London and Moscow, June–July 1941

Harry Hopkins arrived in England to find a land dramatically changed in the six months since his previous visit. The American "soft invasion" had begun. Much of that was a direct result of his efforts. U.S. military "observers" were trickling steadily into London, gathering into an enlarging force centered on the embassy. The Royal Air Force had already flown Flying Fortresses in raids over Germany. The Blitz had ended, German bombing raids into England having ceased in May, and the toll of ship sinkings had fallen off dramatically. Fiercer-than-expected fighting inside Russia, too, cheered morale. Hopkins sensed that if the weight of two years of war, much of that in a lonely fight, had not been enough to crush the English, nothing would. He could justifiably take pride in seeing that his Lend-Lease handiwork had buoyed the British Isles. Germany's Russian turn gave him the impetus to do more than keep them afloat. He was ready to solidify the alliance to win World War Two.

On July 17, Hopkins went to No. 10 Downing Street. He and Churchill sat on the rear terrace enjoying the view toward the sun-drenched trees lining St. James's Park. The smoke from Hopkins's cigarette and Churchill's cigar mingled in the summer air. They now talked not just as national representatives but comfortably as friends with a singular, shared passion to win the war. They discussed the state of the fight, political affairs in both countries, and the accelerating but still uneven buildup of the American war industry. Hopkins pulled out the *National Geographic* map with Roosevelt's line penciled in to show Churchill the enlarged area that the Americans now meant to "police." The prime minister was of course delighted that this latest eastward step would put American navy ships deeper in the North Atlantic shipping lanes, directly on a line with Ireland's western coast. Churchill pushed to define what Hopkins meant by "policing through the zone." Hopkins refused to take the bait to describe this as convoy escort. He impressed upon Churchill Roosevelt's desire that the two leaders meet in person.

Along with extensive meetings with Harriman about Lend-Lease and military advisers about the accreting American presence, plus tours around ports and Lend-Lease intake facilities, Hopkins met twice in London with the Soviet ambassador to Great Britain, Ivan Maisky. Hopkins cared above all about gauging the chances Russia had for holding out against the Germans. Vicious fighting was going on in Smolensk, just 250 miles from Moscow, German forces threatened to encircle Leningrad (St. Petersburg) in the north, and much of Ukraine had been overrun. The Soviet ambassador explained the relative strategic importance of each region and noted that a great deal of Soviet industry had already been relocated beyond the Ural Mountains. Russia intended to fight on even if its major cities fell. Maisky had been pressing the British to open a "second front" to relieve German pressure in the East and asked Hopkins for the same, of course a political impossibility.

Hopkins asked what the Red Army "required" to keep fighting and how best to bring Lend-Lease munitions safely and swiftly to the battlefield. Maisky could not say what Russia had to have; only Stalin could. He encouraged Hopkins to meet with Stalin. This was not part of the president's plan in sending him to Europe. On July 25 Hopkins cabled Roosevelt: "I am wondering whether you think it important and useful for me to go to Moscow." While Hopkins shared the commonly held view that Russia was just a temporary respite for the British, he was keen to deliver whatever Lend-Lease supplies America could offer—and to bolster Soviet morale for a fight he hoped would continue as long as possible to relieve his British friends of their war burden. But the U.S. could ill afford to hand over weapons that would fall into German hands.

Hopkins also took the opportunity while in England to tell the British people personally that they were no longer fighting alone. Speaking from Churchill's estate, Chequers, on Sunday, July 27, Hopkins broadcast a speech which he had written together with the London-based American journalist Quentin Reynolds. His voice went out over BBC radio to the entire United Kingdom and to listeners on the Continent. In his unmistakably Midwestern American voice he declared, "I did not come from America alone. I came in a bomber plane, and with me were twenty other bombers made in America."

He elated listeners all over England and those in Europe who dared to tune in the BBC as he used the kind of fiery tone and leveled insults previously not heard from an American official. "The President," he intoned, "is at one with your prime minister in his determination to break the ruthless power of that sinful psychopath in Berlin." The United States had not entered the war, but the benefits of Lend-Lease and FDR's short-of-war policy were real—and with or without America in the shooting war, FDR had through Hopkins pledged that Hitler and his Thousand-Year Reich would not endure.

Shortly after finishing his radio talk, Hopkins left the prime minister's weekend retreat. A specially arranged train awaited him, as did an American-made RAF PBY Catalina in Invergordon on the east coast of Scotland. His nonstop flight was bound for Archangel, two thousand miles away in northern Russia; from there he would travel six hundred miles south to Moscow. The war in the East was now more than a month old. Badly bloodied, Russia was holding on, but nobody in the West knew for how much longer. The time had come to see what it would take to keep Stalin fighting.

Hopkins was about to leave when he asked the prime minister what personal message he might carry on his behalf to Stalin. "Tell him, tell him," Churchill said as his American friend stepped into his car. "Tell him that Britain has but one ambition today, but one desire—to crush Hitler. Tell him that he can depend upon us. . . ." Hopkins could not know whether Stalin, enigmatic and bloody-handed dictator of a gigantic Soviet empire, would believe those words. Or if he should believe what Stalin might tell him. No high American official had ever before met the leader of the largest nation on earth.

That evening, as Hopkins sped north, Germany retaliated—both for Hopkins's speech and for Britain's steadily intensifying bombing raids on German cities. German bombers blasted London during a raid that lasted two hours without letup. It was the first attack on the city since May 10.

The following day, Churchill telegraphed Stalin to tell him how important Harry Hopkins had proved for Great Britain. "I must tell you," he assured the dictator, "that there is a flame in this man for democracy and to beat Hitler. He is the nearest representative of the president. A little while ago when I asked him for a quarter of a million rifles they came at once. . . ." The same could be true for Russia, he cabled. "You can trust him absolutely. He is your friend and our friend. He will help you plan for the future victory and for the long-term supply of Russia." Harry Hopkins, Churchill told Stalin, traveled on a mission with a single goal: of stopping and, one day, destroying Hitler.

Hopkins left for Russia unsure of what he would find. The war front in Russia had been closed to American reporters and embassy personnel. Based on hearsay and refugees fleeing the advancing German army, the reports from U.S. intelligence officers in Moscow had been unremittingly pessimistic. Flying into the Moscow airport, he could see scattered bomb damage from the first German air raids on the city. On the drive from the airport, he passed through Moscow "streets [which had been] . . . narrowed into lanes by the overflow of thousands of mothers with their children, camped on their sacks of belongings. . . ," reported famed *Life* magazine photographer Margaret Bourke-White, who had come to town just a few days before Hopkins. Refugees fleeing the Nazi advance jammed Moscow while thousands of terrified Muscovites readied to leave. The American ambassador told Bourke-White to keep her bags packed, on alert to go on short notice.

On Hopkins's first night in the American ambassador's elegant neoclassical mansion known as Spaso House, he went to the roof. "The Germans took a hand in welcoming me to Moscow," he recalled when he got back home. Whistling bombs fell and exploded around the city. Antiaircraft fire answered. A week earlier, a German bomb had demolished a theater not fifty yards from the spot where he stood, shattering windows in Spaso House. Parties held in Hopkins's honor were moved into an underground shelter in a subway station specially set aside for him.

Hopkins stepped out of his car at the Kremlin three days after leaving Scotland. "I couldn't believe it," he told a friend later. "There I was, walking up the staircase of the Kremlin, going to talk to the man who ruled one hundred-eighty million people. And I kept asking myself—what are *you* doing here, Hopkins, you, the son of a harness maker from Sioux City?" He fully recognized the significance of his responsibility: "I had executed a number of assignments for the president. None had impressed me more." His bony frame carried the weight of civilization's future.

Stalin knew nothing of Hopkins's unique place in the American leadership firmament before he'd received Roosevelt's telegram inviting him "to treat Mr. Hopkins with the identical confidence you would feel if you were talking directly to me." The Soviet ruler laid out as plush a red carpet as a nation under siege could manage for this tall, shrunken and sallow American who seemed to live in his overcoat—and under a comically oversized hat given to Hopkins by Churchill after he lost his own.

Over the next three days the two men met twice in Stalin's enormous, sparsely furnished, wholly silent Kremlin office. Hopkins noticed that few people dared speak above a whisper anywhere in the Kremlin. Fear of the sixty-two-year-old Stalin who had ruled the Soviet Union for twenty years was palpable. "No man could forget the picture of the dictator of Russia," Hopkins wrote a few months later, ". . . an austere, rugged, determined figure in boots that shone like mirrors, stout baggy trousers, and snug-fitting blouse. He wore no ornament, military or civilian. . . ." His style of speech fit his appearance, found the American: "If he is always as I heard him, he never wastes a syllable. . . . He curries no favor with you. . . ." The two men shared a plainspoken approach and an indifference to the frills of office and accoutrements of power.

As Stalin spoke of Hitler's treachery, his translator relaying his words, he clenched and unclenched his fists. "His hands seemed to feel for something," noticed Hopkins. Stalin appeared momentarily overwhelmed by the effort to keep his fury under control. "We sat in silence until he relaxed again." Hopkins found that "[Stalin's] was a personal hatred [for Hitler] that I have seldom heard expressed by anyone in authority. . . ." Stalin made clear that he would fight the German enemy to the death. But he expected to check the Nazi advance. He confidently predicted, "They will never get to Moscow this year," and, if aid was forthcoming, he said, "we can fight for three or four years."

Hopkins was surprised by the Russian leader's certainty about the future course of the war when the enemy was nearing the distant outskirts of Moscow at that very moment. "He seems to have no doubts," he recalled. "He assures you that Russia will stand against the onslaughts of the German army. He takes it for granted that you have no doubts, either. . . ." Stalin was eager to convey his utter certainty, to convince the American that U.S. aid would enable the Red Army to withstand the powerful Nazi force—and not for just a few months, as many predicted—and would eventually turn the tables and defeat the Germans.

Both men chain-smoked. Hopkins enjoyed the harsh Russian cigarettes, with their long, hollow stems. Stalin preferred the unfiltered American brands, provided for him regularly by the U.S. Embassy. The presidential envoy found he could talk with this man whom most Americans derided, absolute leader of an empire bound within an economic and social system most at home loathed. Hopkins expressed Roosevelt's commitment to defeating the Nazis. Stalin replied through his interpreter, "Therefore our views coincide."

From there, the two were soon immersed in the specifics of the situation at the front, Russian needs (light antiaircraft guns, aluminum for airplane construction, machine guns, rifles, said Stalin), preferred delivery routes (Vladivostok, in the Far East of Siberia), and the aid Washington could realistically provide. The second time the two men met, Hopkins asked for and received what he considered "complete knowledge" of the military situation and details about Red Army weaponry and factory capacity.

Stalin assured Hopkins that the Germans faced far more opposition than they anticipated, and not just of the military sort. "Moving mechanized forces through Russia was very different than moving them over the boulevards of Belgium and France," Hopkins said Stalin explained to him. When he flew over Russia, Hopkins had been impressed at the challenge any invader faced to conquer such a vast, largely roadless land, with its seemingly unending miles of forests and steppes. Stalin detailed the capacities of Russian factories, which were churning out vast quantities of weapons to resupply the armies. Hopkins had seen the Volga River jammed with barges carrying munitions to the front.

While Germany's mechanized army moved fast, strategically little had changed since Napoleon's invasion early in the previous century. The deeper Germany fought into Russia, the more extended its lines of supplies and communications became, rendering them increasingly vulnerable. As Nazi panzer forces advanced, they could be subjected to flanking maneuvers and partisan attack from the rear. Stalin assured Hopkins that once the autumn rains began, the mechanized German units would bog down. By October, when winter weather set in, the attackers would become the defenders. But Russian munitions would wear thin, and by the spring, Stalin admitted, the Red Army would face acute supply shortages. He urged the two Western powers to open a second front in Europe, to relieve his forces, and welcomed American aid in whatever form, he said. Hopkins assured him that the president was ready "to extend all possible aid to the Soviet Union at the earliest possible time." The Communist dictator smiled. He even invited American troops to fight within Russia, under U.S. military leadership, a notion so fabulous that before that instant it would have been impossible to contemplate.

When the front stabilized after the winter, Hopkins assured Stalin, the American president would be prepared to meet the Soviet leader in person. Then, with a swift handshake, a hint of a smile, and few formalities, Stalin prepared to bid Hopkins goodbye. Before the two men parted, though, Bourke-White arrived to shoot several photographs of them together. She managed to capture something close to a smile creasing the Russian autocrat's pockmarked face. But as the portrait session ended, all traces of emotion passed from Stalin, she noted, "as though a veil had been drawn over his features. . . . as if he had been turned into granite. . . ." Bourke-White stayed on several more weeks to produce a photographic spread that ran in *Life* and a book about her journey around Russia at war that would go a long way to humanize the Russians' struggle for Americans.

The frail American flew back to Archangel, carrying with him the detailed notes from his talks with Stalin laying out the Red Army's present positions, Russia's needs for munitions and raw materials, its industrial losses to date and remaining capacity, as well as his impressions of Stalin and the wider strategic outlook. He would carry them to Roosevelt and Churchill. Those notes, and his confidence in Stalin as a leader and as a potential war ally, marked the start to an entirely new relationship among London, Washington, and Moscow. Hopkins

Hopkins and Stalin when they met in the Kremlin in late July as the Soviet front appeared to be near collapse.

clutched in his briefcase what amounted to the foundations of strategic policy and tactical planning for defeating Hitler.

If he made it home.

He flew in the rear of the Catalina through the long Arctic day, sitting on a small saddle seat in the bubble near the tail gunner's position. He was freezing, exhausted after thousands of miles of steady travel—he still hated flying—endless nights in bomb shelters, and long days of unrelieved tension while meeting with the leaders of two besieged nations. He was a man kept alive by nutrient injections, cigarettes, and willpower. Somewhere over the North Sea, his flying boat began to buck, and then it pitched with gut-wrenching force upward. Antiaircraft fire burst around the wings. The pilot never learned the source of the attack, whether friendly fire or German. He zoomed steeply up and safely out of range.

Finally, on August 2, just a week after Hopkins went to Moscow, the aircraft splashed down on the tossing Scapa Flow. Bone-weary, deathly ill, and weak, Hopkins had a military doctor shoot him with drugs to knock him out for the night. Some feared he might never awaken. The following day, though, somewhat revived, he stepped onto a launch from the HMS *Prince of Wales*, the Admiralty's flag battleship. Aboard the big warship, a beaming Winston Churchill greeted his American friend. Virtually his entire foreign affairs staff and military command stood alongside on the deck. Churchill took his friend for a walk around the ship. Despite almost two months in dry dock, she still showed dings and scars, reminders of the shootout with the *Bismarck*.

Gathering about the *Prince of Wales* like bodyguards, escort destroyers moved into formation alongside the great ship. The flotilla churned past the shelter of the Orkney Islands and into the North Atlantic U-boat hunting grounds.

23

The Obvious Conclusion

Washington and Tokyo, June–August 1941

When word of Hopkins's trip to Moscow got back to the United States, an "Eastern Front" in the war of words broke out. Speaking in San Francisco, Lindbergh declared he "would a hundred times rather see my country ally herself with England, or even with Germany with all of her faults, than the cruelty, the godlessness, and the barbarism that exists in Soviet Russia." Under the headline "Harry and Joe in the Kremlin," the *Chicago Tribune* wrote sarcastically, "Strange events have made Joe [Stalin] a champion of [the Four Freedoms]." The editorial writer asked, "Did Harry feel any uneasiness when he found himself in the presence of the veritable Stalin asking him how the United States might aid him wrest Europe from another fellow of the same stripe?" Despite unease with this newfound ally, many newspapers voiced the widely shared conviction, as Hopkins's hometown *Sioux City Journal* wrote, "that Hitlerism must and shall be destroyed." Many might agree, but a large portion of Americans remained unconvinced that Hitler threatened *their* hearth and home.

Across the Pacific Ocean, Japan seemed even more remote—certainly a greater enigma. Russia had far more experience with Tokyo's aggressiveness. With Japan near its far eastern rump and tensions high, the Kremlin under German assault feared that another Axis member would attack. Several hundred thousand Red Army troops remained fixed along the southern Siberian border in expectation that Japanese forces in occupied Manchuria might take advantage of the German invasion to drive off its historic enemy to the north. While in Moscow, Hopkins heard Soviet concerns about Japan. Foreign Minister V. M. Molotov warned him that "the Japanese would not hesitate to strike if a propitious time occurred." The Nazi invasion of the Soviet Union and the Red Army's slowing of the Nazi advance may have clarified the picture in Europe. But the changing situation blew more smoke over the already tenebrous and unsettled situation in the Far East. Japan's next move was anybody's guess.

Roosevelt received regular gleanings from the Magic decodes of radio intercepts, and based on them and on reports from Ambassador Grew in Tokyo and Secretary of State Cordell Hull, who was in negotiations to resolve differences between the countries with Japanese diplomats in Washington, he tried to read the tea leaves. But little clarity emerged. One day the presentiments had it that Japan would soon attack to create an "Asia for the Asians," and the next day that Tokyo was willing to continue negotiations with genuine hope of preventing war with the West.

Should war come, the White House remained uncertain which direction Japan's military might take to break the island nation free from its perceived encirclement by enemies. Some advisers assured the president that Japan would strike north against its historic Russian enemy, given Russia's current preoccupation with the Germans; others predicted that, freed of concern about Russian aggression, Japan would instead push south. Even Japan's Axis ally Hitler—who had not informed Tokyo before launching the invasion of the Soviet Union—did not know Japan's true intention. He anticipated Japan would help precipitate Russian collapse, and told his military leadership at his Eastern Front headquarters in late August that he was "convinced that Japan will carry out the attack on Vladivostok as soon as forces have been assembled."

With America's attention riveted on the European war, above all FDR hoped to avoid armed conflict in the Pacific as long as possible. War might eventually prove inevitable in Asia, but he hoped that his four years of "quarantine" policy would continue to hold Japan's extremist faction in check. To make Tokyo hesitate to provoke a war, he intended to ratchet up the embargo of various vital American products; to position additional bombers, now starting to come off the assembly lines, in Pearl Harbor and the Philippines; and to bolster forward marine garrisons and add to navy air patrols in American Pacific possessions, including Wake and Midway Islands.

The most effective economic weapon in the president's arsenal remained oil and aviation fuel. The U.S. supplied 80 percent of Japanese crude oil and more than 90 percent of its aviation fuel. Stopping their flow would devastate Japan's economy and its war-making capacities. Japan possessed sufficient reserves to meet its needs for just another one and a half to two years. The threat of an American cutoff rattled Japan's already fervently anti-Western military leaders.

The embargo threat, though, produced the opposite effect than the one FDR was expecting. Tightening the cutoff of trade represented an existential threat to Japan. The military in particular was now determined to wrest control of the oil, tin, rubber, and other raw materials of Southeast Asia and to establish a protective moat around Japan through hegemony over China, Indochina, the Philippines, and the South Pacific islands to Australia. War was their response to embargo.

The war faction in the White House pushed for confrontation, weighing in the direction of stronger measures against Japan. The ever-belligerent Ickes urged the president to cut off all oil forthwith. FDR responded that this might "tip the delicate scales and cause Japan to decide to attack Russia or to attack the Dutch East Indies," neither action helping to enhance American defense interests.

On the same day the U.S. and Iceland reached their basing agreement, July 1, Roosevelt sought to explain his dilemma in a letter to a frustrated Ickes, who was increasingly feeling shut out of decision making by the president. At the moment, FDR explained, the best thing the U.S. could do was to sit tight in the Pacific. Thanks to Magic, he knew there was what he called "a real drag-down and knock-out fight" going on among Japanese leadership oligarchs, who were "trying to decide which way they are going to jump—attack Russia, attack the South Seas (thus throwing their lot definitely with Germany), or . . . sit on the fence and be more friendly with us." FDR threw up his hands. He couldn't control the situation, but he also didn't want to force the rash Japanese to act. "No one knows what the decision will be but," he explained, "as you know, it is terribly important for the control of the Atlantic for us to help keep peace in the Pacific. I simply have not got enough Navy to go round—and every little episode in the Pacific means fewer ships in the Atlantic." For now, time was America's, and not Japan's, friend. He needed to win time.

That time might be running out of the hourglass was also on the minds of the imperial leadership of Japan when they met the very next day in an Imperial Conference. Imperial Conferences were rare, generally held solely to provide the emperor's gnomic blessing for war plans. They took place in the First Eastern Hall of the Meiji Palace, within central Tokyo's vast palace compound. The great hall itself was an amalgam of East and West; purple silk with a floral pattern lined the walls, against which stood richly carved wooden furnishings. Japanese crystal patterns on Western-type chandeliers hung from a black lacquered ceiling coffered with gold embossing high over a gleaming parquet floor. In its midst stood a long black conference table draped in brightly colored silks.

The emperor sat at the head of the table in front of a ceremonial gold Meiji screen. Today he wore a military uniform, a dark blue tunic thick with gold shoulder braids, medals, and a sash, befitting his role as head of the army and navy. Despite his uniform and royal authority, his role by tradition was to sit in silence, by his presence to make the will of the Japanese nation and heaven's harmonious assent felt in the earthly proceedings.

Seated around the table benignantly overseen by the emperor, the key state ministers, wearing tails, and military service chiefs in full dress uniform spoke in highly stylized dialogue and presentations. While virtually all matters had been settled in advance, the attendees were expected to make a ritual show before the emperor that decisions had not been taken lightly. Deliberations rarely surprised, but policy advocates were expected to develop their arguments. Even Emperor Hirohito found such gatherings "a curious thing," he later commented. "The emperor had no deciding power," but sat there in silence as a floating figure, like a tableau vivant in the midst of a traditional play, as if this were political Kabuki theater.

The emperor's questions were placed through his emissary, the head of the Privy Council, at the table. Only a few of the men at the table had ever heard Tennō utter a word. They could not help but nervously study the man sitting before them. Nobody in the chamber doubted that he was the "Emperor of Heaven," the sacred embodiment of national unity, a ruler in whose service every Japanese citizen would willingly sacrifice his life and that of his children. The council itself had no formal authority, yet never had its decisions been overturned.

The continued effectiveness of Soviet resistance against the Nazis overcame the arguments of the northern-leaning proponents. After two hours of discussion the conference adjourned, having blessed the predetermined move to occupy French Indochina. France's Vichy government was in no position to resist a force coming in by "invitation" to defend against possible English aggression from Malaysia. The expectation was that violence would not be necessary, but if war came with Britain and the United States, the policy declared, "The Empire shall not flinch. . . ."

When Admiral Isoroku Yamamoto learned about the policy decision, he was shocked. "Are we really ready for an aerial war?" he asked. Navy chief of staff Osami Nagano, the leading voice at the Imperial Conference in support of the southern strategy, reacted as if hidden forces beyond any individual's power to stop had carried the policy to approval. "What can I say?" he answered another worried admiral's query. "The government decided on it."

A few days later, massed Japanese forces occupied French Indochina, effectively positioning them to interdict movement into China over the vital Burma Road and to threaten neighboring British and Dutch territories. Responding to the latest aggression, FDR froze Japanese U.S. bank holdings and halted trade in most American raw materials and manufactured products, but for now he permitted continued sale of aviation-grade petroleum. Ickes thought this brand of "appeasement" amounted to "slip[ping] the noose around Japan's neck and giv[ing] it a jerk now and then." Ickes had been pushing for war since the attack on the *Panay* almost four years before: "Naturally I am in favor of a complete job as quickly as possible. . . . This will be fooling the country again as we fooled it" before, into thinking that somehow war might be avoided.

The president's intention was to squeeze Japan's windpipe just enough to scare, not close it off entirely. Dean Acheson, an assistant secretary in the State Department, decided to pull the noose taut. Ignoring the specifics of FDR's trade interdiction, he used his trade authority to halt all aviation fuel shipments. The embargo intended to hold off war as long as possible now left Japan feeling "like a fish in a pond from which the water was gradually being drained away," said one Japanese official.

Roosevelt would not learn about Acheson's independent action until September, at which point it was too late to reverse the decision. After receiving word of the embargo, U.S. ambassador to Japan Joseph C. Grew recorded privately, "The vicious circle of reprisals and counter-reprisals is on. . . . Unless radical surprises occur in the world, it is difficult to see how the momentum of this downgrade movement in our relations can be arrested, nor how far it will go. The obvious conclusion is eventual war."

He knew from nearly a decade in Tokyo that such a war would be unlike anything modern Americans had experienced. "The Japanese will not crack," Grew contended. "They will not crack morally or psychologically or economically, even when eventual defeat stares them in the face. They will pull in their belts another notch . . . and fight to the bitter end."

24

At Last We've Gotten Together

Argentia Bay, Newfoundland, Canada, August 1941

As the dog days of summer chomped down on Washington, D.C., the withering heat and humidity pressed hard on city residents. On Capitol Hill, the battle over renewing the nation's first peacetime draft added more hot air to the already steamy chambers. Just two months were left until the Selective Service Act and the army's conscription powers lapsed and the first of its nine hundred thousand draftees—the O.H.I.O., for "Over the Hill in October," crowd—would start for home after a year's training for a war that didn't come. Roosevelt warned Congress that it would be held accountable if its members "let America risk the fate which has destroyed the independence of other nations." Those were fighting words among the isolationists on the Hill.

North Carolina senator Robert R. Reynolds led the fight against renewal. The powerful chairman of the Military Affairs Committee and senior Foreign Relations Committee member was notorious not only as the lone Southern isolationist; Unc Bob—Buncombe Bob to opponents—also published the monthly *American Vindicator*, giving a bullhorn and using his Senate franking privileges to disseminate his anti-Semitic, fervently nativist, and anti-Communist viewpoints. The fifty-seven-year-old senator was admittedly distracted during the debate by preparations for his fifth marriage, this one to a twenty-year-old heiress.

Urging an end to the draft, Reynolds accused the administration of whipping up fears of invasion and fascism. He railed against the media for "false propaganda delivered daily" via newsreels, radio, and newspaper, and assailed Hollywood movies that vilified Germans as devious spies out to undermine the nation and Hitler as a psychopathic bumbler and murderer. Reynolds asserted that renewing the conscription act, which declared that America faced "a state of national peril," was as good as giving the president permission to become an "active, participating, shooting ally of Russia and Great Britain."

Despite the fiery words, once speeches were delivered and votes cast, Reynolds slipped out of town for his honeymoon and for fresher climes. With the tar bubbling on Pennsylvania Avenue and syrupy humidity overspreading Foggy Bottom, anyone else who could escape the District of Columbia in the last days of July joined him in getting away.

The president's flag, however, flew steadily atop the White House. Trapped by the global crisis and the push-pull of political infighting raging around him, Roosevelt lived within the whitewashed sandstone prison. He had barely ventured out of Washington since his unsatisfying Florida fishing cruise in March. The effects of his sequestration were telling. After each speech denouncing Hitler's "murder of small nations" or press conference explaining the imperative to arm resisting countries, now including the Soviets, he studied polls to gauge how his words played. Invariably the numbers showed steady support for actions undergirding his "short-of-war" policy of aiding the British and the Chinese; they also indicated that opposition to sending American boys into the fight was still running as high as 80 percent. "All these polls omitted one factor," Stimson complained after a particularly frustrating phone call with the president, "which he seemed himself rather to neglect—namely . . . the power of his own leadership." Harry Hopkins, the man who knew Roosevelt best, agreed "he would rather follow public opinion than lead it" to war.

Feeling unable to move more decisively than "sidewise," after each step over the past two months FDR retreated again to the sanctuary of the White House second-floor living quarters and his family's place in Hyde Park to ponder the next step. Treasury's Morgenthau found the president slumped "into a state of innocuous desuetude again," possibly due to the political trap he was in, but also perhaps because of chronic bleeding hemorrhoids as a result of sitting too long in his wheelchair. Thus, nobody around the West Wing was much surprised when, in late July, word circulated that, despite the important and vitriolic debate in Congress over the selective service renewal bill, the president was taking a vacation. The White House announced to the press that Roosevelt was going fishing. He was heading out August 3 for ten days of cruising around Cape Cod.

Nothing cheered FDR like the prospect of time on the water. He came to work "with a flare-up of the old gusto," remarked brain truster Rexford Tugwell after he met with the president. He took charge of the August 1 Cabinet meeting with a feistiness rarely seen of late. Much of the meeting was devoted to the seemingly desperate Soviet situation. Hitler was fastening his death grip around a badly wounded Russia. Smolensk had fallen; Kiev was under bombardment; German forces were closing on Moscow itself; a million Red Army troops had already fallen or been taken prisoner. At the meeting, FDR hammered home the need to reprioritize a shipment of planes crated up and just now being loaded for transshipment to Great Britain. He ordered the precious aircraft—190 P-40 fighters and 10 B-17 bombers—instead flown across the country and over the Pacific to the Red Army in Siberia—"right off with a bang next week," insisted Roosevelt.

Stunned by another example of the president's style of policy making, as Stimson criticized it, "with a cigarette holder," he protested that the English were barely holding on in North Africa, putting the Nazis in position to take the vital Suez Canal, and were depending on those airplanes. Moreover, he protested, sending them to the collapsing Red Army would almost certainly result in their being lost to the Nazi onslaught, probably within days of reaching the front. He quickly regretted his words.

Despite what Stimson may have read in the newspapers and intelligence briefings, Roosevelt knew things nobody else at the table knew. He had heard from envoy Hopkins, flying back at that moment to Britain from his just-completed mission to Stalin and the Kremlin. Hopkins had cabled FDR "that I feel ever so confident about this front. The morale of the population is exceptionally good. There is unbounded determination to win." Stalin had convinced his trusted aide that the Red Army could hold off the Germans for longer than anyone outside Russia believed. Hopkins urged the president to make an immediate concrete demonstration of real support for Stalin. Along with the signal that the U.S. meant what Hopkins had told Stalin, a substantial addition to the Red Army air force could help extend Hitler's Eastern Front diversion into a painful sojourn on the Russian steppes.

The Cabinet sat in stony silence while FDR lectured for forty-five minutes on the disposition of forces along the Eastern Front and described the difficulties even Hitler's mighty army faced in conquering the Soviets. By the end of the meeting, Stimson was looking "thoroughly miserable," noted Morgenthau.

"The only answer I need to hear is that it is under way," said the president about the fighter shipment. He jabbed a finger at Stimson: "Use a heavy hand—act as a burr under the saddle and get things moving." He added a last kick in the pants of the elder statesman: "Step on it!"

The weight of the world seemed to have dropped from his shoulders. *Time* magazine's White House correspondent reported on the president's closing up shop before his vacation. "Franklin Roosevelt," he wrote, "patted his perspiring forehead and glanced at his cluttered desk. There was the same old optimistic cast in his eye. It was still possible to hope, in spite of all, that the U.S. would not have to get in a shooting war." Roosevelt's timing was just right, the reporter thought: ". . . it was a good time to take a vacation."

Congressional isolationists found an easy target for their acid over the president's heading out onto the water. On the Senate floor, John A. Danaher, a Republican from Connecticut, read a newspaper headline: "President Departs on Carefree Vacation." In a voice dripping with sarcasm, he intoned, "Congress is asked to declare a state of national peril and the president goes on a cruise."

At eleven in the morning on Sunday, August 3, 1941, the White House flag came down. Before closing the doors to his railcar, Roosevelt regaled a few reporters tagging along with his delight at the prospect of catching sailboat races, hooking fish, and savoring "the wonderful rest and quiet away from people and telephones," off Cape Cod. By seven-thirty in the evening, Roosevelt boarded the waiting presidential yacht *Potomac*. *The New York Times* reported, "It was no more than the start of a vacation for a man who has, amid the cares of his official duties, longed for some sea air, and tonight he got it at last, the first since March."

FDR spent the following day at the helm of a motorboat darting about sparkling Buzzards Bay, just below Cape Cod, accompanied by exiled members of the Danish and Norwegian royal families. In the afternoon, he waved a jovial goodbye to his friends. The following day's newspapers prominently featured pictures of the beaming president at the wheel of his Chris-Craft runabout with two pretty young Scandinavian princesses. He returned to *Potomac* and, together with its coast guard escort *Calypso*, went out to sea.

By dawn the next morning, the slender white *Potomac* slid amid a flotilla of eight hulking gray warships, coming alongside USS *Augusta*, flagship of the Atlantic Fleet. *Augusta*'s sister ship *Tuscaloosa* and five destroyers formed a protective cordon around the president's cutter while Roosevelt's party transferred over to *Augusta*. The great ship had been specially equipped with ramps and even a two-story portable elevator. Coming aboard, FDR saluted the principal officers of the United States Armed Forces: the army chief of staff, General

George Marshall; the navy chief, Admiral "Betty" Stark; the Army Air Forces' General "Hap" Arnold; and the Atlantic Fleet's commander in chief, Admiral Ernest J. King. The flotilla quickly set out to sea. Operating under wartime convoy and escort orders, the ships did not stop even when *Augusta*'s outboard antimine gear fouled and needed to be jettisoned.

On the *Potomac*, a convincing-enough-looking double rolled on deck smoking from a long cigarette holder as the ship made her way back to Buzzards Bay. The coast guard kept other boaters away while "the president" occasionally cast for fish and sailors dressed like vacationers in natty whites lounged under a canopy. The presidential yacht stuck close enough to shore for excited vacationers to point out FDR to one another.

Back in Washington, with virtually the entire military leadership supposedly out west on inspection tours and out of reach, Stimson complained the day after FDR left that nobody remained in town to assist him in carrying out his charge to have the Lend-Lease airplanes that were formerly bound for England uncrated and reassembled for the long flight to Russia. "So," the secretary of war grumbled, "I had to do a lot of shooting around myself with subordinates to help me, the Heads of the Departments being in so many cases absent."

Augusta and its escorts beat a northerly heading. In the early hours of August 7, FDR's naval convoy steamed into Canadian waters, where the battleship *Arkansas* and eight more destroyers completed the impressive presidential "task force." The flotilla steamed up spacious Placentia Bay, a bear paw–shaped indentation carved out of the southeastern coast of Newfoundland, and then around the Argentia headland into Little Placentia Sound. *Augusta* and its sister cruiser *Tuscaloosa* slipped into Ship Harbour, a fjord less than a mile wide. Dropping anchor, the warships loomed up over the docks and house peaks of the tiny fishing village of Ship Harbour, nestled amid trees and green hills rising from the rocky shore. Across the fjord rose the impressive eight-hundred-foot gray granite escarpment of Sugar Loaf Hill.

Not long after *Augusta* arrived, Ensign Franklin D. Roosevelt, Jr., on board the destroyer *Mayrant* in the bay, was ordered to see the commander in chief on the *Augusta*. He wondered why Admiral King "would want to haul me on the carpet," but soon discovered the commander in chief was the real boss, his father. When FDR's equally uninformed second son, Elliott, an Army Air Forces officer, flew in to Argentia from his post at Gander Bay, he was "amazed and puzzled" by the sight of "the bay . . . filled with warships and a lot of them, big too." He shortly learned why when he was piped over the side of *Augusta*.

On the morning of August 9, shadowy through the mist, the great bulk of HMS *Prince of Wales* steamed into view.

On the battleship's quarterdeck, Winston Churchill, dressed in his double-button navy blue Royal Yacht Squadron jacket and hat, danced about excitedly, occasionally grabbing at Harry Hopkins's arm. The prime minister was a man with a keen sense of history, personally involved in or witness to a number of the world's most momentous events for nearly five decades. Here, he told his American friend, was "something really big." Hopkins later said, "You'd have thought Winston was being carried up into the heavens to meet God!" It wasn't God, but to Churchill's and many of his countrymen's minds, it was the man who would save the U.K. from Nazi hell. The question foremost on the prime minister's mind, though, seemed almost that of a teenager preparing for his first date: Will the president like me? he worried.

Meeting for the first time as national leaders at sea certainly seemed propitious. Each man, of course, styled himself a naval expert and nowhere more at home than at sea. Meeting in the North Atlantic was also a dramatic and historically symbolic locale for these two nations separated by an ocean—and a symbolic slap at Hitler's war to throttle Atlantic shipping. Churchill, the supplicant and the head of government, came hat in hand to see the president, the Old World again making the long sea journey to gain riches from the New. For Roosevelt, trysting with Churchill in foreign territory could keep up the façade of American neutrality while holding the British P.M. away from a press eager for a scoop about U.S. war commitments made in secret.

Hopkins, the go-between with the ear of each man, had managed to arrange the sea party. Here finally was the moment he had envisioned since January, "a full meeting of minds" between the two most important leaders in the free world. The fuse Hopkins lit over the months of literally living with the two men had finally reached the charge. "Bringing together President Roosevelt and the prime minister on a ship would cause the biggest explosion ever seen," he'd thought earlier. All three men knew the world would never be the same after this.

After Hopkins's Moscow trip, he boarded *Prince of Wales*, where he was met by most of London's military and Foreign Ministry heads—including First Sea Lord admiral Dudley Pound, Chief of the Imperial General Staff general John G. Dill, and Air Chief Marshal W. R. Freeman, plus their deputies. Churchill carried along a significantly larger delegation than Roosevelt had waiting for them across the ocean. Bending his agreement with the president, Churchill invited two "writers," not "journalists," along. One of them, H. V. Morton, well known for his travelogues, accepted a Ministry of Information invitation for a three-week foreign junket of unspecified destination—just bring a dinner jacket, he was told. The secret preparations and travel to Scapa Flow went off "like the opening of a good [John] Buchan spy novel," he wrote.

British summit preparations, if surreptitious, were of necessity more widely discussed within the government. With Parliament in session, Churchill required permission of his king and cabinet to depart the country. He also informed the prime ministers of all the Dominion Lands, the present and former colonies fighting with the British in the war, as much in an effort to encourage their hopes that here, finally, was the longed-for American commitment to a war alliance as to keep them apprised of wartime diplomacy. At the very least, Churchill expected he and FDR would issue a joint statement drawing a clear red line over which the Japanese dare not move farther southward without war. And, as for the Germans, he noted the date on which he set sail and telegraphed a last message to FDR before radio silence commenced. It was the twenty-seventh anniversary of the day the "Huns began their last war. We must make a good job of it this time. Twice ought to be enough."

As *Prince of Wales* sailed through the U-boat hunting grounds, Churchill scoffed when one member of the party observed, "Hitler would give fifty divisions to capture the British Prime Minister—or kill him." He longed for the latest German battleship, *Tirpitz*, to come out for some action, but he said, "I fear there will be no such luck." British intelligence would make sure of that. In March 1941, British naval forces had captured an armed German trawler off Norway that carried encoding machines and codebooks. That opened the previously indecipherable German naval Enigma code to decryption. Royal Navy radio intercepts from Germany to North Atlantic U-boats enabled the P.M.'s convoy to skip around them.

However, two anxious days ensued when heavy seas sent wave tops spraying over the decks and proved dangerously rough for the last two destroyers escorting the battleship. Both turned back. The *Prince of Wales* plunged on alone through the tossing ocean, zigging and zagging away from U-boat positions until, near Iceland, three Canadian destroyers picked up the British flagship and escorted her for the final leg to Newfoundland.

At nine on Saturday, August 9, *Prince of Wales*, White Ensign and Union Jack aloft, steamed slowly up the Ship Harbour to her anchorage. Dense mist shrouded the camouflage-painted ship as she dropped anchor in the smooth green water. Thousands of British and American eyes strained to pierce the glowing whiteness. Beneath the low-hanging white clouds, patrol aircraft flew overhead. Then, almost as if answering to the will of the prime minister, the mist dissolved in an instant, revealing a dazzling panorama. On blue-green water surrounded by low green and gray hills, *Prince of Wales* stood strong, backed at the Ship Harbour mouth by nearly a score of American and Canadian warships. A great cheer rang out from thousands of American sailors. The assembled British swabbies answered in return, as the ship's band played.

Motoring over to *Augusta* shortly after noon, Churchill stood on the deck of the admiral's barge, cigar in mouth, grinning broadly. He held aloft his two fingers to form the familiar V for Victory. Again loud, echoing cheers. Alongside him stood a tall, slender man, Harry Hopkins, looking laughable in Churchill's gray homburg, which hung over his ears. As Churchill came over *Augusta*'s side, a drummer played ruffles and flourishes and the ship's band struck up "God Save the King." Invited aboard, the prime minister walked to the deck to where the President of the United States awaited him. In suit, tie, and hat, Franklin Roosevelt stood upright, supported by his son Elliott's arm, the ensign staring ahead stiffly at attention. Churchill reached out his hand to the president, who saluted. With his highest-wattage smile, FDR said, "At last we've gotten together."

No sooner had formalities ended than FDR surprised Churchill. Roosevelt had more on his mind than figuring out how to move ships through the Atlantic safely. The drama of their encounter—the setting at sea, the first meeting of the nations' two great leaders, the evidence of their unity—would electrify the world, and that, along with a formal warning Churchill hoped would be issued to the Japanese, would have been enough for the first summit. But the president wanted something more resonant: a message "to the enslaved peoples of the world." He also wanted to shepherd American opinion and galvanize a gridlocked Congress by using the occasion to dramatize the global struggle between good and evil, between militarized powers that gobbled up smaller nations and democratic nations that traded freely.

Here, too, was an opportunity to underscore for those at home— especially Anglophobes skeptical of the U.K.'s and arch-imperialist

Roosevelt and Churchill secretly met August 9 off the coast of Newfoundland aboard the USS Augusta. *Franklin Roosevelt, Jr., is at left and Elliott Roosevelt at right.*

Churchill's goals in the war—that the fight was not about the New World's coming in to rescue the Old World's empires, but rather an attempt to forge a post-colonial future for the entire planet. FDR wanted his and Churchill's first meeting to end with a declaration, according to Churchill, "laying down certain broad principles which should guide our policies along the same road" after the war, when he expected American leadership to reshape the global order.

FDR had asked that a brief mutual statement of their common war and postwar mission be drafted. After its release, the document came to be known as the Atlantic Charter. (Churchill claimed after the war to have set out the initial declaration, but who was responsible for drafting it remains in dispute.) The two leaders struggled over its wording: Churchill called for an international organization along the lines of the League of Nations, and FDR rejected that notion, with the ghost of Woodrow Wilson hovering nearby. Roosevelt insisted on equal access to markets and raw materials; Churchill feared such a statement would undermine the preferential trade protocols among the Dominion Lands and presage the dissolution of the British Empire (which it did).

After Assistant Secretary of State Sumner Welles (pointedly, FDR had left Secretary Cordell Hull behind in favor of his friend) and British foreign ministry head Alexander Cadogan massaged the language, the two leaders agreed upon an eight-point declaration making clear that the nations shared a unified vision of the postwar international order. That brief statement set forth principles underlying the protection of national sovereignty, freedom of trade and open seas, advancement of individual well-being and rights, and disarmament of aggressor nations—along with the destruction of Nazi tyranny—that would serve as the guiding document for future international relations. In effect, FDR's "Four Freedoms" were now enshrined as postwar global goals.

The Atlantic Charter was not a treaty—"not a law, but a star," Churchill later termed it—but instead a handshake in the form of a joint public statement, signed by neither man and endorsed by neither nation's legislative bodies. Yet the Atlantic Charter was the cornerstone for the twenty-six-nation United Nations Declaration to oppose the Axis powers (drafted by Hopkins for Roosevelt and Churchill) six months later on New Year's Day of 1942, and the underpinning at the foundations of the postwar North Atlantic Treaty Organization (NATO), General Agreement on Tariffs and Trade (GATT), and the United Nations (UN) Organization, after the war. The joint statement marked an international New Deal tailored to the postwar world and underscored the democracies' stark contrast with the Axis nations. The Atlantic Charter would take its place alongside the Magna Carta, the Declaration of Independence, the Bill of Rights, and just a few other seminal documents as an essential statement of human freedoms and global ideals.

Over the next four days of summitry, the men and their diplomatic and military delegations met and discussed how their anticipated escort alliance would come about. Those face-to-face discussions facilitated an inevitably complex set of future operations. Sailors, too, spent time aboard one another's ships, catching glimpses of the great men in motion, giving the dry-navy Americans British rations of rum and the Royal Navy crewmen American smokes and sweets they desperately missed on war-restricted rations at home. At Hopkins's suggestion, the very first evening after dinner Churchill led one of his impressive seminars on the war's strategic situation for the Americans. The following rainy afternoon, the people of the village of Ship Harbour paid little heed when the short, stout, cigar-smoking man motored over for an amble along the rocky shore and through the misty hills.

The shipboard meetings brought minds into concert, but Americans refused to go beyond that. The United States was not at war; England was not an ally. The British men at the summit quickly grasped just how different their two worlds, though separated by the same ocean, still were. The war seemed barely to impinge on American life, while the British were engaged in a life-and-death struggle and came from a land pushed to the brink. Even American military brass seemed oblivious to the brutal realities of the war.

Nothing brought home this profound division more dramatically than the news that arrived from Washington. Like a torpedo amidships came word on August 12 that the House of Representatives had renewed selective service by a single vote margin, 203-202. If anyone in the *Prince of Wales* and *Augusta* meeting rooms was wondering, a statement from Montana senator Burton K. Wheeler, from Roosevelt's own party, pointed out the obvious: "This vote," he declared, "clearly indicates that the Administration could not get a resolution through the Congress for a declaration of war. It is notice to the War Department that the Congress does not approve of their breaking faith with the draftees. It is also notice that the Congress does not take seriously the cry of the Administration that the so-called emergency is greater now than it was a year ago." To underscore matters, Wheeler, chairman of the Interstate Commerce Committee, announced he would investigate "interventionists" in the motion picture industry and the role of foreign agents' "propaganda" films in shaping American opinion.

The continued flexing of muscles by congressional isolationists threw cold water on British hopes that the meeting in Argentia would mark a decisive turning point in U.S. entry into the war. Even the British delegation's goal to win an American signature on a statement warning that further Japanese aggression would lead the U.S. into war proved out of the question. FDR steadfastly refused to issue any post-summit declarations, only promising the dismayed foreign ministry delegates that on his return he would meet with the Japanese ambassador and convey the strength of American commitments to the region. He did assure Churchill that he could "baby" Japan for another three months, time enough to ready U.S. forces to repulse further Japanese advances.

With virtually all their hopes for definitive steps toward formal alliance with the U.S. drifting off into the Canadian Maritimes fog, the glum British delegation prepared to depart, almost in despair over the lack of concrete accomplishments. The Americans were far from ready to go to war.

Despite the disappointment, though, the summit's main purpose had in fact been accomplished, and, by all accounts, more fully than many had anticipated. The common-law marriage that Harry Hopkins had previously brokered was, if nowhere signed into a formal document, consummated in spirit. Roosevelt and Churchill passed nearly twenty-four hours together. Though much of the time was spent in ceremonial events and banquets, the pair had had several hours of one-on-one conversation. They'd dispensed with formality and overcome questions about personal distance. While duty-bound never to overstep their fenced-off national interests as leaders of sovereign nations, each now understood that his nation would grow stronger as the two men grew closer in the struggles that surely lay ahead.

FDR assured his son Elliott that he and Churchill came away with "a deep and intimate contact." Churchill concurred that the something big he had hoped for had indeed happened at Argentia. He had established "warm and deep personal relations with our great friend." After this, one match would light the president's cigarette in its holder and the prime minister's long cigar. The two men's personal amity would make possible all other national alliances to come.

A grand ceremonial gathering cemented the nations' and their leaders' enduring bond. Fifteen hundred sailors, officers, and government officials of both countries intermingled aboard the *Prince of Wales* for Sunday morning's church service. Some thought of it as a marriage ceremony of sorts. The prime minister had orchestrated every minute of the occasion. All saluted as Roosevelt walked the length of the ship, slowly and painfully, leaning on his son's arm. Those aboard witnessed the longest walk he had made since being stricken by polio almost two decades before. The American president took his place of honor, seated side by side with the British prime minister on the quarterdeck. The two nations' flags draped the pulpit. The big ship's guns angled up overhead. The leadership of American and British military forces bowed their heads in prayer together.

Two nations' men and their civilian and military heads sang "Onward, Christian Soldiers" in chorus, their voices ringing out over the tranquil fjord. No moment in the relations between the two English-speaking lands had compared in its grandeur and significance since the dissolution of America's place within the British Empire 165 years earlier. The bright, wary, sunken eyes of Harry Hopkins watched over the two leaders. He knew that the "special relationship" between them and their nations was sealed.

On August 12 at four forty-five in the afternoon, Winston Churchill stood alone on the *Prince of Wales* fantail. He waved to Franklin Roosevelt, who sat on *Augusta*'s deck next to his leadership delegation. As the great British battleship passed alongside the American warship and then steamed out of Ship Harbour, its band played "Auld Lang Syne." The American ship's band responded by playing "There'll Always Be an England" as the lone figure in his blue yachting uniform grew steadily smaller in the distance.

Four months later, on December 10, *Prince of Wales* would be sunk in a Japanese air attack; 327 of the men present at Placentia Bay would die in the ship's last fight.

Roosevelt did not believe Congress or the American people were ready to go to war. He knew the isolationists would accuse him of arranging the clandestine conference to make secret promises. He insisted nothing of the kind had taken place. Roosevelt returned home saying the nation was "no closer to war."

Ignoring disappointment that the Americans would not issue a warning to the Japanese, Churchill arrived in London, where he told his

FDR and Churchill aboard HMS Prince of Wales *on August 10. U.S. Navy Admirals Ernest King (left) and Harold "Betty" Stark stand behind the two leaders while Hopkins looks on warily.*

War Cabinet that from here on the American president "would become more and more provocative . . . [and] would look for an 'incident' which would justify him in opening hostilities." That may have been wishful thinking; or Roosevelt may have told him that sotto voce.

But however uncertain the formal alliance of their nations might remain, Roosevelt and Churchill now felt confident in their relationship as national leaders and reassured about their ability to work together in the trials to come. They did not put their names to the Atlantic Charter, yet their joint declaration went out to the entire world. They shared "certain common principles . . . on which they base their hopes for a better future for the world." These included a definitive call for the "final destruction of the Nazi tyranny." And the sole realistic, as yet undeclared, path to achieving that goal lay in American entry into the shooting war.

Returned to London, Churchill reported proudly to his king and Parliament that together the two nations would lead mankind "forward out of the miseries into which they have been plunged, back to the broad highroad of freedom and justice." And when Churchill walked smiling through the cheering benches of Parliament the following week, he raised his fingers in the same "V for Victory" sign he'd flashed to the American president he now called his friend.

25

The Rattlesnakes of the Atlantic

Washington, Des Moines, and the North Atlantic, September 1941

The president had determined that his navy would now patrol every shipping lane from North America all the way to about two hundred miles east of Iceland in the north, down to Cape Verde in the mid-Atlantic, and from there south. The U.S. Neutrality Zone now covered more than three quarters of the entire Atlantic Ocean. Despite the meeting of minds and hearts aboard the *Prince of Wales*, FDR had yet to make public his greatly enlarged policing orders. He promised Churchill that once the North Atlantic patrols began operation later in August, he would announce the new patrol policy. Still he hesitated, concerned that without an incident he would lose public support.

He did not have long to wait.

Early on September 4, a calm and sunny morning, a British Hudson bomber patrolling about 125 miles southwest of Iceland spotted *U-652* cruising several miles distant through the whitecaps of the green North Atlantic. Seeing the RAF aircraft approach, the German submarine dived. The RAF pilot flew on until it met the U.S. destroyer *Greer* steaming ten miles off. She was bound for the new marine base in Iceland, carrying supplies, mail, and some officers. Using a cockpit lamp, the bomber signaled the *Greer* that a U-boat lurked ahead. Under the new orders to shadow and report U-boat activity, *Greer's* captain closed on her last location. The general quarters gong sounded.

U-652's captain knew Hitler's standing orders not to attack American ships. Hitler was constant in his commitment "to avoid having the U.S.A. declare war while the Eastern Campaign is still in progress." However, pressed by naval chief Admiral Raeder, the Führer promised, "[I] will never call a submarine commander to account if he torpedoes an American ship by mistake." Sniffing glory, U-boat captains were eager to bag the first American naval vessel.

Reaching near to where the Hudson circled overhead, the *Greer* began a sonar search at around nine-thirty in the morning. A tinny sound returned: dead ahead, moving away slowly, the sub. A pursuit began in which the *Greer* ranged between two hundred and twelve hundred yards from *U-652*. *Greer's* commander blinked out a message to let the British bomber crew know they were trailing the silent running sub. The British pilot asked if the Americans would attack. Under the commander in chief's orders, they would not fire first.

Flying overhead, the British patrol bomber was running low on fuel. Needing to return home, the Hudson dropped four depth charges on the sub's suspected location before flying from the scene. They missed, but the explosions rocked *U-652*, startling its crew. Rising to periscope depth, the sub skipper sighted the *Greer*. No markings distinguished British from American destroyers, and the captain could not discern the ship's flag. The U-boat assumed the destroyer had dropped the depth charges. Now at about two thousand yards, the two vessels continued to run in tandem for more than two hours.

Shortly after midday, the German commander decided to attack. He turned to get broadside to the destroyer. *Greer's* sonar man picked up the U-boat's maneuver. The commander ordered full speed and *Greer* tacked away, forcing the sub to fire a torpedo before being fully lined up. "Captain!" a lookout shouted. "Something in the water off the starboard bow. One thousand yards!" The ship surged ahead full and veered hard.

The torpedo wake passed on a visible track, streaming by parallel to the ship about one hundred yards off.

The U-boat motored below the ship, milky bubbles indicating her passage. She came about to a new firing position. *Greer* answered by rolling eight depth charges off the stern. Another torpedo streaked past. White plumes shot into the air from the exploding depth charges. Below the ocean, the bursting bombs rattled *U-652* enough to smash out her interior lights, but caused no serious damage.

The turbulence caused *Greer* to lose sonar contact. She continued to search, but by evening the destroyer left off and made for Reykjavik. *U-652* surfaced alone on the darkening, empty sea.

When Roosevelt learned of the battle, he immediately called in Hopkins to prepare his speech. He had his incident.

A week later, on the evening of September 11, Charles Lindbergh stood offstage in the Des Moines Coliseum. He held the typescript of the red-meat speech he had been working on for several weeks. He was going to lay out just who was dragging America into war. Here was a chance to point fingers and put America's true enemies, the ones pushing for war, on notice. Des Moines was no great friend to the isolationists; not only America Firsters, but a sizable contingent of their opponents as well, were among the eight thousand shouting, hooting, and whistling around the arena.

An announcer finally stepped to the podium. Instead of introducing the night's first speaker, though, he announced that the President of the United States would address the nation first, speaking over radio from the White House. A few seconds later, Roosevelt's familiar voice echoed out ghostly and hollow from the loudspeakers. Eight thousand pairs of ears perked up. Across the nation, throughout the Western Hemisphere, over the BBC and from there throughout Europe and the dominions of the British Commonwealth, more than a billion people gathered about radios and listened along with the Iowans to FDR's words. (Churchill was in bed when the broadcast went over the BBC, but heard a rebroadcast in the morning.) Billed as a "Fireside Chat," it had little of the reassuring warmth one usually heard in the president's voice during these talks.

A Nazi submarine, in broad daylight on the open seas, had attacked a U.S. destroyer, the USS *Greer*, which was doing nothing more belligerent than "carrying American mail . . . [and] flying the American flag." His voice rose in righteous indignation: "In spite of what any American obstructionist organization may prefer to believe, I tell you the blunt fact that the German submarine fired first upon this American destroyer without warning, and with deliberate design to sink her." Every person in the Des Moines arena knew the president was speaking to them; he, of course, knew that the true circumstances were not as he described. "This attack on the *Greer*," he declared, "was no localized military operation in the North Atlantic." Rather, he insisted, this was but "one determined step" toward world conquest.

"This Nazi attempt to seize control of the oceans," he warned, "is but a counterpart of the Nazi plots now being carried on throughout the Western Hemisphere—all designed toward the same end. For Hitler's advance guards—not only his avowed agents but also his dupes among us—have sought to make ready for him footholds [and] bridgeheads in the New World, to be used as soon as he has gained control of the oceans." He was referring to the many business agents and others with Axis connections in South America, now blacklisted and in some cases jailed as a result of the Rockefeller Shop's and the British Security Coordination's efforts. He clearly also had "dupes" in Des Moines in mind.

Every eye in the crowd looked inward as the president declared, "The danger is here now—not only from a military enemy but from an enemy of all law, all liberty, all morality, all religion."

The president was not declaring war, but, he said, "when you see a rattlesnake poised to strike, you do not wait until he has struck before you crush him." The Nazis were, he intoned, "the rattlesnakes of the Atlantic. . . ."

He had ordered his navy to "shoot on sight." He declared, "The time for active defense has come," and warned, ". . . if German or Italian vessels of war enter the waters . . . they do so at their own peril." He did not make public the order he issued the day after he learned of the *Greer* incident: The navy would finally begin escorting convoys. As he always insisted, the U.S. had not fired the first shot, but was now free to shoot. Active combat in the undeclared war had begun.

The Iowans stirred about uneasily, and then a buzz rose up. The crowd grew noisy and was soon on the verge of pandemonium. Standing behind a curtain waiting for Roosevelt's talk to end, Lindbergh felt unnerved. He now faced, he penned, "about as bad a setting as we could have had for our meeting." Not sixty seconds after Roosevelt signed off, he and his party walked onstage. After the lead-in speeches, heckling and booing mixed with restrained applause as Lindbergh stood at the microphone. He looked out into what he called "the most unfriendly crowd of any meeting to date, by far." He would also claim that "paid shouters" had been strategically placed to disrupt his speech. Hecklers hooted at him; boos and applause warred in the air.

Then the loudspeakers failed. He stood mute and uncomfortable before the restive crowd for several minutes while they were fixed.

Finally, he spoke. Here it was. Everything he had predicted was coming to pass. But almost as if FDR had timed his own talk to preempt the impact of Lindbergh's speech, the moment of truth seemed lost.

Still, Lindbergh was determined to point the finger of accusation at the people driving the nation to war. These were not real Americans, but those he called "other people" who cared for their own needs, not America's. "That effort," he said, "has been carried on by foreign interests, and by a small minority of our own people. . . ." Ignoring the booing and heckling, he lumped together Roosevelt's administration with "the British and Jewish races . . . [which] for reasons which are not American, wish to involve us in the war. . . ." As he spoke these lines, loud cheers erupted and he received a standing ovation. He focused mostly on the Jews, who, he said, "Instead of agitating for war . . . should be opposing it in every possible way for they will be among the first to feel its consequences." Their control over propaganda vehicles and sway in Washington and on unsuspecting people, he said, endangered Americans: "Their greatest danger to this country lies in their large ownership and influence in our motion pictures, our press, our radio and our government."

Those agitating for war had formed an insidious conspiratorial cabal that, he stated, ". . . planned: first, to prepare the United States for foreign war under the guise of American defense; second, to involve us in the war, step by step, without our realization; third, to create a series of incidents which would force us into the actual conflict." And now, this very evening, Roosevelt had proved the plain truth for all to see. The conspirators' plan was dangerously close to fruition. "You see the first of these [incidents] already taking place, according to plan," he said.

Applause, shouts, and boos drowned Lindbergh out for several seconds. Several times he was forced to repeat a word before his voice rose above the din. "We are on the verge of war, but," he insisted, "it is not yet too late to stay out. It is not too late to show that no amount of money, or propaganda, or patronage can force a free and independent people into war against its will." Heckling and booing continued to battle applause and shouts of support inside the arena. Fights broke out. The most celebrated and revered American of the age looked bewildered by the mass of people boiling over before the stage.

Polls over the next few days showed overwhelming support for the president's "shoot-on-sight" order. News about Lindbergh's speech convulsed the nation. A deluge of criticism seemed to sweep away talk of overseas intervention and replace it with talk of intolerance and prejudice at home. Wendell Willkie called Lindbergh's "the most-un-American talk made in my time by any person of national reputation." The former "Public Hero No. 1," wrote one columnist, had transformed himself into "Public Enemy No. 1." The reliably interventionist *New York Herald Tribune* termed his speech an invitation to unleash "the dark forces of prejudice and intolerance." Even the most forceful isolationist pages of the *Chicago Tribune* condemned Lindbergh's "impropriety," and the almost equally anti-interventionist Hearst papers termed his talk "intemperate and intolerant."

Leading anti-interventionist senator Robert Taft stated in a private letter that he disapproved entirely of Colonel Lindbergh's speech, and "particularly the part attacking the Jews." He condemned Lindbergh for having "referred to the Jews as if they were a foreign race, and not Americans at all, a grossly unjust attitude." However, he did not criticize him in public, because he considered "his intolerance . . . more than matched by the intolerance" of his critics "toward him and his views."

While Lindbergh continued to speak at chapter events, the Des Moines talk put America First into a tailspin. Desperate to push back against the charges of anti-Semitism, national director Bob Stuart sent a letter to chapter chairmen. He inveighed against "one more attempt to divert attention of Americans from the issue of peace or war . . . .the war promoters having deliberately raised the false issue of anti-Semitism. Let us nail down this false charge now for the willful fraud that it is. . . . We challenge anyone to find one anti-Semitic sentence in [Lindbergh's Des Moines speech]. Though the charges are baseless, they are nevertheless dangerous." He feared that "certain elements which seek to promote racial and religious intolerance may mistakenly conclude that they will now be welcomed in the ranks of America First."

Even now, while a significant American majority approved FDR's "shoot-on-sight" order, polls showed that by an even larger margin they still opposed going to war in Europe or Asia. Americans knew they wanted Hitler stopped but were unwilling to accept the necessity of carrying the war through to the end. In a national radio broadcast a few days after the president's bellicose "chat," Herbert Hoover decried FDR's "edging our warships into danger zones" without congressional authorization, "steps to war unapproved and undeclared. . . ." He blamed the president for the attack on the *Greer*, "the consequence of violating the spirit of the Neutrality Act."

Berlin and Rome made little note of Roosevelt's talk, but picked up and broadcast portions of Hoover's, pointing out in their press statement that the former president had criticized FDR's aid to the English and dispatch of warships into danger zones, feeling it would "lead directly to war."

After a summer of quiescence, ravenous U-boat wolfpacks went back on the attack. On September 9, the captain of a sub alerted other U-boats that he'd discovered a Liverpool-bound sixty-five-ship convoy carrying iron ore, wheat, lumber, and oil south of Cape Farewell, Greenland. For three days the sky was lit red as eight U-boats ripped apart the freighters. Before the attack broke off, fifteen were sunk and four more damaged; one ship turned back. A sixteenth ship from the convoy was torpedoed and sunk off England. In all, almost three hundred crewmen were lost. American ships raced in, but too late to stop the carnage.

Sailors aboard U.S. navy ships in the front lines of the undeclared war had more than enough imagination to figure out what they faced. Few were pleased. Donald Hugh Dorris had left Vanderbilt University the previous spring to enlist in the navy. The day the wolfpack struck the Liverpool-bound convoy, the green ensign's cruiser, USS *Vincennes*, was already on escort duty, among the very first U.S. Atlantic Fleet escorts, accompanying ten merchant ships bound for the U.K. via the Reykjavik turntable. "We now have orders to open fire immediately on sighting 'enemy' warships," recorded Dorris, looking out on the darkening North Atlantic. Firing began quickly. One of the other destroyers saw what she believed to be a periscope and let off depth charges.

Dorris confided in the personal logbook he kept on the *Vincennes*, "We know what the public does not know, namely, that F.D.R. is deliberately doing all he can to make an incident which will unite public opinion in support of 'all out' aid to Britain." He was cynical about the prospect, but fully expected "F.D.R. will get his incident."

After the initial elation over his summit meeting with the president, Churchill realized no concrete action was forthcoming, and despair had set in. After Roosevelt's shoot-on-sight address, though, Churchill's sense of desperation turned to satisfaction. "U.S. to Guard Our Ships," declared the *Daily Mail*'s front-page banner headline the day after FDR's speech. With the eased American restrictions on engagement, Churchill announced that the "mixed up together" British, Canadian, and American navies would share in escorting and patrolling the declared German war zone through to Iceland. Within three weeks, American naval ships in the North Atlantic rivaled the entire Pacific Fleet.

Still, the ocean was vast and Atlantic Fleet commander Ernest J. King had only thirty-three destroyers ready for merchant escort duty, though another sixteen were scheduled to be ready to set sail at the end of October. That left him with only a skeletal escort for his own warships to meet the wolfpacks. But notwithstanding the dangers, the U.S. was now covering most of the Atlantic Ocean, relieving the Royal Navy of the burden and permitting transfer of scores of British ships to other fronts.

The implications went much further. "Hitler will have to choose," an ebullient Churchill wrote to Imperial War Cabinet member and field marshal Jan Smuts just three days after the president's talk, "between losing the Battle of the Atlantic or coming into frequent collisions with United States ships and warships." In all but signature on an alliance document, Churchill had his ally.

Hitler understood this. He and his entire High Command, along with Foreign Minister Ribbentrop, met at Wolfsschanze—or "Wolf's

Lair," the Eastern Front headquarters—a week after Roosevelt's speech. Dealing with the changed situation in the Atlantic as a result of FDR's "shoot-on-sight" order was the first item of business. The aggressive Raeder reminded the Führer that American ships were no longer "employed merely for reconnaissance" but now provided convoy service, "including escort of British ships." The admiral recognized the consequences of the presence of the American naval warships. Even if Germany sought to avoid U.S. ships, "German forces," he explained to the gathering, "must expect offensive war measures by these U.S. forces in every case of encounter. There is no longer any difference between British and American ships." The combat zone almost fully overlapped the U.S. Neutrality Zone. Roosevelt, he said, had extended the American zone "indefinitely to the east according to the whims of the U.S.A. . . ." In response, he asked that Hitler stop the charade and permit U-boats to attack any ship sailing within twenty miles of the American coast.

Unnerved by the continuing fight in Russia, Hitler said no. He had a war to win in the East, and the Red Army, despite its supposedly racially inferior composition, was proving far more able to fight than predicted. He was still satisfied that "the great decision in the Russian campaign" would come within a month. Until then he asked the *Kriegsmarine* to exercise "care . . . to avoid any incidents . . . before the middle of October."

But Hitler's expected victory over Russia did not come to pass by his forecast date. Italian foreign minister Ciano traveled to Germany in late October to meet with Hitler and Ribbentrop at the Wolfsschanze headquarters. The specter of Roosevelt in the White House across the Atlantic infested their minds. Fighting on the Eastern Front was ferocious, and the Nazi leader, found Ciano, would "do nothing that will accelerate or cause America's entry into the war." Effectively, he had ceded the Atlantic to the Anglo-American forces for now.

On the last day of their conclave, Ribbentrop spoke at a lunch. He launched into a blistering series of sophomoric insults aimed at the American president. "I have given orders to the press," he proclaimed, "to always write 'Roosevelt, the Jew.'" He prophesied, "That man will be stoned in the Capitol by his own people." After two full years of war, Ciano had wised up to the value of the blowhard Ribbentrop's forecasts. "I personally believe," he sardonically thought, "that Roosevelt will die of old age, because experience teaches me not to give much credit to Ribbentrop's prophecies."

Back in Rome, Mussolini remained confident that the U.S. could do nothing to change the outcome of the war in Europe. Ciano's father-in-law told him he would never see an American soldier in Europe. "It is quite clear," said the Duce, "that Roosevelt is barking because he cannot bite."

Ciano felt increasingly doubtful: "Could he be right?" he pondered. He felt much less certain than Mussolini.

26

Tennō

Tokyo, Washington, and Honolulu, September–November 1941

September 5 proved a fateful day in other places across the planet. At about the same time President Roosevelt learned about the *Greer* incident and ordered U.S. warships to shoot "the rattlesnakes of the Atlantic" on sight, the entire Japanese leadership oligarchy gathered once again for an Imperial Conference. It was September 6 in Tokyo when they came together before Tennō: Hirohito, the 124th emperor of Japan, the third to ascend the throne following the Meiji restoration, the heavenly sovereign at the head of the people and the Shinto religion.

Hirohito seemed an unlikely object for such veneration. At forty years old, he was slight and bespectacled. The Son of God sported a wispy mustache. He enjoyed studying marine biology and relaxed by reading poetry. The commander in chief of Japan's armed forces seemed a gentle soul, a contemplative scholar who espoused pacifism as a family heritage. Yet since his ascension to the "Chrysanthemum Throne" in 1926, his country had known almost nothing but war. Now, a nation embroiled in a brutal war in China for a decade was contemplating vastly enlarging that war.

When the Imperial Conference began at precisely ten in the morning, Hirohito knew well the gravity of the gathering's agenda. The preceding day he had met with his prime minister, Prince Fumimaro Konoe, and both the army's and the navy's chiefs of staff. The four men discussed the subject to come before the Imperial Conference, a document known as "Essentials for Carrying Out the Empire's Policies." The Essentials called for war, a move to oust the United States, Great Britain, and the Netherlands from their colonial territories, to commence at the end of October. The document's policies dictated that only a halt to British and American aid to Chiang Kai-shek's Nationalist force and their acknowledgment of Japanese hegemony in China could prevent war. The Western powers would also have to agree to end their military presence in the region and cooperate in securing permanent sources of oil for Japan. The chiefs of staff recognized the virtual impossibility that London or Washington would agree to such terms.

The dominant militarists would accept no alternative: Just the week before, a cabinet minister in Prime Minister Konoe's government known to have drawn close to U.S. ambassador Grew somehow survived six bullets from an assassin's gun, including one to the head. Increasingly nervous at the prospect of world war, Prince Konoe understood what he was up against should he dare to oppose those itching for war with the Western powers.

The armed forces felt increasingly confident about their chances for success. The occupation of French Indochina had gone off without resistance. British forces had their hands full fighting Germany, and Singapore was within easy striking distance. A little more than a month before, at the end of July, the navy chief of general staff, Admiral Osami Nagano, had gone to see Hirohito. America had just raised the specter of a cutoff in oil supplies. Nagano warned the emperor that without renewed U.S. deliveries his country faced drastic shortages and, before many months, complete depletion of its fuel storages. In the logic of this oil squeeze, if war became unavoidable, Nagano said to the emperor, Japan had "no choice but to strike" quickly.

Hirohito asked him if Japan might expect "a big victory," such as in the 1904–1905 war with Russia. Nagano hesitated. "I am uncertain as to any victory. . . ."

Hirohito was stunned. "What a reckless war that would be!" he declared. But at the moment when he might have stopped such reckless-ness, he permitted snowballing war preparations to continue.

The emperor was nonetheless shocked that Nagano and the others intended to push a national grand strategy at the September 6 Impe-rial Conference focused almost entirely on waging a war he had so recently labeled "reckless" and perhaps unwinnable. At the meeting the day prior to the conference, the emperor asked the army chief of staff, Field Marshal Hajime Sugiyama, how long he anticipated hostilities with the Americans would last. Sugiyama replied that South Pacific operations would take no more than three months. Visibly perturbed, Hirohito reminded Sugiyama that he had been minister of war when Japan attacked China in 1937. At the time he had promised the emperor that the "China Incident" would last at most one month. Fighting has continued to this day, Hirohito scolded. How would this war with far more powerful enemies spanning the vast Pacific Ocean prove any easier? The shamed Sugiyama hung his head in silence.

Nagano finally spoke up. He had previously warned that victory might not be possible. But, he said, the time had come when Japan must prepare for war. The nation was like "a patient suffering from a serious illness . . . so critical that the question of whether or not to operate had to be deter-mined without delay." He claimed "the High Command desires diplomatic negotiations to reach a successful conclusion." Any further delay in making a decision, Nagano maintained, would be fatal for the patient. ". . . I am afraid," he said, "that we must pluck up enough courage and operate."

Repeating his question from their previous meeting, Hirohito de-manded, "Will we win? Can you say we will definitely win?"

Nagano replied, "I cannot say 'definitely' because it depends not on just manpower but on divine power, too." Thus he thrust responsibility for victory away from the military and into the emperor's pliant lap. The divinity did not intervene.

Hirohito pressed, however, until he won assurance from the chiefs of his armed forces that they would support negotiations until the impasse proved truly unbridgeable. But the sands were running out of the hour-glass. The military men insisted upon a fixed policy and date for war.

Sitting in the palace's resplendent hall at the brilliant-hued silk-covered Imperial Conference table, Yoshimichi Hara, president of the Privy Council, who served as the emperor's surrogate in posing questions, asked the Army High Command to discuss its readiness to negotiate a settlement. Sugiyama sat in silence. His silence spoke louder than words. Nagano also remained quiet.

Suddenly all eyes turned upon the emperor, at the head of the table in front of his ceremonial golden screen. "Struck with awe," Konoe recalled in later years, several of the men at the table gasped audibly. Tennō spoke. "It is regrettable," Hirohito said, "that both chiefs of the general staff are unable to answer." The emperor reached into his tunic pocket and pulled out a paper. He had jotted out a poem written by his late grandfather, the revered Meiji, at the start of the Russo-Japanese War more than thirty-five years earlier. Hirohito recited:

In all four seas all are brothers and sisters.
Then why, oh why, these rough winds and waves?

Tennō was indicating his desire for peace, intimating his perspective in almost mystical terms. All sat with eyes averted, dumbstruck, as if turned to stone. After a long silence, Admiral Nagano spoke. He assured the emperor that his navy favored diplomacy. If negotiations failed, however, he called for a quick, decisive strike on the Western powers. The Imperial Council adjourned precisely at noon, the national policy having been adopted.

The countdown to war had begun, and Prince Konoe left the September 6 Imperial Conference with a sense of dread. The prime minister drove—alone in an unmarked car—to a secretly arranged meeting with the American ambassador, Joseph Grew. Konoe pleaded with Grew to arrange a summit between him and President Roosevelt; together the two could iron out their nations' differences. A ship stood ready to carry Konoe to wherever the president chose to meet. Without having to say why, he warned Grew that time was growing short.

The ambassador cabled the State Department. The prince spoke sincerely, Grew claimed. But the signals coming to Washington pointed in the other direction. Konoe's willingness to negotiate seemed to contradict Japanese diplomats' rigidly restated positions in their meetings with Hull in Washington: Number one, they insisted upon recognition of Japanese sovereignty in Manchuria; number two, they called for a halt to Western support for the Chinese Nationalist army; and three, they demanded an end to the embargo, with a commitment to renew delivery of raw materials and aviation fuel.

With Magic intercepts further undermining Konoe's reputation for influence among the military's leadership, Secretary of State Hull doubted bringing together the highest civilian leadership could reliably resolve differences while extremists held control over the military. Hull went to Stimson when he heard about the Konoe overture. Stimson doubted the prime minister's government would survive long should the U.S. respond positively to the summit overture. Additionally, distrustful of what he called FDR's "private government," Stimson was concerned that the president, were he to meet with the Japanese prime minister, might make "concessions" that would be "highly dangerous to our vitally important relations with China." They teamed up to convince FDR to abandon the half-baked idea for a war-or-peace summit and rebuffed Grew and the prime minister.

The day after the Imperial Conference, Honolulu's *Star-Bulletin* proclaimed, "A Japanese attack on Hawaii is regarded as the most unlikely thing in the world, with one chance in a million of being successful. Besides having more powerful defenses than any other post under the American flag, it is protected by distance. . . . The Japanese fleet . . . would have so far to come that American patrols would spot it long before it arrived."

Less than three weeks later, on September 25, Admiral Yamamoto wrote Nagano that he intended to lead his forces "to achieve considerable success in initial battles." But he added that the war to follow would be "protracted . . . [and] . . . will last for several years. . . . Japan will be impoverished." So though he thought his gamble would pay off at first, he admonished that nonetheless, "A war with so little chance of success should not be fought." Japanese leaders' optimism about a quick war was so strong, the forces weighing in favor of military conflict so heavy, that he failed to heed his own rational assessment.

He watched aboard his flagship *Nagato* two weeks after expressing his grim outlook while officers and aides ran through five days of map maneuvers—tabletop war games—of the attack he had planned for Pearl Harbor. After they concluded on October 14, he met with his Combined Fleet's commanding officers, nearly all of whom had known nothing beforehand about the intended attack on Pearl Harbor; many were still in shock at the prospect. "Some of you may have objections," affirmed Yamamoto, "but so long as I'm C. in C. I'm intent on going through with the raid on Hawaii." He would not be deterred by doubts, not even his own.

He realized that he was gambling everything on a long shot. In the midst of the map maneuvers, on October 11, he reflected in a letter to one of his closest friends, Rear Admiral Teikichi Hori, "My present situation is very strange. Because I have been assigned the mission, entirely against my private opinion. . . ." The most reluctant proponent of war was the man chosen as architect of his nation's strategic approach and tactics for the attack. "In Japan today," he lamented, "the circumstance seems to be such that only the emperor pays his utmost concerns about the situation, and also that he would be the only and the last man who could check the tide. But even his decision, if made, would be difficult to be effective in present Japan."

Admiral Yamamoto preparing
for the Pearl Harbor attack.

Tennō had receded into enigma and meditative reflection rather than take the responsibility of placing himself and his authority against the onrushing tide of war. The high command of both the army and navy were determined upon war. An increasingly gloomy Konoe sought to convince them that partially withdrawing from China, and avoiding the consequences of possible war with both the U.K. and the U.S., might be in the national interest. The prime minister met on the evening of October 7 with General Hideki Tojo, his army minister. Konoe expressed a willingness to withdraw from the nation's pledges under the terms of the Tripartite Pact. He pressed Tojo, "Can we not find a way to stick to the substance of military occupation and still agree to troop withdrawal?"

Tojo told the prince that the U.S. would not agree to such a situation. And after the deaths of tens of thousands of soldiers in China, he was personally unwilling to make such a huge concession. Realizing all was lost, Konoe said glumly, "Military men take wars too lightly."

"Occasionally," Tojo responded, "one must conjure up enough courage, close one's eyes, and jump off the platform of the Kiyomizu." The general was referring to a famed plunge from a Kyoto temple. According to myth, if the jumper survived the fall, the gods would grant him a fabulous wish for his bravery.

But in the face of such daunting odds, would Japan's going to war be bravery or suicidal recklessness? Should an entire nation be forced to take such a plunge into the unknown? A defeated Konoe looked at Tojo and muttered that an individual might decide to make such a leap, "but if I think of the national polity that has lasted twenty-six hundred years and of the hundred million Japanese belonging to this nation, I, as a person in the position of great responsibility, cannot do such a thing." He would not take the nation to the edge of the precipice—but nor could he stop those who would plunge his nation into the abyss. Konoe decided he could no longer govern Japan with his eyes closed.

War's momentum infected the two countries on either side of the Pacific while diplomatic talks continued in Washington. Even if Roosevelt's policy aimed to avoid war with Japan—or delay it by "babying" the Japanese as long as possible, as he had promised Churchill—war was on everyone's mind. In early August, Stimson and Hull met and, to Stimson's satisfaction after four years of beating the drum for confronting Japan, shared their recognition that "the period of appeasement is over in respect to Japan."

Over the summer, FDR decided to increase the U.S. force of advanced B-17s based in the Philippines as a deterrent to the Japanese. With some 220 of them set to roll off the assembly lines over the next six months, the heavy bombers were Washington's new "big stick." One hundred sixty-five Flying Fortresses, half of all the B-17 bombers the U.S. possessed, would deploy to the Philippines. On August 25, the very first of the beefed-up Flying Fortresses rolled out of the massive new Boeing plant in Seattle. Stimson projected that the full force of B-17s would be based in the Philippines by the first of the coming year or shortly thereafter.

Belief in the power of the Flying Fortresses to redress regional force imbalance washed through Washington like a refreshing shower after a sweltering heat wave. Stimson shared the general belief that when the new bombers reached the Pacific, the U.S. would induce Japan "to keep away from Singapore and perhaps, if we are in good luck, to shake the Japanese out of the Axis. . . ." He also made plans to station more fighter aircraft throughout the western Pacific. Japan would not dare risk bomber strikes on Tokyo.

Roosevelt's chief objective in the Pacific was checking Japan's push for war in order to buy time for the navy to enlarge its limited firepower in the Atlantic. He encouraged Secretary Hull and the Japanese ambassador's desultory meetings to seek a diplomatic solution through the fall. Those sessions merely reaffirmed that Washington demanded a Japanese rollback from China and that Tokyo refused to budge without Washington's meeting its preconditions. This stalling suited Washington and Tokyo. Confided Stimson, the Japanese gambit in pursuing diplomacy was "merely a blind to keep us from taking definite action." Both Japan and the U.S. were playing a complex game to gain the upper hand in a war both expected likely at the end.

Roosevelt sent a note to King George on October 15 describing himself as "a bit worried" over the Pacific situation. Based on Magic, Ambassador Grew's notes, and his own strategic assessment, he told the king, "The emperor is for peace I think, but the jingoes are trying to force his hand." Roosevelt and many advisers around him believed that if Japan did strike, it was likeliest to attack northward, into Siberia, given the Soviet preoccupation with the Nazis on the outskirts of Moscow. While FDR told most people that he believed Russia would hold out, into the last week of November he fretted behind the scenes that Russia was on the verge of "falling." Marking time with the Japanese until American Asia-Pacific defense capabilities were sufficiently secure—and

Atlantic forces strong enough to engage a powerful Germany—seemed his sole recourse in the region.

On September 24, the consul general of the Japanese Consulate in Hawaii, Nagao Kita, handed Vice Consul Tadashi Morimura decoded Message No. 83 from Navy Intelligence, stamped "STRICTLY SE-CRET." Of course, "Tadashi Morimura" was the alias by which the Naval Intelligence spy Takeo Yoshikawa had gone since his arrival from Japan. To date, Yoshikawa's reports corresponded to Tokyo's interest in fleet movements. Message No. 83 changed that focus entirely. From here on his goal would be to observe ships in Pearl Harbor and to pinpoint them within a designated five-area grid. Within those grids, Navy Intelligence called on him to identify the ships, their types, classes, and moorage. The Japanese spy did not know when an attack would come, but the call for "items of immediate tactical significance" meant, he was certain, that "the date was rapidly approaching"—and that Pearl Harbor was, shockingly likely, the target. The spy went to work.

27

The Undeclared War

Atlantic and Pacific, September–November 1941

British and American intelligence gave Washington mixed signals about Japanese intentions. Magic intercepts included commands to Japanese agents to report on coastal defenses in the Philippines. However, Tokyo was aware of American monitoring of its radio transmissions and deliberately communicated messages indicating no change in Japan's strategic planning, particularly about the locations of its naval task forces. The Magic decryption of Message No. 83 from September 24 sparked a brief flurry of concern among analysts that "the Japanese were showing unusual interest in the port at Honolulu." The cable stood out as Tokyo's first request to agents to gather intelligence focusing not on ship movements but instead on their stationary positions in port.

The document circulated in early October, along with many other Magic intercepts covering the entire Far East. Amid the confusing noise of so many transmissions—some only partly decrypted due to limits of the Magic decoding systems—and the ongoing efforts by Japan to deny information to commanders within its navy in order to avoid detection of changing strategies and deceive American monitors, the singular focus on Pearl Harbor largely disappeared from Washington's concerns.

His desperate bid for a summit with the American president having been rejected, Prince Konoe and his entire cabinet resigned on October 16. When Roosevelt heard about the fall of the Konoe government—and his replacement by the known extremist General Hideki Tojo—he canceled a meeting of his own Cabinet scheduled for the same day. Instead, he brought together the inner circle he now relied upon as his War Council, the six men he kept closest to the Oval Office in the crisis days: Stimson, Hull, Knox, Admiral Stark, General Marshall, and Hopkins. The president expected the new Japanese government would prove "much more anti-American."

With no obvious signs of immediate attack, questions lingered in Roosevelt's mind "whether Japan was playing poker or not." He confessed a month later to Ickes that he was still "not sure . . . whether or not Japan had a gun up its sleeve." Ickes urged him to fire the first shot, saying to the president, ". . . when I knew that I was going to be attacked, I preferred to choose my own time and occasion." But Ickes saw that "the president had not yet reached the state of mind where he [was] willing to be aggressive as to Japan." FDR, he found, expected Japan to "draw herself in" rather than strike out.

Grew predicted war: On November 3, he telegrammed that Japan did have a gun—in the form of "obvious preparations to implement a program of war"—and Tokyo would almost certainly use it "if her peace program fails." He warned that Japan's military might launch an "all-out, do or die attempt, actually risking national hara-kiri," by lashing out "with dangerous and dramatic suddenness" in the hope of making the nation "impervious" to foreign pressures. He still hoped to see some sort of diplomatic reversal, but neither government seemed ready to come to terms without its preconditions having first been accepted.

Within the administration, pressure mounted from Stimson and Morgenthau to declare war on Germany, while Ickes favored war with Japan. But declaring war against any power in the Axis alliance ran a nightmare risk: a two-front war. General Marshall advocated holding off war with Japan. He needed just a couple more months to reach what he termed "impressive strength," the air firepower arriving in short order to pose a "positive threat" against a southward move by Japan. The army chief of staff urged "clever diplomacy," even suggesting that Roosevelt consider relaxing oil restrictions for a period in order to slow the pressure building within Japan for war, until the threat of retaliation on Tokyo itself worked to block attack. Under the radar, Chennault's AVG pilots were sailing for Burma to begin aerial operations against Japanese installations from the airstrip he'd had built over the border in China.

The shadow war in the Pacific was a photographic negative of the undeclared war in the Atlantic; the U.S. hoped to avoid attack by Japan for as long as possible while seeking a German strike that might precipitate open war in the Atlantic. Foreign relations through the unusually warm Washington autumn thus became, in Secretary Stimson's words, "diplomatic fencing"—thrust and parry, thrust and parry, holding off the opponent for as long as possible, not striking a touch until the opponent bloodied him first. Informed Americans recognized that the nation's days of peace were numbered. On November 10, William Shirer told a large audience in Milwaukee "that the showdown between Japan and the United States would come within four weeks. . . ."

Time was indeed running short. On November 15, a Magic intercept confirmed November 25 as Japan's avowed final date for reaching an accord with the West, a date described as "absolutely immovable." In Japan, Yamamoto solidified the plan of attack. War games and target practice focused on sea targets. The Japanese press threw off the gloves. In the past, news outlets would scold the U.S. and then hold out an olive branch. The olive branch had withered. One newspaper insulted the American "soul of a prostitute." Another freely wrote that Japan's "war structure" was being readied for "armed clash in the Pacific." U.S. and British intelligence reported that Japan's military had begun positioning troops, aircraft, and carriers at bases and ports in the South Pacific Islands.

On Tuesday, November 25, Roosevelt met with his War Council, minus Hopkins, who was back in the Naval Hospital trying to regain his strength. The president told the men that an attack was likely, perhaps to come as early as the following Monday. He thought the Japanese would carry out their initial move without declaring war, saying they were "notorious for making an attack without warning." He raised the possibility of "maneuver[ing] them into the position of firing the first shot without allowing too much danger to ourselves."

Some consider this exchange within the War Council a decision to open the door to an attack by Japan, raising the disturbing specter of FDR knowing in advance of the Japanese plan to attack Pearl Harbor without taking steps to ensure its having been adequately defended. However, documents from the period show nothing of the kind, instead demonstrating FDR's continued focus on arousing public opinion to push him into war, with no specific foreknowledge about the targets Japan was then mobilizing to attack. The Oval Office discussion that day centered on the grounds the U.S. had for going to war with Japan. Japan had been warned the previous summer that moving into Thailand would be "violating our safety," recalled Stimson. Hull would tell the Japanese ambassador that enlarging Japan's occupation zone in southeastern Asia further would bring war with the United States.

When Stimson got back to his War Department offices, military intelligence informed him that Japan's forces were, in fact at that very instant, on the move. Five army divisions had embarked on as many as fifty transports that were now heading south. Stimson phoned FDR. The president responded with shock, describing the movement as "evidence of bad faith on the part of the Japanese," whom he accused of negotiating a truce involving withdrawal from Indochina while mobilizing this large military force.

In the month and a half from mid-September, when FDR ordered the navy to begin escorting convoys, to the end of October, Atlantic Fleet warships brought fourteen convoys, composed of some 675 ships in total, across the North Atlantic. Several times the convoys encountered

U-boats. The German submarine fleet had tripled in size over the past year. The newer submarines were being christened at the rate of four per month. They had a cruising range of more than ten thousand miles, and each packed twenty-two torpedoes.

On October 16, American escorts, together with British and Canadian warships, were bringing over a slow eastbound convoy. Suddenly, at around eight in the evening, as they were chugging through the blackness of the long North Atlantic night, an explosion lit up the dark. It was the beginning of a gauntlet of terror and death throughout the night—and the first American deaths in the undeclared war. A Norwegian freighter sunk before anyone aboard could escape. Flares and star shells sparkled against the black sky, casting a pale glow over the sea and the dozens of ships arrayed on the edge of the eerie phosphorescent light. Protective depth charges were dropped, deep booms rolling over the ocean. Sighting nothing in the gloaming, the convoy moved on.

A bit more than an hour later, though, a tanker exploded, turning into a gargantuan blowtorch, the flames reaching more than three hundred feet into the sky. Less than two minutes later, another ship was blasted and sank. Nobody saw or spotted an enemy vessel in the surface reflection of the fires and illumination shells. Two more ships exploded almost simultaneously. Nothing. At exactly midnight, another tanker burst into flames that ran its entire length. The great column of fire lit up the entire convoy in a hellishly flickering red glow.

At the mauled convoy's trailing end the USS *Kearny* twice dropped depth charges, hoping to shoo off unseen U-boats following behind the convoy. A thousand yards back, *U-568* prowled off the convoy's stern flank. The glare of the burning tanker, visible for fifty miles, silhouetted *Kearny* as sharply as a noontime shadow. *U-568* loosed three torpedoes in a fan pattern. *Kearny*'s bridge watch spotted the iridescent white snakes approaching through the water. Her captain ordered a full halt. Every breath aboard ship stopped.

The first shot passed slightly forward of the bow. The skipper ordered full ahead. The second torpedo slipped by the stern. At ten minutes past midnight, October 17, the third torpedo pierced the hull slightly forward of amidships, penetrating the steel plates below the waterline. The explosion blew out the forward boiler room. Seven men there were killed instantly. Four more sailors died and many others were wounded when the blast blew through the main deck, knocking a stack askew and ripping apart the rear of the bridge. Tons of seawater rushed into the gaping hole in the ship. By sealing off compartments, the repair crew managed to save the *Kearny*. Slowly she churned on. Another tanker in the convoy was hit. More depth charges thumped out in the black ocean night.

As gray dawn finally arrived, the attackers seemed to have left. A British corvette crammed with survivors turned back to assist *Kearny* and the other stragglers. A waiting U-boat sunk the Royal Navy warship. Nobody sighted or heard her going under. Another British destroyer shepherding the last of the surviving merchants exploded. Not a single one of the five submarines participating in the slaughter was even damaged.

Kearny finally limped into the Reykjavik harbor for repairs, care for the wounded, services for the dead. The eleven men killed on the USS *Kearny* were the first official American military combat casualties of the war.

"The shooting war has started," a somber Roosevelt intoned at the annual Navy Day speech on October 27. "And history has recorded," the president declared, "who fired the first shot. In the long run, however, all that will matter is who fired the last shot." He added, ". . . it can never be doubted that the goods will be delivered by this nation, whose Navy believes in the tradition of 'Damn the torpedoes; full speed ahead!'" Fine words, fiery phrases, yet Roosevelt still lacked the confidence to charge at full speed into Congress. And at sea, his green navy men, confided Stimson, remained "thoroughly scared about their inability to stamp out the sub menace."

Hoping to fan war fever at home further, Roosevelt sought to raise public alarm about Nazi intentions in America's own hemisphere. Hitler continued to deny any interest in extending his empire beyond Europe. Americans had made abundantly clear they would not go to war to defeat Hitler there. However, polls showed that more than 85 percent of Americans considered an attack anywhere in the Western Hemisphere a casus belli.

In the Navy Day speech, Roosevelt also denounced Hitler's claims "that his plans for conquest do not extend across the Atlantic Ocean." He possessed a map—"a secret map made in Germany by Hitler's government—by the planners of the new world order," FDR declared. "It is a map of South America and a part of Central America, as Hitler proposes to reorganize it." The map, he said, showed that the Germans planned to turn the present fourteen separate countries into "five vassal states, bringing the whole continent under their domination." One of "these new puppet states includes the Republic of Panama and our great life line—the Panama Canal." Any who still believed Hitler's ambitions did not reach across the Atlantic were thus shown to be wrong—or fascist dupes. "This map makes clear the Nazi design not only against South America but against the United States itself."

During his press conference the next day in the Oval Office, reporters asked where the "secret map" was. FDR pointed: The map, he said, is "in my basket at the present time." Reporters asked to see it. He refused. He told them the document had "certain manuscript notations" which if revealed "would in all probability disclose" its source.

Along with being "exceedingly unfair to a number of people"— presumably meaning it would put American intelligence agents in danger—laying it out for public scrutiny might "dry up the source of future information," FDR said. The reporters questioned the reliability of the source. One asked if the map might not be "a forgery or a fake of some sort" concocted by some unknown antifascist agitators. Roosevelt sought to sidestep the question. Finally, he insisted it came from "a source which is undoubtedly reliable. There is no question about that."

Here, he insisted, was evidence that Hitler meant to bring the Western Hemisphere within his dominion. He had yet to attack, but the "secret map" indicated that Germany was already planning for the future after it had conquered South and Central America. What Roosevelt did not say, and perhaps did not know, was that the map was counterfeited by William Stephenson's British Security Coordination agents.

FDR was aware that British sources had provided the map. If he did not ask about its authenticity, he knew he should. Speaking to Treasury Secretary Henry Morgenthau, Jr., about relations with Argentina a little over six months later, FDR revealed much about his thinking regarding strategic matters. "I may be entirely inconsistent," he said, "and furthermore, I am perfectly willing to mislead and tell untruths if it will help us win the war. . . ." He had yet to find the right formula for winning American support, but he was not done experimenting, even resorting to lies, deceit, and tricks in his search to find ways to arouse the nation for war.

Berlin reacted almost instantly to the "infamous statements" by "the Jewish faker" Roosevelt. They called on him to identify his sources. After that no further word was heard of the map, in Berlin or in Washington.

Events at sea continued to push well ahead of public opinion at home. On October 31, a German U-boat slipped a torpedo into the center magazine of the destroyer *Reuben James*. Unlike the *Kearny*, she split in two and sank in seconds. One hundred fifteen sailors and officers went down with her. Rueful memories of the U.S. entry into World War One, driven by the same *drip-drip-drip* of torpedoed ships sinking beneath the Atlantic waves, muted the public outcry for revenge. As with the *Panay* on the Yangtze, many Americans continued to fault their own nation for having placed American ships in harm's way.

After the attack on the *Kearny*, FDR had called on Congress to permit arming of merchant ships and to let U.S. vessels sail into declared combat zones and on to belligerent—British—ports, overturning the last of the Neutrality Acts still in effect. Ohio senator Robert Taft denounced these moves as a tacit declaration of war. Illinois Republican representative George W. Gillie urged colleagues "to serve notice to the world . . . that the Yanks are not coming, that our sailors are not going to be sent to die in European waters, and that eighty percent of the American people are still firm in their resolve not to become involved in a shooting war on foreign soil." Congress, nonetheless, voted to end the last restrictions of the five-year-old Neutrality Act—although by thin margins (50-37 in the Senate and 212-194 in the House).

Armed American merchant ships in convoys, escorted by American warships, now carried American-made war munitions through U-boat-infested war zones in the North Atlantic and the Irish and North Seas, to Liverpool, Southampton, and Archangel, and across the Pacific through the Sea of Japan to Vladivostok. If they encountered German or Italian vessels, they would fire on sight. The difference between this and war was only a formal declaration, a vote by the House of Representatives and a presidential signature. But even now, the latest vote showed that short of a direct attack, the people's representatives in Washington were not ready to declare war.

Deeply frustrated by the nation's continuing refusal to face reality, Admiral Stark wrote to his friend at the helm of the Asiatic Fleet, Admiral Thomas Hart, "The Navy is already in the war of the Atlantic, but the country doesn't seem to realize it. Apathy, to the point of open opposition, is evident in a considerable section of the press. . . . Whether the country knows it or not, *we are at war.*"

With his singular focus on the Atlantic, Stark did not realize that Hart, with his fleet in the Philippines, was, in fact, on the front lines of World War Two. On November 26, the most powerful combined air and sea force ever assembled, the *Kidō Butai*, the First Air Fleet, under the command of Vice Admiral Chuichi Nagumo on his flagship *Akagi*, sailed out from Hito-kappu Bay in the Kurile Islands. The Japanese carrier strike force consisted of six carriers carrying 414 fighters and bombers, accompanied by two battleships, three cruisers, nine destroyers, eight tankers, 23 submarines and eight mini-submarines. That same day (November 25 in Washington), Secretary of State Hull handed Japan's ambassador, Kichisaburō Nomura, and the special Japanese emissary for the Washington talks, Saburō Kurusu, a ten-point American proposal largely reiterating the U.S. position to date. Proposals in what became known as the "Hull Note" included a nonaggression agreement and Japanese withdrawal from China in return for a gradual resumption of economic relations with Japan. Hull suggested a ninety-day stay-of-hostilities while the two governments established, per the president, a modus vivendi leading to "a peaceful settlement in the entire Pacific area." The two Japanese emissaries agreed to bring the Hull Note to the government in Tokyo. No one in Washington knew that the First Air Fleet was now steaming toward Hawaii, but they were aware that the Hull Note offered no path away from war. The Americans understood this: Hull said later that "we had no serious thought that Japan would accept our proposal."

On November 27, with time running out, in a last, highly public bid to resolve the nations' differences, Hull escorted the two Japanese diplomats to meet with the president in the Oval Office. The men began cordially enough, with smiles for the press and cigarettes shared. The two sides restated their positions. But after forty-five minutes, the men knew they were at an impasse, and they knew what that meant. His face gone hard and eyes steely, Roosevelt warned the diplomats that Japan would be "the ultimate loser" if its leaders "decide to follow Hitlerism and courses of aggression." Japan, he said, must stop its "opposition to the fundamental principles of peace and order." As the grim-faced men parted ways, they knew that the charade of negotiations had come to an end.

The following morning *The New York Times* reported, "All United States efforts to solve differences with Japan appeared exhausted yesterday and the next move—either diplomatic or military—seemed up to Tokyo."

Running in silence through the Pacific, the *Kidō Butai* pressed toward X-Day.

28

Son of Man, Son of God

The Pacific, Honolulu, and Washington,
November–December 6, 1941

In Honolulu, on December 2, Captain Irving H. Mayfield, the Naval Intelligence officer in charge of Hawaii, closed the wiretaps he had placed on the Japanese Consulate's telephones twenty-two months before. They were illegal. Rather than risk "any possibility of international complications," he told his counterespionage team, to shut them off. With war news filling the headlines, nervous locals were already on edge. Who knew what Tokyo might do if the wiretaps were revealed? Nobody wanted to spark the fuse for war.

Honolulu's Federal Bureau of Investigation chief Robert Shivers did not share the military's diplomatic concerns. Even now the G-man's five-agent team was closing in on the fox den–like consulate. Several times Shivers paid Consul General Kita visits. In their icy exchanges, social niceties slicing about like knives, each man wondered who was cat and who mouse. Shivers faced others' constitutional scruples in trying to trap the spies—his attempts to read the consulate's radio transmissions, broadcast to Tokyo from an off-site commercial shortwave office, were rebuffed by the local broadcast company, citing privacy concerns.

He was sure that personnel in the Japanese Consulate were up to something more important than just pushing paperwork to speed visa requests. Two weeks earlier, FBI director J. Edgar Hoover sent word to

Shivers that Japan and the U.S. had for all practical purposes broken off negotiations to stave off war. Ignoring the Constitution and the military intelligence officers' orders, Shivers put his own tap on a consulate telephone line. A translator listening in told him that the consulate had ordered its staff to burn code books and other papers. Shivers asked, Why? Why now? He couldn't just arrest the wily Kita, or the dissembling Morimura for pretending to be a hard-drinking, loose-limbed tourist squiring tittering painted whores in kimonos around town, while always keeping the navy and army installations and the Pearl Harbor basin in his sights. Shivers felt certain Kita and Morimura were spies, and likely just part of a nest of spies, possibly the hub of an intelligence network spread throughout the islands. He wanted some hard evidence to bring it down.

Shivers did not know that he should question Kita about the two crewmen he had met with several times aboard the Japanese passenger liner *Taiyo Maru* after it arrived in Honolulu Harbor on November 1. In sailing for Oahu, the liner had followed an unusual course in from the north. As the ship approached Oahu, Lieutenant Commander Suguru Suzuki and Sublieutenant Keiu Matsuo, intelligence officers disguised as stewards, had kept day-and-night watch as the liner steamed along the approach laid out for it by the Japanese navy. About two hundred miles out of Oahu, for the first time in the voyage, they observed a U.S. reconnaissance patrol and made note of the most distant line the flight covered.

Once their ship docked in Honolulu, Consul General Kita came aboard, where he retrieved ninety-seven detailed questions the two men had for Yoshikawa. Fearing Yoshikawa's detection, Kita served as the courier between the men. The information requested included what day of the week most ships would be in Pearl Harbor—Sunday—and how many seaplanes patrolled Pearl Harbor dawn and dusk—about ten that Yoshikawa had observed. Yoshikawa gave Kita most of the answers, as well as sketches and maps, even photographs, which Kita passed on to Suzuki and Matsuo.

Things had sped up since then. Tokyo relayed orders for Yoshikawa to report every three days on the presence of ships in Pearl Harbor and, just a few days ago, twice each day. "We knew then," he said, "that things were building to a climax and that my work was almost done."

American intelligence had picked up signals that Japanese naval fleets were on the move. A large task force last known to be in the remote Kurile Islands was in all likelihood on a southerly heading—though an attack on Siberia could still not be ruled out. General Marshall and his navy counterpart Admiral Stark sent out top-secret "war warning" orders in late November to the highest command levels in the Pacific, with the alert that "Japan is expected to make an aggressive move within the next few days." The most likely attack would come "against either the Philippines or the Kra Peninsula [Isthmus] or possibly Borneo." Four thousand miles from Japan on Oahu, "the strongest fortress in the world," those orders translated to mean "watch out for saboteurs."

And thus, the series of messages that flowed through the army and navy's Pacific Command headquarters warning of a "possible" Japanese amphibious attack in the last week of November and first week of December did not seem to apply to Pearl Harbor. However, with "acts of sabotage and espionage probable," watches were extended, leaves curtailed, and aircraft while on the ground rolled together, wings folded up, in a straight line like a closed zipper down the center of the runway, giving guards a clear line of sight for watch over them against attempts at sabotage. Unthinkingly, those orders set the aircraft closely together, as if fastened in a long chain. No approaching airplane could miss such a target.

Harry Hopkins spent most of November in a sickbed in the Naval Hospital. He turned over day-to-day control of the Lend-Lease program, but monitored its progress from bed. As often as he could, he taxied the short distance to the White House for dinner. Even getting out of bed to sit in pajamas and robe with the president required enormous effort. His physicians urged him to stay clear of stress. Yet every significant in- or outbound White House memorandum and report passed through him. The president sent orders to the hospital with messages scratched on them for Hopkins to take care of matters. By December 3, Hopkins had regained enough strength to move back to his Lincoln Study bedroom suite in the White House.

Three days later, on Saturday, December 6, *New York Times* editors were readying the following morning's newspaper. The main war-news analysis pointed to an apparent relaxation in previously warlike statements out of Tokyo. The next morning's headline would read: "Japan Rattles Sword but Echo Is Pianissimo." Tokyo, wrote the *Times*, seemed to be seeking time, possibly to prepare for war—or, more likely, "Japan does not wish the war." The latest issue of *Life* magazine pointed out that, while Japan might talk tough, thanks to the severe American embargo its military was in no position to take on another enemy. "Japan is desperate and getting weaker every day," the popular weekly trumpeted. A Gallup Poll at the start of the month found that slightly more than 50 percent of respondents expected war with Japan. If war came, "Americans felt confident, rightly or wrongly, that the Japs were pushovers," *Life*'s review of the past week's news proclaimed. Cover date: December 8, 1941.

A week earlier, on December 1 (November 30 in Honolulu) in Tokyo, the country's ruling oligarchy came together for an unprecedented fourth Imperial Conference in five months. The time had come to approve the final decision to attack. Tension, an air of doubt, even desperation filled the Eastern Hall. Everyone rose and bowed as the emperor entered the room. The ritual began. Dour-faced, the men, in their assigned order, spoke one by one. Points were raised about the Hull Note and the impossibility of accepting such demands. This, as at the previous Imperial Conferences, served ceremonial purposes. Last to speak came the new prime minister, General Tojo. "We are fully prepared for a long war," he said. The goal, though, was ". . . to do everything we can . . . to bring the war to an early conclusion." The gathered momentum for war, the closed thinking process of the ruling oligarchy, and hubris based on past victories—the conviction that a stone thrown at a tiger's head will drive off the beast—obliterated any hope for rational consideration of the calamity upon which they were embarking.

"At the moment our Empire stands at the threshold of glory or oblivion," Tojo told the conferees. "His Majesty reaches a decision to commence hostilities, [and] we will all strive to repay our obligations to him, bring the Government and the military ever closer together, resolve that the nation united will go on to victory, make an all-out effort to achieve our war aims, and set his Majesty's mind at ease." The nation would, as he had previously urged, "jump off the platform of the Kiyomizu."

The emperor nodded as he gave his blessings to the decision: "The Empire," he assented with his silence, "will go to war with the United States, Britain, and the Netherlands." As Hirohito departed, Field Marshal Hajime Sugiyama, the army chief of staff, noted, "He seemed to be in an excellent mood, and we were filled with awe."

The next day, December 2, Admiral Yamamoto stood on the bridge of the *Nagato*, which hung at anchor in the Inland Sea, near Hiroshima. Word came that the emperor had given imperial blessings on December 8 (December 7 in the United States) as "X-Day." He sent out a radio message to Vice Admiral Nagumo's First Air Fleet, which would shortly cross the international date line. "Climb Mount Niitaka 1208," the message read. Mount Niitaka looms high over the island of Formosa (Taiwan), then the tallest peak in the Japanese Empire. War to rid Japan of its Western foes would begin on December 8.

On Saturday, December 6 (7 in Japan), President Roosevelt cabled a personal message from the White House through Ambassador Grew in Tokyo directly to Emperor Hirohito. He reiterated the proposals made in the Hull Note two weeks earlier and appealed to Tennō's sense of "a sacred duty to restore traditional amity and prevent further death and destruction in the world." After dinner, Eleanor Roosevelt brought two people she'd met with that evening to the president's study to wish him good night. FDR shared his gallows humor with the three of them. "Well," he said, ". . . this son of man has just sent his final message to the Son of God."

Half an hour later, FDR and Harry Hopkins lounged and smoked in their pajamas and robes in the president's study. A navy captain arrived with the day's Magic briefing. While the officer waited, Roosevelt reviewed the decrypted transcripts. His face darkened. He handed the pages to Hopkins, who read them while walking slowly back and forth in front of the president. Hopkins handed them back. Roosevelt finally said what both men were thinking: "This means war." The Japanese had rejected FDR's earlier call for a modus vivendi.

A year of diplomatic fencing had reached its end. A sword blow was about to fall. The Japanese might attack anywhere, and very soon, said Hopkins. Perhaps, he suggested, the time had come for the U.S. to "strike the first blow and prevent any sort of surprise."

A solemn FDR pointedly demurred. "No, we can't do that," he insisted. "We are a democracy and a peaceful people." He would not cede to the impulse for preemptive war—or his political reflexes refused to move in that way. The full implications of what lay ahead hit the two friends like a punch to the chest. Roosevelt felt he had done everything he could to prevent war with Japan. He raised his voice and said: "But we have a good record!"

The Japanese task force pressed on through heavy seas toward Oahu. More than ever, the *Kidō Butai* required last-minute information about American military activities on the island. Tokyo cabled the Honolulu Consulate for immediate information about "the movements of the fleet subsequent to the fourth." On Saturday, December 6 (December 7 in Tokyo), Yoshikawa left his office around ten in the morning for

Pearl Harbor. Returning at two that afternoon, he wrote out a message for transmission. He went through possible air defenses, noting that he had seen no signs of barrage balloons anywhere, nor torpedo nets around the battleships. "I imagine," he cabled, "that in all probability there is considerable opportunity left to take advantage for a surprise attack against these places."

He headed back out and returned in the evening to write up his final cable of the day. He read his dispatch: "No barrage balloons sighted. Battleships are without crinolines [torpedo netting]. No indications of air or sea alert wired to nearby islands." He made note that the carriers *Enterprise* and *Lexington* had gone to sea. Yoshikawa recalled later on, "I knew that the message I was working on might well be the last which the Japanese attack force commander would receive before the attack."

He buzzed the radio room code clerk. Japan's secret agent in Hawaii paused before handing him the paper. He knew, "I held history in the palm of my hand."

His messages for the day reached Admiral Yamamoto aboard the *Nagato*. The intelligence staff forwarded Yoshikawa's observation that Pearl Harbor showed "no indication of any changes in U.S. Fleet or anything unusual." Magic intercepts, decryptions, and translators would not unlock his message for a few days.

Aboard the *Akagi*, Nagumo received word from Tokyo based on Yoshikawa's transmission. He ordered his carriers, now moving slowly through rolling, vacant seas four hundred miles off and bearing southward toward Oahu, to turn into the wind and prepare their aircraft to launch before daylight.

The USS *Utah* was among the ships whose position Yoshikawa had detailed in that day's penultimate message to Tokyo. She was berthed at a fixed mooring about a hundred yards northwest of Ford Island. As it happened all three Pacific Fleet carriers were at sea, so the *Utah* had moored on what some called "Carrier Row." For the past two days the crew of the *Utah* had grumbled as they'd shouldered and stacked the tree-thick timbers that had shielded her decks into stacks eight feet high topside. They were being readied for off-loading on Monday. After nine weeks at Pearl Harbor, *Utah* was heading for the West Coast, where another training rotation awaited. The seamen from California couldn't wait to get back home.

As night settled over the still harbor, Navy reservist John Vaessen, the former shipyard worker from Sonoma, settled into his rack. It had been a frustrating evening for the twenty-five-year-old unmarried sailor. Earlier he had joined the famous "river of white," the moving, roiling flow of white-uniformed sailors along Hotel Street on Saturday night liberty. Vaessen had quickly abandoned the chase for whatever action a young man making thirty-six dollars a month might find in the bars, dance halls, shooting galleries, and whorehouses. After wandering around, drinking a beer and avoiding the MPs, Vaessen caught the early bus and liberty boat back to ship. He needed a night's sleep anyway. He had early watch in the dynamo room.

In Compartment 3C near Vaessen's, twenty-two-year-old fellow reservist Don Green climbed into his berth. He, too, needed to be sharp in the morning. The Iowan would play first base for the ship's team in the Pacific Fleet championship game at the diamond on Ford Island. Orders came down from the bridge for the baseball team to be ready to leave the ship at "zero aight unnerht shop," he mocked—eight in the morning on the dot.

Pete Tomich, the chief water tender, made his last inspection of the fiery boiler room deep in the ship's bowels. He kept a head of steam in Boiler No. 2 to ready the ship to motor over to the yard on Monday to off-load her stacks of timbers before heading stateside.

Across Ford Island and its airstrip and hangars, now closed up tight, eight-year-old Charlotte Coe lay in bed, trying to fall asleep, in her family's Quarters J house. She could hear the films being shown that Saturday night and see the lights flickering aboard the USS *Arizona* on

*Reserve Ensign Donald Green
had this portrait made while
stationed aboard USS* Utah *in
Pearl Harbor.*

Battleship Row. Charlotte and her brother Chuckie were home with a
sitter. That evening her father, Lieutenant Commander Charles L. Coe,
Ford Island's third in command, and his wife had gone out for dinner,
possibly to the Ramseys' place, just the other side of Admiral Patrick
Bellinger's house at the top of the married officers' quarters' loop. Captain Logan Ramsey was Bellinger's chief of staff. As the evening ended,
Ramsey called out to the departing guests, "Well, let's hope the Japs
wait until after Christmas before they start raising hell in the Pacific."

As he often did before going to bed, Yoshikawa strolled among the
consulate's carefully tended garden beds, palm trees, fragrant flowering

hibiscus, and plush lawns. Stars glimmered in the dark sky above. He had heard a PBY on patrol buzzing overhead earlier in the evening. It had departed the scene. Only the sound of his footfalls and the fluttering leaves penetrated the sweet Honolulu night.

"It was a quiet Saturday night," he observed, "and all seemed normal."

29

East Wind, Rain

Pearl Harbor, December 7, 1941

Shortly before eight in the morning, Sunday, December 7, still half asleep, Yoshikawa sat down for breakfast. A distant explosion snapped him awake. He thought it might be a navy exercise. A second explosion quickly followed. Then another. Consul General Kita rushed in. The two tuned in Radio Tokyo over the shortwave. The routine eight a.m. news came on. During the weather forecast, the announcer slowly stated, "East wind, rain." He repeated the words. The two men looked at each other in stunned silence. Those were the code words announcing that the war had begun.

In the routine quiet of early Sunday morning in Pearl Harbor, Don Green was pulling on his flannel baseball pants on the USS *Utah* alongside a few other half-dressed, bleary-eyed men. He took a step and the compartment and everyone and everything in it heaved fifteen feet sideways and upward before sighing back. Green found himself in the air and then within a tangle of arms, legs, and footlockers. At the bottom of the pile, a fellow Iowan cracked to Green, "I like ordinary reveille better."

The bewildered sailors climbed back to their feet. Green went back to pulling on his uniform, rushing to be ready to leave ship for the game. With no public address system aboard the old ship, they listened for a bosun's pipe, a bugle call, or a coxswain's scream from down a hatch to let them know what could have just shoved 21,825 tons of ship dead starboard against her cement moorings before her overstretched lines tugged her back to port.

The second explosion split 3C's after bulkhead open like a coconut shell from deck to ceiling. The blast lifted the deck up in what seemed like slow motion, and then it dropped away as if a trapdoor had been sprung beneath the men's feet. Green swiped for a passing girder as he fell. He came to rest amid a jumble of debris and stunned, cursing men. Seeing his footlocker toppled nearby, he reached in and buckled on the precious fifty-dollar Elgin Special wristwatch for which he had plunked down five dollars in San Diego and been paying off the rest at the rate of two dollars a week ever since. The watch read seven fifty-five.

The ship lurched hard back to port, and now he could see the bilgy green water of Pearl Harbor sloshing over the combing around the adjoining compartment's doorway. Feet were drumming overhead and a babble of voices echoed about the off-kilter ship without him being able to make any sense of them. "I could hear no order, no authority, no control," he realized. "This wasn't the Navy I knew."

A few moments later, the coxswain's voice rang down the ladder, "The Japs are attacking! No shit this time!" The old and tired target ship *Utah* had been among the very first ships in Pearl Harbor the Japanese attackers struck. Green had to get out, but with the ship listing over hard and much of the interior twisted into an incomprehensibly distorted wreck, he did not know which way was out. He raced through several compartments and passageways. He felt the deck beneath him, which had been leaning, begin to roll. Everything—footlockers, racks, tables, and all their contents—began sliding and skidding; metal shrieked, bolts popped and equipment flipped and slammed into the bulkheads. He found a clear escape ladder and scrambled topside.

From the steeply leaning maindeck, he watched as a plane with red circles on its lower wings dropped a bomb that hit the water with an explosion. Another fighter flew in with tracers bursting out of its wing guns. Green could see that the plane's canopy was open. The pilot's long white scarf fluttered out in the wind. He was grinning as he fired at a target on the beach. Green started to follow other sailors lowering themselves hand over hand along the mooring ropes running from the ship. Another fighter zoomed in, strafing. Green dropped back on the listing ship. Another sailor's hand reached out and grabbed him, pulling him to cover as bullets zipped and pinged nearby. The *Utah* rolled over entirely on her side. Finding himself in the water, Green swam for shore. Scrambling for cover, he looked at the Elgin Special on his wrist: eight ten.

Inside the dying *Utah*, chief water tender Pete Tomich called out above the ear-rending racket of tearing steel, muffled explosions, screaming men, and chaotic motion, "Get out!" He could feel the ship rolling and knew that in moments any hope of escape would vanish. "Get topside! Go. . . . The ship is turning over! You have to escape now!" he ordered his crew of firemen in Boiler Room 2. As the ship listed more than forty degrees, scalding steam was whistling out through the antiquated valve cocks and turning the always tropical engine room into a steam cooker. With the room tilting about them, the other tenders crowded up the ladder, praying that up still led out. They looked back at Tomich, who remained behind, trying to shut the fired-up boilers down. If they blew, the entire ship would go.

That was the last anybody saw of Tomich, who would receive the Medal of Honor posthumously for his heroism, though no next of kin would be found to accept the award for another sixty-five years.

Fifteen minutes after the first bomb hit, the ship lay upside down in the oil-black, burning water. John Vaessen, who had been settling into his morning watch in the dynamo room deep amidships, had no idea what had happened aboard the *Utah* as he made his way down through the labyrinthine belowdecks darkness. Down had now become up. He lit the way with a flashlight he carried with him from the dynamo room. Climbing through wreckage and twisted metal, he reached the bilge crawlway beneath the hull. By luck, he found a heavy wrench.

Within minutes of the first torpedo strike, the Utah *started capsizing at its mooring off Ford Island.*

He started to pound on the steel hull overhead. He heard rapid knocks answering his taps. He didn't know they were Japanese bullets striking the hull while strafing the men who had scrambled up onto it.

After what seemed like an eternity of knocking and waiting in the dark space breathing the stifling, foul air, a blowtorch opened a small square in the hull. Vaessen climbed blinking through the passage to the surface of Pearl Harbor. He emerged into an utterly changed world from the one he thought he knew and gaped at the devastation surrounding the overturned USS *Utah*. Thick black smoke covered Pearl Harbor like storm clouds; he could see dark hulks burning on the water; smoking ships lay beached; even the water was on fire. Bodies floated amid the debris in the black water. The home of the Pacific Fleet was barely recognizable. Looking out at the sunshine paradise gone to hell, he asked the first sailor he saw, "What happened?"

"We're at war!" one of his rescuers shouted above the noise.
"Who with?"
"Japan."

Yoshikawa and Kita hurried to their offices. They began burning the last of the code books, diplomatic cables, intelligence instructions, and any other evidence of espionage that had not yet been thrown into the fire. A newspaper reporter knocked at the consulate doors asking for comment about the attack. Walking him politely but quickly back to the compound gate, Yoshikawa looked up. A Japanese navy dive-bomber roared overhead. His mission had achieved the emperor's purpose. His heart swelled as he watched the plane "with its red Rising Sun insignia streaking into the dense smoke clouds now rolling towards the city from the harbor."

Outside the compound fence, a line of armed soldiers had gathered. He ran back to his office and locked the doors while he and Kita completed burning anything incriminating. Soon the American soldiers stormed in. Military police followed. They began rifling through the consulate files.

All they found was ash. As they led Kita and Yoshikawa away, an overlooked scrap of paper in the trash can caught the master spy's eye. On it he had drawn the locations of the capital ships of the Pacific Fleet, many now burning or sunk, in Pearl Harbor.

A resounding explosion awoke Charlotte Coe from a sound sleep. The eight-year-old hazily thought the navy was dredging up coral in the harbor again. Her father was already up, following his usual routine of making his Sunday morning pancakes for the family. He shouted, "Get up! The war's started." The children and their mother threw on their robes and slippers and ran outside. Charlotte looked up as they stepped out the door. A khaki-colored airplane with red circles under its wings zoomed past so low she could see the pilot's face. For some reason he did not strafe them.

The Coes had practiced this drill. They sprinted the hundred yards to Admiral Bellinger's house and down the curved driveway to the old gun emplacement below it, Charlotte's father carrying her five-year-old brother Chuckie the whole way. They scurried into their scary Dungeon playhouse. Lieutenant Commander Coe set down his son so he could talk to the admiral, who had run in with them. Chuckie could not resist all the Fourth of July explosions, flames, and noise going on outside. He raced back out of the Dungeon. This time Japanese bullets zinged about him. His father chased him down and brought him back, kicking and crying. His mother pinned him tightly to the floor.

Lieutenant Commander Coe ran home to dress. Just as he got to the door, a massive pressure wave blew through him, followed by a tremendous, deafening detonation. The explosion sent him sprawling and knocked the wind out of him. Steel plates, chunks of superstructure, debris from the USS *Arizona* showered across the lawn. A brick-size chunk of steel ripped through the garage's two layers of wood and smashed in the bumper of his car. Nothing hit Coe. The *Arizona* was reduced to a flaming, twisted hulk. He didn't know it yet, but Admiral Isaac C. Kidd, who had been such a favorite of his children, had been killed.

Coe dressed and left the house. As he did he saw "a sight beyond belief . . . the most awful thing I had ever seen." Through the billowing black smoke, he could make out farther along Battleship Row that the *Oklahoma* was capsizing. As the monstrous battleship turned turtle, he thought of the men trapped inside. It hit him like another bomb blast: "War had come to Hawaii." He drove away with Admiral Bellinger. As the attack continued, his family did not know if he was still alive until he returned twenty-four hours later.

In the Dungeon shelter, Charlotte watched as her neighbors filed in and crowded together, away from the big openings. Explosions rocked the concrete walls and floors. Charlotte stood next to her mother, who held her brother tightly. Charlotte felt the need to do something: She

Pearl Harbor shortly after the start of the attack, viewed from a Japanese airplane. The Utah *lists on the near side of Ford Island while a torpedo explodes against the USS* West Virginia *at the far side of the island. The USS* Arizona *is tied in just above her and the USS* Oklahoma *just below on Battleship Row. The Coe family lived in married officers' housing at the eastern part of the island (here shown at the top left).*

raised her fist and shouted, "Those dirty Germans!" Her mother below her said quietly, "Hush, ChaCha. It's the Japanese."

Before long, survivors who made it ashore from the burning battle-ships began to filter into the shelter of what had once been the children's playhouse of horrors. They were wide-eyed, scared, coated in oil. They were the lucky ones. Others had been hit by the blasts or caught in the oil burning on the water. Many were barely alive; burnt flesh hung off them in ribbons. Charlotte had not known that skin could crisp and melt. Grown men in shock sat or lay down, their empty eyes gazing into space. Several men died while the children struggled to follow their mother's orders not to look. Neighbors ran out during a lull in the attack and brought blankets, sheets, anything to clean wounds and wipe off the oil that clung to the men. Charlotte looked at a naked and shivering sailor propped against a wall next to her. She unzipped her blue quilted bathrobe and handed it to him. He wrapped his bare body and thanked her.

Charlotte's mother went up to a young marine nearby. She asked him to step aside so she could speak to him. She knew about the atrocities the Japanese had inflicted on Chinese women and children. She implored him that if the Japanese came ashore for what all expected would be a full-scale invasion, he should save three bullets in the pistol he carried. She told him forcefully: "When I am sure that my children are dead, then you will shoot me."

"Yes, ma'am."

Oily black smoke pouring out of the burning *Arizona* floated into the Dungeon. The children's playhouse had saved their lives. When Charlotte finally went out, she saw gigs and barges buzzing about, fires burning, bodies lying unrecognizable as human on the grass and pier where she and her brother and friends had played so often. Pearl Harbor was utterly transformed. Shocked, barely able to comprehend all she was seeing, the thought occurred to her: "A lot of those men I'd seen coming along the dock from their ships were never coming again."

On December 7, Secretary Henry Stimson went to his War Department office early. He hadn't seen the Magic decrypts yet and noted in his diary, "Today is the day that the Japanese are going to bring their answer" to the Hull Note and the modus vivendi offer. The secretary of war met that morning with Secretary of State Cordell Hull and Secretary of the Navy Frank Knox. The three old men of the Cabinet shared their certainty that "the Japs are planning some deviltry," and they were "all wondering where the blow will strike."

At two that afternoon, President Roosevelt called Stimson. "Have you heard the news?" he asked. Stimson thought he meant that the Japanese were advancing into the Gulf of Siam. "Oh, no," came the president's

Seemingly still in shock, Charlotte Coe, left, with her mother and brother, Chuck, in a newspaper photo taken shortly after their return to the mainland U.S. following the attack on Pearl Harbor.

voice, "I don't mean that. They have attacked Hawaii. They are now bombing Hawaii."

Twenty minutes before Roosevelt called Stimson, the president and Hopkins had been eating lunch in the Oval Office. Knox had phoned to tell them an air raid was on in Hawaii. Hopkins had turned to the president and said something to the effect of "There must be some mistake . . . surely Japan would not attack in Honolulu."

According to Hopkins, the president remarked that he thought the report "was probably true." This, he said, "was just the kind of unexpected thing the Japanese would do. . . ." He and Hopkins discussed the president's efforts to keep the country out of the war. Hopkins jotted down afterward that FDR expressed "his earnest desire to complete his administration without war. . . ." Now, he said, if the reports coming in "were true it would take the matter entirely out of his own hands, because the Japanese had made the decision for him."

A bit later, Eleanor came in to see her husband. She noticed immediately his "deadly calm . . . almost like an iceberg." Messages had started to reach the White House that described the blow the Pacific Fleet and the airfields had taken on Oahu. The armed forces there were devastated. FDR's bitterness over the attack was evident, as was his realization of what lay ahead. "I never wanted to have to fight this war on two fronts," he told her. "We haven't got the navy to fight in both the Atlantic and the Pacific . . . so" a long buildup of forces would be required, and ". . . that will mean that we will have to take a good many defeats before we can have a victory." He anticipated those defeats would inflict more losses and terrible pain, but he knew, as he told a Joint Session of Congress the following morning, "we will gain the inevitable triumph. . . ." He finally asked for, and received, a declaration of war.

That day, under the headline "We All Have Only One Task," Robert McCormick's *Chicago Tribune*, the most influential isolationist paper in the country, wrote in a front-page editorial, "All that matters today is that we are in a war and we must face that fact." War abroad meant unity at home. A week later, the December 15 issue of *Time* magazine encapsulated the significance for the nation of the Japanese attack on Pearl Harbor and along the entire U.S. Pacific island-bridge to Asia. "The war," the editors wrote, "came as a great relief, like a reverse earthquake, that in one terrible jerk shook everything disjointed, distorted, askew back into place. Japanese bombs had finally brought national unity to the U.S." The bitter fight, the uncertain hours, the indecision were over. The United States was at war.

Unity, too, dawned that day in Berlin and Rome. Overnight on December 8, German foreign minister Ribbentrop called his Italian counterpart

Ciano. Ciano recorded that the foppish German was "jumping with joy about the Japanese attack. . . ." In the morning Ciano went to see Mussolini; the Duce "was also happy" that the attack had succeeded in "clarifying the position between America and the Axis." The next day Ribbentrop told Italy's ambassador to Berlin, Dino Alfieri, "The essential thing was that Japan was now in the fighting on the side of the Axis. . . . It was the most important event since the beginning of the war." That day the order went out to begin all-out attacks against U.S. ships. Assuring that the war would overspread the globe and believing that war would pin down American power, Hitler fulfilled his country's Tripartite Pact obligations and his own ambitions. He went to the Reichstag on December 11 to declare war on the United States. Italy followed Germany at once.

The shadow war was over. World War Two had begun in full.

Epilogue

Rendezvous with Destiny

Charles and Anne Lindbergh were at their home on Martha's Vineyard at the time of the attack. When Anne told Charles what she had heard on the radio, he found it beyond belief that an air attack could have penetrated Pearl Harbor's defenses. "How did the Japs get close enough, and where is our navy?" he asked. The man who had forecast the age of unstoppable aviation warfare could not imagine airplanes getting through a stoutly defended military installation.

When Congress declared war, he ruefully pointed to American actions as the cause: "We have been asking for war for months." He was certain that America First had kept war away for as long as possible: "If the President had asked for a declaration of war, I think Congress would have turned him down with a big majority. But now we have been attacked, and attacked in home waters. We have brought it on our own shoulders, but I can see nothing to do under these circumstances except to fight. If I had been in Congress, I certainly would have voted for a declaration of war."

He went to Washington eager to find a place in the military, but the White House made clear to him that his services were not welcome. He saw Stimson at his War Department office and asked to resume his commission in the Army Air Corps. Stimson's face tightened. He told Lindbergh to go home, that he was "unwilling to place in command of our troops as a commissioned officer any man who had such a lack of faith in our cause as he had shown in his speeches." Eventually the Ford

Motor Company hired Lindbergh to advise it on engineering bombers. He and Anne moved to Detroit. As the war went on, he test piloted aircraft, and went to the Pacific where he flew reconnaissance and combat missions, though as a freebooter, never being allowed to regain his Army Air Corps commission.

Most of his America First Committee associates agreed the time had come to fight. The organization that had proved such a brake on American entry into the war closed its doors. Both Bob Stuart and Kingman Brewster, its Yale student founders, enlisted, Stuart in the army, Brewster the navy.

Among those who immediately buried the hatchet were the commander in chief and his distant cousin, Theodore Roosevelt, Jr. A few days after the attack on Pearl Harbor, FDR signed off on a promotion for his political foe to brigadier general. Ted went to see Franklin in the White House. Upon leaving the Executive Mansion after their private meeting, Ted told waiting reporters he had gone to "pay my respects" to the president, with whom they knew he had feuded and battled for the better part of two decades. Everything had changed, he explained to the reporters. "Remember," he said, "it is our country, our war and our president." Truly his father's son, Ted Roosevelt, Jr., would win the Medal of Honor for his heroics as a fighting general, rousing his battered men on bloody Utah Beach to push up the landing beach in the face of withering German machine gun fire on D-Day, the invasion of Europe, June 6, 1944.

Neither FDR nor TR, Jr., would live to see the end of the war; both Roosevelts succumbed to heart disease.

Others struggled to remove the hatchet with less success. Harvard architecture student Philip Johnson, widely recognized as the most brilliant designer in his class, was drafted into the army in early 1943. He was almost thirty-seven years old. The year before he had tried to enlist in Naval Intelligence, hoping to put his German-language fluency to work, but the navy got word of his past associations with Nazi Germany and fascist organizations in the U.S. He was turned away. He then tried for a federal job that would make use of his language skills. When the interviewing officer read his FBI dossier, he was sent promptly back to school in Cambridge. FBI agents followed up with Johnson there not long after to learn more about his onetime mentor, Lawrence Dennis, his fellow guiding light in the American Fellowship Forum. Dennis and twenty-seven codefendants would soon go on trial for sedition.

Johnson had managed to avoid indictment. Shortly after being inducted into the army he was sent to Fort Ritchie in Maryland, which housed a German prisoner-of-war camp. He was assigned to interrogate German prisoners. When what was known as the Great Sedition Trial of 1944 finally reached court three years after the original indictments, Johnson was again interrogated about Dennis and the numerous cash gifts he had made to him. In fact the prosecutor hoped to prove that Johnson's money had not been enough to support Dennis, hoping to show Dennis received direct support from Germany.

As a result of the sedition trial depositions, Army Intelligence learned about Johnson's numerous connections to the suspected foreign agents. He was relieved of his duties interrogating prisoners and sent off to Fort Belvoir, to clean kitchens and latrines while awaiting word whether he, too, faced indictment. He managed to stay clear of the court and, after the war, began to design buildings that led to his emergence as one of the most prolific and influential architects of the postwar years.

Military police took Japanese Consulate consul general Nagao Kita and Takeo Yoshikawa, known still as Vice Consul Tadashi Morimura, into custody, along with hundreds of Japanese and Japanese American citizens, not one of whom had helped the Japanese Imperial Navy carry out its attack. U.S. authorities never discovered Yoshikawa's true identity or his role in the attack. He, Kita, and the entire consulate staff were held until August 1942, when they were exchanged for interned American diplomats being held in Japan. Back home he worked in Naval Intelligence for the remainder of the war.

After Japan surrendered in August 1945, fearing reprisals if American occupation forces learned of his spying at Pearl Harbor, he once again assumed a false identity. For several years, he posed as a Buddhist monk living in the countryside. His work as the Imperial Navy's spy at Pearl Harbor remained secret until December 1953, when a former Japanese navy officer spoke of Yoshikawa's role during an interview with a provincial Japanese newspaper. Yoshikawa had expected when his espionage work was revealed to the public he would be lionized for his courage in fulfilling his unique mission for the emperor. In the wake of the war's devastation, his countrymen rejected him. Scorned by neighbors, he ran a succession of small businesses that failed. He reportedly began to drink heavily.

In the 1960s, CBS News found Yoshikawa and persuaded him to return with them to Honolulu and the Shuncho-Ro Teahouse, where he had spent many nights spying on Pearl Harbor. They filmed him there for a television program. However, after locals found out who he was, newsman Walter Cronkite, who accompanied him, said, ". . . we barely got him out of town before the lynching." The Pearl Harbor spy returned to Japan, where he died penniless and largely forgotten in 1993.

Almost exactly four years after he left Germany, CBS Radio journalist William Shirer caught up with the U.S. First Army in Aachen, Germany, on November 8, 1944. It was the same German frontier city from which he had followed the German advance through Holland and Belgium into northern France in 1940. My father, Bernard Wortman, one of millions of American soldiers fighting around the world, was at Aachen with the First Army at about the same time. Another six months of hard, dogged, brutal fighting, from the west and the east, remained before

Berlin would fall and the Third Reich would finally cease to exist. My father arrived at the Buchenwald concentration camp not long after its liberation and saw the horrific vestiges of Nazi barbarity.

Five years after Shirer left Nazi Berlin, he went back to the devastated capital of the would-be Thousand-Year Reich. Adolf Hitler was dead. Berlin, most of Germany, much of Europe and Asia lay in ruins. Most of those among Hitler's henchmen who had not been killed, fled, or committed suicide now awaited trial for war crimes in Nuremberg, scene of Shirer's and Johnson's introductions to Hitler and where Shirer would report on the fate of the murderous men who had once dictated life and death for millions. Much of what Shirer had sought to convey within the limits of the censors' rule while reporting from Nazi Germany had come to pass. The world, infected and darkened by brutality, terror, and war, would never be the same.

On November 5, 1945, for the first time in five years, Shirer reported over the radio from Berlin. He found it a "strange" experience. No censors reviewed his script before the broadcast; no minders watched over him to stop him from telling the truth as he once again spoke the words, "Hello, America. This is Berlin."

Acknowledgments

We live in an era in which U.S. intervention in foreign conflicts has become the norm, very often to our eventual national regret. I wrote this book to understand better the time in which my parents and their generation lived, when the United States was a country that habitually stayed *out* of war, when, in hindsight, earlier interventions in Europe and Asia might have saved countless innocent lives. My views evolved during the nearly five years I worked on this book as a result of reading, archival research, countless conversations, and other communications with many people with diverse viewpoints. I am indebted to the many historians and authors who have written on this subject, starting with Robert E. Sherwood's superb 1948 *Roosevelt and Hopkins: An Intimate History*, which after nearly seventy years remains the richest book on that special, complex bond between two extraordinary men who reshaped the world.

I am deeply grateful to the New York Public Library for granting me a fellowship that gave me time to read through papers of the newsletter *Uncensored* and the Writer's Anti-War Bureau and to explore other materials from the period in that great library's collections. Research there crystallized my understanding of the depth and breadth of anti-interventionist sentiment and the political and social complexities of the time that help to explain Americans' unwillingness to enter World War Two. I am particularly grateful to Carolyn Broomhead, Thomas Lannon, and the staff of the Library's Manuscripts and Archives Division for making my time there so fruitful.

Several other archival research centers aided me. The FDR Presidential Library and Museum provided me with much assistance. Thanks to Bob Clark, Matthew Hanson, Paul Sparrow, and others there for their assistance. A visit to Hyde Park still gives us a true sense of FDR the man and the president.

Coe College in Cedar Rapids holds the William L. Shirer Papers and provided me with housing, congenial help, and ongoing assistance. I am particularly grateful to Jill Jack, chief archivist, Carla Frazer, and Kim Pribyl-Hulme. Ms. Jack introduced me to Linda Shirer Rae who thoughtfully answered questions about her father and provided me with wartime photos of him, some of which appear in this book.

The highly professional staff of Yale University's Manuscripts & Archives department has helped me many times over the years. William Massa and Judith Schiff in particular deserve my thanks.

Reading the Library of Congress's Theodore Roosevelt, Jr., Papers opened my eyes to a conflicted man and nation that had yet to grasp how to utilize its might, as well as to the Hyde Park vs. Oyster Bay Roosevelt family rivalries. The nation's library's staff helped me in many ways. I want to thank Roosevelt's grandson, Theodore Roosevelt IV, for sharing his insights into the man and family. Thanks to The American Legion and its archivist Howard C. Trace for help in looking into Roosevelt's role in that organization. Heather Cole, curator of the Theodore Roosevelt Collection at Harvard University's Houghton Library, also assisted me, as did Laurence Pels, executive director of the Theodore Roosevelt Association.

Other help came from the Federal Bureau of Investigation and the National Archives and Records Administration; the History of Aviation Collection at the University of Texas at Dallas; and the Intrepid Society and its director, Col. Gary Solar.

Countless conversations, letters, and emails have aided me throughout the process of writing this book. In many cases people did not even realize the importance of their help. I apologize to those whose names I have not included by accidental oversight. My thanks, in no particular order, go to David Kaiser, Richard Alexander, Jim Green, Richard Latture, Will Howarth, David Harrington, Franz Schulze, Eric Lamond, Zach Morowitz, Nathaniel Philbrick, Darroch Greer, Ron King, Michael Fitzsousa, Robbie Harris, Skip Lehman, Marco Epstein, Rick Clarke, Lee Branch, Larry Cenotto, Tom Frail, Bob Wilson, Peter Mersky, Bud Patten, Richard Breitman, Timothy Snyder, and Bernard Wasserstein. Thank you to the Honorable Bruce Smith, son of Lieut. Leonard "Tuck" Smith, for providing me with his flight logs and photographs from the war.

I am especially grateful for having had the opportunity to interview the late Charlotte Coe Lemann at length twice before her death. Her harrowing childhood memories of that awful day at Pearl Harbor, December 7, 1941, brought home the reality of the experience.

The Daily Beast literary editor, Lucas Wittmann, and his successor, Malcolm Jones, assigned me to write several review essays that helped organize my thinking on various aspects of the period. Thanks to both of you.

Peter McGuigan and Foundry Literary + Media represent me and my book. Thank you.

Grove Atlantic, as an independent publisher, carries on a noble fight as it contends with an increasingly consolidated industry. They do so with aplomb, professionalism, personal care, and a sense of collegiality and fun. It's a good home for this author. I have enjoyed help in publishing this book from the entire team there, but in particular from Sal Destro, Charles Rue Wood, Zachary Pace, Amy Hundley, Deb Seager, and Julia Berner-Tobin. My deepest gratitude goes to my editor, Joan Bingham. Joan is a kind and encouraging person as well as a formidable presence and a demanding editor who made this book far better and more readable through her work on it.

I want to thank the players on the numerous youth baseball teams I've coached over the last several years. Nothing like working with young players on making cutoffs to take your mind off writing.

My parents, brother, and sister have been supportive in any way they can be. My parents answered many questions I posed about their lives in America before the war that changed everything. Thank you.

Finally, my deepest and most enduring gratitude goes to my wife, Jodi Cohen, and my children, Rebecca and Charlie. Few households have somebody holed up in a book-crammed study from which a sometimes agonized writer emerges with a faraway look after dwelling many hours in another time and place day after day. They put up with that, my occasional extended absences for research, and worse. Our love and delight in each other sustain me in every way and ever more.

               Marc Wortman
               September 21, 2015
               New Haven, Connecticut

Endnotes

Abbreviations for Frequently Cited Sources

Archival Sources

CAL Papers: The Papers of Charles A. Lindbergh, Yale University Library, Manuscripts & Archives

FDR Press Conferences and Papers: Press Conferences of President Franklin D. Roosevelt, 1933–1945, FDR Library and Museum

FDR Speeches: Presidential Speeches and Addresses of Franklin D. Roosevelt and Others: http://www.presidency.ucsb.edu/ws/

HH Papers: Harry Hopkins Papers, FDR Library and Museum

Johnson FBI Report: FBI report, "Philip Cortelyan [sic] Johnson," online: http://www.scribd.com/doc/219654052/Architect-Philip-Johnson-FBI-File-Part-1 and -2

Shirer Papers: William L. Shirer Papers, Coe College, Stewart Memorial Library

Stimson, Diary: Henry L. Stimson Diary, Yale University Library, Manuscripts & Archives

TR, Jr., Papers: The Papers of Theodore Roosevelt, Jr., Library of Congress

Newspapers and Periodicals

CT: *Chicago Tribune*

NYT: *New York Times*

SJ: *Social Justice*

Published Sources

C&R Correspondence: Warren F. Kimball ed., *Churchill & Roosevelt: The Complete Correspondence, Alliance Emerging, October 1933–November 1942*, Volume 1 (Princeton, NJ: Princeton University Press, 1984)

Ciano, *Diary*: Galeazzo Ciano, *Diary, 1937–1943*, trans. V. Umberto Coletti-Perucca (New York: Enigma Books, 2002, edition of Doubleday 1946)

DGFP: *Documents on German Foreign Policy, 1918–1945. From the Archives of the German Foreign Ministry. Series D (1937–1945)*. Multiple vols. (Washington, DC: United States Government Printing Office, 1962)

FCNA: Jak P. Mallmann Showell, *Fuehrer Conferences on Naval Affairs* (London: Chatham Publishing, reprint of 1948, 2005)

Ickes, *Diary*: *The Secret Diary of Harold L. Ickes*, III, *The Lowering Clouds, 1939–1941* (New York: Simon & Schuster, 1955)

Morgenthau Diaries: John Morton Blum, *Morgenthau Diaries*, II, *Years of Urgency, 1938–1941* (New York: Houghton Mifflin, 1965)

Shirer, *Berlin Diary*: William L. Shirer, *Berlin Diary: The Journal of a Foreign Correspondent, 1934–1941* (New York: Alfred A. Knopf, 1941)

"Top Secret Assignment": Anonymous (Yoshikawa), "Top Secret Assignment," *Proceedings*, Volume 86, December 1960, 27–36

Secondary Works

Abbazia, *Mr. Roosevelt's Navy*: Patrick Abbazia, *Mr. Roosevelt's Navy: The Private War of the U.S. Atlantic Fleet, 1939–1942* (Annapolis, MD: Naval Institute Press, 1976)

Berg, *Lindbergh*: A. Scott Berg, *Lindbergh* (New York: G. P. Putnam's Sons, 1998)

Collier, *The Roosevelts*: Peter Collier with David Horowitz, *The Roosevelts: An American Saga* (New York: Simon & Schuster, 1994)

Evans, *The Third Reich at War*: Richard J. Evans, *The Third Reich at War* (New York: Penguin Press, 2009)

Friedländer, *Prelude to Downfall*: Saul Friedländer, *Prelude to Downfall: Hitler and the United States, 1939–1941*, trans. Aline B. and Alexander Werth (New York: Alfred A. Knopf, 1967)

Gilbert, *Finest Hour*: Martin Gilbert, *Winston S. Churchill, Vol. VI: Finest Hour, 1939–1941* (Boston: Houghton Mifflin Company, 1983)

Heinrichs, *Threshold of War*: Waldo Heinrichs, *Threshold of War: Franklin D. Roosevelt and American Entry into World War II* (New York: Oxford University Press, 1988)

Hotta, *Japan 1941*: Eri Hotta, *Japan 1941: Countdown to Infamy* (New York: Alfred A. Knopf, 2013)

Kaiser, *No End Save Victory*: David Kaiser, *No End Save Victory: How FDR Led the Nation into War* (New York: Basic Books, 2014)

Lash, *Roosevelt and Churchill*: Joseph P. Lash, *Roosevelt and Churchill, 1939–1941: The Partnerships That Saved the West* (New York: W. W. Norton & Company, 1976)

Olson, *Those Angry Days*: Lynne Olson, *Those Angry Days: Roosevelt, Lindbergh, and America's Fight Over World War II, 1939–1941* (New York: Random House, 2013)

Prange, *At Dawn We Slept*: Gordon W. Prange, in collaboration with Donald M. Goldstein and Katherine V. Dillon, *At Dawn We Slept: The Untold Story of Pearl Harbor* (New York: Penguin Books, 1981)

Roll, *The Hopkins Touch*: David L. Roll, *The Hopkins Touch: Harry Hopkins and the Forging of the Alliance to Defeat Hitler* (New York: Oxford University Press, 2013)

Schulze, *Philip Johnson*: Franz Schulze, *Philip Johnson, Life and Work* (New York: Alfred A. Knopf, 1994)

Sherwood, *Roosevelt and Hopkins*: Robert E. Sherwood, *Roosevelt and Hopkins, An Intimate History* (New York: Harper & Brothers, 1948)

Stimson, *On Active Service*: Henry L. Stimson and McGeorge Bundy, *On Active Service in Peace and War* (New York: Harper & Brothers, 1948)

The Undeclared War: William L. Langer and S. Everett Gleason, *The Undeclared War, 1940–1941* (New York: Harper & Brothers, 1953)

WSC, *The Second World War*: Winston S. Churchill, *The Second World War*: *The Gathering Storm* (New York: Houghton Mifflin, 1948); *Finest Hour* (1948); *The Grand Alliance* (1950); *Closing the Ring* (1951)

Notes

Introduction: *1941*

1 The following day . . . : Citations of presidential speeches and other major public addresses will only be given when conflicting texts or matters of interpretation are involved. For sources, go to: http://www.presidency.ucsb.edu/ws/

2 "The American Century": Henry R. Luce, "The American Century," *Life*, February 17, 1941, pp. 61–65, and elsewhere.

Chapter 1: *Foreign Correspondents*

5 "tanks": Richard M. Ketchum, *The Borrowed Years 1938–1941: America on the Way to War* (New York: Random House, 1989), 211.

6 "the sickening sweet smell": Shirer, *Berlin Diary*, 212. Shirer is referring to the aftermath of a battle involving Polish cavalry in the Tuchola Forest near Krojanty on the first day of the Nazi invasion. The Polish cavalry drove off German infantry, but never charged German tanks. The German armored counterattack killed or wounded a third of the Polish fighters. For an analysis of the battle, see: https://en.wikipedia.org/wiki/Charge_at_Krojanty.

9 That was when: Throughout this book, along with many original sources, I have drawn on Richard J. Evans's final volume in his magisterial trilogy of histories of the rise and fall of the Third Reich, *The Third Reich at War*. Except where differences of opinion or interpretations may exist and are duly noted, or where original sources are referenced, descriptions of historical incidents and facts about Germany in the world war are drawn from this book and will not be cited. Several different attacks occurred within minutes of the 4:45 a.m. start time of the invasion. Given Danzig's prominence, the Westerplatte attack is generally memorialized as site of the first attack. However, that is not correct.

9 "Go, kill": Richard J. Evans, "Europe's Killing Fields," in *The Third Reich in History and Memory* (New York: Oxford University Press, 2015), 390.

9 "off to the 'front'": Shirer, *Berlin Diary*, 212.

10 "sort of baptism," etc.: Shirer, *Berlin Diary*, September 4–10, 1934, 17–22; and William L. Shirer, *20th Century Journey*, Vol. II, *The Nightmare Years, 1930–1940* (Boston: Little, Brown, 1984), 119–128, 351.

11 "used every ruse": "Shirer the Superb," no source, February 1941, Shirer Papers, Romeike originals 1941, Box 1.

12 "This is a truth": Shirer, *Berlin Diary*, May 16, 1940, 343.

12 "didn't have the patience": Ibid. and e-mail communication, September 3, 2014, Jill Jack, Coe College, Stewart Memorial Library, Director of Library Services.

12 "my closest and dearest": Martha Dodd, *Through Embassy Eyes* (New York: Harcourt, Brace and Company, 1939), 108.

13 "The clash": Shirer, *Berlin Diary*, December 1, 1940, 592.

13 "where the killing": Ibid., 214–217, and *This Is Berlin*, 91–92.

13 "repellent": Shirer, *Berlin Diary*, August 26, 1940, 488.

16 "none of us can": Shirer, *Berlin Diary*, September 18, 1939, 213. Johnson FBI Report, 12/2/41.

Chapter 2: *A New World*

17 "handsome, always": "Forms Under Light," *The New Yorker*, May 23, 1977.

19 "totally febrile": Schulze, *Philip Johnson*, 89–90.

20 "If in the arts": *The Hound and Horn* 1 (October–December 1933), 137–139, in Schulze, *Philip Johnson*, 107.

20 "Lack of leadership": SJ, July 24, 1939, 5.

21 A light-skinned: "The Fascist Who Passed for White," *The Guardian*, April 4, 2007.

21 "America's No. 1": "The Ism of Appeasement," *Life*, January 20, 1941, 26–27.

22 "Two Forsake": NYT, December 18, 1934, 23.

22 "I'm leaving": Schulze, *Philip Johnson*, 116–117.

23 "for elimination": Lincoln Kirstein letter, January 5, 1944, in ibid., 164.

23 In February of 1936: On Johnson and Long, ibid., 113–119. On Long and Coughlin, see Alan Brinkley, *Voices of Protest: Huey Long, Father Coughlin & the Great Depression* (New York: Random House, Vintage, 2011); on Johnson and Coughlin, Schulze, *Philip Johnson*, 275–276.

24 As the Depression: "Father Coughlin Airs Open Break with Roosevelt," CT, November 18, 1935, 5.

25 "American Christians": SJ, July 18, 1938, 5. On the Christian Front and other fascist groups, see Kramer, "The American Fascists," *Harper's*, June 1, 1940, 386–389. See also, Francis MacDonnell, *Insidious Foes: The Axis Fifth Column and the American Home Front* (Guilford, CT: The Lyons Press, 2004, reprint of 1994 Oxford University Press edition), 34–39.

25 "America was seeing": Kramer, "The American Fascists," 390.

25 "Front of Reason": Shirer, *Berlin Diary*, September 22, 1939, 220.

25 "Coughlinism is the thread": Kramer, "The American Fascists," 384.

26 A reported 80,000: "Boston Packed for Roosevelt as at Chicago," CT, October 24, 1936, 13. "Coughlin Declares Rome Report a Lie," NYT, September 7, 1936, 1. SJ, June 30, 1941, 8–9.

27 "form your battalions": "Charles Coughlin, '30s 'Radio Priest,' Dies," NYT, Oct. 28, 1979. SJ, December 5, 1938, 19. Video of Coughlin at the 1936 Chicago rally: http://www.ushmm.org/wlc/en/media_fi.php?MediaId=2517. Gene Fein, "Twisted Social Justice: Father Coughlin & the Christian Front," *The Forum on Public Policy*, 2009.

27 "special stand": CT, September 7, 1936, 4.

27 Johnson arrived: On Johnson's contacts with the German Foreign Ministry, see various entries from interviews with him contained in his FBI File.

28 "This is the first day": Shirer, "Letter from Munich," SJ, September 2, 1939, 4.

28 Sticking beside Shirer: Shirer, *Berlin Diary*, September 18, 213. On the German Propaganda Ministry's relations with Johnson including Shirer's reaction to his presence on the Polish war front press trip, see Johnson FBI Report, "Re: Philip Cortelyan [sic] Johnson," February 1, 1945, 1.

28 "the region of some awful plague": "Letter from Munich," SJ, September 2, 1939, 4.

29 "not be solved": "Poland's Choice Between War and Bolshevism Is a 'Deal' with Germany," SJ, September 11, 1939, 4.

29 "The German green uniforms": Schulze, *Philip Johnson*, 139.

29 He concluded: "*Mein Kampf* and the Businessman," *The Examiner*, Summer 1939, vol 2, no 3, 291–296, in ibid., 140–141.

30 "we want to protect": Evans, *The Third Reich at War*, 16.

30 It was the first camp: Martin Gilbert, *The Holocaust: A History of the Jews of Europe During the Second World War* (New York: Holt, Rinehart and Winston, 1985), 115.

30 "the Nazi policy": Shirer, *Berlin Diary*, November 19, 1939, 250.

30 "Black-out, bombs": Ibid., October 8, 1939, 233.

Chapter 3: *"That Prophecy Comes True"*

31 "[Berlin's] war aims": "This 'Sitdown' War," SJ, November 6, 1939, 5.

32 England possessed a naval fleet: Royal Navy: http://www.naval-history. net/WW2Campaign RoyalNavy.htm; Kriegsmarine: http://www.naval-history. net/WW2CampaignsGermanWarships.htm

33 Raeder regarded his fleet: Reflections of the C.-in-C., Navy, on the Outbreak of War, September 3, 1939, FCNA, 38.

34 "WINSTON IS BACK": On Churchill's eight months as First Lord of the Admiralty, see *Gilbert, Finest Hour*, 3–284.

34 "have sustained a defeat": http://hansard.millbanksystems.com/ commons/1938/oct/05/policy-of-his-majestys-government

34 "Never for one moment": WSC, *The Second World War: Closing the Ring*, 6.

34 "to purchase destroyers": Gilbert, *Finest Hour*, 32–33. WSC, *The Second World War: The Gathering Storm*, 367, 387–388.

36 "This business of carrying on": FDR Press Conferences, #528, March 7, 1939, 177–179.

36 Roosevelt kept America's security: See Mark M. Lowenthal, "Roosevelt and the Coming of the War: The Search for United States Policy 1937–42," *Journal*

of Contemporary History, Vol. 16, No. 3, The Second World War: Part 2 (July 1981), 413–440. Charles A. Beard, *President Roosevelt and the Coming of the War, 1941* (New Haven, CT: Yale University Press, 1948), remains the original and clearest statement of the view that FDR sought to bring the U.S. into the war from the beginning.

37 That distrust of Churchill: See Sherwood, *Roosevelt and Hopkins*, 350–351.

37 "one of the few men": Michael Beschloss, *Kennedy and Roosevelt: The Uneasy Alliance* (New York: Norton, 1980), 200.

37 He had begun: On Roosevelt's role at the Navy Department, see Lash, *Roosevelt and Churchill*, 44–51.

38 In late 1939: On Roosevelt's decision and challenges in seeking a third term as president, see Susan Dunn, *1940: FDR, Willkie, Lindbergh, Hitler—the Election Amid the Storm* (New Haven, CT: Yale University Press, 2013), and Richard Moe, *Roosevelt's Second Act: The Election of 1940 and the Politics of War* (New York: Oxford University Press, 2013).

38 "a map mind": Abbazia, *Mr. Roosevelt's Navy*, 80.

39 But just how far from shore: FDR Press Conference #523, February 3, 1939, 8–9, #525, February 17, 1939, 8–10, 17–18.

40 "It is because you": C&R Correspondence, September 11, 1939, 24. On the importance of the first message from FDR, see Lash, *Roosevelt and Churchill*, 23ff.

41 Sitting with the king: On Roosevelt's thinking on the neutrality zone in 1939, see Lash, *Roosevelt and Churchill*, 63–65.

42 Churchill understood: C&R Correspondence, October 5, 1939, 27. On the redrafting of Churchill's original, see Gilbert, *Finest Hour*, 52–53.

Chapter 4: *Unneutral Acts*

43 The initial mission: Lash, *Roosevelt and Churchill*, 80ff.

44 "If Britain wins": Memorandum to Frank Knox, secretary of the navy, November 12, 1940, in Gregory J. Florence, *Courting a Reluctant Ally: An Evaluation of U.S./UK Naval Intelligence Cooperation, 1935–1941* (Washington, DC: Center for Strategic Intelligence Research, Joint Military Intelligence College, 2004), 41.

44 "He could sit": Joseph E. Persico, *Roosevelt's Centurions: FDR and the Commanders He Led to Victory in World War II* (New York: Random House, 2013), 51.

45 "to make the following orders clear": Abbazia, *Mr. Roosevelt's Navy*, 68.

46 For three long months: Abbazia, *Mr. Roosevelt's Navy*, 71–74.

47 Word of the great German liner's: "Luxury Ship Burns," NYT, December 20, 1939, 1.

47 "we do not desire": Abbazia, *Mr. Roosevelt's Navy*, 74.

48 On December 13, an Allied squadron: "Churchill Praises British Sea Deeds," "Captain Says Graf Spee Sailed for a Time Disguised as Renown," NYT, December 19, 1939, 6, 5. For German account of *Graf Spee* battle, see FCNA, 67–72. On the *Graf Spee* incident, see Gilbert, *Finest Hour*, 116–117.

50 "Nobody can expect": "Reich Warns US," NYT, May 26, 1941, 1.

50–51 "The earlier and the more ruthlessly": Report of the C.-in-C., Navy, to the Führer on October 10, 1939, at 1700, FCNA, 46.

51 "the psychological effect": Friedländer, *Prelude to Downfall*, 65.

51 "Nothing," the Führer dictated: "From notes, undated and unsigned, on a memorandum on the intensification of the war at sea against Britain" in Office of United States Chief Counsel for Prosecution of Axis Criminality, *Nazi Conspiracy and Aggression,* Supplement A (Washington, DC: United States Government Printing Office, 1947), C-100, 845.

51 "the United States' Army's lack": The Embassy of the United States to the Foreign Ministry, August 25, 1939, DGFP, VII, 275–276.

Chapter 5: *Scooping Hitler*

53 "American arms production": Conversation, Swedish navy commander in Chief Tamm, April 16, 1940, DGFP, IX, 182.

53 "the recurring undertone": Letter to Mussolini, May 3, 1940, ibid., 275.

53 "I felt," he recalled: WSC, *The Second World War: The Gathering Storm,* 596. Much has been written describing the historic days leading to Churchill's becoming prime minister; see for instance, Gilbert, *Finest Hour*, 306–318. On the immediate aftermath of the debacle in France, see John Lukacs, *Five Days in London, May 1940* (New Haven, CT: Yale University Press, 1999).

56 "the grand scope": Churchill listens to broadcast, Gilbert, *Finest Hour*, 492. June 11, 1939, C&R Correspondence, 43.

56 Poll results: September 1939 Roper Poll results in Sherwood, *Roosevelt and Hopkins*, 127–128; "American Opinion and the War" and "Impact of the War on the Nation's Viewpoint," NYT, June 2, 1940.

57 "It's a terrible thing": Roosevelt to Reid, June 6, 1940, quoted in Susan Dunn, *1940: FDR, Willkie, Lindbergh, Hitler—the Election Amid the Storm*, 39.

57 "Poor Paris": Shirer, *Berlin Diary*, June 14 and 17, 1940, 404–405, 409, 412.

57 The National Socialist Party newspaper: Dunn, *1940*, 103.

58 In his years of watching: Shirer, *Berlin Diary*, June 21, 1940, 422, and June 28, 1940, 443ff. William L. Shirer, *20th Century Journey*, Vol. II, *The Nightmare Years, 1930–1940* (Boston: Little, Brown, 1984), 530–543.

59 "Some of those who helped us": Shirer, *Berlin Diary*, June 28, 1940, 442–443.

59 By fall 1940: Shirer Papers, General Correspondence 1940–1943, telegram, no date. "Like that," Diaries, Entry, November 6, 1940, ibid.

60 A few days before departing: "An Interview with William L. Shirer," *NYT Book Review*, January 18, 1942, 2.

60 At Christmastime 1940: Shirer, *Berlin Diary*, December 13, 1940, 604–605.

Chapter 6: *Blitzkrieg Propaganda*

62 "Our 'neutral' press": "War and the Press," SJ, November 6, 1939, 12.

62 According to the AFF brochure: "Dr. Auhagen," *Boston Globe*, October 23, 1940, 14.

63 In October 1940: Ibid.

64 Among his talks: Investigation of un-American propaganda activities in the United States: Hearings before a Special Committee on Un-American Activities, House of Representatives, Seventy-fifth Congress, third session–Seventy-eighth Congress, second session, on H. Res. 282, 28. On Johnson's life after his return to the U.S., see Schulze, *Philip Johnson*, 141ff.

65 In May 1940: On the BSC, Stephenson, and Anglo-American intelligence cooperation, see Jennet Conant, *The Irregulars: Roald Dahl and the British Spy Ring in Wartime Washington* (New York: Simon & Schuster, 2008), 65ff. Fleming quote, ibid., 84–85.

66 Federal Bureau of Investigation: Douglas M. Charles, "Informing FDR: FBI Political Surveillance and the Isolationist-Interventionist Foreign Policy Debate, 1939–1945," *Diplomatic History*, 24 (Spring 2000), 211–232; and Kenneth O'Reilly, "A New Deal for the FBI: The Roosevelt Administration, Crime Control, and National Security," *Journal of American History*, Vol. 69, No. 3 (December 1982): 638–658.

69 Through data collected: On BSC propaganda and public relations operations, see Thomas E. Mahl, *Desperate Deception: British Covert Operations in the United States, 1939–1944* (Dulles, VA: Brassey's Inc., 1998), 27ff. On Ogilvy and Gallup in the BSC, ibid., 196ff. See also, Francis MacDonnell, *Insidious Foes: The Axis Fifth Column and the American Home Front* (Guilford, CT: The Lyons Press, 2004, reprint of 1994 Oxford University Press edition), 93ff.

71 Assistant Secretary of State: Berle to Sumner Welles, March 1941, in Nicholas John Cull, *Selling War: The British Propaganda Campaign Against American "Neutrality" in World War Two* (London: Oxford University Press, 1996), 145.

71 Berle eventually complained: Berle to FDR, February 5, 1942, in MacDonnell, *Insidious Foes*, 98. Sherwood, *Roosevelt and Hopkins*, 270.

71 During the fall 1940 campaign: Mahl, *Desperate Deception*, 108ff, 155ff.

Chapter 7: *Shadowed by the G-Men*

74 After the fall of France: See *The Undeclared War*, 593–624.

75 At its height: "Nelson A. Rockefeller," *Life*, April 27, 1942, 80–90. For a general introduction to the formation and workings of the OIAA, see Gisela Cramer and Ursula Prutsch, "Nelson A. Rockefeller's Office of Inter-American Affairs (1940–1946) and Record Group 229," *Hispanic American Historical Review*, Vol. 86, No. 4 (November 2006): 785–806.

75 He also kept a fund: See Paul Kramer, "Nelson Rockefeller and British Security Coordination," *Journal of Contemporary History*, Vol. 16 (January

1981): 73–88. "Trade 'Black List' Covers Axis Links in Latin America," NYT, July 12, 1941, 1.

76 The success of the Rockefeller Shop's: Shirer, *Berlin Diary*, July 25, 1940, 460.

77 Roosevelt was by then: Francis MacDonnell, "The Search for a Second Zimmermann Telegram: Franklin Roosevelt, British Security Coordination, and the Latin-American Front," *International Journal of Intelligence and Counterintelligence* (Winter 1990): 487–505. Berle to Welles, July 7, 1941, MacDonnell, *Insidious Foes*, 96; Berle smear campaign, ibid., 97–99.

78 Getting wind of this: On FDR's attitude and actions against fifth column subversion, see ibid., 137ff. Taft quote in Charles Peters, *Five Days in Philadelphia: The Amazing "We Want Willkie" Convention of 1940 and How It Freed FDR to Save the Western World* (New York: Public Affairs, 2005), 21.

79 On November 21, 1940: "Dr. Kertess Held as Head of Nazi Smuggling Ring," *New York Herald Tribune*, November 7, 1942, 26. "Held in Smuggling of Metal to Nazis," NYT, November 7, 1942, 17. See also, "Excerpts from White Paper on Nazi Activities Here Released by the Dies Committee," NYT, November 22, 1940, 12.

80 According to FBI agents: FBI Report, February 1, 1945.

80 On January 14, 1940: "18 Seized in Plot to Overthrow U.S.; Arms Found Here," NYT, January 15, 1940, 1. "Coughlin Condemns Group," NYT, January 15, 1940, 3; "Coughlin Supports Christian Front," January 22, 1940, 1. On the arrest of the New York City Christian Front chapter members, see Kramer, "The American Fascists," 386–389. See also, Francis MacDonnell, *Insidious Foes*, 34–39.

81 Implicated in the Dies Committee investigation: "Dies Agents Making Raids in Eight Cities," *New York Herald Tribune*, November 22, 1940, 1; "Dies Raiders in Boston Today," *Boston Globe*, November 22, 1940, 1. "Auhagen Is Indicted by U.S. as German Propaganda Agent," *New York Herald Tribune*, March 4, 1941, 15. "Kertess Conviction Is Upheld," NYT, January 7, 1944, 19. "Mass Sedition Case Dismissed by Court," NYT, November 23, 1946, 1. Dennis cowrote a 1947 book about the case, *A Trial on Trial: The Great Sedition Trial of 1944*.

Chapter 8: *The Roosevelt Brand*

82 As pressure to intervene in Europe: On Butler's antiwar campaign, see Hans Schmidt, *Maverick Marine: Smedley D. Butler and the Contradictions of American Military History* (Lexington: University Press of Kentucky, 1987), 241–245.

83 Among those who wanted: On Eddie Rickenbacker's initial isolationist outlook and eventual shift to an interventionist stance, see W. David Lewis, *Eddie Rickenbacker: An American Hero in the Twentieth Century* (Baltimore: Johns Hopkins University Press, 2005), 359–364. See also, Justus D. Doenecke, "American Isolationism, 1939–1941," *Journal of Libertarian Studies*, Vol. 6, Nos. 3–4 (Summer/Fall 1982): 206–207. York quoted in "Sergeant York Hopes We Will Avoid Wars," NYT, November 11, 1934, 2. York eventually reversed his views about intervention in World War Two; his life would serve as the subject of an immensely popular 1941 movie some criticized as pro-British war propaganda.

83 His father, Teddy Roosevelt: http://www.pbs.org/wgbh/americanexperience /features/timeline/rushmore/

83 Ted wrote his first cousin: January 14, 1938, TR, Jr., Papers, Box 30.

84 "Dante," he fumed: Theodore Roosevelt, *America and the World War* (New York: Charles Scribner's Sons, 1915), xi.

84 The youngest, most adored: On the death of Quentin, see Edward J. Renehan, Jr., *The Lion's Pride: Theodore Roosevelt and His Family in Peace and War* (New York City: Oxford University Press, 1998), 34, 4–5. On the Roosevelt sons in the Great War, see Collier, *The Roosevelts*, 196ff.

85 "I feel exactly": To Major John (Jack) Thomason, July 26, 1938, TR, Jr., Papers, Box 30.

85 "He is a maverick": Quoted in "Col. T. Roosevelt Will Go on Stump," NYT, July 31, 1932, 17. See also, Linda Donn, *The Roosevelt Cousins: Growing Up Together, 1882–1924* (New York: Alfred A. Knopf, 2001), 171–173.

85 Wherever Ted went: *New York Herald Tribune*, June 7, 1924. On Theodore Roosevelt, Jr.'s postwar political career and run for the governorship, see Collier, *The Roosevelts*, 276–330.

86 They refused to accept: Conversation with Theodore Roosevelt IV, December 9, 2013.

86 On the very day the European war: To Alice R. Longworth, TR, Jr., Papers, Box 9. University of Virginia speech, "Say Our First Duty Is to Avoid War," NYT, July 7, 1939.

86 He did not need: "Next War Will Be Worse Than Hell," article, no source or date, TR, Jr., Papers, Box 73.

87 "I'd rather vote for": Quoted in Collier, *The Roosevelts*, 394.

87 "Franklin Roosevelt," said Ted: *Seattle Post-Intelligencer*, October 15, 1940.

87 With two weeks still: To Stewart E. White, September 25, 1940. "Col. Roosevelt Visits Campus," College of Boise newspaper, no date. TR, Jr., Papers, Box 31.

88 Ted cabled: To Willkie's wife October 21, 1940; to Willkie, October 29, 1940, ibid.

88 He wrote his son: November 1, 1940, ibid., Box 9.

88 "When your boy": Radio script quoted in Sherwood, *Roosevelt and Hopkins*, 198.

89 His speechwriter: Ibid., 201.

Chapter 9: *Cassandra*

90 At midday on a clear: On the *Panay* Incident and other events preceding the attack on Pearl Harbor, see Manny T. Koginos, *The Panay incident: prelude to war* (Lafayette, IN: Purdue University Studies, 1967). See also, Samuel Eliot Morison, *History of United States Naval Operations in World War II*, Vol. 3, *The Rising Sun in the Pacific, 1931–April 1942* (Annapolis, MD: Naval Institute Press, 2010 (original edition 1948), 16–18.

91 "Certainly war with Japan": Ickes quote in Jean Edward Smith, *FDR* (New York: Random House, 2007), 421.

92 "Unhappy [in the] temperamentally": Stimson, *On Active Service*, 307.

92 "I held the great statesman": Joseph Alsop, *I've Seen the Best of It* (New York: W. W. Norton, 1992), 143.

93 "If we lie down": Stimson, *On Active Service*, 232–233.

93 He said of himself: Ibid., 196.

93 He embodied in full: On the rise of the "Establishment" from the Ivy League and Wall Street, see Walter Isaacson and Evan Thomas, *The Wise Men: Six Friends and the World They Made* (New York: Simon & Schuster, 1986; Touchstone, 1988), 26–139.

94 "a man [I] knew and liked": Stimson, *On Active Service*, 303. On Stimson's views of and relations with Roosevelt before 1940, see ibid., 297–305.

95 "I believe that": "Ex-Secretary Stimson's Letter on Foreign Relations," NYT, March 7, 1939.

95 At his news conference: Press Conference #145, October 6, 1937.

96 He issued a presidential: On American relations with Japan prior to 1941, see Hotta, *Japan 1941*, 24ff.

96 Chinese Nationalist officials: Edward R. Stettinius, Jr., *Lend-Lease: Weapon for Victory* (New York: The Macmillan Company, 1944), 15ff.

97 Congress would go: Quoted in Maury Klein, *A Call to Arms: Mobilizing America for World War II* (New York: Bloomsbury Press, 2013), 54.

97 Less than six months later: Shirer, *Berlin Diary*, 412.

98 That same evening: "Stimson Demands Military Training," NYT, June 19, 1940, 17.

99 Clark's "ridiculous idea": Stimson, Diary, June 25, 1940, 55. On the effort to create the Selective Service System and to bring Stimson into the administration, see Olson, *Those Angry Days*, 197ff, and Susan Dunn, *1940: FDR, Willkie, Lindbergh, Hitler—the Election Amid the Storm* (New Haven, CT: Yale University Press, 2013), 167ff. See also, Stimson, *On Active Service*, 319–320.

Chapter 10: *A Rising Sun*

100 "struck fire," in Richard Moe, *Roosevelt's Second Act: The Election of 1940 and the Politics of War* (New York: Oxford University Press, 2013), 161.

100 The president told him: Stimson, Diary, June 25, 1940.

101 "path [that] leads": Quoted in Kaiser, *No End Save Victory*, 74. "I would do anything": "Knox Urges Every Possible Aid to Great Britain Short of War," NYT, July 3, 1940, 1. "Knox Appointment Is Approved, 9–5," NYT, July 4, 1940, 8.

101 "Your ridiculous plot": Quoted in Olson, *Those Angry Days*, 205.

101 His former Republican friends: "Vote for Stimson," "Stimson Assailed, Praised in the Senate," "Stimson Confirmed by Vote of 56–28 Despite Attacks," NYT, July 3, 9, and 10, 1940, 1.

102 FDR charged Stimson: Statistics from William L. Langer and S. Everett Gleason, *The Challenge to Isolation: The World Crisis of 1937–1940 and American Foreign Policy* (New York: Council on Foreign Relations, 1952), 471, 473. "We have so little": Stimson, Diary, September 9, 1940.

102 "the greatest British military defeat": Quoted in Thomas Parrish, *To Keep the British Isles Afloat: FDR's Men in Churchill's London, 1941* (New York: HarperCollins, 2009), 93.

103 "that the voice and force": May 15, 1940, C&R Correspondence, 37.

103 For the first time: June 11, 1940, 43; June 15, 1940, ibid., 50–51.

104 Allied shipping losses: Samuel Eliot Morison, *History of United States Naval Operations in World War II*, Vol. 1, *The Battle of the Atlantic, September 1939–May 1943* (Edison, NJ: Castle Books, 2001) (original edition 1947), 22–26.

106 When the massive bombing: Quoted in Warren F. Kimball, *Forged in War: Roosevelt, Churchill, and the Second World War* (New York: William Morrow and Company, 1997), 63.

106 "becom[e] a vassal state": June 15, 1940, C&R Correspondence, 50.

107 As France capitulated: June 22, 1940, WSC, *The Second World War: Finest Hour*, 200.

107 The planners projected: "Joint Army and Navy Basic War Plan—Rainbow no. 4," in Kaiser, *No End Save Victory*, 63.

107 Senator David Walsh: See Warren F. Kimball, *The Most Unsordid Act: Lend-Lease, 1939–1941* (Baltimore: The Johns Hopkins Press, 1969), 55.

108 The British purchasing agent: Gilbert, *Finest Hour*, 463.

108 "Mr. President," he concluded: C&R Correspondence, 57.

109 He would consider *leasing*: Quoted in Parrish, *To Keep the British Isles Afloat*, 102.

109 It was a big political risk: Kimball, *The Most Unsordid Act*, 70. "Ruling by Jackson," NYT, September 4, 1940, 1.

109 FDR and Stimson traveled: "U.S.-Canada Ties Welded by President and Premier," "Joint Board to Act," NYT, August 18 and 19, 1940, 1. Stimson Diary, August 17, 1940.

110 That night, Stimson: Ibid., August 17, 1940.

111 "Mr. Roosevelt today": "Dictator Roosevelt Commits an Act of War," *St. Louis Post-Dispatch*, September 3, 1940, 2B.

111 Critics left off: "Willkie for Pact, but Hits Secrecy," NYT, September 4, 1940, 1.

112 Later, he would call: "The Few," Speech of August 20, 1940, House of Commons. WSC, *The Second World War*, Finest Hour, 404.

112 "Although the transfer": September 22, 1940, DGFP, XI, 150–152.

112 Mussolini told German: Ciano, *Diary*, September 4, 1940, 380.

113 The Duce was largely: September 19 and 20, 1940, ibid., 383.

113 The arrival of those fifty destroyers: Report of the C.-in-C., Navy, to the Führer on the afternoon of September 6, 1940, FCNA, 134.

Chapter 11: *Prairie Fire*

115 Ribbentrop could barely contain: Ciano, *Diary*, September 19, 1940, 383. Video of the signing ceremony is available online: http://www.ushmm.org/wlc/en/media_fi.php?MediaId=151

116 Britain, he reflected: Shirer, *Berlin Diary*, September 27, 1940, 532ff.

116 "Our policy has succeeded": "Japan Treaty Stirs Senators," CT, September 28, 1940, 1.

117 "The U.S. is isolated": Stimson, Diary, September 27, 1940; November 25, 1940.

118 "I believe it is better": Konoe press conference quote in Hotta, *Japan 1941*, 54. On Konoe's life and attitudes toward the West, see ibid., 28ff.

118 "America has been": Conversation, Hitler-Mussolini, October 4, 1940 DGFP, XI, 245ff.

118 While in Berlin: September 22, 1940; September 27–28, 1940, Ciano, *Diary*, 384, 385.

119 The newspaper mouthpiece: Quoted in Jonathan Marshall, *To Have and Have Not: Southeast Asian Raw Materials and the Origins of the Pacific War* (Berkeley: University of California Press, 1995), 85.

120 Ambassador to Tokyo Joseph Grew: Grew letter in ibid., 92–93.

120 "Every day that we": Stark quoted in Lash, *Roosevelt and Churchill*, 225 and 227.

121 Still, isolationists: "Marching Down the Road to War: Peace Time Conscription a Menace to our Liberties," National Broadcasting Company, August 15, 1940, in *Vital Speeches of the Day*, Vol. VI (City News, 1940), 689–692.

121 In his testimony: "Grave Peril Seen" and "Text of Stimson's Appeal for the Compulsory Service Bill," NYT, August 1, 1940, 1, 14. On the draft fight, see Olson, *Those Angry Days*, 196–219; see also, Kaiser, *No End Save Victory*, 87–90.

121 The powerful North Dakota: Ernest K. Lindley, "News Behind News in Washington," *Brooklyn Eagle*, August 5, 1940, 16.

122 Anger over conscription: "The Bitter End," *Time*, September 16, 1940.

Chapter 12: *"Aviation, Geography, and Race"*

125 The final outcome: On the 1940 election, see Richard Moe, *Roosevelt's Second Act: The Election of 1940 and the Politics of War* (New York: Oxford University Press, 2013), and Susan Dunn, *1940: FDR, Willkie, Lindbergh, Hitler—the Election Amid the Storm* (New Haven, CT: Yale University Press, 2013).

125 "Well, the election": November 12, 1940, and December 5, 1940, TR, Jr., Papers, Box 9.

126 "'Democracy' as we have known it": November 5, 1940, December 3, 1940, and May 1, 1941, CAL Papers, Diaries, Series V, Box 209, Series V, Box 210. Numerous diary entries concerning Jews were edited or excised from *The Wartime Journals of Charles A. Lindbergh* (1970).

127 Lindbergh was eager: Letter to Henry Breckinridge and speech, July 23, 1936, quoted in Berg, *Lindbergh*, 357.

128 Shirer was surprised: July 23, 1936, Shirer, *Berlin Diary*, 64.

128 The ultimate significance: Berg, *Lindbergh*, 359–360.

129 In reality: *Luftwaffe* aircraft totals cited in Albert Fried, *FDR and His Enemies* (New York: St. Martin's Press, 1999), 178.

129 "It is no longer possible": Berg, *Lindbergh*, 357.

129 The Berlin Olympics: July 23, 1936, Shirer, *Berlin Diary*, 63–66.

130 "The organized vitality": Charles A. Lindbergh, *Autobiography of Values* (New York: Harcourt Brace Jovanovich, 1978), 147.

130 Shortly after leaving: Berg, *Lindbergh*, 361.

130 ". . . I have never in my life": Anne Morrow Lindbergh quoted in Andrew Nagorski, *Hitlerland: American Eyewitnesses to the Nazi Rise to Power* (New York: Simon & Schuster, 2012), 206.

132 On the night that Lindbergh: On the Lindberghs' years in Europe, see Berg, *Lindbergh*, 345ff. On the awarding of a German service medal, ibid., 377ff. Quotes in ibid., 379–380.

133 ". . . I was seeing in Germany": Lindbergh, *Autobiography of Values*, 156.

134 Lindbergh asked: Charles Lindbergh, "Aviation, Geography, and Race," *Reader's Digest*, November, 1939, 64–67; "What Substitute for War?" *Atlantic Monthly*, March, 1940, 305–307; Berg, ibid., 383.

134 Even before the German: Wayne S. Cole, *Charles A. Lindbergh and the Battle Against Intervention in World War II* (New York: Harcourt Brace Jovanovich, 1974), 76.

134 "We are in danger of war": "The Air Defense of America," delivered May 19, 1940, Mutual Broadcasting System.

135 Reverend Coughlin: SJ, cover note, June 3, 1940.

135 The day after Lindbergh's: FDR quotes in Cole, *Charles A. Lindbergh and the Battle Against Intervention in World War II*, 128–129.

136 Afterward Stuart had a long talk: From R. Douglas Stuart, Jr. ("Bob Stuart"), August 5, 1940, CAL Papers, Series 1, Box 1 (America First Comm Nat HQ folder).

136 He would remain unaffiliated: On Lindbergh's associations with various anti-interventionist organizations before formally becoming part of America First, see Cole, *Charles A. Lindbergh and the Battle Against Intervention in World War II*, 103ff.

138 "We have started to train": "FDR Addresses 2000 Admirers in Elm City Visit," *Yale Daily News*, October 31, 1940, 1.

138 "Every seat was taken": Richard M. Ketchum, *The Borrowed Years 1938–1941: America on the Way to War* (New York: Random House, 1989), 512–514. October 25–November 21, 1940, Diary, Entry for October 30, Yale speech: Woolsey Hall, CAL Papers, Diaries, Series 209. On Yale during the Great War, see Marc Wortman, *The Millionaires' Unit: The Aristocratic Flyboys Who Fought the Great War and Invented American Air Power* (New York: PublicAffairs, 2006).

138 America should pursue: "Lindbergh Sees U.S. Unprepared to Change Course of War Abroad," *Yale Daily News*, October 31, 1940, 1.

139 Learning about the success: Letter from R. E. Wood, November 1, 1940, CAL Papers, Series 1, Box 1. Sherwood, *Roosevelt and Hopkins*, 299.

139 German embassy's chargé d'affaires: Thomsen to Foreign Ministry, November 30, 1940, DGFP, XI, 751–752.

Chapter 13: *Indictments*

140 He spoke to groups: To Cornelius, January 20, 1941, TR, Jr., Papers, Box 9.

140 "empire complex": "Dr. Tugwell in Puerto Rico," CT, November 20, 1942, 14.

140 He told his closest friend: March 3, 1941, TR, Jr., Papers, Box 31.

141 His advocacy for tolerance: 1941 letter quoted in Eleanor Roosevelt, *Day Before Yesterday: The Reminiscences of Mrs. Theodore Roosevelt, Jr.* (Garden City, NY: Doubleday & Company, 1959), 418.

141 "No small group": University of Virginia speech, "Say Our First Duty Is to Avoid War," NYT, July 7, 1939.

142 On Friday night: To Cornelius Roosevelt, January 10 and 20, 1941 TR, Jr., Papers, Box 9.

142 Shirer, who had come back: "An Interview with William L. Shirer," *NYT Book Review*, January 18, 1942, 2.

142 Pendleton (OR) *East Oregonian*, "Plenty of Danger, " July 1, 1941. Shirer Papers, Romeike originals 1941, Box 1; Bound Columns & Articles: Newspaper Clippings, 1927–1961 Bulk '40s.

143 When Shirer embarked: "Britain Must Increase Power and Get More U.S. Aid to Win, Shirer Informs Syracusans," *Syracuse Post-Standard*, April 18, 1941. Ibid.

143 He told a huge audience: "U.S. Must Face Hitler Alone in Five Years if England Falls: Shirer," Cedar Rapids *Gazette*, June 8, 1941. *Memphis Press-Scimitar*, "U.S. Must Make Up Mind on How Far It Will Aid," April 25, 1941. Milwaukee, no source, November 10, 1941: "Halt the Nazis, Shirer Warns." Ibid.

144 "You know my position": To Cornelius, December 12, 1940, TR, Jr., Papers, Box 9.

145 President Roosevelt's wife: "My Week," July 11, 1941, no source. ibid.

146 Johnson seemed to panic: Johnson's entry and pro-interventionist activities at Harvard Graduate School of Design, Schulze, *Philip Johnson*, 147–152. Manny letters in ibid., 153.

146 The investigators reported: Memorandum, July 31, 1941, Special Agent E. F. Enrich, Johnson FBI Report.

147 Nonetheless, a year later: April 12, 1942, ibid.

147 Two years younger: Schulze, *Philip Johnson*, 115.

147 She reportedly said: Quoted in ibid., 143.

148 Shirer figured the committee's: Diary entry, January 25, 1941, Shirer Papers, Diaries, Loose Pages 1930–1997.

Chapter 14: *The Garden Hose*

149 Churchill knew that: December 7, 1940, C&R Correspondence, 102ff.

151 London would have a bill: British debt, Warren F. Kimball, *The Most Unsordid Act: Lend-Lease, 1939–1941* (Baltimore: The Johns Hopkins Press, 1969), 116–117.

151 Amid what Morgenthau: Diary entry, December 11, 1940, quoted in ibid., 115.

151 "Then one evening": Sherwood, *Roosevelt and Hopkins*, 224. The actual genesis of the program may have differed from Hopkins's description: see Kimball, *The Most Unsordid Act*, 119.

152 A month earlier: November 9, 1940, Ickes, *Diary*, 367.

153 On his first day back: FDR Press Conference #702, 350ff.

154 Harry Hopkins may have suggested: Several alternate stories relate the possible originator of the "Arsenal of Democracy" slogan. See Lash, *Roosevelt and Churchill*, 265.

155 Lanky, bright-eyed, caustic: On Hopkins's life, character, and relationship to Roosevelt, I have relied on two superb books on their relationship during the war period: Sherwood, *Roosevelt and Hopkins*, and Roll, *The Hopkins Touch*.

156 Some were openly jealous: April 12, 1941, Ickes, *Diary*, 471.

157 "I can understand that you": Quoted in Sherwood, *Roosevelt and Hopkins*, 2–3.

158 "His mind," a frustrated: Stimson, Diary, December 17 and 18, 1940; February 27, 1941.

159 Even before legislation: "Wheeler Defines His 'Just Peace,'" NYT, December 28, 1940, 7.

160 A poll of Yale students: "Faculty, Students Split in Reaction to Poll," *Yale Daily News*, February 10, 1941, 1; "Risk-Involvement Polls Plurality In 'News' Survey, But Majority Shows Non-Interventionist Leanings," February 8, 1941, 1.

161 The twenty-two-year-old college senior: "Senate Calls Brewster to Hearing," February 8, 1941, ibid., 1.

162 Wheeler threatened: Sherwood, *Roosevelt and Hopkins*, 260–262. Lindbergh, Willkie, and CT quoted in Olson, *Those Angry Days*, 280–281.

163 "We might not have had": Sherwood, *Roosevelt and Hopkins*, 355. *The Undeclared War*, 279–280.

163 In effect, Secretary Stimson: Stimson, Diary, March 17, 1941.

163 Shortly after the big victory: Ibid., March 20 and 24, 1941.

164 "Probably we would have": April 20, 1941, Ickes, *Diary*, 485.

164 "Congratulations!" Early said: Sherwood, *Roosevelt and Hopkins*, 231. Sherwood mistakenly indicates the date as January 5.

Chapter 15: *How Do You Do?*

165 Many hurdles and bottlenecks: See http://usgovernmentspending. blogspot.com/2009/03/world-war-ii-us-defense-spending.html

165 Roosevelt tasked Harriman: Quoted in W. Averell Harriman and Elie Abel, *Special Envoy to Churchill and Stalin, 1941–1946* (New York: Random House, 1975), 3.

166 Harriman was to be: FDR Press Conference, #719, February 18, 1941. On other emissaries' foreign missions during this period, see Michael Fullilove, *Rendezvous with Destiny: How Franklin D. Roosevelt and Five Extraordinary Men Took America into the War and into the World* (New York: The Penguin Press, 2013).

166 "The mere thought": *Lynchburg News*, March 12, 1941; "Brain Trusters Back in Saddle; Run Arms Show," CT, March 28, 1941, 26; "Wheeler Flays F.D. 'Advisers,'" Washington *Times-Herald*, July, 20, 1941. HH Papers, Scrapbook, 1933, January–August 31, 1941, Box 348.

167 "Harry has not successfully": March 13, 1941, Ickes, *Diary*, 459.

168 He knew how power worked: Jason Scott Smith, *Building New Deal Liberalism: The Political Economy of Public Works, 1933–1956* (New York: Cambridge University Press; 2006), 87f.

168 "Our people," he wrote: "Hitler Won't Win," *The American Magazine*, July 1941, 24ff. Scrapbook, 1933, January–August 31, 1941, HH Papers, Box 348.

169 The defeatist Joseph Kennedy: Beschloss, *Kennedy and Roosevelt*, 229.

169 No, FDR insisted, Hopkins: Press Conference #706, January 3, 1941.

169 He wrote to tell Ickes: Roosevelt to Ickes, January 4, 1941, Elliott Roosevelt ed., *F.D.R.: His Personal Letters, 1882–1945*, IV (New York: Duell, Sloan & Pearce, 1947), 1100.

170 Hopkins arrived in England: On Hopkins's first London visit including quote to Murrow and following Churchill quote, see Sherwood, *Roosevelt and Hopkins*, 234ff. See also Roll, *The Hopkins Touch*, 78ff; and Lash, *Roosevelt and Churchill*, 273ff.

171 The president, Hopkins: WSC, *The Second World War: The Grand Alliance*, 23–24.

172 The answer to one question: Winston Churchill and Martin Gilbert, eds., *The Churchill War Papers, III, The Ever-Widening War, 1941* (New York: W.W. Norton, 2001), 76ff. Claridge's stationery, HH Papers.

172 Extending his originally: A film clip of Hopkins and Churchill visiting dockyards in the south of England can be seen at: http://www.britishpathe.com/video/churchill-on-tour/query/Hopkins

173 He was delighted: February 8, 1941, Ickes, *Diary*, 429.

174 "It's a real connection": March 5, 1941, Stimson, Diary. On his initial reactions after Hopkins's return from London, see February 26 and 27, 1941.

175 Berlin's official policy: Secretary of State Weizsäcker, circular, November 8, 1940, DGFP, XI, 499.

175 The armed forces general staff: Quoted in Friedlander, *Prelude to Downfall*, 157–158.

176 In public he showed: Thomsen to Foreign Ministry, March 9, 1941, DGFP, XII, 251–252.

176 This was necessary: Friedlander, *Prelude to Downfall*, 171, 175.

177 "If the Russian threat": "Report on Conferences with the Fuehrer and Supreme Commander of the Armed Forces at the Berghof (Obersalzberg) on January 8 and 9, 1941," FCNA, 169ff.

177 In early March: "Number 125. Directive of the High Command of the Wehrmacht. Number 24. Regarding Cooperation with Japan," March 5, 1941, DGFP, XII, 219–220.

177 The Communist government: On Hitler's long-standing planning to take land to the east for German economic use, Richard J. Evans, *The Third Reich in Power* (New York: The Penguin Press, 2005), 358ff.

178 "Bolshevism," he said: October 4, 1940, Ciano, *Diary*, 387.

178 "You have only to kick": On Hitler's racial thinking about the invasion of the Soviet Union, see Evans, *The Third Reich at War*, 160ff. Hitler quotes in ibid., 161, 162; and in Lash, *Roosevelt and Churchill*, 348.

Chapter 16: *Intolerence*

179 Results from Gallup Polls: *The Undeclared War*, 441–442.

179 America First rallies: October 6, 1941, 20.

180 Its directors asked Charles Lindbergh: On Lindbergh's becoming part of the AFC, see Wayne S. Cole, *Charles A. Lindbergh and the Battle Against Intervention in World War II* (New York: Harcourt Brace Jovanovich, 1974), 120ff.

180 He told the fevered: Text of Address, New York Public Library, Uncensored Papers, Box 17, Folder Printed Matter America First Committee. Stuart quotes, Cole, 122, 124.

181 The crowd went wild: "Lindbergh Joins in Wheeler Plea to U.S. to Shun War," NYT, May 24, 1941, 1.

182 Eleanor served as the evening's: "One U.S. Life Put Above British Aid," NYT, April 15, 1941, 9.

183 "I have an abiding fear": To Major John (Jack) Thomason, October 24, 1939, Box 30; To Aleck, February 26, 1941, March 31, 1941, TR, Jr., Papers, Box 31.

183 He told his son: February 13, 1941, ibid., Box 9.

184 "Being as strong as I am": To Archie, April 9 1941, ibid.

184 According to family members: Conversation with Theodore Roosevelt IV, December 9, 2013.

185 FDR made sure: Collier, *The Roosevelts*, 397.

185 She wrote Woollcott: Eleanor Roosevelt to Alexander Woollcott, no date; TR, Jr., Papers, Box 9. Archibald Roosevelt, Jr., quote in Collier, *The Roosevelts*, 399.

186 He wrote to Bob Stuart: Geoffrey Kabaservice, *The Guardians: Kingman Brewster, His Circle, and the Rise of the Liberal Establishment* (New York: Henry Holt and Company, 2004), 83.

Chapter 17: *Good Americanism*

187 Interior Secretary Harold Ickes: "Ickes Offers a List Of Nazi 'Tools' Here," NYT, April 14, 1941, 19.

188 Even the Pulitzer Prize–winner Sherwood: Sherwood, *Roosevelt and Hopkins*, 152–153.

188 FBI director J. Edgar Hoover: Douglas M. Charles, "Informing FDR: FBI Political Surveillance and the Isolationist-Interventionist Foreign Policy Debate, 1939–1945," *Diplomatic History*, 24 (Spring 2000): 211–232.

189 At his press conference: Press Conference #738, April 25, 1941.

189 When Lindbergh read: Diary entry, April 25, 1941, CAL Papers, Diaries, Series V, Box 210. Letter of resignation, "Lindbergh Seeks Roosevelt Inquiry," NYT, July 18, 1941, 1.

190 Lindbergh met on July 11, 1941: October 6, July 11, 1941, Diaries, Series V, Box 210.

Chapter 18: *Living a Nightmare*

191 By the spring of 1941: Sherwood, *Roosevelt and Hopkins*, 270ff.

192 Tizard also carried: On the Tizard Mission and the cavity magnetron, see Paul A. Redhead, "The Invention of the Cavity Magnetron and Its Introduction into Canada and the U.S.A.," *La Physique au Canada*, November/December 2001, 321.

192 War secretary Henry Stimson: October 2, 1940, Stimson, Diary.

192 The MAUD report: On the development of the atomic bomb following the MAUD committee report, see Richard Rhodes, *The Making of the Atomic Bomb* (New York: Simon & Schuster, 1986), 368ff.

193 After meeting with Bush: November 6, 1941, Stimson, Diary.

193 Even before Lend-Lease passed: On ABC-1 and quotes, see Kaiser, *No End Save Victory*, 174–177, 179–181. The full text of the report appears in

U.S. Congress, *Hearings Before the Joint Committee on the Investigation of the Pearl Harbor Attack*, 79th Congress, 1st session (Washington, DC: U.S. Government Printing Office, 1946), 15: 1485–1550.

193 Churchill pleaded with Roosevelt: Churchill letters of February 15, March 19, C&R Correspondence, Vol. 1, 150.

194 Secretary of the Navy Frank Knox: Knox to FDR, March 21, 1941, in Kaiser, *No End Save Victory*, 181. Stark quote, Stetson Conn and Byron Fairchild, *The Framework of Hemisphere Defense* (Washington, DC: Center of Military History United States Army, 1989), chapter 5, footnote 13. March 24, 1941, Stimson, Diary.

194 As he had previously explained: FDR to Stark in Heinrichs, *Threshold of War*, 46.

195 The men became seasick: April 12, 1941, Harold L. Ickes, *Diary*, 465ff.

195 On March 30, 1941: March 8, 1941, and April 12, 1941, ibid., 453, 473–474. Sherwood, *Roosevelt and Hopkins*, 277–278.

196 "Piracy!" Berlin screamed: "U.S. Uses First Force to Win Bloodless Victory in the Battle of the Atlantic," *Life*, April 14, 1941, 23–27.

196 Polls showed: Armament, poll numbers, Walker and Perkins in Heinrichs, *Threshold of War*, 45–46. Morgenthau Diary entry in Kaiser, *No End Save Victory*, 183.

196 Writing to Lindbergh: Stuart to Lindbergh, April 25 and May 9, 1941, CAL Papers, Series 1, Box 1.

197 Admitting he felt: April 21, 1941, Stimson, Diary.

197 "I believe": Roosevelt to Grew, January 21, 1941, United States Department of State, *Foreign Relations of the United States Diplomatic Papers, 1941. The Far East* (1941), 6–8.

199 With Churchill's plea: April 10, 17, and 25, 1941, Stimson, Diary.

200 "You could draw": Press Conference #739, April 29, 1941.

200 Roosevelt condemned: "Piracy Is Assailed," NYT, June 21, 1941, 1.

200 Asked now to beef up: On fleet transfer, Samuel Eliot Morison, *History of United States Naval Operations in World War II*, Vol. 1, *The Battle of the Atlantic,*

September 1939–May 1943 (Edison, NJ: Castle Books, 2001; original edition 1947), 56–57. April 24, 1941 Stimson, Diary.

201 Stimson proposed: May 24, 1941, ibid.

202 While less than he hoped: May 28, 1941, ibid.

202 Ickes's response: May 30, 1941, Ickes, *Diary*, 527.

203 Thomsen felt: Thomsen to Berlin, May 27, 1941; *Völkischer Beobachter*, May 29, 1941, in Friedlander, *Prelude to Downfall*, 212–213.

203 In Rome: May 28, 1941, Ciano, *Diary*, 429–430. Conversation, Hitler-Mussolini, June 2, 1941, DGFP, XII, 940ff.

204 "It has been as if living": Harriman to Hopkins, quoted in Sherwood, 276. Harriman to FDR, April 10, 1941, W. Averell Harriman and Elie Abel, *Special Envoy to Churchill and Stalin, 1941–1946* (New York: Random House, 1975), 31.

204 "He says that he means": Alsop and Kinter column and accompanying Stuart to Lindbergh letter, June 4, 1941, CAL Papers, Series 1, Box 2.

205 Some interventionists: "Foil Pro-War Clique's Gag on Col. Lindbergh," CT, May 29, 1941, 1. "Lambertson Assails Censorship," NYT, May 22, 1941, 11.

205 Despite the limits: "Lindbergh Assails Roosevelt Speech," NYT, May 30, 1941, 1.

206 Lindbergh noticed: May 29 and 31, 1941, *Diary* May 12–June 3; *Diary* June 9, June 4–July 8, CAL Papers, Series V, Box 210.

206 "I am waiting to be pushed": *Morgenthau Diaries*, 254. May 25, 1941, Ickes, *Diary*, 523.

Chapter 19: *Volunteers*

209 Corcoran heard out: Martha Byrd, *Chennault: Giving Wings to the Tiger* (Tuscaloosa: University of Alabama Press, 1987), 114ff. Stimson, Diary, October 2, 1941.

210 "I don't expect them": Navy Secretary Frank Knox to FDR, March 21, 1941, Sherwood Collection, Box 297, FDR Library.

210 They reported to Washington: Captain Leonard B. "Tuck" Smith, USN (Ret.), "Naval Air's Role in Sinking the Bismarck," *Naval Aviation Museum Foundation, Inc.*, Vol. 3, No. 2 (Fall 1982): 32–35. "I Was There!—How Our Catalina Shadowed the Bismarck," *The War Illustrated*, Vol 4, No. 94 (June 20, 1941): 621.

211 Five days after Smith: On the dispatching and aftermath of the *Bismarck* from the German perspective, see FCNA, 196ff.

213 "Enemy is exploding": Ibid.

213 "Electrified" U.S. sailors: Abbazia, *Mr. Roosevelt's Navy*, 188.

213 Speechwriter Robert Sherwood: Sherwood quote from June 4, 1941, letter to a friend, in Lash, *Churchill and Roosevelt*, 324.

214 Sherwood recollected: Sherwood, *Roosevelt and Hopkins*, 294–295.

214 For the entire following day: "Survivor's Report (Rescued by U.74), in FCNA, 214ff.

215 Although not officially: Captain Leonard B. "Tuck" Smith, USN (Ret.), "Naval Air's Role in Sinking the Bismarck," *Naval Aviation Museum Foundation, Inc.*, Vol. 3, No. 2 (Fall 1982): 32–35.

216 He was the first American: Other Americans, not in U.S. armed forces uniform, flew previously for the RAF Eagle Squadron.

217 "We had the impression": "Survivor's Report," 218.

217 As the battle raged: Gilbert, *Finest Hour*, 1095.

217 On the other side: May 30, 1941, Ickes, *Diary*, 427–428.

217 No public announcement: Conversation with Bruce Smith, son, May 23, 2013. Leonard Smith navy flight logs, courtesy of Bruce Smith.

218 He likely didn't know: "Reich Warns U.S.," NYT, May 26, 1941, 1. "Report of the C.-in-C., Navy, to the Fuehrer on June 6, 1941, at the Berghoff," FCNA, 218. Conference, June 21, 1941, ibid., 219–220.

Chapter 20: *The Strongest Fortress in the World*

220 Japan made no secret: On Japanese anti-Westernism and militarists' pressure for ousting the colonial powers, see Hotta, *Japan 1941*, 23ff.

221 Those who merely questioned: Unnamed anonymous source quoted in Hiroyuki Agawa, trans. John Bester, *The Reluctant Admiral: Yamamoto and the Imperial Navy* (New York: Kodansha International, 1979), 202.

221 Yamamoto knew the United States: On Yamamoto's early life in the U.S. and opposition to the Tripartite Pact, see Hotta, *Japan 1941*, 98ff; and Agawa, *The Reluctant Admiral*, 185ff.

222 "Today, as chief": Yamamoto quotes in ibid., 186–187, 180.

223 On January 7, 1941: "Opinions on War Preparations," January 7, 1941, Donald M. Goldstein and Katherine V. Dillon, eds., *The Pearl Harbor Papers: Inside the Japanese Plans* [Washington, DC: Brassey's [US], 1993,) 115–118. On the evolution of Yamamoto's thinking about such an attack, see Agawa, *The Reluctant Admiral*, 193ff.

224 After initial resistance: On Japanese tactical preparations and maintenance of secrecy, Robert J. Hanyok, "How the Japanese Did It," *Naval History*, Vol. 23, No. 6 (December 2009).

225 Although only the top navy heads: Grew quoted in Samuel Eliot Morison, *History of United States Naval Operations in World War II*, Vol. 3, *The Rising Sun in the Pacific, 1931–April 1942* (Annapolis, MD: Naval Institute Press, 2010; original edition 1948), 60–61.

225 He wrote his commanding general: Marshall to Lt. Gen. Walter C. Short, February 7, 1941, Henry C. Clausen and Bruce Lee, *Pearl Harbor: Final Judgement* (New York: Da Capo Press, 2001 reprint of 1992), 422–423.

226 In a memorandum: Marshall memorandum in Prange, *At Dawn We Slept*, 122–123.

226 "hotbed of espionage": Quoted in ibid., 70.

226 Takeo Yoshikawa grew up: On Yoshikawa, see Edward Savela, "The Spy Who Doomed Pearl Harbor," *MHQ* magazine, published online November 8, 2011: http://www.historynet.com/the-spy-who-doomed-pearl-harbor.htm; Walter L. Hixson, ed., *The American Experience in World War II: Pearl Harbor in History and Memory* (New York: Routledge, 2002), 274; and "Top Secret Assignment."

231 "The key information": Yoshikawa quotes, "Top Secret assignment."

231 Back at the consulate: On the Japanese Consulate's espionage support, see Prange, *At Dawn We Slept*, 70ff; and "200 Japanese in Consulate Operated Freely as Spies," NYT, January 25, 1942, 8, 148–149.

232 One U.S. Army intelligence official: Quotes from *Investigation of the Pearl Harbor Attack* in Prange, *At Dawn We Slept*, 152–153. Shivers and Kita dialogue in ibid., 155.

232 "We felt free," etc.: Conversation with Charlotte Coe Lemann, January 24, 2013.

235 USS *Utah* description and photographs: http://www.history.navy.mil/danfs /u2/utah.htm; and http://www.oocities.org/historypost/Utah/utahpage.htm

235 Twenty-two-year-old Don Green: Donald A. Green, "Nowhere to Go but Down," *Naval History*, Vol. 22, No. 6 (December 2008): 48–53.

235 Berthed close by: "The Reminiscences of Mr. John B. Vaessen, Pearl Harbor Survivor," interviewed by Paul Stillwell, *The Jerseyman 3Q-2012*, Oral History Supplement (Annapolis, MD: U.S. Naval Institute, 2012), 1–42.

236 Pete Tomich: Clyde Haberman, "After 65 Years, a Hero's Medal Finds a Home," NYT, May 30, 2006.

Chapter 21: *Geographers*

237 As early as April 9: Churchill in House of Commons, April 9, 1941, Gilbert, *Finest Hour*, 1056.

237 The Kremlin received: On Russian attitude toward U.S. and British warnings, see Lash, *Roosevelt and Churchill*, 346ff. See also, Evans, *The Third Reich at War*, 166ff.

239 The army was racing: Heinrici, July 11, 1941; soldier, June 27, 1941: ibid., 179, 182.

238 German foreign minister: July 5, 1941, June 21, 1941, Ciano, *Diary*, 441, 437.

239 "This is a war": Quoted in Evans, *The Third Reich at War*, 175.

240 "Whole districts are being": Winston Churchill to *Jewish Chronicle*, November 14, 1941, in Winston Churchill and Martin Gilbert, eds., *The*

Churchill War Papers, III, The Ever-Widening War, 1941 (New York: W. W. Norton, 2001), 1454.

241 "There is no question": November 10, 1941, report, HH Papers, Military Intelligence Division Reports, 1935–1941, Box 188. On the FDR administration's attitudes and actions in response to the Holocaust, see Richard Breitman and Alan J. Lichtman, *FDR and the Jews* (Cambridge, MA: Harvard University Press, 2013). On G-2 bulletin, see Richard Breitman, *Official Secrets: What the Nazis Planned, What the British and Americans Knew* (New York: Hill and Wang, 1999), 124.

241 In early November 1941: "Halt the Nazis, Shirer Warns," no source, November 10, 1941, Shirer Papers Bound Columns & Articles: Newspaper Clippings, 1927–1961 Bulk '40s.

242 An attack appeared imminent: Gilbert, *Finest Hour*, 1118–1119.

243 Hitler's attack on his former ally: June 22, 1941, Stimson, Diary; Stimson to FDR, June 23, 1941, Stimson Papers. Knox to FDR, June 23, 1941, Kaiser, *No End Save Victory*, 236–237. Stark, ibid. 237.

243 Early intelligence reports: "Military Intelligence Division Reports, 1935–1945 U.S.S.R. Report of June 30, 1941, signed "Yeaton," Container 190, HH Papers.

244 "Stalin is on our side": "Russia as an Ally," NYT, August 6, 1941, 16.

244 "A tremendous victory": "Forts Delay Nazis," ibid., July 18, 1941, 1.

245 That led to the first U.S. "combat": On the *Niblack* incident see Abbazia, *Mr. Roosevelt's Navy*, 191ff.

247 Churchill told the House of Commons: Quoted in Robert Dallek, *Franklin D. Roosevelt and American Foreign Policy, 1932–1945: With a New Afterword* (New York: Oxford University Press, 1995), 276.

247 When Roosevelt formally: "Icelandic and 'Irish' Bases Assailed in Senate by Foes of Intervention," NYT, July 11, 1941, 1.

247 "Mr. President," a reporter queried: July 8, 1941, Press Conference #753.

248 "Roosevelt has occupied": Quoted in translation, July 14, 1941, G-2 military report, HH Papers, Box 188, Military Intelligence Division Reports, 1935–1941.

248 In his diary, Lindbergh: July 8, 1941, Diaries June 4–July 8, July 8–August 12, CAL Papers. "This Changing Hemisphere," "Uncensored," July 12, 1941, No. 93, Uncensored Papers, BOX 17, Folder Printed Matter America First Committee, NYPL.

249 "... Obviously," he wrote: "This Changing Hemisphere," "Uncensored," July 12, 1941, No. 93, Uncensored Papers, BOX 17, Folder Printed Matter America First Committee, NYPL.

249 National polls continued: Poll numbers cited in Lynne Olson, *Those Angry Days*, 342ff. July 11, 1941, Diaries July 8–August 12, CAL Papers.

249 Infuriated by the White House's: July 11, 1941, Diaries July 8–August 12, CAL Papers.

249 At an America First rally: "Lindy Gets Big Ovation," *Reading Eagle*, June 21, 1941, 3.

250 Hopkins and Roosevelt huddled: David L. Roll, *The Hopkins Touch*, 114–115. Sherwood, *Roosevelt and Hopkins*, 308–310.

Chapter 22: *Son of a Harness Maker*

252 He and Churchill sat: WSC, *The Second World War: The Grand Alliance*, 424ff; and Roll, *The Hopkins Touch*, 117.

253 Along with extensive meetings: Sherwood, *Roosevelt and Hopkins*, 309ff.

254 In his unmistakably Midwestern: Ibid., 320–321.

255 "I must tell you": Prime Minister to Moscow, July 28, 1941, in Gilbert, *Finest Hour*, 1143–1144.

256 On the drive from the airport: Margaret Bourke-White, *Shooting the Russian War* (New York: Simon and Schuster, 1942), 64, 66.

256 "The Germans took a hand": Harry Hopkins, "The Inside Story of My Meeting with Stalin," *The American Magazine*, December 1941, 14ff.

256 For Hopkins's meetings with Stalin, I have relied on Hopkins, "The Inside Story of My Meeting with Stalin"; Sherwood, *Roosevelt and Hopkins*, 323ff; Roll, *The Hopkins Touch*, 122ff; and Bourke-White, *Shooting the Russian War*, 205ff.

259 She managed to capture: Bourke-White, *Shooting the Russian War*, 217.

Chapter 23: *The Obvious Conclusion*

262 When word of Hopkins's trip: Lindbergh in Justus D. Doenecke, *In Danger Undaunted: The Anti-Interventionist Movement of 1940–1941 as Revealed in the Papers of the America First Committee* (Stanford, CA: Hoover Institution Press, 1990), 30. "Harry and Joe," CT, August 6, 1941, 12. *Sioux City Journal* in Sherwood, *Roosevelt and Hopkins*, 346.

263 He anticipated Japan: "Conference of the C.-in-C., Navy, with the Führer in the Wolfsschanze in the Afternoon of August 22, 1941," FCNA, 229.

264 At the moment, FDR: Ickes, *Diary*, 567.

266 "The emperor had": Imperial Conference description and quotes, Hotta, *Japan 1941*, 130–135.

267 Ickes thought: July 27, 1941, Ickes, *Diary*, 588.

267 Dean Acheson: On Acheson's and the State Department's role in making the embargo total, see Heinrichs, *Threshold of War*, 176–179. Japanese official, ibid., 182.

267 After receiving word: Grew in Jonathan Marshall, *To Have and Have Not: Southeast Asian Raw Materials and the Origins of the Pacific War* (Berkeley: University of California Press, 1995), 133–134. Joseph Grew, "Report from Tokyo," *Life*, December 7, 1942, 82.

Chapter 24: *At Last We've Gotten Together*

268 North Carolina senator: "Selects Will Be Retained, Leaders Feel," *Washington Post*, July 28, 1941, 1. On Reynolds and his marriage, see Robert Coughlan, " 'Our Bob' Reynolds," *Life*, September 8, 1941, 47ff.

269 "All these polls": July 30, 1941, Stimson, Diary.

270 Treasury's Morgenthau found: *Morgenthau Diaries*, 264.

270 Much of the meeting: August 1, 1941, Stimson, Diary. See also, August 2, 1941, Ickes, *Diary*, 592–593.

271 "Franklin Roosevelt," he wrote: "Time for Vacation," *Time*, August 11, 1941.

272 On the Senate floor: "Two-Year Limit on Draft Beaten in Senate, 50–21," NYT, August 7, 1941, 1.

272 *The New York Times* reported: "President Sails for Week's Rest," NYT, August 4, 1941, 1.

272 Coming aboard, FDR: I have benefited throughout this chapter from Theodore A. Wilson, *The First Summit: Roosevelt and Churchill at Placentia Bay, 1941* (Lawrence: University of Kansas Press, Revised Edition 1991). Unless otherwise indicated, quotations and descriptions from the Atlantic Conference come from Wilson.

273 "So," the secretary of war: August 4, 6, 1941, Stimson, Diary.

274 When FDR's equally uninformed: Elliott Roosevelt, *As He Saw It* (New York: Duell, Sloan and Pearce, 1946), 16.

274 Hopkins later said: On Hopkins and Churchill aboard *Prince of Wales*, see Robert Sherwood, *Roosevelt and Hopkins*, 349ff.

275 One of them, H. V. Morton: H. V. Morton, *Atlantic Meeting an Account of Mr. Churchill's Voyage in H.M. S. Prince of Wales in August, 1941* (New York: Dodd Mead & Company, 1943), 5.

277 There are differing versions from various witnesses of this first meeting.

278 FDR wanted: WSC, *The Second World War: The Grand Alliance*, 433.

278 Churchill claimed: Ibid., 433.

280 If anyone in the *Prince of Wales*: "Fight on Draft Ends in Senate, Due to Act Today," NYT, August 14, 1941, 1.

281 He had established: WSC, *The Second World War: The Grand Alliance*, 447.

283 Ignoring disappointment: August 19, 1941, quoted in Martin Gilbert, *Churchill and America* (New York: Simon & Schuster, 2008), 234.

284 Returned to London: *The War Speeches of Winston S. Churchill, O.M., C.H., P.C., M.P., Volume Two: From June 25, 1941 to September 6, 1943* (London: Cassell & Company, 1965), 60.

Chapter 25: *The Rattlesnakes of the Atlantic*

286 Hitler was constant: "Conference of the C.-in-C., Navy, with the Fuehrer in the Wolfsschanze in the Afternoon of July 25, 1941," FCNA, 222.

287 When Roosevelt learned: Naval Staff to Foreign Office, September 12, 1941, ibid., 230. Abbazia, *Mr. Roosevelt's Navy*, 223–229.

289 He now faced: September 11, 1941, Diary, September 11–October 8, CAL Papers, Series V, Box 210.

289 "That effort," he said: http://www.charleslindbergh.com/americanfirst/speech.asp

290 Wendell Willkie called: Reactions to Lindbergh speech, Wayne S. Cole, *Charles A. Lindbergh and the Battle Against Intervention in World War II* (New York: Harcourt Brace Jovanovich, 1974), 171ff; Berg, *Lindbergh*, 428ff; Olson, *Those Angry Days*, 387ff.

291 He inveighed against: Stuart to "all chapter chairmen," September 23, 1941, CAL Papers, Series 1, Box 2.

291 In a national radio broadcast: "Hoover Says Wait Till Hitler Loses," NYT, September 17, 1941, 1.

292 "We now have orders": September 8, October 1, 15, 1941, Donald Hugh Dorris, *A Log of the Vincennes* (Louisville: Standard Printing, 1947), 88, 96, 100.

293 "Hitler will have to": September 14, 1941, in Winston Churchill and Martin Gilbert, eds., *The Churchill War Papers, III, The Ever-Widening War, 1941* (New York: W. W. Norton, 2001), 1214.

294 The aggressive Raeder: "Conference of the C.-in-C., Navy, with the Fuehrer in the Wolfsschanze in the Afternoon of September 17, 1941," FCNA, 231–233.

294 Fighting on the Eastern Front, etc.: October 25–29, 30, 1941, Ciano, *Diary*, 458–459, 460.

Chapter 26: *Tennō*

297 A little more than a month before: Hotta, *Japan 1941*, 172–175.

299 Sitting in the palace's resplendent hall: Ibid., 175–176.

300 Konoe pleaded with Grew: Waldo Heinrichs, Jr., *American Ambassador: Joseph C. Grew and the Development of the American Diplomatic Tradition* (Boston: Little Brown, 1966; Oxford University paperback, 1986), 354ff.

300 Stimson doubted: "Memorandum of Conference Between Secretary Hull and Secretary Stimson, October 6, 1941," Stimson Papers.

300 The day after the Imperial Conference: Prange, *At Dawn We Slept*, 206.

301 Less than three weeks later: Hotta, *Japan 1941*, 192.

301 "Some of you may": Hiroyuki Agawa, trans. John Bester, *The Reluctant Admiral: Yamamoto and the Imperial Navy* (New York: Kodansha International, 1979), 230–231.

301 In the midst of the map maneuvers: October 11, 1941, Donald M. Goldstein and Katherine V. Dillon, eds., *The Pearl Harbor Papers: Inside the Japanese Plans* (Washington, DC: Brassey's [US], 1993), 124. Yamamoto expressed similar concerns in a letter, October 24, 1941, to the navy's new minister, Shimada, *The Pearl Harbor Papers*, 118–120.

302 The prime minister met: Hotta, *Japan 1941*, 201ff.

303 In early August: August 7, 1941, Stimson, Diary.

304 Stimson shared the general belief: October 28, 1941, ibid.

304 Confided Stimson: August 9, 1941, ibid.

304 Roosevelt sent a note: http://www.fdrlibrary.marist.edu/_resources/images/psf/psfa0335.pdf

305 The Japanese spy: "Top Secret Assignment."

Chapter 27: *The Undeclared War*

306 The Magic decryption: Prange, *At Dawn We Slept*, 248ff. Robert J. Hanyok, "How the Japanese Did It," *Naval History*, Vol. 23, No. 6 (December 2009).

307 He confessed a month later: November 23, 1941, Ickes, *Diary*, 649.

307 Grew predicted war: Waldo Heinrichs, Jr., *American Ambassador: Joseph C. Grew and the Development of the American Diplomatic Tradition*, 355.

308 On November 10, William Shirer: "Halt the Nazis, Shirer Warns," November 10, 1941. No source.

308 One newspaper insulted: Heinrichs, *Threshold of War*, 202.

309 The president told the men: November 25, 1941, Stimson, Diary.

309 Some consider this exchange: On the controversy over FDR's possible foreknowledge of the attack and the definitive investigation into it, see Henry C. Clausen and Bruce Lee, *Pearl Harbor: Final Judgement* (New York: Da Capo Press, 2001 edition of 1992).

309 When Stimson got back: November 25 and 26, 1941, Stimson, Diary.

311 *Kearny* finally limped: *Kearny* attack, Abbazia, *Mr. Roosevelt's Navy*, 265ff.

311 And at sea, his green navy: October 23, 1941, Stimson, Diary.

312 The map, he said: Press Conference #779, October 28, 1941.

313 FDR was aware: John F. Bratzel and Leslie B. Rout, "FDR and the 'Secret Map,'" *Wilson Quarterly* 9 (1985): 167–173.

313 Berlin reacted almost instantly: Press conferences, October 28, 29, 1941, in Friedländer, *Prelude to Downfall*, 301.

314 Illinois Republican representative: Congressional debate, October 16, 1941, quoted in Charles A. Beard, *President Roosevelt and the Coming of the War, 1941* (New Haven, CT: Yale University Press, 1948), 167.

314 Deeply frustrated: November 7, 1941, Abbazia, *Mr. Roosevelt's Navy*, 306.

315 The Americans understood: Hotta, *Japan 1941*, 267.

315 On November 27: "Memorandum by the Secretary of State," November 27, 1941, U.S. Department of State, *Papers*, 2: 770–772.

315 The following morning: "Talks Are Bogged," NYT, November 28, 1941, 1.

Chapter 28: *Son of Man, Son of God*

316 They were illegal: Prange, *At Dawn We Slept*, 124–125.

317 Ignoring the Constitution: Ibid., 148–156.

318 Tokyo relayed orders: "Top Secret Assignment." Prange, *At Dawn We Slept*, 313–319.

318 General Marshall and his navy counterpart: Henry C. Clausen and Bruce Lee, *Pearl Harbor: Final Judgement* (New York: Da Capo Press, 2001 edition of 1992), 438–439.

318 However, with "acts of sabotage": Clausen and Lee, *Pearl Harbor*, 438ff.

319 Three days later: NYT, December 7, 1941. "U.S. Cheerfully Faces War with Japan," *Life*, December 8, 1941, 38.

319 Last to speak: Prange, *At Dawn We Slept*, 432–433. Hotta, *Japan 1941*, 278.

320 He sent out a radio message: Ibid.

320 He reiterated the proposals: Prange, *At Dawn We Slept*, 467–468. Lash, *Roosevelt and Churchill*, 486–487.

321 A navy captain arrived: L. L. Schultz testimony, *PHA*, pt. 10, 4662–4663. Sherwood, *Roosevelt and Hopkins*, 426–427.

322 Returning at two that afternoon: "Top Secret Assignment." Prange, *At Dawn We Slept*, 70ff.

322 Aboard the *Akagi*: "Top Secret Assignment." Prange, *At Dawn We Slept*, 472–473.

323 Donald A. Green, "Nowhere to Go but Down," *Naval History*, Vol. 22, No. 6 (December 2008): 48–53. Charlotte Coe Lemann, interview with the author, January 24, 2013. Mary Ann Ramsey, "Only Yesteryear," *Naval History*, Winter 1991, online http://www.ussblockisland.org/Beta/V2-Memories /Other_Memories_files/ONLY%20YESTERDAY%20by%20Mary%20Ann %20Ramsey.pdf

Chapter 29: *East Wind, Rain*

326 During the weather forecast: "Top Secret Assignment." Prange, *At Dawn We Slept*, 562. Gordon W. Prange with Donald M. Goldstein and Katherine Dillon, *December 7, 1941: The Day the Japanese Attacked Pearl Harbor* (New York: McGraw-Hill, 1988), 344–345.

326 Donald A. Green, "Nowhere to Go but Down," *Naval History*, Vol. 22, No. 6 (December 2008): 48–53. About the *Utah* and the attack at Pearl Harbor, go to: http://www.oocities.org/historypost/Utah/utahpage.htm

328 Inside the dying *Utah*: Clyde Haberman, "After 65 Years, a Hero's Medal Finds a Home," *NYT*, May 30, 2006.

328 John Vaessen, who had been settling: *The Jerseyman* 3Q-2012, Oral History Supplement, "The Reminiscences of Mr. John B. Vaessen, Pearl Harbor Survivor," interviewed by Paul Stillwell (Annapolis, MD: U.S. Naval Institute, 2012), 1–42.

330 As they led Kita: "Top Secret Assignment."

330 A resounding explosion: Charlotte Coe Lemann, interview with the author, January 24, 2013.

331 As he did he saw: Prange et al., *December 7, 1941*, 167–168.

333 He hadn't seen the Magic: December 7, 1941, Stimson, Diary.

334 Twenty minutes before: Sherwood, *Roosevelt and Hopkins*, 430ff.

335 She noticed immediately: Doris Kearns Goodwin, *No Ordinary Time: Franklin and Eleanor Roosevelt: The Home Front in World War II* (New York: Simon & Schuster, 1994), 289–290.

335 Ciano recorded: Ciano, *Diary*, 472. Friedländer, *Prelude to Downfall*, 308–309.

Epilogue: *Rendezvous with Destiny*

337 Charles and Anne: December 7, 8, 12, 1941, Diary November 23, 1941–January 3, 1942, CAL Papers, Series V, Box 211. Berg, *Lindbergh*, 436ff. Stimson quote in ibid., 437.

338 Ted went to see Franklin: "So Home Will Be Empty This Year," N.d. *World-Telegram*, TR, Jr., Papers, Box 73.

338 Harvard architecture student: Johnson FBI Report. Franz Schulze, *Philip Johnson*, 160ff.

339 Military police took: "Top Secret Assignment."

340 However, after locals found: Fred L. Schultz, "The U.S. Naval Institute," *Proceedings*, October 2006, Vol. 132/10/1,244.

340 Almost exactly four years: William Shirer, *20th Century Journey: A Memoir of a Life and the Times*, II, *The Nightmare Years, 1930–1940* (Boston: Little, Brown, 1984), 617ff.

Picture Acknowledgments

Page 14: William Shirer: Courtesy of Linda Shirer Rae.

Page 15: William Shirer: Courtesy of Linda Shirer Rae.

Page 21: Philip Johnson: Courtesy of the Van Vechten Trust.

Page 26: Father Charles Coughlin: Library of Congress, Prints & Photographs Division, New York World-Telegram and the Sun Newspaper Photograph Collection.

Page 67: Sir William Stephenson: Courtesy of the Intrepid Society.

Page 123: President Roosevelt and Secretary of War Henry Stimson: FDR Library Photograph Collection, Franklin D. Roosevelt Presidential Library and Museum, Hyde Park, New York.

Page 137: Lindbergh, Kingman Brewster, and Richard M. Bissell: Library of Congress, Prints and Photographs Division, New York World-Telegram and the Sun Newspaper Photograph Collection.

Page 171: Harry Hopkins: Library of Congress, Prints and Photographs Division, New York World-Telegram and the Sun Newspaper Photograph Collection.

Page 173: Hopkins, Churchill, and Vice Admiral Gordon Ramsey: FDR Library Photograph Collection, Franklin D. Roosevelt Presidential Library and Museum, Hyde Park, New York.

Page 218: Lieutenant Smith: Courtesy of Bruce Smith.

Page 251: Map: Courtesy of FDR Library, Harry Hopkins Papers: Sherwood Collection.

Page 260: Hopkins and Stalin: FDR Library Photograph Collection, Franklin D. Roosevelt Presidential Library and Museum, Hyde Park, New York.

Page 278: Roosevelt and Churchill: FDR Library Photograph Collection, Franklin D. Roosevelt Presidential Library and Museum, Hyde Park, New York.

Page 283: FDR and Churchill: Aboard the HMS *Prince of Wales:* U.S. Naval Historical Center Photograph.

Page 302: Admiral Yamamoto: U.S. Naval Institute Archives.

Page 324: Donald Green: Courtesy of James Green.

Page 329: The *Utah:* U.S. Naval Historical Center Photograph.

Page 332: Pearl Harbor: U.S. Naval Historical Center Photograph.

Page 334: Charlotte Coe with her mother and brother: Courtesy of Charlotte Coe Lemann.

Index

Note: Page numbers in *italics* indicate photographs or illustrations.

Lindbergh seen as Nazi by FDR, 135
modern art seen as degenerate by, 20
Federal Bureau of Investigation (FBI)
  Christian Front members arrested by,
    80–81
  cooperation with BSC by, 71
  duped by BSC, 77
  in Honolulu, 232, 316–317
  Johnson and, 80, 147
  in Latin America, 76
  Nazi supporters arrested by, 81
fifth column
  AFF as, 64
  Americans' fears about, 78
  arrests in U.S., 80–81
  British operatives countering, 64–65,
    67, 73
  FDR's warning to Bolivia about, 77
  origin of term, 64
  sabotage threatened by, 195
  in South America, 67
Fight for Freedom Committee, 69
Fish, Hamilton, 72
Fleming, Ian, 66
Flying Fortresses, 303–304
Flying Tigers, 209, 210
Flynn, John T., 181
Four Freedoms, 159, 182, 262, 279
France
  fall of Paris, 54, 57–58
  surrender of, 58–59, 97, 107
Frankfurter, Felix, 99, 100
Freeman, W. R., 275
French Indochina invasion, 119, 209,
    220, 266–267
Funk, Walter, 76–77

G
Gallup, George, 69
"garden hose" speech, 153–154
George VI, King, 41, 304

Germany
  anger at Iceland occupation, 248
  censorship in, 11–12, 59
  Kristallnacht pogrom, 132
  Latin American relations with,
    73–74
  Lindbergh's praise for, 130
  naval weakness of, 32–33
  nonaggression pact with Russia, 9,
    176
  Poland invaded by, 5–6, 7, 9
  precision of the military, 16
  Red Cross and, 59
  Tripartite Pact, 115–119, 220, 336
  war declared on U.S. by, 336
Gillie, George W., 314
Goebbels, Herr, 75
Golden Hour of the Shrine of the Little
    Flower, 23–24
Good Neighbor Policy, 73
Göring, Hermann
  Lindbergh hosted by, 127, 128, 129,
    131–132
  Lindbergh praising Germany and,
    130
  Luftwaffe overestimated by, 128, 129
  medal awarded to Lindbergh by,
    131–132
  plan for exterminating Jews
    demanded by, 240
Graf Spee (scuttled cruiser), 48–49, 50
Great Britain. See England
Green, Don, 235, 323, 324, 326–328
Greer destroyer, attack on, 285–287,
    288–289
Grew, Joseph
  FDR's reliance on reports from, 263,
    304
  FDR's strategic viewpoint
    summarized to, 197
  Konoe's secret meeting with, 300

Jodl, Alfred, 176
Johnson, Hugh S. "Iron Pants," 83
Johnson, Philip Cortelyou, *21*
  Abby Rockefeller's benevolence
    toward, 147
  accused by HUAC, 79
  AFF co-founded by, 62
  Allies belittled by, 31–32
  anti-Semitism of, 20
  architecture championed by, 18–19,
    145–146
  "Architecture in the Third Reich,"
    20
  attempt to change his image, 146–
    147
  Coughlin admired by, 25
  Dennis supported by, 21–22
  described, 6, 17–18
  desire for fascist America, 21
  early end to war predicted by, 31
  early life of, 7
  electorates rejection of, 64
  England blamed for war by, 31
  European culture loved by, 7–8, 18,
    19
  excitement about war in, 7
  fame of, 8
  fascism idealized by, 19–22
  feared by war reporters, 16
  first sight of Hitler by, 19–20
  followed by FBI, 80, 147
  at the front in Poland, 28
  generosity of, 18
  German actions defended by, 62, 64
  German victory in Poland praised by,
    29–30
  Hitler admired by, 17
  Hitler's racism defended by, 133
  Hitler's rallies loved by, 27–28
  indictment avoided by, 81, 147–148,
    339

  list of people to be eliminated kept
    by, 23
  as Long's Minister of Fine Arts,
    22–23, 147
  MoMA architecture show curated by,
    1932, 18
  Nazi flaws overlooked by, 20
  Nazi restrictions on homosexuality
    and, 20
  Nazism course taken by, 27
  Nazism idealized by, 19–22, 27–28,
    62
  Nietzsche's superman esteemed by, 19
  passion for art world, 8, 16, 17, 18,
    19
  on power politics, 29
  pro-Nazi activities of, 80
  service during war, 338–339
  Shirer compared to, 6–8
  Shirer disliked by, 8
  Shirer interrogated by, 28
  Shirer's book exposing, 145, 146
  Thompson's criticisms of, 64
  as writer for AFF, 64

K
Kearny, attacked by U-boats, 310–311
Kennedy, Joseph P., 37, 131, 169
Kertess, Ferdinand, 79, 81
Ketchum, Richard, 138
Kidd, Isaac C., 233
Kierstein, Lincoln, 23
King, Ernest J., 200, 273, *283*
King, Mackenzie, 107, 109–110
Kita, Nagao
  arrest of, 330, 339–340
  espionage info sent through, 231,
    305, 317
  evidence burned by, 330
  exchanged for American prisoners,
    340